THE IMAGINARY LINE

See page 152 - "1889 _∞. I. B. C. . . . . "

THE IMAGINARY LINE

A History of the United States and Mexican Boundary Survey
1848–1857

JOSEPH RICHARD WERNE

TEXAS CHRISTIAN UNIVERSITY PRESS • FORT WORTH, TEXAS

Library of Congress Cataloging-in-Publication Data

Werne, Joseph Richard, 1943-
  The imaginary line : a history of the United States and Mexican boundary
survey, 1848/1857 / by Joseph Richard Werne.
     p. cm.
  Includes bibliographical references and index.
  ISBN-13: 978-0-87565-338-9
  ISBN-10: 0-87565-338-3
  1. United States—Boundaries—Mexico. 2. Mexico—Boundaries—United
States. 3. Mexican-American Border Region—Surveys. 4. Surveyors—
Mexican-American Border Region—Biography. 5. Surveyors—United
States—Biography. 6. Mexican-American Border Region—Description and
travel. 7. Southwest, New—Description and travel. 8. Natural history—
Southwest, New. 9. Indians of North America—Southwest, New—History—
19th century. 10. Southwest, New—History, Local. I. Title.

F786.W44 2007
972'.1—dc22
                              2006027539

Cover and text design by Bill Maize; Duo Design Group

TCU Press
P. O. Box 298300
Fort Worth, TX 76129
817-257-7822
http://www.prs.tcu.edu/

To order books: 1-800-826-8911

For Patricia

TABLE OF CONTENTS

MAPS

⊰✦ PREFACE ✦⊱

The United States and Mexican boundary survey is a little-known event crowded out of history by the war that made it necessary and the larger events that later overshadowed it in both countries. Scarcely had the Joint United States and Mexican Boundary Commission put the finishing touches to its maps in 1857 when the devastating War of the Reform broke out in Mexico, and the United States began rushing toward the Civil War. When these great struggles were finally over, Mexico needed a long rest and the United States entered upon the peaceful conquest of its newly won empire. The boundary survey was but a dim memory next to such momentous affairs. Nor could those who decades after wished to study the tracing of the international line do so effectively. The only accessible public record of the survey was that left by the officers of the United States commission, marked by confusion and quarrels unending, and very much one-sided. To read the last United States commissioner's final report is to receive the impression that Mexico played no part in it at all. Strengthening this bias was the almost complete absence of any Mexican account of the Joint Commission's labors. Presenting an objective view of the boundary survey was therefore difficult at best.

The recent availability of the documents relating to the Mexican Boundary Commission in the Archivo de la Secretaría de Relaciones Exteriores, and the opening of the files of the Archivo Histórico de la Defensa Nacional, however, have made it possible to reconstruct the story of the United States–Mexican boundary survey on firmer ground. The efforts and activities of the Mexican surveying team can now be made known to us. Still, there are fewer materials on hand for an investigation of the Mexican commission than for that of the United States. The Mexican commission did not generate the volume of controversy that the United States section of the Joint Commission did in producing a large amount of conflicting testimony. While this has made achieving a balance in relating the work of both survey teams challenging, there are gaps in the documentary record presented by the United States commission as well as the Mexican. Credit for unearthing the records of the Mexican Boundary Commission must go to Harry P. Hewitt of Midwestern State University, whose research and writing on the survey has been pioneering and thorough, and without which my own work would not have been possible.

This study has been supported by a number of generous research grants from Southeast Missouri State University, which permitted several rewarding stays in the archives of Mexico City, Washington, D.C., and elsewhere. No research is ever accomplished without the pleasant assistance of archivists and librarians who generously give the time and insight that makes historical investigation a pleasure. I would therefore like to express my deep gratitude to the directors and staffs of: the Archivo de la Secretaría de Relaciones Exteriores, the Archivo General de la Nación, and the Archivo Histórico de la Defensa Nacional in Mexico City; the National Archives and Library of Congress in Washington, D.C.; the Archivo del Ministerio de Asuntos Exteriores in Madrid; the Beinecke Library, Yale University; the University of Texas Archives and the Barker Library of the Texas State Historical Society; the De Golyer Library, Southern Methodist University; the Cleveland Public Library and the Western Reserve Historical Society Library in Cleveland; the Oklahoma Historical Society; and the Missouri Historical Society.

Portions of certain chapters of this study have previously appeared in the *Southwestern Historical Quarterly*, *Historia Mexicana*, and the *Journal of the Southwest*, which merit acknowledgment.

JOSEPH RICHARD WERNE

INTRODUCTION

*"I have considered that the time has come
when hypothetical geography should cease."*

**William Hemsley Emory, Major, United States
Army Corps of Topographical Engineers**

The new international boundary between Mexico and the United States following the war of 1846–1848 coursed through unexplored terrain, virtually unknown to science. Every chart of the region was erroneous to a degree, and the descriptions of the old boundary between the Californias and that dividing Chihuahua and New Mexico were so divergent as to cause confusion in all who unfolded a map of the area. Yet the statesmen who framed the Treaty of Guadalupe Hidalgo were confident that the boundary they described would be clear to any surveyor. It simply consisted of a straight line dividing the two Californias, the Gila River, the southern and western boundaries of New Mexico, and the Río Grande. Nevertheless, as though the Sonoran Desert had become a quagmire, the effort to trace this line on the ground brought forth a controversy so perplexing that only an entirely new treaty could resolve the matter.

The great goal for the United States was a transcontinental railroad, which many experts of the day insisted could only cut through to the Pacific slightly south of the thirty-second parallel, and this the treaty did not grant. Mexico's patriotic pride cared nothing for a railroad along its far northern frontier, and having accepted a punishing peace was unwilling to bend the treaty line simply to accommodate its northern neighbor.

While the boundary line was manifestly clear to the treaty negotiators, it was sufficiently vague to everyone else as to give rise to different interpretations. This gave life to the controversy that in the end enabled the United States to throw the line farther south and gain the much desired rail route. Later surveys proved that the Gadsden Purchase was not needed for a railroad to the Pacific, but in 1854 the availability of the southern route was a necessity for political if not engineering needs. One objective of this study is to unravel this tangled skein, explore the several threads of the boundary dispute, and demonstrate how they led to the Gadsden Treaty and the completion of the survey. An important element was the combination of partisan politics in the United States and Mexico's political instability during those years. These two forces caused such disruption within the Joint United States and Mexican

Boundary Commission that it is a wonder the engineers of both nations were able to survey the line at all, no matter where it fell. While the new boundary was not the only aspect of the Treaty of Guadalupe Hidalgo and the Gadsden Purchase, such questions will be dealt with only as they affect the international survey.

The general objective of the two treaties was to resolve all existing difficulties between Mexico and the United States, yet the border became and has remained a continuing problem to the present day. The treaty framers sought to draw a line through land that was devoid of people and economic activity, but it was an arbitrary boundary eventually destined to run through a populous and economically important region. The problems became binational from the beginning as the Apache recognized no boundary at all, raiding and taking refuge on both sides of it. The refusal of the Río Grande to remain within its banks, thereby changing the boundary itself, began causing problems even before the international survey was completed. Today such issues as migration, drug trafficking, use of the waters of the Colorado River for irrigation, air pollution, and other environmental questions continue to plague the two nations. Thus the surveyors who drew the boundary were unknowingly witnesses to the beginning of a border controversy, not the end of one.

A further objective of this study is to explore the actual work of the surveyors themselves as they braved the privations under which they suffered during this difficult multiyear task. Enduring floods and sandstorms, earthquakes and Indian attacks, abandoned and left destitute by their governments, one can only admire their courage and fortitude.

As far as possible this work has been based on the wealth of materials found in the public archives of Mexico and the United States, but also upon the private papers of the men who played the principal roles in surveying the boundary. An effort has been made to bring to life the engineers who were involved in the work of the survey over so many years, especially on the part of Mexico. While the treaty negotiators and men of the United States commission are generally known to historians of the American West, the Mexican engineers and diplomats until recently seemed barely visible at all. As if the Mexican commission had no part in carrying the survey to its conclusion, it was seen but dimly, as through a desert fog. Even the Mexican statesmen who negotiated the Treaty of Guadalupe Hidalgo have appeared as empty men, and the only monograph on the Gadsden Treaty simply refers to two of the Mexican treaty framers as nameless "engineers." It is hoped this work will bring forward the importance of their efforts and demonstrate that they were equal to those of the United States.

The final objective of this study is to tell the whole story of the survey of the new boundary between the United States and Mexico, to relate the successes and failures, the delights and frustrations, of the men who labored long years to trace a line from the Gulf of Mexico to the Pacific Ocean. There were also incidents of humor as well as tragedy that are perhaps not essential to understanding the boundary survey, but do indeed instill sympathy for the afflictions and obstacles the men of both commissions faced nearly every day. These too have been included in this moment, this tracing of an imaginary line through the desert sands.

GUADALUPE
HIDALGO

"What is my line of duty to my government & country, in this most extraordinary position in which I find myself?"

**Nicholas P. Trist, the only American
signatory of the Treaty of Guadalupe Hidalgo**

The Advanced Guard of the Army of the West had crossed and recrossed the Río Gila several times during its march into Mexico, but now found it necessary to leave its bed to avoid a canyon. This led the party over very broken country, with huge volcanic dikes and walls of basalt traversing it, the ground strewn with fractured pieces of this same hard rock. A hot, dry wind swept the moisture from the lieutenant's eyes as he looked out over the surrounding country from the peak of one of the mountains around which his small surveying party now passed. The rugged mountains coursed from northwest to southeast, rising abruptly from the plateau to form long, narrow, disconnected ridges that appeared as trap dikes on a great scale. He noticed that these mountain chains came to an end some distance south, giving a route near the thirty-second parallel for a wagon road or rail passage from the Río Grande del Norte west to the Gila.

Harsh and beautiful, the Sonoran Desert, with its block-faulted mountains never out of sight from the arid outwash plains between them, challenged the lieutenant, whose gaze was more accustomed to the green of his tidewater Maryland home. Yet the varicolored volcanic rock, granite, feldspar, and red sandstone of the mountains enchanted him. The cloudless sky above invited the sun to bake the desiccated plains, mockingly searing away any moisture that might comfort the human eye. The engineering party camped the following day on a bluff well above the Río Gila, in full view of a pinnacle that the troops quickly named Steeple Rock. The desert temperatures rose and fell as sharply as the rock before their eyes. That late October night the lieutenant's party went to sleep with the temperature at 70° Fahrenheit and with hopes of their first sprinkle of rain in a month, which the overcast heavens seemed to promise. Instead they awoke shivering in their blankets under a clear sky with the thermometer reading a cold 25°.[1] The temperatures would become yet more extreme and the terrain ever more fantastic as the lieutenant carried the reconnaissance down the Río Gila and westward to the Pacific Ocean.

William Hemsley Emory had been detailed as chief engineer to Colonel Stephen W. Kearny's Army of the West on 5 June 1846. While Kearny's objective was to strike a blow at Mexico's northern territories between the Río Grande and the Pacific, Emory's task was to collect data that would give the government an idea of the country traversed, particularly the New Mexico territory. Before Emory's reconnaissance, not one point of latitude or longitude in that vast region had been determined, the entire area virtually unknown. His numerous astronomical observations and barometric readings produced the first map of the area to show the exact position of fixed points on the earth's surface.[2] Once in California, Emory's duties as a topographical engineer ceased with the outbreak of hostilities. He proved his bravery and bold spirit at the battle of San Pascual, where he saved Kearny's life during the fray, but this was the least important aspect of his reconnaissance.[3] If the war gave California and the New Mexico territory to the United States, a railroad binding them to the rest of the nation would be of the utmost importance.

At the outbreak of the war with Mexico, Emory was principal assistant engineer on the survey of the northeastern boundary and had served in the United States Army Corps of Topographical Engineers since 1838. Emory was born on 7 September 1811 to a military family whose home was an estate called Poplar Grove in Queen Anne's County, Maryland. His father, Thomas, had served in the army and fought in the War of 1812, and his grandfather in the Revolutionary War.[4] Along with this military tradition, the family had political ties that were of considerable value. The Emorys were close friends with the Clays of Kentucky, with whom the young Emory spent many fond summer hours. Henry Clay Jr. and Jefferson Davis had been Emory's friends since boyhood and remained his closest associates during their years at the military academy.[5]

In part through the influence of John C. Calhoun, Emory received an appointment to The United States Military Academy at West Point, where he enrolled as a cadet in 1826.[6] While at the academy he earned the quite appropriate nickname "Bold," a characteristic that was to suit him all his life.[7] Graduating as a brevet second lieutenant in the Fourth Artillery, Emory was eager to get into the Black Hawk War that broke out in 1832.[8] Perhaps the disappointment in being turned down for such exciting duty had some influence on his decision to resign his commission. Even the regrettable campaign against the Creek Indians was closed when he left the service in 1836.[9]

During his brief interlude as a civilian, Emory married Matilda Wilkens Bache, the great-granddaughter of Benjamin Franklin. Matilda's father was Alexander Dallas Bache, later superintendent of the United States Coast Survey, and her great uncle, George Mifflin Dallas, was to become vice president in the Polk administration. Thus Emory had allied himself to the influential Bache

William Hemsley Emory, Courtesy National Archives, Washington, DC.

and Dallas families of Pennsylvania, thereby widening his circle of political friends. On more than one occasion Matilda Emory would marshall her political connections to shield her husband from Washington, D.C.'s flared tempers, which his ill-considered dispatches from the far frontier at times provoked. Her calm advice was an important strength upon which Emory could rely.[10]

Emory soon secured a position as chief engineer with the Eastern Shore Rail Road Company, but his restless nature caused disenchantment with civilian life. He seemed to be floundering about for a suitable career, when he sought and at length obtained an appointment to the Corps of Topographical Engineers at the rank of first lieutenant, but not without some difficulty. It would appear that his earlier resignation from the service caused enough murmuring that Thomas Hart Benton saw to the tabling of his nomination in the Senate; an act that earned the senator Emory's everlasting enmity. So distraught was Emory that to avoid the stigma of rejection, he was willing to give up the appointment once the Senate had granted it.[11] Matilda Emory thought her husband's consideration of a second resignation from the army would open himself to censure, "as it looks like fickleness to have allowed himself to be nominated unless he meant to enter the corps."[12]

Despite his frustrations, Emory secured the nomination to the corps, where his exceptional mathematical ability promised him a successful career.[13] Hotheaded and blunt in speech and written word, Emory was an explosive personality; a prima donna who found it difficult to get along with his fellow officers in the Topographical Engineers as well as his superiors. Yet he was to do yeoman work on the northeastern boundary survey where he honed his skills as surveyor and engineer. The scientific knowledge, bold nature, and powers of observation he possessed would serve Emory well throughout the decade that began in 1846 and ended with the delineation of the new boundary between Mexico and the United States. In this he was to play a key role.

Emory's report on his military reconnaissance had great influence on Secretary of State James Buchanan, who drafted the original treaty proposal that the United States presented for Mexico's consideration. Emory had observed that a railroad to the Pacific could be built through New Mexico along the Río Gila, although both banks of the river would be required. Even before war was a certainty, Buchanan was adamant that the Río Grande was the western line of Texas and wanted all of New Mexico and California. While there was never any question of withdrawing from the Río Grande, the question of additional territory became pressing after the outbreak of a lengthy war accompanied by considerable losses in men and treasure. Buchanan began to see the cession of New Mexico and California as an indemnity. In any case the war could not be allowed to drag on forever, and the Polk administration was eager to bring it to a close as quickly as possible.[14]

With this in mind the president appointed Nicholas Trist, the able chief clerk of the Department of State, as commissioner with the authority to conclude a treaty of peace with the Republic of Mexico.[15] A native of Charlottesville, Virginia, Trist appeared to be well along the path toward a respectable career in public service when his name was placed before Polk. He had read law under Thomas Jefferson and married Jefferson's granddaughter, Virginia Jefferson Randolph. Appointed as a clerk in the Department of the Treasury, he later served briefly as private secretary to Andrew Jackson, with whom he developed a fast friendship. From 1833 to 1841 Trist was United States Consul at Havana where he perfected his knowledge of Spanish and gained an understanding of Hispanic character.[16] While at Havana he also demonstrated an independence of thought and attitude that would have an important influence on his mission to Mexico.[17] Intellectually Trist was the heir of Jefferson and the protégé of Jackson. He was conscientious and possessed industry and integrity, and although scholarly, Trist was cursed with verbosity. Too quick to give advice to presidents and secretaries of state whether solicited or not, he was honest and a slave to justice for others and himself, a trait that sometimes brought him into conflict with men of lesser intellectual bent than he.

Trist's post as chief clerk of the Department of State brought him into close association with Buchanan and Polk. With the secretary he became intimate; the bachelor Buchanan was always welcome for tea at the Trists. With Polk he was candid and had little in common with the president save the desire to end the war as quickly as possible.[18] Polk considered Trist a good choice as the messenger of peace to Mexico. He was a Democrat of long standing and as chief clerk held a position of no political importance. His appointment would offend no faction of the Democratic Party, and as commissioner he could easily be replaced by a full diplomatic mission should the occasion arise. Trist's experience, education, and obvious capacity for work easily recommended him to Polk and Buchanan. Receiving his instructions on 15 April 1847 Trist departed the next day and reached Veracruz on the sixth of the following month.[19]

The line Buchanan instructed Trist to negotiate began in the mouth of the Río Grande, followed that river to the southern boundary of New Mexico, and along that line and the territory's western boundary until it struck the Río Gila. It then followed the course of the Gila and that of the Colorado to the Gulf of California, giving both Californias and the entire New Mexico territory to the United States. The secretary cautioned Trist that Baja California was not a sine qua non to the conclusion of a treaty, and if it could not be obtained Trist was authorized to seek the dividing line between the two Californias that he believed ran somewhat north of the parallel of thirty-two degrees, striking the Pacific Ocean south of the port of San Miguel. The acquisition of Alta

California was therefore an essential condition to the conclusion of peace.[20] For his further instruction, Buchanan provided Trist with a copy of a map of Mexico published by J. Disturnell whereon the dividing line between the two Californias was clearly demonstrated.[21]

In a subsequent dispatch to Trist, Buchanan urgently expressed his belief in the necessity of securing thirty-two degrees north latitude. He informed Trist that a conversation with Lieutenant Emory had convinced him of the importance of this modification. While in California Emory had determined that San Diego and the mouth of the Río Gila were both north of the thirty-second parallel. Thus, Buchanan had concluded that the most favorable boundary would be 32° north latitude from the Río Grande to the Gulf of California, or if Baja California could not be obtained, directly to the Pacific shore. Important as this modification was, Buchanan insisted that the thirty-second parallel was not an absolute condition to the conclusion of a treaty of peace.[22] Above all Buchanan wanted an uninhabited desert and mountain boundary and would be amazed at the increasingly urban and populous border region of today.

Trist meanwhile had been working his way toward the opening of peace negotiations, and by the end of August thought a treaty could be had with very little delay.[23] After the great battle of Churubusco, with Antonio López de Santa Anna's army dispersed and the forces under Winfield Scott having dwindled through disease and battle, the opposing commanding generals agreed to an armistice. The ostensible purpose of the agreement signed on 23 August 1847 was to explore the possibility of making peace. Both Scott and Trist, who had become close friends sharing their innermost thoughts, believed in the sincerity of Santa Anna's expressed desire for peace.[24]

Armed with his treaty and Buchanan's modifications, Nicholas Trist met with the Mexican treaty commissioners on 27 August 1847 at the house commonly known as that of the Inquisitor Alfaro in the town of Atzcapotzalco in the environs of Mexico City. Senators José Bernardo Couto and Miguel Atristáin, ex-President José Joaquín de Herrera, and General Ignacio Mora y Villamil represented Mexico.[25] These men were all known to be advocates of peace. Herrera in particular was considered the leader of those who were then known as the peace party. His appointment gave the coming negotiations a certain respectability as he possessed a reputation of honor and virtue and was the very symbol of impartiality.[26] The Mexican commissioners found Trist's first proposals inadmissable.[27] From an intercepted dispatch of Buchanan's, they had learned that Trist was not to consider Baja California and the thirty-second parallel as a sine qua non to the conclusion of peace.[28] Here they were on firm ground. When the plenipotentiaries of both nations met again on the first and second of September, Trist found the Mexican commissioners adamant in their determination to retain the territory between the Río Grande and the Río Nueces, and equally desirous of keeping New Mexico.[29]

At the following negotiations on 6 September, the Mexican commissioners assented to the loss of Texas, but held that Mexico could not cede the territory between the Río Grande and the Nueces since it had never been part of Texas. They also refused to relinquish Baja California and insisted that a part of Alta California be retained as a land bridge to the mainland. With this said they presented Trist with a counterproposal that would establish the boundary at the Río Nueces and retain for Mexico all of Alta California and New Mexico south of the thirty-seventh parallel.[30]

The proposed boundary was so divergent from Trist's instructions that he felt it proper to break off negotiations. It was now clear to both sides that Mexico's refusal to cede all of Alta California and New Mexico had brought the negotiations to an impasse. According to the terms of the truce, the armistice was now at an end and the war resumed. Though ending in failure, these negotiations had prepared the ground for a renewal of the discussions that would ultimately lead to peace.[31]

Hearing that Trist's mission had failed, President Polk reacted by ordering Buchanan to recall the commissioner. If Mexico was not willing to accept his conditions, the war must be prosecuted until the defeated nation sued for peace. Buchanan ordered Trist to return to Washington at the first opportunity, and bring a treaty should he have one, but, if he were merely involved in negotiations, to suspend them immediately.[32] When Trist received word of his recall on 16 November, Mexico City was in General Winfield Scott's possession, and the Chief Justice of the Supreme Court, Manuel de la Peña y Peña, had replaced the disgraced and defeated Santa Anna in the presidency and established a de facto government at Querétaro. This was no easy task since the war party desired to continue the struggle and disrupted his efforts as best it could.[33] Sparing and lofty in speech, Peña y Peña was a respected and erudite lawyer who had held various government and diplomatic posts with ability, and had received a number of accolades including the presidency of the Academy of Jurisprudence. He had been in favor of negotiating a solution to the Texas question and was known to be a proponent of peace. Of "mild, benignant expression … ," Peña y Peña possessed the cautious wisdom that his country now so desperately needed.[34]

Under these circumstances, Trist had made a gesture toward reopening negotiations on 20 October, believing that the prospect of concluding a peace treaty was at the moment very good. The new minister of foreign relations, Luis de la Rosa, was a noted journalist, one of the editors of the famous *Siglo XIX*, a legislator, and another advocate of peace. He had a profound hatred for militarism, often remarking that one could make anything of a soldier except a rational man. De la Rosa and Peña y Peña, with only moral force at their disposal, had established the new government in which for a time de la Rosa held all portfolios.

Not given to lengthy discussion or argument, de la Rosa soon responded to Trist's proposal with a promise to appoint a commission to resume negotiations. During the ensuing month the Moderado, or moderate liberal party, worked assiduously to establish a legally constituted government committed to the cause of peace. At length the Querétaro Congress elected the tall, bony-framed and monosyllabic Pedro María Anaya president ad interim, and Peña y Peña, now serving as foreign minister, informed Trist that Anaya had appointed Couto, Atristáin, General Manuel Rincón, and Luis Gonzaga Cuevas, also a senator, to reopen the discussions. It soon appeared, however, that all their efforts had come to nothing, for Trist's recall had made any official negotiations an impossibility.[35]

Peña y Peña believed the moment at hand was the last chance to make a treaty and preserve Mexico as a nation. The new government was in place and the peace commissioners chosen. Indeed the very character of the government had changed. He was certain that Trist's recall would only give added strength to the enemies of peace.[36] Convinced that Trist had confidential instructions that would allow him to remain in Mexico and treat for peace, the foreign minister argued that Trist had had full powers when he offered to renew negotiations and Mexico had responded in good faith.[37] Trist was very disturbed by all this and wrote to Buchanan his sincere belief that this moment was the last chance for a peace treaty, recommending that the president appoint his successor immediately.[38] But this would take time and time was running out. After wrestling with his conscience, his patriotism, and his sense of the moment, Trist decided on 4 December 1847 to disobey his recall and resume negotiations if Mexico could agree to begin with his original treaty proposal.

He realized that his government would be displeased with his actions and was doubly disturbed as his family had been very close to Buchanan— a relationship he sensed would now change.[39] Though anxious over the reaction to his decision in Washington, Trist was confident he had acted in the best interests of his country. He soon learned that Minister of War Mora y Villamil had expressed his government's sincere desire to begin negotiations based on Trist's original proposal.[40] It was with greater confidence, therefore, that Trist explained his actions to Buchanan. Trist was convinced that his recall had been based upon an incorrect understanding of the condition of affairs in Mexico, and yet he had received no new instructions from Washington indicating his boundary proposal would not be acceptable.

The question in Mexico, on the other hand, was whether there would be immediate peace or indefinite war. Both the ad interim Anaya government and that which was to replace it in January were in favor of a settlement, but to gain ratification any treaty would have to be made quickly. Trist was convinced that, should this government of the Moderado party fail, anarchy would follow and there would be no one with whom to negotiate. If adopted, the new boundary would cost the nation half her territory, but however defenseless a nation may become, Trist argued, there was a limit to what it could accept, and Mexico had reached that limit. A treaty asking for more could not be ratified by her government, but would bring it down. Here was the real danger for the United States. As these anxious days followed one another, Trist became increasingly sure of his momentous decision.[41] Buchanan, meanwhile, feared the chaos in Mexico would demand a lengthy military occupation before a lasting peace could be had.[42] Peña y Peña also realized that if peace were not concluded now, Mexico faced not only further humiliation, but the possible extinction of her sovereignty. Her armies were defeated and dispersed, her capital in the hands of the invader.[43]

The commissioners for both nations knew that time was limited when they met to begin negotiations on Sunday evening, 2 January 1848. The Mexican treaty framers were José Bernardo Couto, Luis Cuevas, and Miguel Atristáin, Manuel Rincón having withdrawn due to illness. Of those remaining, Couto was the most notable. He had studied law and the humanities at the renowned Colegio de San Ildefonso and had served in the legislatures of Veracruz state and the republic, and then as minister of justice in the Herrera administration. Couto was one of the most notable jurists of his day, a disciple of Mexico's great liberal philosopher, José Luis Mora. With his deep-set and penetrating eyes, Couto was a striking personality. He accepted his appointment to the commission because he believed that no patriot could refuse to serve his country in its time of dire need. He brought to the negotiations not only his patriotism, but also his modest simplicity, profound wisdom, and clear intelligence. Couto was the principal negotiator for Mexico and wrote most of his government's proposals to Trist. He was to serve his country with honor in the negotiations at hand.[44]

Cuevas was another product of San Ildefonso, where he had studied law and won fame for early brilliance. Following a long and successful diplomatic career, he had served as chargé d'affaires at Mexico's legations in Berlin and London, and on more than one occasion as minister of foreign relations. He was regarded as a man of capacity, integrity, and vision. Cuevas and Couto were staunch advocates of peace, but it was mainly Couto who brought spiritual serenity and unfailing energy to the negotiations.[45] Peña y Peña, Cuevas, and Couto had been political associates and close friends all their lives, and now faced the most difficult work of their careers.[46]

Atristáin appears to have been a much less notable figure, although he was adept in financial affairs. His eyes spying from behind thick, gold-rimmed glasses, he spoke ineffectively and in a monotone, but was distinguished by his probity and circumspection. Atristáin was somewhat tarnished by his close association with the English banking house of Manning & Marshall, represented in Mexico City by British consul Ewen C. Mackintosh. He was also affiliated with the government bond speculator Francisco Iturbe y Anciola, who along with Mackintosh seems to have urged his appointment.[47] He appears to have played a silent role in the negotiations.

The instructions that Peña y Peña gave the Mexican commissioners on 30 December called for a boundary that did not differ greatly from Buchanan's original proposal. While it was clear that Alta California and New Mexico were lost, they were restricted to treat for a boundary that would serve as a natural barrier to further aggression. However, Peña y Peña's instructions were not to be considered absolutely binding, the government reserving the right to make modifications if the commissioners believed them necessary for the successful conclusion of the negotiations. Under no circumstances, Peña y Peña cautioned them, were humiliating conditions to be placed upon Mexico, or her honor impugned.[48]

Trist began the negotiations in earnest when he proposed a boundary following the Río Grande to the thirty-second parallel and along that line to the Pacific Ocean. Such a boundary, the Mexican commissioners rejoined, would leave a mere mathematical line as a barrier between Mexico and the United States. They feared it would tear away such important possessions as El Paso del Norte and the left bank of the Gila, and cut the land communication between Baja California and Sonora. They vigorously opposed the suggested line and pressed upon Trist the impossibility of negotiating from such a base. They therefore returned to the line Trist had proposed in the earlier negotiations of 2 September, with the understanding that indispensable modifications would be required.[49] The Mexican commissioners were determined to retain San Diego, the Gila River, El Paso del Norte, and the Río Grande. Under no circumstance was any part of Sonora or Chihuahua to be ceded.

While Trist understood the force of this last point, he was willing to make the middle of the Río Gila the boundary instead of insisting on both banks of the river, as his instructions suggested. He could not, however, give up any part of Alta California or any territory north of the Río Grande. Couto, Cuevas, and Atristáin appeared to acquiesce on the question of the Río Grande, and in fact their instructions had called for a boundary following the middle of the two rivers. Therefore they could easily give in on this point, having once more expressed their attitude regarding the territory north of the Río Grande and having driven Trist from the left bank of the Gila. Nevertheless, they were adamant on the land bridge to Baja California and the harbor of San Diego. To this they declared they were so absolutely restricted by their instructions that Trist agreed to consult his own, at which point the discussion adjourned until the next day.[50] Trist then proposed a line following the Río Grande to the southern boundary of New Mexico and along that line to the ridge of the Sierra de los Mimbres; thence south to the thirty-second parallel and on to the Pacific Ocean, leaving San Diego and all of Alta California to the United States. After a long discussion, the Mexican commissioners agreed to accept the southern boundary of New Mexico from the Río Grande running westward until it struck the first branch of the Gila and down that river to the Río Colorado, but were not yet able to agree on the boundary dividing the two Californias.[51]

Trist noted that Buchanan had permitted him to fall back to the dividing line between the two Californias as it appeared on John Disturnell's map, which would leave San Diego within the United States. Couto, Cuevas, and Atristáin, however, insisted that the town of San Diego and its port had always been part of Baja California, claiming they had never heard of such a boundary as that drawn on Disturnell's map. In fact the Mexican commissioners had found that the various maps and descriptions of the line were so discordant that it was difficult to present any one of them as the correct boundary. The line itself was not the question; all that mattered was that San Diego remain with Mexico.[52]

Trist believed this was the only obstacle to making a treaty, and proposed getting around it by drawing an entirely new line between the two Californias that would give San Diego and its harbor to the United States. He insisted that unless he obtained such a line he could make no treaty, and would suspend negotiations.[53] Trist had been negotiating from great diplomatic strength. If he were to break off negotiations, peace would have been delayed for an indefinite period, the war would remain, and Polk would likely demand more territory as an indemnity.[54] This Couto and his colleagues knew.[55]

It was now clear to the Mexican government that the port of San Diego would have to be sacrificed if a treaty of peace were to be signed. Trist could not be expected to give up such a prize as San Diego Bay, which he knew, and the Mexican commissioners later admitted, had always been a part of Alta California.[56] On 9 January the Mexican commissioners presented Trist a treaty draft that ran the line from the mouth of the Gila to a point on the California coast south of San Diego Bay.[57] The line now offered was a compromise. San Diego was lost forever to be sure, but the port of San Miguel and the Bay of Todos Santos to the south of it fell to Mexico.[58] Even Baron Alexander von Humboldt, they admitted, had run the line between the two Californias to the middle of the Bay of Todos Santos.[59]

With the boundary essentially agreed upon, it was now but a matter of putting the finishing touches to the treaty on which Trist, Couto, Cuevas, and

Atristáin had spent many laborious hours. Trist, who had no clerk to assist him, had done all the rewriting and copying himself, but by the end of January expected to sign the treaty. He informed Secretary of State Buchanan of his conviction that the government formed by the Moderado party with whom he had been negotiating was "perfectly and absolutely *constitutional* in all respects ... ," thus guaranteeing the surest legality of any treaty that government might ratify.[60] He further related to the secretary that he had intended to insist upon 32° north latitude from the Río Grande to the Pacific, but soon realized that any cession of territory from Sonora or Chihuahua would have made it impossible for the Mexican Congress to ratify such a treaty. No delegate could have voted for it and maintained his self-respect and honor as a patriot. Had the treaty failed, the Moderado government would have fallen and with it the best chance for peace.[61]

The final sticking point was the concern of the Mexican government as to whether the southern boundary of New Mexico actually ran north of El Paso del Norte as the treaty framers intended. The law of 6 July 1824 describing the boundaries of the state of Chihuahua was sufficiently vague as to leave the question in doubt. Fearful of citing a parallel that might inadvertently place El Paso del Norte in the United States, Couto, Cuevas, and Atristáin chose the southern line of New Mexico as it appeared on Disturnell's map, where it ran a few miles above the town.[62] They considered El Paso del Norte the key to Chihuahua and believed the line on this map could give no question as to its inclusion within that state.[63]

Trist meanwhile had grown impatient and informed his Mexican counterparts that unless they signed the treaty by the beginning of February, he was prepared to break off negotiations. His intention was to hurry the pace as he expected that Buchanan might suspend his actions at any moment.[64] His fear was unwarranted, for as soon as Mexico's concern over El Paso del Norte was aired and calmed, the treaty commissioners for both nations affixed their signatures to the treaty on 2 February 1848 at the town of Guadalupe Hidalgo, with its shrine to the Virgin of Guadalupe making it the most sacred place in Mexico. That same day Trist dispatched the treaty to Washington.[65] In its final form Article V of the treaty described a boundary consisting of the Río Grande, the southern line of New Mexico, the Gila River, and a line running from the confluence of the Gila and Colorado rivers to the Pacific Ocean one marine league south of the southernmost point of the bay of San Diego.[66]

Couto, Cuevas, and Atristáin had obtained the most favorable line possible for their defeated and occupied country. There had never been any hope of obtaining the Río Nueces as the boundary. The land between that river and the Río Grande had never been adequately settled or defended by

Mexico; on this question hinged war or peace. This they knew. They had pre-
served their nation's hold on the important point of El Paso del Norte and
the territory south of the Gila along with Baja California and its land bridge
to Sonora, so critical if the nation were to maintain its grip on the peninsula.
This was to prove no easy task as Manifest Destiny attempted to wrest the
peninsula from the nation well into the twentieth century. The California
line could also be seen as something of a victory. The Mexicans failed in their
effort to keep San Diego, which they recognized as never having been within Baja California, but they had kept that portion of Alta California that
gave San Miguel and the Bay of Todos Santos to Mexico. Indeed, they came
very near to fulfilling their instructions of 30 December 1847 from the
Anaya government, which called for a boundary consisting of the Río
Grande, the southern line of New Mexico and the Gila to its junction with
the Colorado, and thence to the Pacific. They were particularly instructed to
ensure that El Paso del Norte and San Diego remain with Mexico. Only
regarding the latter did they fail.[67] Considering the new boundary as a
whole, they saw the Río Grande and the Gila as a natural and secure barrier, an indestructible line subject to no future controversy. The rest of the line
they believed held fewer advantages as a natural barrier. The Mexican commissioners had in fact done well, yet they themselves did not excuse their
nation's sorrowful and tremendous loss.[68]

President Polk received the treaty on 19 February, but was displeased
with the manner in which Trist had conducted the negotiations, his disobedi-
ence, and the resulting treaty itself. After the fall of Mexico City, Polk had
come to desire much more of Mexico's territory than the Treaty of Guadalupe
Hidalgo gave. However strongly the president disliked the treaty, he felt
obligated to submit it to the Senate, where his party had an uncertain majority. Trist, after all, had followed Buchanan's instructions and obtained New
Mexico and Alta California; should Polk reject the treaty, the Whigs were sure
to condemn him for waging a war of conquest. The opponents of slavery in
both parties would surely fear and condemn unrelenting acquisition of territory to the south.[69]

Worse still, the haunting specter of a protracted guerrilla war resulting
from the treaty's rejection would make "Mr. Polk's War" increasingly unpop-
ular. That, of course, could only serve the Whigs. The Whig-controlled
House, replete with a number of professed abolitionists, might well refuse to
vote additional funds to prosecute the war and the army would have to be
withdrawn from Mexico. Meanwhile a war-weary nation was preparing itself
for the 1848 elections and Polk was apprehensive over the political appeal of
the war hero, General Zachary Taylor, whom the Whigs favored to lead their
party. Finally, the Wilmot Proviso, intended to keep slavery out of the lands

ceded to the United States, was inflaming an old sore that could ruin the Democratic Party. Though he believed a greater indemnity should be exacted, it was clear that more territory could not now be had from Mexico. With these thoughts in his mind, Polk presented the treaty to the Senate, realizing that he would at least gain New Mexico and California.[70]

While there were certain questions that would surely be raised in the upper house, the only senators who might oppose the treaty were the most ardent opponents of the extension of slavery, but they had also been the most sincere in their desire for peace. When discussion on the treaty ran its course, the Senate's modifications proved relatively minor, the most important dealing with land grants and the property rights of Mexican citizens in the new territories. It seems the desire for peace in the Senate was greater than objections within that body to Trist's efforts, and the Senate voted to ratify the treaty on 10 March 1848 by a margin of thirty-eight to fourteen.[71]

While Polk and the Senate had been deliberating on the treaty, the condition of affairs in Mexico had remained unchanged with the Moderado government at Querétaro awaiting the news from Washington. The boundary had emerged from the Senate unaltered, but the amendments to the treaty left the question of Mexico's ratification in some doubt.[72] On opening the session of the new Congress in Querétaro on 7 May, Peña y Peña, who had returned to the interim presidency when Anaya's term came to a close, affirmed that his belief in the need for peace was greater than ever. Despite the alterations made in the treaty by the United States, he believed Mexico should accept it because new negotiations were impossible. It was his espoused opinion that a continuation of the war would result in greater losses for Mexico.[73]

In presenting the treaty to the Congress two days later, Minister of Foreign Relations Luis de la Rosa noted that the treaty should be viewed not in terms of what the nation lost by the war, but by what Mexico had recovered by the peace, and the imminent danger of losing her sovereignty and nationality if the war continued. The war could not be prolonged indefinitely. Mexico had suffered defeat after defeat, her coast under blockade, her army dispersed, her cities and fortresses occupied; the nation seemed to be disintegrating.[74] Couto, who was the primary author of the apologia for the treaty, considered the open frontier of Alta California and New Mexico to have been lost on the day the first shot of the war was fired. Without allies or sufficient military and naval forces, and exhausted after twenty-six years of civil revolt, the Mexican people were unable to offer new and greater sacrifice. The loss of territory, he held, was decisive and inevitable, but Mexico had retained her sovereignty and independence.[75]

After a discussion of Mexico's limited alternatives, and having heard the report of the minister of war on the deplorable state of the army, the committees on foreign relations of the Chamber of Deputies and the Senate asserted that the treaty was a national urgency. Both committees reported in favor of the treaty's ratification, believing its acceptance could well be the nation's salvation and the beginning of its regeneration.[76] The government's greatest concern for the fate of the treaty lay in the uncertain Chamber of Deputies where a number of members were known to be in opposition, but after much animated discussion the chamber approved the treaty fifty-one to thirty-five. Debate on the treaty then began in the Mexican Senate where a large majority in favor of peace easily passed the treaty by a margin of thirty-three to four.[77] The object of the treaty had been to allay all points of controversy between the two nations, but as later decades were to prove, this was not achieved. Although Mexico's remorse could scarcely have been greater, the war was over at last. Ratifications were exchanged on 30 May 1848, and both nations began preparations for the survey of the new boundary, which ran through territory in certain stretches inhospitable, and in others utterly unknown. But would the treaty provide the rail route to the Pacific the United States so desperately needed? This was now the great unanswered question.

CHAPTER I NOTES

[1]   Lieut. Col. William H. Emory, *Notes of a Military Reconnoissance, from Fort Leavenworth, in Missouri, to San Diego, in California, Including Part of the Arkansas, del Norte, and Gila Rivers*, 30th Cong., 1st sess., 1848, H. Ex. Doc. 41 (Serial 517), pp. 7–8, 62–63; Roger Dunbier, *The Sonoran Desert* (Tucson: 1968), pp. 5, 15, 18, 26–30.

[2]   Emory, *Notes of a Military Reconnoissance*, pp. 7–8; Ross Calvin, ed., *Lieutenant Emory Reports* (Albuquerque: 1951), pp. 12–13.

[3]   William H. Goetzmann, *Army Exploration in the American West 1803–1863* (New Haven: 1959), p. 140.

[4]   Calvin, *Lieutenant Emory Reports*, p. 8; Goetzmann, *Army Exploration*, pp. 128–29.

[5]   Albert Gleaves, *The Life of an American Sailor: Rear Admiral William Hemsley Emory, United States Navy* (New York: 1923), pp. 9–10; Goetzmann, *Army Exploration*, pp. 128–29.

[6]   Emory to John C. Calhoun, 28 May 1823, Folder 9, William Hemsley Emory Papers (Beinecke Library, Yale University); Gleaves, *Life of an American Sailor*, pp. 14–15.

[7]   Henry Clay Jr. to Emory, 29 Dec. 1842, Folder 10, Emory Papers.

[8]   Emory to Thomas Emory, 24 Jul. 1832, Folder 9, ibid.

[9]   Emory to "My dear Munroe," 15 Jul. 1838, ibid.

[10] Calvin, *Lieutenant Emory Reports*, p. 8; James P. Shenton, *Robert John Walker: A Politician from Jackson to Lincoln* (New York: 1961), pp. 9–10; Gleaves, *Life of an American Sailor*, pp. 12–15; Merle M. Odgers, *Alexander Dallas Bache, Scientist and Educator, 1806–1867* (Philadelphia: 1947), pp. 2–8.

[11] Emory to "My dear Munroe," 15 Jul. 1838, Emory to Col. B. K. Pierce, 15 Jul. 1838, Emory to Gen. Scott, 15 Jul. 1838, Emory to Capt. Cooper, 15 Jul. 1838, Matilda Emory to Anna M. Emory, 31 May 1839, Folders 9, 10, Emory Papers; Calvin, *Lieutenant Emory Reports*, p. 8.

[12] Matilda Emory to Anna M. Emory, 13 Feb. 1839, Folder 10, Emory Papers.

[13] Calvin, *Lieutenant Emory Reports*, p. 8; Matilda Emory to Anna M. Emory, 13 Feb. 1839, John James Abert to Emory, 11 May 1839, Folder 10, Emory Papers.

[14] Emory, *Notes of a Military Reconnoissance*, pp. 35–36, 62; Buchanan to Charles S. Todd, 26 Sep. 1845, Series II, The Papers of James Buchanan (The Historical Society of Pennsylvania, Philadelphia); Buchanan to Slidell, 10 Nov. 1845, Container 9, The Papers of Nicholas Trist (Library of Congress, Washington, D.C.).

[15] Polk to Trist, 15 Apr. 1847, ibid.

[16] Robert Arthur Brent, "Nicholas Philip Trist, Biography of a Disobedient Diplomat" (Ph.D. diss., University of Virginia, 1950), pp. 64–65, 69–79.

[17] Eugene K. Chamberlin, "Nicholas Trist and Baja California," *Pacific Historical Review*, XXXII (Feb., 1963), pp. 57–58.

[18] Louis Martin Sears, "Nicholas P. Trist: A Diplomat with Ideals," *Mississippi Valley Historical Review*, XI (Jun., 1924), pp. 85–92; Brent, "Nicholas Philip Trist," p. 119; Chamberlin, "Nicholas Trist and Baja California," pp. 57–58; Norman A. Graebner, "The Treaty of Guadalupe Hidalgo: Its Background and Formation," (Ph.D. diss., University of Chicago, 1949), pp. 303–304.

[19] Norman A. Graebner, "Party Politics and the Trist Mission," *Journal of Southern History*, XIX (May, 1953), p. 140; Brent, "Nicholas Philip Trist," pp. 127–29.

[20] Buchanan to Trist, 15 Apr. 1847, Container 9, Trist Papers.

[21] *Mapa de los Estados Unidos de Méjico, segun lo organizado y definido por las varias actas del congreso de dicha república: y construido por las mejores autoridades. Lo publicán J. Disturnell.* Rev. ed. Nueva York, J. Disturnell, 1847. (Map Division, Library of Congress, Washington, D. C.); Buchanan to Trist, 13 Jul. 1847, Series II, Buchanan Papers.

[22] Buchanan to Trist, 19 Jul. 1847, Container 9, Trist Papers.

[23] Trist to Buchanan, 24 Aug. 1847, Container 10, ibid.

[24] Trist to Virginia Trist, 18 Oct. 1847, Container 2, ibid.; David M. Pletcher, *The Diplomacy of Annexation. Texas, Oregon, and the Mexican War* (Columbia: 1973), pp. 518–19; Ramón Alcaraz, et. al., *Apuntes para la historia de la guerra entre México y los Estados Unidos* (México: 1848), pp. 260–64. When Santa Anna later returned to power, he condemned this work as dishonoring the nation, as calumny, and ordered all copies to be seized and burned. Decreto del Presidente Antonio López de Santa Anna, 1 Feb. 1854, Gobernación, Sección s/s, C: 433-E. 18 (Archivo General de la Nación, Mexico City; Hereafter cited as AGN, Gob., Sec. s/s).

[25] "Exposición de motivos presentada por los Comisionados de México," in *Algunos documentos sobre el Tratado de Guadalupe y la situación de México durante la invasión americana*, No. 31 of *Archivo histórico diplomático mexicano* (México: 1971), p. 146; José María Roa Bárcena, *Recuerdos de la invasión norteamericana (1846–1848) por un joven de entonces* (México: 1947), II, 317–18, 321–22; Guillermo Prieto, *Memorias de mis tiempos, 1840–1853* (México: 1948), II, 8–9.

[26] Alcaraz, *Apuntes para la historia de la guerra*, p. 268; Thomas Ewing Cotner, *The Military and Political Career of José Joaquín de Herrera, 1792–1854* (Austin: 1949), pp. 158–59.

[27] Roa Bárcena, *Recuerdos*, II, 328–29; "Puntos que deberán tratarse … ," in, *The Treaty between the United States and Mexico* … , 30th Cong., 1st sess., 1848, S. Ex. Doc. 52 (Serial 509), pp. 355–56; "Instrucciones para los comisionados del gobierno mexicano … ," in, ibid., pp. 369–73; Herrera, Couto, Atristáin and Mora y Villamil to Pacheco, 31 Aug. 1847, Pacheco to Herrera, Couto, Atristáin and Mora y Villamil, 30 Aug. 1847, in, ibid., pp. 369–73.

[28] Pletcher, *The Diplomacy of Annexation*, p. 516.

[29] Trist to Buchanan, 4 Sep. 1847, Container 10, Trist Papers; "Exposición de motivos … ," in *Algunos documentos*, p. 148.

[30] Alcaraz, *Apuntes para la historia de la guerra*, pp. 278–86.

[31] Herrera, Couto, Mora y Villamil and Atristáin to Trist, 6 Sep. 1847, Trist to Herrera, Couto, Mora y Villamil and Atristáin, 7 Sep. 1847, Container 10, Trist Papers; Roa Bárcena, *Recuerdos*, II, 344–50; Graebner, "The Treaty of Guadalupe Hidalgo," p. 329.

32 Buchanan to Trist, 6 Oct. 1847, Container 10, Trist Papers; Milo M. Quaife, *The Diary of James K. Polk During His Presidency, 1845–1849* (Chicago: 1910), III, 186.

33 Roa Bárcena, *Recuerdos*, III, 233–39; Alberto María Carreño, *México y los Estados Unidos de América* (México: 1922), p. 199.

34 Henry Augustus Wise, *Los Gringos: Or, An Inside View of Mexico and California* … (New York: 1849), p. 269; Prieto, *Memorias de mis tiempos*, II, 118–19, 180; Francisco Sosa, *Biografías de mexicanos distinguidos* (México: 1884), pp. 800–802; Pletcher, *The Diplomacy of Annexation*, pp. 532–33; Carreño, *México y los Estados Unidos*, pp. 237–38.

35 Wise, *Los Gringos*, p. 269; Trist to Buchanan, 7 Nov. 1847, Container 10, Trist Papers; Roa Bárcena, *Recuerdos*, III, 233–39, 259–61; Sosa, *Biografías de mexicanos distinguidos*, pp. 548–50; Prieto, *Memorias de mis tiempos*, II, 56, 94–96, 180–81.

36 Edward Thornton to Trist, 22 Oct. 1847, Container 10, Trist Papers; Alice Katherine Schuster, "Nicholas Philip Trist: Peace Mission to Mexico," (Ph.D. diss., University of Pittsburgh, 1947), p. 134.

37 "Notes, etc. regarding United States relations with Latin America," 5 Jan. 1848, Series II, Buchanan Papers; Peña y Peña to Trist, 22 Nov. 1847, Trist to Thornton, 24 Nov. 1847, Trist to Peña y Peña, 24 Nov. 1847, Container 10, Trist Papers; Manuel Dublán y José María Lozano, eds., *Legislación mexicana ó colección completa de las disposiciones legislativas expedidas desde la independencia de la república* (México: 1876–1890), V, 305; Roa Bárcena, *Recuerdos*, III, 261.

38 Trist to Buchanan, 27 Nov. 1847, Container 10, Trist Papers.

39 "Notes, etc.," 5 Jan. 1848, Series II, Buchanan Papers; Trist to Virginia Trist, 28 Nov., 4 Dec. 1847, Trist to Thornton, 4 Dec. 1847, "Statement by Nicholas P. Trist written at Philadelphia this fourth day of November 1857," Containers 1, 10, 6, Trist Papers; Norman A. Graebner, *Empire on the Pacific: A Study in American Continental Expansion* (New York: 1955), p. 205.

40 Thornton to Trist, 5 Dec. 1847, Container 10, Trist Papers.

41 Trist to Buchanan, 6, 20 Dec. 1847, Thornton to Trist, 11 Dec. 1847, *ibid.*; Graebner, "The Treaty of Guadalupe Hidalgo," p. 379.

42 "Notes, etc.," 5 Jan. 1848, Series II, Buchanan Papers.

43 Winfield Scott, *Memoirs of Lieut.-General Scott, LL.D. Written by Himself* (New York: 1864), II, 576; Roa Bárcena, *Recuerdos*, III, 261–64, 274; Frederick Merk, *The Monroe Doctrine and American Expansionism, 1843–1849* (New York: 1966), pp. 186–87; Sears, "Nicholas P. Trist: A Diplomat with Ideals," pp. 96–98; Graebner, "Party Politics and the Trist Mission," pp. 148–49.

44 Ricardo Couto, *Homenaje a don José Bernardo Couto* (México: 1949), pp. 10–13, 19; Roa Bárcena, *Recuerdos*, II, 318; Wise, *Los Gringos*, p. 269; Prieto, *Memorias de mis tiempos*, II, 119; Alcaraz, *Apuntes para la historia de la guerra*, pp. 268–69.

45 Luis G. Cuevas, *Porvenir de México. Introducción de Francisco Cuevas Cancino* (México: 1954), pp. x–xiv; *Diccionario Porrúa de historia, biografía y geografía de México*. Tercera ed. (México: 1971), I, 570–71; Couto, *Homenaje*, p. 22.

46 José Rojas Garcidueñas, *Don José Bernardo Couto, jurista, diplomático y escritor* (Xalapa: 1964), p. 15.

47 Prieto, *Memorias de mis tiempos*, II, 182; Cotner, *The Military and Political Career of José Joaquín de Herrera*, p. 159; Alcaraz, *Apuntes para la historia de la guerra*, pp. 269–70; *Diccionario Porrúa*, I, 1,090.

48 "Instrucciones…," in, *Algunos documentos*, p. 107; "Discurso del señor Peña y Peña…," in ibid., p. 283–84; "Conferences with the Mexican Commissioners," 2 Jan. 1848, Container 10, Trist Papers; Roa Bárcena, *Recuerdos*, III, 282–83.

49 "Exposición de motivos…," in, *Algunos documentos*, p. 149. El Paso del Norte is present day Ciudad Juárez.

50 "Conferences with the Mexican Commissioners," 3 Jan. 1848, Container 10, Trist Papers; "Instrucciones … ," in, *Algunos documentos*, p. 107; Luis G. Zorrilla, *Historia de las relaciones entre México y los Estados Unidos de América, 1800–1958* (México: 1965), I, 221.

[51] "Conferences with the Mexican Commissioners," 4 Jan. 1848, Container 10, Trist Papers; Couto, Atristáin, and Luis Genaro to Ministro de Relaciones, 6 Jan. 1848, "Tratado de paz, amistad, límites y arreglo definitivo de México y los Estados Unidos de A.-Firmado en Guadalupe Hidalgo, D. F., el 2 de febrero de 1848.-Correspondencia relacionada con los límites entre ambos paises," Expediente H/351 (72:73) "848"/21 (Archivo de la Secretaría de Relaciones Exteriores, Mexico City; Hereafter cited as ASRE, Exp. 21), p. 2.

[52] "Memorandum," 4 Jan. 1848, Container 10, Trist Papers; "Exposición de motivos ... ," in Algunos documentos, pp. 149–50.

[53] "Memorandum," 4 Jan. 1848, Container 10, Trist Papers; "Instrucciones ... ," in Algunos documentos, p. 107; "Exposición de motivos ... ," in ibid., pp. 149–50.

[54] Pletcher, The Diplomacy of Annexation, p. 545.

[55] "Memorandum," 7 Jan. 1848, Container 10, Trist Papers.

[56] "Exposición de motivos ... ," in Algunos documentos, p. 151; Pletcher, The Diplomacy of Annexation, p. 545; Graebner, Empire on the Pacific, p. 208.

[57] "Treaty Draft," 9 Jan. 1848, Container 10, Trist Papers.

[58] Modern Ensenada lies on the Bay of Todos Santos.

[59] "Exposición de motivos ... ," in Algunos documentos, p. 151.

[60] Trist to Buchanan, 25 Jan. 1848, Container 11, Trist Papers.

[61] Ibid.; Trist to Scott, 28 Jan. 1848, ibid.

[62] Couto, et. al., to Ministro de Relaciones, 25 Jan. 1848, Ángel Trías to Ministro de Relaciones, 4 Feb. 1848, ASRE, Exp. 21, pp. 41, 132.

[63] "Exposición de motivos ... ," in Algunos documentos, pp. 152–54.

[64] Trist to Couto, Atristáin, and Cuevas, 29 Jan. 1848, Container 11, Trist Papers.

[65] Trist to Buchanan, 2 Feb. 1848, ibid.

[66] Charles I. Bevans, comp., Treaties and Other International Agreements of the United States of America, 1776–1949 (Washington: 1972), IX, 813.

[67] "Instrucciones ... ," in Algunos documentos, p. 107.

[68] "Exposición de motivos ... ," in ibid., pp. 148–56; Jack Nortrup, "Nicholas Trist's Mission to Mexico: A Reinterpretation," Southwestern Historical Quarterly, LXXI (Jan., 1968), p. 346; Zorrilla, Historia de las relaciones entre México y los Estados Unidos, I, 228–29.

[69] Pletcher, The Diplomacy of Annexation, pp. 557–58, 562–63.

[70] Quaife, The Diary of Polk, III, 343–48; Charles J. Ingersoll to Buchanan, 11 Nov. 1846, Series I, Buchanan Papers; Congressional Globe, 7 Dec. 1847, 30th Cong., 1st sess., p. 7; Graebner, "The Treaty of Guadalupe Hidalgo," pp. 411–12.

[71] Pletcher, The Diplomacy of Annexation, 562–63; The Treaty between the United States and Mexico ... , 30th Cong., 1st sess., 1848, S. Ex. Doc. 52 (Serial 509), pp. 43–44; Congressional Globe, 22 Dec. 1847, 30th Cong., 1st sess., p. 62.

[72] Roa Bárcena, Recuerdos, III, 327–33; Pletcher, The Diplomacy of Annexation, p. 564.

[73] "Discurso del señor Peña y Peña ... ," in Algunos documentos, pp. 281–82, 287–88; Circular, 15 May 1848, AGN, Gob., Sec. s/s, C: 348-E. 5.

[74] "Exposición con que el Ministro de Relaciones presenta al Congreso Nacional ... ," in Algunos documentos, pp. 168–69.

[75] "Exposición de motivos ... ," in ibid., pp. 139–40.

[76] "Aprobación del tratado de Paz ... por la Comisión de Relaciones ... , in ibid., pp. 193, 202–204; "DICTAMEN de la Comisión de la Cámara de Senadores ... , in ibid., pp. 206, 225–26; "Memoria del General Anaya, Ministro de la Guerra, acerca de la situación del Ejército," in ibid., pp. 51–58.

[77] Pletcher, The Diplomacy of Annexation, p. 567; Alcaraz, Apuntes para la historia de la guerra, pp. 393–95.

ALTA CALIFORNIA

"Flores, faltan."

**José Salazar Ylarregui,
Surveyor, Mexican Commission**

The Treaty of Guadalupe Hidalgo specified that the two nations were each to appoint a commissioner and a surveyor who would meet in San Diego one year from the date of the exchange of ratifications. From that point the Joint United States and Mexican Boundary Commission was to survey the new international boundary without interruption, through its entire course, to the mouth of the Río Grande.[1] Yet the provisions of the treaty were not fulfilled. Neither government fully understood the difficulties of the terrain through which the boundary was to be drawn, nor could they have foreseen that the California gold rush would strip the survey teams of laborers and engineers and make a mockery of their cost estimates. Over these obstacles Washington and Mexico City had no control. All they could do was to organize their respective commissions as efficiently as possible and support their efforts in the field. In this both governments failed their surveyors in the meanest way imaginable, all too often leaving surveying parties on the frontier without pay, military escort, or even the wherewithal to define the boundary. The greater fault lay with the United States, which unwisely created a mixed commission of bungling political appointees and strutting military engineers whose nearly constant quarrels caused such delay as to bring the Joint Commission to a state of disintegration. Partisan politics served to complete the dismal picture, all of which proved a great disadvantage to Mexico, ultimately resulting in a further loss of territory.

It fell to the irascible President Polk to seek the proper legislation from Congress for organizing the United States commission. The Democratic Senate easily met with Polk's request, but the bill was brought before the House at so late a time that it expired without Congress having acted upon it.[2] That session did provide $50,000 for the expenses of the boundary commission, and Polk believed this and the authority of the treaty would allow him to appoint a commissioner and surveyor.[3] Because of William Emory's knowledge of the area to be surveyed, Polk offered him the post of United States boundary commissioner. Ever fearful of undue military influence, Polk stipulated that Emory, recently breveted to major, resign from the army. As a second resignation from the service would mean the end of his career, the major declined the offer and Polk appointed an Ohio Democrat, John B. Weller, commissioner. Still wishing to avail himself of Emory's expertise, the president then attached Emory to the commission as chief astronomer and commander of the military escort. To fill the post of surveyor, Polk appointed the experienced Andrew Belcher Gray, a Texas Democrat.[4]

John B. Weller had recently lost the gubernatorial race in Ohio by the narrowest of margins, and his appointment may be viewed as a reward for long service to the party. Tall, strong, and hearty, the thirty-seven-year-old Weller was a successful politician despite his recent defeat at the polls and appears to have been a rather brilliant man. Ohio born, Weller attended Miami University at Oxford, "but left the institution with more reputation for frolicksomeness than scholarship ... ," the accolade of brilliance apparently arriving a bit later in life.[5] At eighteen, he began the study of law and before reaching his majority was admitted to the bar. Weller was soon nominated to run for prosecuting attorney for the Democratic Party, easily winning the race. In 1838 Weller, though barely of legal age, was elected to the House of Representatives from Ohio's second congressional district, maintaining his seat for three terms. Weller then retired to the practice of law until the outbreak of the war with Mexico when he volunteered as a private. He was elected captain of his company which became part of the First Ohio Regiment of Volunteers, in which he was quickly elected lieutenant colonel. He led his men through the streets of Monterrey and to victory in the war, earning a reputation for gallantry and bravery under fire; excellent credentials for a man who now decided to reenter politics.

Weller returned a war hero and won the Democratic nomination for governor in the 1848 election.[6] He spoke in seventy-eight counties and "stumped the State to the confusion of the Whigs ... ," but suffered his first and bitterest defeat, losing the election by a mere 345 votes.[7] Weller was an eloquent speaker, and had given the Ohio Whigs a good scare.[8] He was later described as "a ready, fluent, agreeable and popular speaker..., was witty, and being a man of strong passions, would sometimes, when excited, speak in a really impressive manner."[9] John B. Weller was a scrapper, a fighter, determined to vindicate himself before public opinion at all costs. His appointment as United

States boundary commissioner certainly offered him the opportunity, for now he would be acting on a much larger stage.

Secretary of State James Buchanan instructed Weller to organize the boundary commission as he saw fit, to guard his expenses, and to employ as few persons as might be compatible with the successful completion of the task at hand. The commission was solely to survey the line, although Buchanan encouraged the incidental collection of information regarding a road along the Gila. Buchanan lastly reminded Weller that the line run and marked by the

John B. Weller, Courtesy San Diego Historical Society.

Joint United States and Mexican Boundary Commission would have the same force as the treaty.[10]

In addition to Gray and Emory, the government assigned two Topographical Engineers, Lieutenant Amiel Weeks Whipple of Portsmouth, New Hampshire, and Brevet Captain Edmund La Fayette Hardcastle of Maryland as Emory's assistants. The mixed nature of the commission gave rise to frequent bickering between the civilian and military members throughout the course of the survey and ultimately caused much delay. Also attached to the commission were a variety of assistant surveyors, tradesmen, and an interpreter, Dennis Gahagan. Frederick Emory and Charles Weller, brothers of the chief astronomer and commissioner, were included as well.[11]

Having received his instructions, Weller got his commission to San Diego in several small parties. The commissioner himself left for Panama by the end of February 1849 in company of a few assistant surveyors on the steamer *Alabama*.[12] Captain Hardcastle was sent around Cape Horn with the heavier of the commission's instruments, while Lieutenant Whipple remained in Cambridge gathering and calibrating instruments used on the northeastern boundary survey, as well as others from West Point and the Smithsonian Institution. Major Emory and his assistants left from New York on the steamer *Northerner*, while Gray and other members of the commission, including Frederick Emory and the young George Clinton Gardner, reached Panama by way of New Orleans. Gray's party, after being nearly stranded in cholera-ridden New Orleans for want of money, reached Panama City on 12 April 1849.[13]

While the members of the commission had reached the midpoint of their journey safely, serious obstacles began to present themselves.[14] Weller reported to Secretary of State John M. Clayton of the newly installed administration of President Zachary Taylor that the charges for transportation across the isthmus of Panama were enormous. News of the discovery of gold in California had brought an invasion of gold seekers and caused the price of passage on the steamers to become exorbitant. He noted there was no means of transportation at Panama at the moment and doubted whether he could get the commission to San Diego in time to fulfill the stipulation in the treaty.[15]

Fortunately, Weller, Gray, Emory, and a few assistants secured passage on the *Panama* in mid-May, the very ship Weller had taken to the isthmus and upon which Captain Hardcastle had continued around the Horn with the instruments. After a rather disagreeable voyage they reached San Diego on 1 June.[16] The gold fever had not yet reached San Diego and did not attain epidemic proportions until some months later. Only this delay in the arrival of the disease enabled Weller and Emory to keep the enlisted men of the escort and laborers of the commission together.[17]

Yet there was a worse danger than the miasmas of the gold rush confronting the United States section of the Joint Commission. Shortly after arriving in California, Weller reported to Clayton that the unexpected costs of the commission would exhaust the $50,000 Congress had appropriated for the survey soon after the work got under way.[18] Weller had reason to be concerned, for Congress had as yet failed to provide for the organization of the commission, appropriate money for its needs, or fix the salaries of the commissioner or surveyor. The Whigs, who held a majority in the House, resented Polk's appointment of Democrats as commissioner and surveyor when the inauguration of the Taylor administration was so close at hand. When the Senate bill providing for the expenses and personnel of the commission came before the House, the Whigs introduced amendments limiting members of the commission to the Topographical Engineers and providing that no funds appropriated for the survey be used to defray the salaries of persons appointed to the commission without the assent of Congress. Both amendments passed the House by a strictly partisan vote.[19] The Democratic Senate refused to accept the amended bill, which left the commission lacking funds and its members without salaries.[20] The United States survey team, therefore, found itself in rather serious financial constraints even before its Mexican counterpart reached the shores of California.

The Mexican Boundary Commission, meanwhile, had organized with less haste and seemingly more care. Minister of Foreign Relations Mariano Otero requested legislation for the organization of the commission in September 1848. In addition to the positions of commissioner and surveyor required by the treaty, Otero asked for four assistant engineers to aid the surveyor, as well as a secretary who could also serve as interpreter. For such an important task as the survey, Otero suggested 6,000 pesos annually as the commissioner's and surveyor's salaries.[21] The committees of foreign relations and treasury of the Chamber of Deputies believed the commissioner would have a function that would have a diplomatic character and thus should have the salary of a diplomatic agent of the nation, 10,000 pesos per year. Other considerations were the difficulties of the frontier and the danger from the Indians, which would make the task particularly arduous. This was approved in committee and sent on to the Chamber of Deputies on 17 October 1848.[22] With only minor changes in salaries the bill was sent to the Senate the following day, and after some discussion, on 2 November 1848 the Senate approved everything the lower house suggested, even increasing the appropriation for instruments to 10,000 pesos.[23] The next day the enabling legislation was in the hands of Foreign Minister Mariano Otero.[24]

The government offered the post of Mexican boundary commissioner to General Pedro García Conde, an engineer and cartographer of renown, who readily accepted the appointment, which the Senate quickly confirmed.[25] More than anyone else, Pedro García Conde was aware of the tremendous task upon which he was about to embark, and therefore obtained a conference with the cabinet to make sure the government understood the difficulties he would encounter, and to ensure that the requisite support would be forthcoming. To fill the important post of surveyor, García Conde proposed José Salazar Ylarregui, professor of geodesy in the Colegio de Minería. As first assistant engineers, he suggested Francisco Jiménez, professor of mechanics, and Francisco Martínez de Chavero, professor of fortifications, both of the Colegio Militar. As second assistant engineers, he requested his son, Agustín García Conde, professor of geodesy and astronomy of the Colegio Militar, and Dr. Ricardo Ramírez. The general believed his selections possessed ability and only required practice. Before accepting the posts, Jiménez, Martínez de Chavero, and Agustín García Conde petitioned that they be allowed to retain their positions at the Colegio Militar. Their request was granted and the government assigned them to the posts García Conde had proposed. In addition the government named Felipe de Iturbide, son of the former emperor, as interpreter. First engineer Martínez de Chavero was also to serve as the secretary of the commission.[26] The commissioner thought there should be attached to the surveying team a mineralogist, zoologist, and a botanist, but in this he was disappointed. To fill this need García Conde charged Dr. Ramírez with double duty as zoologist and botanist.

A request of more immediate concern was an escort of cavalry of no fewer than a hundred men. The expedition, including commissioner, surveyor, engineers, servants, laborers, and escort would consist of nearly 150 men. He explained to the cabinet that they would need all the necessary equipment, campaign tents, and provisions for a full year. García Conde expected that the entire survey from San Diego to Matamoros would require two years to complete. The plan of operation presented to the cabinet was to fix the two points of the California line, trace that line, and then follow the course of the Río Gila to its origin and thence on to the Río Grande.[27]

The government's ultimate allocation for the survey amounted to 124,323 pesos. This sum included 10,000 pesos for instruments which were immediately ordered from Europe, but when surveyor Salazar Ylarregui inspected them shortly before the commission's departure for California, he found many of them defective and inaccurate. Salazar Ylarregui believed the Mexican government had not received the instruments actually purchased in Paris; that after Mexico's minister to France had assured himself of their quality, other, defective instruments had been shipped to Mexico in their stead. All that could be done at the moment to rectify this distressing situation was to gather a few additional instruments from the Colegio Militar and the Colegio de Minería.[28]

It was unfortunate that the quality of the Mexican Commission's instruments did not match the superior quality of the engineers who composed it.

At dawn on the eighteenth of April 1849 the Mexican Boundary Commission left Mexico City by coach and reached Guadalajara on the twenty-fourth without incident except for a terribly rough road, which upset the coach and caused the wagons of the baggage train to break down almost daily. At San Blas, García Conde secured passage for his entourage of engineers on the English frigate *Caroline*, and on 24 May the ship raised her sails for San Diego. The same day Colonel José María Carrasco, commander of the escort, departed by land with his contingent of dragoons.[29] With a sense of melancholy, José Salazar Ylarregui, surveyor and engineer, reflected upon the beauty of his nation along the arduous journey between Mexico City and San Blas, accentuated by the "flight of the coach and the monotonous pace of the wagons ... ," filling him with a national pride that only the poet and the artist could express.[30]

Pedro García Conde had hoped to embark on the Pacific mail steamer, but on learning from the United States Consul at San Blas that it would not stop at that port, he secured passage on the more peaceful yet slower sailing vessel.[31] The forty-one-day voyage to San Diego gave him ample time for reflection. Like his father, and indeed his entire family, Pedro García Conde had spent his life in the service of his nation. Born in Arizpe, Sonora, on 8 February 1806, he began his military career at the age of eleven as a cadet in the Compañía Presidial de San Carlos at Cerro Gordo, Durango. When he reached Mexico City with his father, Field Marshall Alejo García Conde, in 1822, he enrolled in the Colegio de Minería. He obtained the grade of captain in the Corps of Engineers in 1828, serving in that branch of the army through most of his career.[32] He was posted to Chihuahua in 1833 with the objective of constructing a map of that state. This he completed along with a statistical report, both works providing the most accurate knowledge of the geography of Chihuahua available at that time.[33] While there, he also served as *jefe político* of El Paso del Norte, and inspector of the civil militia. Named director of the Colegio Militar, of which he is considered to be the true founder, he returned to Mexico City in 1837. There, among many other tasks, he carried out the topography of the federal district and supervised the reconstruction of the Palacio Nacional.[34]

A tall man with dark hair, pale complexion, and verdigris-colored eyes, Pedro García Conde possessed a pleasant, gentlemanly manner and spoke with the particular accent of his native Arizpe, Sonora. Credited as being very capable, possessing valor, excellent military conduct, and robust health, he rose easily in the ranks and was promoted to brigadier general in 1837. By then he was already well known for his productive work at the Colegio Militar and as an excellent engineer and man of science who was constantly occupied with his maps and charts.[35]

While first and foremost an engineer, García Conde could not avoid the political instability that afflicted Mexico in the 1840s. He was a deputy of the

Pedro García Conde, Courtesy Benson Latin American Collection, University of Texas at Austin.

PEDRO GARCIA CONDE
Militar e Ingeniero -- Patriota Distinguido

National Assembly that named the moderate José Joaquín de Herrera president, and served in the new government as minister of war and marine.[36]
Resigning his post in the government in 1845, García Conde occupied a seat
in the Senate the following year. When the dictator Antonio López de Santa
Anna returned to lead Mexico's forces against the invading North Americans,
García Conde, who ever had been his enemy, considered fleeing the country,
but soon received orders to march to Guanajuato where he was to serve as
military commander at Yrapuato. Before he could take up his duties at that
post, the minister of war ordered him to proceed to Chihuahua and report to
General José Antonio Heredia to construct fortifications for the defense of
Chihuahua City. Claiming a variety of excuses, the most plausible of which
was the lack of men and resources to build such defensive works, García
Conde stubbornly refused to obey the order. Bristling at this insubordination,
Santa Anna at length issued orders for García Conde to leave for Chihuahua
within forty-eight hours or be taken there under arrest. Arguing that Santa
Anna was persecuting him, García Conde, after three and one-half months of
verbal fencing, left to join Heredia under arrest on his word of honor, escorted
by ten soldiers. Once there General Heredia, apparently agreeing with García
Conde about the lack of resources for the construction of fortifications,
placed him in command of the cavalry, in which post he conducted himself
well.[37] At the end of hostilities, he was elected a senator in the provisional
government at Querétaro, but soon left his seat to assume the post of
Mexican boundary commissioner. General Pedro García Conde fulfilled his
duties as commissioner with dispatch and patriotism, on several occasions
supplementing the meager funds of his commission with his own resources
in order to avoid an interruption of the work.[38]

García Conde was a natural choice for the post. He had been an engineer for most of his career, was a prominent member of the Sociedad
Mexicana de Geografía y Estadística, and had prepared maps and statistical
tables concerning the geographical features of Chihuahua, the section of
Mexico with which the boundary commission was most concerned. Moreover
he was familiar with Major Emory's *Military Reconnoissance*, and perhaps
looked forward to meeting the only man who could have matched him in
knowledge of the topography of the area through which the new boundary
would pass.[39]

As the sun rose on 3 July 1849, the *Caroline* slowly entered the bay of
San Diego and dropped its anchor. Major Emory soon arrived and the Mexican
commission proceeded to San Diego with Emory's troops serving as escort. On
reaching the plaza, the entire United States Commission turned out to receive
them and toast the arrival of the Mexican engineers. After a dinner hosted by
Emory, García Conde and his team returned to spend the night aboard the

Caroline. The following day they joined the United States commission in a Fourth of July celebration graced with a dance in the evening.[40]

With these festivities at an end, the Mexican section of the Joint Commission established itself in "una miserable casa" of San Diego, the entire team occupying a single room.[41] On the same day, 6 July, García Conde and Salazar Ylarregui met with Weller and Gray at Weller's residence to exchange credentials and organize the Joint Commission to run and mark the new international boundary. During the next few days, the Joint Commission authorized the surveyors to formulate a general plan of operations to determine the southernmost point of the bay of San Diego and the initial point of the line on the Pacific Ocean. Gray and Salazar Ylarregui agreed to fix the two extreme points of the California line, mark them with monuments and determine the azimuth, or straight line, connecting them. Meeting on the ninth, the Joint Commission approved the plan, agreeing that each commission would work independently.[42]

On the same day Major Emory established his observatory near Punta Loma, naming it Camp Riley after General Bennett Riley, the commander of United States troops in California. With the aid of his assistants James Nooney and George Gardner, Emory took personal charge of the determination of the latitude and longitude of Camp Riley and the triangulation by which that point was to be carried to the initial point on the Pacific.[43] Salazar Ylarregui's observatory was also soon established and he and Emory met to calibrate their chronometers and compasses. Salazar Ylarregui's assistants now joined him, and he informed Surveyor Gray that he was prepared to begin the determination of the initial point of the line on the Pacific Ocean.[44]

The great question was to locate the southernmost point of the bay of San Diego. Mexico's minister of foreign relations, Luis Cuevas, in his instructions to García Conde, noted that the line was to be fixed in accord with the 1782 map of Don Juan Pantoja. The California line was a purely mathematical boundary, Cuevas noted, and must be marked with great care. In reply, the general did not believe there would be great difficulty as the treaty was clear, but when the Joint Commission began work on 18 August, it found that Pantoja's map did not quite match the configuration of the bay of San Diego.[45] United States Surveyor Gray, assisted by Charles J. Whiting, William A. Taylor, and John H. Forster, surveyed the shoreline of the bay, while Salazar Ylarregui and First Assistant Francisco Jiménez made a like effort on the part of the Mexican section.[46]

Changes in the topography from natural causes and the peculiar features that the map represented brought a difference of opinion between the surveyors. Salazar Ylarregui considered the southernmost point of the port to be farther north than Gray believed Pantoja's map represented it. A difference in the season of the year, Gray thought, in which the two surveys were made, 1782 and 1849, might have made a difference in the appearance of the port. Gray solved the problem by determining the position of a range of bluffs bordering the low salt flats in which time seemed to have made no change and proved the identity of this range on Pantoja's map. Salazar Ylarregui agreed, and the two surveyors established the southernmost point of the bay by measuring one marine league south from the highest point at which they noticed indications of the overflow of salt water.[47]

With this point determined, the Joint Commission met on 10 October 1849 to establish the initial point of the California boundary on the Pacific, marking the place with a post until a monument of marble could be erected.[48] Salazar Ylarregui felt that the initial point favored Mexico to the extent of 168 meters, and that had the treaty framers not attached Pantoja's map to the treaty, he and Gray would have fixed the initial point on the Pacific even farther to the north.[49]

Thus far the members of the Joint Commission had worked well together, assisting one another on several occasions.[50] There were difficulties within each of the two commissions however. A great concern on the part of the United States commissioner was a serious lack of funds, which caused much delay in the work. On this critical subject Weller had received no news whatever, his last communication from Secretary of State Clayton having the date of 15 March 1849.[51] Mexico's immediate problem was the inferior quality of the instruments. Some Salazar Ylarregui found useless, while others had been broken on the rough road from Guadalajara to San Blas. This he found a bitter complaint.[52] Nevertheless both sections of the Joint Commission continued as best they could under adverse conditions.

Before the initial point on the Pacific had been officially established, a surveying party under Lieutenant Whipple composed of Edward Ingraham and Dr. Charles Christopher Parry set out on 8 September to the junction of the Gila and Colorado rivers to determine that point. Parry, though officially serving as an assistant engineer, was charged with geological and botanical investigations to illustrate the physical geography of the country in the commission's final report.[53] Escorted by Lieutenant Cave Johnson Couts' company of dragoons, Whipple's party experienced a journey that was at best arduous for men and mules alike because of the extreme temperatures and lack of water and grass.[54] Toward the end of their march, after traveling in heat that soared to 108° Fahrenheit in the shade, and at times 120° in the sun, they were forced to resort to night marches. On one occasion they were subjected to a storm that first struck them with blinding sand and then rain, hail, and lightning.[55] Whipple and his small surveying party reached the confluence of the Gila and Colorado rivers on 29 September 1849, where he was greeted by

Colonel José María Carrasco of the Mexican escort attached to the commission.[56] After a brief reconnaissance, Whipple found an excellent hill for his observatory, the same suggested to him by Major Emory before his departure from San Diego.[57]

Whipple now entered upon his task in earnest, observing the stars every night and making his computations by day. Often the work was made difficult when high winds blew over the campaign tents and the camp itself became host to an unending stream of immigrants on their way to California.[58] On occasion the visitors were interesting, as was the case when John W. Audubon, son of the naturalist, appeared in camp and dined with Whipple, who no doubt enjoyed the company. Tragedy visited the camp the following day, however, when Whipple, who could not swim, helplessly watched several immigrants drown while attempting to cross the Colorado.[59] If the river flowed treacherously, the dryness of the climate had a surprise or two for Whipple as well. All the boxes in which the instruments had originally been packed on the Atlantic coast were being destroyed by dryness and had so shrunk as to make it nearly impossible to repack them. On one evening when Whipple was reading the micrometer of his zenith telescope, he was startled when the dried and shriveled horn that encased the reading lens snapped into three pieces and flew some distance from his hand. Despite the pleas of the immigrants, which threatened to despoil the surveying party of its provisions, the drownings, sleepless nights, and the tricks played on him by the climate, Lieutenant Whipple completed his observations and determined the point where the Gila enters the Colorado. He now eagerly awaited the arrival of the Mexican section of the Joint Commission.[60]

Following the establishment of the initial point on the Pacific on 10 October, the Mexican commission prepared for the march to the Colorado River. As the wagons were in need of repair and the mules and horses required rest, a delay until the end of October was unavoidable. The commission left San Diego on 1 November and arrived at the Río Colorado on the twenty-ninth, after a difficult journey.[61] Learning of their arrival, Whipple invited Salazar Ylarregui to join in deciding on the point where the Gila meets the Colorado, and make an accurate survey of the azimuth line from that point to where it crossed the Colorado.

Whipple informed Salazar Ylarregui that Commissioner Weller was confined to the sickbed and that he desired that Whipple determine the eastern end of the line in conjunction with the Mexican surveyor. It appeared that neither the United States commissioner nor the United States surveyor were to be present for that important duty. While García Conde agreed to Weller's request, Salazar Ylarregui correctly held the opinion that Weller had no authority to appoint Whipple to treat with the Mexican surveyor, rather, Gray should have been present. He also believed García Conde should not have agreed to such a request.[62] Nevertheless, Salazar Ylarregui bowed to the general's wishes, and on the morning of 30 November met with Whipple at the intersection of the two rivers and accepted the latitude and longitude Whipple had already determined as the initial point. The surveyor also accepted the beginning of the azimuth line, which the lieutenant had marked with a stone pillar. Unknown to the treaty framers, the Colorado turns north and west after receiving the waters of the Gila, which enter the Colorado from the south. After flowing west for seven miles, the Colorado resumes its southward course, unexpectedly throwing both its banks into the United States for that distance. This not only blocked Mexico's access to the mouth of the Gila, but also included nearly the same territory on both banks of the Colorado below its junction with the Gila that Trist had wanted for the United States. For this he had offered the middle of the bay of San Diego as the initial point on the Pacific, but the Mexican negotiators had refused, not willing to cede any territory below the mouth of the Gila. García Conde later held that a strict adherence to the letter of the treaty would defeat the intentions of the treaty framers and wished to present the matter to Washington and Mexico City, but Weller would not agree. The treaty placed the eastern point of the California line at the junction of the Gila and Colorado; the course the rivers took beyond that point was irrelevant. García Conde dropped the issue, but the episode does demonstrate his determination to miss no opportunity to protect Mexico's honor. For the moment however, García Conde contented himself with an examination of the confluence of the two rivers and the map Whipple had made of the area, giving his approval.[63] Having completed his task, Whipple turned his camp and observatory over to the Mexican Commission, and at midday on 1 December departed for San Diego.[64]

United States Boundary Commissioner Weller had a very good reason for his failure to make an appearance at the Gila, for he had recently received a gunshot wound in the leg. George Gardner woefully related that at a gathering of the members of the United States commission, some of the gentlemen, among whom were Weller and Gray, had become not a little drunk. Over some trifle, the two entered into a heated dispute during which Weller tried to strangle Gray, and in the scuffle Gray shot Weller in the thigh. This dismal scene occurred on 29 October 1849 and certainly prevented Weller from meeting with García Conde at the Río Gila.[65] Why Andrew Gray failed to do so is uncertain.

Left alone thereby on the banks of the Gila, the Mexican commission occupied itself in fixing a number of points to determine the course of the Gila for a short distance above its junction with the Colorado, and the course of the latter river until it struck the boundary line itself. The engineers of the

Mexican section also measured the area of land between the Colorado and the azimuth line. In addition the surveying party determined the latitude and longitude of the observatory, finding that their calculations differed little from those of Whipple's party. The Mexican commission began its work on 1 December 1849, engineers Francisco Jiménez and Francisco Martínez de Chavero, as well as Agustín García Conde, the general's son, laboring with competence and dedication under the direction of Salazar Ylarregui.

With the work nearly finished, García Conde, in company with the assistant engineers, departed for San Diego on 1 January 1850, leaving Salazar Ylarregui and the able Ricardo Ramírez to assist him in the final operations at the mouth of the Gila. Having completed their work on 20 January, the two engineers broke camp the next day and marched to San Diego, arriving on 3 February.[66] There the Mexican surveyor discovered that the Joint Commission had met, in his absence, on 28 January, and ratified the initial point upon which Salazar Ylarregui and Whipple had agreed.[67]

The Joint Commission met again the following day, agreeing to place the task of completing the survey of the azimuth line and erecting the monuments in the hands of the two surveyors. Seven monuments were to be erected along the line, one at each end and five at intermediate points chosen by the Joint Commission. This act was modified slightly on 15 February when the two commissioners decided that one of the intermediate points was to be decided jointly by Emory and Salazar Ylarregui; a second point already having been determined by the Mexican surveyor, leaving three points to be fixed by the engineers whom the two commissioners should appoint to remain in California to oversee placement of the seven monuments. Salazar Ylarregui considered this addendum to the original 29 January decision illegal—that he should have worked jointly with United States Surveyor Gray, not Emory, who held no official position on the Joint Commission under the treaty. Gray agreed, and protested the action, but Salazar Ylarregui felt he had no option other than to obey the Mexican commissioner.[68]

To comply with the general's orders, Salazar Ylarregui and his assistant, Martínez de Chavero, needed to verify that portion of the azimuth line from Camp Riley to Mount Tecate, about thirty miles, that Emory had determined while the Mexican section was occupied at the junction of the Gila and Colorado. This busied the two engineers from 18 February to 27 March, during which time they were hindered by rain nearly every day. At one point it rained incessantly for three days, filling the arroyos and making the terrain impassable. The last point to be fixed was at Mount Tecate, accessible only with great difficulty. The Mexican surveyor also found himself inadequately supplied with instruments, among which he counted a sextant borrowed from Major Emory and a theodolite rendered partially unserviceable when it fell into a flooded arroyo with Martínez de Chavero, who nearly drowned.[69]

When Salazar Ylarregui returned to San Diego at the end of March, nine months had elapsed since the day the Joint Commission had entered upon its labors, and the California line still remained to be run and marked throughout its entire length, a task that would not be completed until July 1851. The Joint Commission had in fact adjourned on 15 February 1850, without completing its mission. In consideration of the upheaval in California caused by the gold fever, the Joint Commission decided that it would be impractical to advance the line beyond the Colorado, and therefore agreed to reunite in El Paso del Norte, Chihuahua, on the first Monday in November 1850.[70]

It was the United States section that proposed the adjournment, for Commissioner John B. Weller found himself completely bereft of funds as well as credit. Early on in the work he had apprised Secretary of State Clayton of the great expense the commission had incurred in simply getting to San Diego and that without a further appropriation he could not push the survey beyond the confluence of the Gila and Colorado rivers. Not only had Weller no money, he had no credit either since Clayton declined to pay any further drafts upon the department made by the commissioner until his vouchers had been received and his accounts brought up to date. This would seem to be a rather abrupt attitude when the great distance and difficulties of communication between California and the Atlantic states at that time are taken into consideration. Indeed, one is inclined to suspect the play of partisan politics.[71] Therefore, in early January 1850, Weller informed Clayton that an adjournment of the Joint Commission would take place as soon as he could exchange communications with García Conde. With bitterness he pointed out that $11,000 was due the employees of the United States commission, and that he had no way to pay them, adding, "It is hard, indeed, that gentlemen who have served the government faithfully, at rates less than one-half that paid to other employés in this country, should now be left destitute, six thousand miles from their homes."[72]

Greatly affecting Weller's ability to obtain credit for the commission in California was the persistent rumor that he had been removed from office. Weller was aware of the rumor as early as August 1849, but received no official confirmation until early 1850.[73] Weller in fact had scarcely set foot in California when Clayton replaced him with John C. Frémont, the pathfinder and protégé of Senator Thomas Hart Benton of Missouri. Former Whig governor of Kentucky Robert Perkins Letcher had earlier written confidentially to Clayton that Benton was inclined to support the recently installed Taylor administration and that a kind gesture or two might win him over. Letcher also informed the secretary that Benton would like to see his "darling Frémont . . ." at the head of the California government.[74]

Whether this influenced Clayton or not is uncertain, but a few weeks later, on 20 June 1848, the secretary appointed Frémont United States boundary commissioner. With his appointment, he received a letter dismissing Weller, which he was to deliver as soon as he entered upon his duties. Frémont, who was in San Francisco, accepted the appointment immediately. Since he was hoping to obtain a Senate seat from California he did not enter upon his duties as boundary commissioner and therefore failed to deliver Clayton's letter of dismissal to Weller, though for a time he saw him daily while Weller was in San Francisco. The only bright spot in this for Weller was that Frémont assisted him in negotiating a draft for $10,000 so the employees of the commission could be paid. Without this the United States commission would have been paralyzed. This draft was itself later repudiated by the department.[75]

With Weller's dismissal common though not yet official knowledge in California, his funds exhausted, no new appropriations forthcoming, and his drafts repudiated by the Department of State, it is no wonder the United States commission had no credit. Compounding the misery of the commission was the tremendous cost of everything in gold-crazed California. Even before the finances of the commission had become desperate, Major Emory believed it would have been impossible to progress the survey beyond the Colorado because most of the resources of the country had been drawn to the gold mines. Moreover there was little food for man or mule between the Colorado and the Río Grande.[76]

At this juncture the Taylor administration transferred the oversight of the boundary commission from the Department of State to Interior, whereupon Secretary Thomas Ewing sent a second letter of dismissal to Weller, ordering him to turn all the property of the commission over to Major Emory.[77] When Emory received charge of the United States commission it "was without one cent of money, without a mouthful to eat, and without a hoof or wheel for transportation...."[78] The cost of everything had by now become prohibitive. And then there was the gold. One by one, employees of the commission left until only four remained. Emory reported that had he been a civilian he too would have left.[79] Aside from the lack of money, Emory's immediate complaint was his loss of the command of the escort. Indeed, much of the work would have gone undone had he not the free use of the soldiers of the escort to assist in the day-to-day labors of the commission.[80]

Another problem that had been smoldering for some time within the United States commission was the friction between civilian surveyor Andrew B. Gray and the Topographical Engineers. Colonel John James Abert of the Corps expressed his fear that Emory would be embarrassed by his new relationship to the surveyor who was recognized in the treaty. He wrote a friendly letter to Emory saying that Emory ought not anticipate problems nor compare this new assignment with the northeastern boundary survey where the Corps had had sole charge.[81] The fire now burst into flames as Gray claimed the Topographical Engineers should be placed under his direction, and refused to recognize Emory's exercise of authority.[82]

Another approach to this minor feud is to note that Emory was not an easy man to serve. Emory's assistant, James Nooney, left the commission because Emory was so difficult, and George Gardner later threatened to do so. Bitter feelings between Emory and Gray continued as well and Frederick Emory departed from the commission because of it, while Gray simply withdrew to sulk in San Diego.[83] The young Gardner stated the commission's situation poignantly when he wrote, "we are out here without a cent and would starve were it not for the little hard bread and pork which we can beg from the commissary department of the Army."[84]

The final disintegration of the United States commission took place as Emory received orders to turn over all instruments no longer needed to finish the California line to Gray, who was to proceed by the shortest route to El Paso del Norte. This meant an arduous trek up the Gila Valley and across the entire New Mexico Territory at a time when the commission had neither money, wagons, nor mules. Emory therefore took the responsibility of ordering Whipple to proceed to El Paso del Norte with the instruments by way of Panama, New Orleans, and the smooth wagon road across Texas. With this done, and no money to be expected, Emory placed Captain Hardcastle in charge of finishing the line and repaired to Washington to plead his case.[85]

Meanwhile General Pedro García Conde and most members of the Mexican commission departed by steamer for Mexico City on 4 March, and one month later José Salazar Ylarregui and the remainder of the commission left as well.[86] The survey did not come to a complete halt, however. The Joint Commission had agreed in its meeting of 29 January that Francisco Jiménez was to work with Hardcastle in finishing the survey of the line and the placing of the monuments.[87] At length it was not Jiménez, but Ricardo Ramírez who worked with Hardcastle in completing this task. After an arduous effort of four months they held their final meeting on 14 July 1851 at the monument marking the initial point on the Pacific coast.[88] The monuments on the California line were few, but no one at the time imagined the population that would be there a century and a half later.

When Hardcastle and Ramírez finished the California line, the labors of the Joint United States and Mexican Boundary Commission had been under way for a full two years—the same amount of time García Conde had estimated for the entire length of the boundary from San Diego to Matamoros. The disorganization of the United States commission, caused in part by the hysteria of the gold rush, but in much greater part by the failure of the government to

Old Monument No. I (marble), view to the southeast, before being recut by the 1891-1896 commission. Photographed by D. R. Payne, 1893-94. Reproduced by J. Robert Willingham of Southeast Missouri State University, from Report of the Boundary Commission upon the Survey and Re-marking of the Boundary between the United States and Mexico..., Album, 55th Cong., 2nd sess., 1898, S. Ex. Doc. 247 (Ser.3613).

Monument No. 258 as repaired in 1892 (marble), view to the southeast. This is Old Monument
No. I on the Pacific Ocean, which was recut by the 1891-1896 commission because it was so
mutilated. Photographed by D. R. Payne, 1893-1894. Reproduced by J. Robert Willingham
of Southeast Missouri State University, from Report of the Boundary Commission upon the
Survey and Re-marking of the Boundary between the United States and Mexico..., Album, 55th
Cong., 2nd sess., 1989, S. Ex. Doc. 247 (Ser. 3613).

provide adequate money and credit, is largely to blame for the delay. Very
early in the work, when the Joint Commission had not yet been in the field a
full three weeks, García Conde complained to his government of the slowness
of the United States commission. At this point he was prepared to begin running the line toward the Río Colorado, but the United States section had no
desire to do so. In his view the United States survey team perceived the difficulties of proceeding up the Gila as insuperable unless they could procure
extraordinary resources in dollars and hooves.[89]

What the general found even more unforgivable was the failure of the
United States section to remove itself from San Diego, apparently having little
desire to penetrate the desert. With some astonishment, García Conde reported
that neither Commissioner Weller, Surveyor Gray, nor Chief Astronomer
Emory joined him at the junction of the Gila and Colorado; only a lieutenant
of the Topographical Engineers, Whipple, was present at the confluence.
Having agreed to the point at the junction of the two rivers with Whipple,
García Conde desired to return upon the line with the United States section,
but Whipple had departed in haste for San Diego and Weller was unable to
send another party to the Gila.[90] When García Conde returned to San Diego
from his work on the Gila, he found the United States commission "completely

dissolved...," and that Weller had been relieved and was preparing to go to San Francisco with no intention of returning to San Diego.[91]

Under these circumstances, García Conde agreed to adjourn to El Paso del Norte.[92] The Mexican commission had by now used up all its resources as well, and nearly all its escort had left for the gold fields. The adjournment had in fact relieved the general from an embarrassing position. With his own commission lacking all resources, he could now gracefully depart for Mexico City and reorganize, allowing the onus of the adjournment to fall upon the United States commission.[93]

News of the adjournment should have come as no surprise in Mexico City, for as early as 22 July 1849 García Conde had informed the Ministry of Foreign Relations of the probable need to shift the survey to El Paso del Norte because of the financial distress of the United States section.[94] The adjournment caused something of a flurry in Mexico City since García Conde had no instructions to agree to anything of the kind. It also brought forth an official protest from the Mexican Legation in Washington. Envoy Luis de la Rosa pointed out to Secretary of State Clayton that it was not Mexico's fault that the survey had been postponed, and that Mexico desired a more rapid completion of the work.[95] Moreover, the shift to El Paso del Norte would be to the disadvantage of Mexico as Emory had foreseen.

Emory believed that running the survey eastward and searching for a branch of the Gila that would comply with the treaty would cause the Joint Commission to strike the western boundary of New Mexico north of the rail route he believed existed in the southern part of that territory. All the streams to the south of that latitude have their sources in the mountains and disappear in the desert before reaching the Gila. Working eastward the most diligent explorer would fail to notice them. Pushing the survey westward from El Paso del Norte, however, the Joint Commission would strike the sources of the streams themselves, and, while they may be mere arroyos, fulfill the terms of the treaty and throw the boundary farther south. Emory also noted the inaccuracies of the map attached to the treaty and that the boundary between Chihuahua and New Mexico had never been defined. He believed the two commissioners would have to negotiate and might well adopt the thirty-second parallel running from the Río Grande to the San Pedro, an affluent of the Gila. This he believed would provide the only practical rail route from ocean to ocean within the territory of the United States.[96]

Emory considered the river boundaries unimportant by comparison and had expressed these views before leaving Washington for San Diego. In his belief, beginning the survey at the mouth of the Gila "would end in failure, if not in disaster ...."[97] Colonel Abert of the Bureau of Topographical Engineers agreed with Emory that the line from El Paso del Norte to the Gila was the more important and that its survey should be the next task of the Joint Commission.[98]

And so the first great effort of the Joint Commission had failed. Defeated by the difficulties of the terrain, the gold fever in California, and the blundering effort of the United States government in organizing its commission and failing to support it, the Joint Commission was forced to move its headquarters to El Paso del Norte, ensuring that the boundary would fall farther south, ultimately causing Mexico to lose another sizeable piece of territory.

CHAPTER II NOTES

[1] Bevans, *Treaties and Other International Agreements*, IX, 813.

[2] *Congressional Globe*, 30th Cong., 1st sess., 1848, pp. 901, 902, 1,043–1,052, 1,064.

[3] United States Statutes at Large … , 30th Cong., 1st sess., 1848, IX, 301.

[4] *Report on the United States and Mexican Boundary Survey…*, 34th Cong., 1st sess., 1857, S. Ex. Doc. 108 (Serial 832), p. 1 [Hereafter cited as SED 108 (832)].

[5] *Alta California* (San Francisco), 4 Aug. 1857; Erwin H. Price, "The Election of 1848 in Ohio," *Ohio Archaeological and Historical Quarterly*, XXXVI (Apr., 1927), pp. 270–72.

[6] Bert Surene Bartlow, ed., *Centennial History of Butler County, Ohio* (n. p.: 1905), pp. 914–15; *Butler County Telegraph*, 23 Mar. 1848; *Daily Enquirer* (Cincinnati), 22 Jan. 1848; *Plain Dealer* (Cleveland), 3 Feb. 1848; Joseph Richard Werne, "Partisan Politics and the Mexican Boundary Survey, 1848–1853," *Southwestern Historical Quarterly*, XC (Apr., 1987), pp. 334–35.

[7] *Plain Dealer* (Cleveland), 24 Jan. 1849; *Daily Enquirer* (Cincinnati), 12, 17 Oct. 1848; Bartlow, *History of Butler County*, p. 915.

[8] *A History and Biographical Cyclopaedia of Butler County, Ohio …* (Cincinnati: 1882), p. 160.

[9] *Alta California* (San Francisco), 4 Aug. 1857; *Telegraph* (Hamilton), 28 Jun. 1849.

[10] Buchanan to Weller, 24 Jan., 13 Feb. 1849, *Report of the Secretary of the Interior…*, 31st Cong., 1st sess., 1850, S. Ex. Doc. 34 (Serial 558), pt. 1: 2–5 [Hereafter cited as SED 34 (558)].

[11] Weller to Emory, 1 Apr. 1850, Folder 25, Emory Papers.

[12] Weller to Clayton, 20 Mar. 1849, SED 34 (558), pt. 1: 24–25; Official Journal, p. 25, The Mexican Boundary Commission Papers of John Russell Bartlett (The John Carter Brown Library, Brown University).

[13] SED 34 (558), pt.1: 1–2; Emory to Gardner, 13 Feb. 1849, Gardner to Charles K. Gardner, George Clinton Gardner Papers (The De Golyer Library, Southern Methodist University).

[14] Official Journal, p. 25, Bartlett Papers.

[15] Weller to Clayton, 20 Mar. 1849, SED 34 (558), pt. 1: 24–25; Gardner to Alida A. Gardner, 8 May 1849, Gardner Papers; *Congressional Globe*, 31st Cong., 2nd sess, 1850, pp. 40, 82.

[16] SED 108 (832), p. 3; Weller to Clayton, 16 Jun. 1849, SED 34 (558), pt. 1: 27.

[17] SED 108 (832), p. 3.

[18] Weller to Clayton, 16 Jun. 1849, SED 34 (558), pt. 1: 27.

[19] *Congressional Globe*, 30th Cong., 2nd sess., 1849, pp. 617–24.

20 Ibid., pp. 667–68; Clayton to Weller, 15 Mar. 1849, SED 34 (558), pt. 1: 6–7.

21 Otero to Cámara de Diputados, 23 Sep. 1848, Oficina de Límites y Aguas Internacionales, 1847–49. "Límites entre México y los Estados Unidos de A." Expediente X/221 (72:73) "847"/22 (Archivo de la Secretaría de Relaciones Exteriores, Mexico City; Hereafter cited as ASRE, Exp. 22), pp. 3–5.

22 Minutes, Sala de Comisiones de la Cámara de Diputados, 14, 18 Oct. 1848, ASRE, Exp. 22, pp. 6–8, 14–15.

23 Minutes, Sala de Comisiones del Senado, 25 Oct. 1848, ASRE, Exp. 22, pp. 17–26; Decreto del Presidente, 2 Nov. 1848, AGN, Gob., Sec. s/s, C: 343-E.1.

24 Comisiones de Relaciones y segundo de Hacienda to Senado, 30 Oct. 1848, Minutes, Sala de Comisiones del Senado, 30 Oct. 1848, Otero to Secretarios del Soberano Congreso, 3 Nov. 1848, ASRE, Exp. 22, pp. 32–40; José Salazar Ylarregui, *Datos de los trabajos astronómicos y topográficos ... en la línea que divide esta república de la de los Estados-Unidos* (México: 1850), pp. 8–9.

25 Manuel Larráinzar and Manuel Nobredo to Ministro de Relaciones, 28 Dec. 1848, Secretaría del Senado to Ministro de Relaciones, 9 Jan. 1849, ASRE, Exp. 22, pp. 63, 67; Francisco R. Almada, *Diccionario de historia, geografía y biografía chihuahuenses* (Chihuahua: 1927), p. 282; Joseph Richard Werne, "Pedro García Conde: el trazado de límites con Estados Unidos desde el punto de vista mexicana (1848–1853)," *Historia Mexicana*, XXXVI (julio-septiembre, 1986), pp. 113–29.

26 García Conde to Ministro de Relaciones, 25 Jan., 21 Feb. 1849, Cuevas to Senado, 21 Feb. 1849, Secretaría del Senado to Ministro de Relaciones, 28 Feb. 1849, Salazar Ylarregui to Cuevas, 4 Mar. 1849, Ministro de Relaciones to García Conde, 1 Mar. 1849, García Conde to Ministro de Relaciones, 12 Mar. 1849, Cuevas to García Conde, 13 Mar. 1849, Iturbide to Ministro de Relaciones, 30 Mar. 1849, García Conde to Ministro de Relaciones, 22 Apr. 1849, ASRE, Exp. 22, pp. 71–78, 95–99, 105, 108–109, 122, 130; Archivo de Cancelados, Expediente 8–13896, folio 1, Exp. 4–3868, folios 28,170, 174–88, Exp. 5–2470, folios 7, 47, (Archivo Histórico de la Defensa Nacional, Mexico City; Hereafter cited as AHDN, Cancelados); Arista to Ministro de Relaciones, 7 Jul. 1848, José María Tornel to Ministro de Relaciones, 17 Jan., 7 Mar. 1849, AGN, Gob. Sec. s/s, C: 349-E. 15, C: 360-E. 11, 12; Salazar Ylarregui, *Datos de los trabajos*, p. 8. [Salazar Ylarregui's name is also spelled Ilarregui. His preference seems to have been Ylarregui, and is that adopted here.]

27 García Conde to Ministro de Relaciones, 25 Jan. 1849, Ministro de Relaciones to Ministro de Hacienda, 3 Sep. 1849, ASRE, Exp. 22, pp. 71–78, 134.

28 García Conde to Ministro de Relaciones, 30 Mar. 1850, ASRE, Exp. 22, pp. 328–31; Salazar Ylarregui, *Datos de los trabajos*, pp. 9–10; SED 108 (832), p. 5.

29 Salazar Ylarregui, *Datos de los trabajos*, pp. 10–11; Official Journal, p. 23, Bartlett Papers; *El Siglo XIX* (Mexico City), 16 May 1849.

30 Salazar Ylarregui, *Datos de los trabajos*, p. 11.

31 Official Journal, pp. 23–25, Bartlett Papers.

32 Francisco R. Almada, *Diccionario de historia, geografía y biografía sonorenses* (Chihuahua: 1952), pp. 294–95; AHDN, Cancelados, Exp. 2–284, I, folios 1–6; Almada, *Diccionario chihuahuenses*, p. 281; Alberto María Carreño, *Jefes del ejército mexicano en 1847* (México: 1914), pp. 160–62; Sosa, *Biografías de mexicanos distinguidos*, p. 398.

33 Almada, *Diccionario sonorenses*, p. 298; AHDN, Cancelados, Exp. 2–284, I, folio 30; Pedro García Conde, *Ensayo estadístico sobre el Estado de Chihuahua* (Chihuahua: 1842).

34 Almada, *Diccionario sonorenses*, p. 298; AHDN, Cancelados, Exp. 2–284, I, folios 92–94, 123–24, 188, 206, 219; Sosa, *Biografías de mexicanos distinguidos*, p. 399; Enriqueta de Parodi, *Sonora: hombres y paisajes* (México: 1941), p. 33; Gabriel Cuevas, *El glorioso Colegio Militar Mexicano en un siglo (1824–1924)* (México:1937), p. 59.

35 Prieto, *Memorias de mis tiempos*, II, 114, 167; AHDN, Cancelados, Exp. 2–284, I, folios 3, 243; Almada, *Diccionario sonorenses*, p. 298; John Russell Bartlett, *Personal Narrative of Explorations and Incidents ... Connected with the United States and Mexican Boundary Commission ...* (New York: 1854), I, 455–56.

36 Prieto, *Memorias de mis tiempos*, II, 114, 164, 167; Almada, *Diccionario sonorenses*, p. 298; Carreño, *Jefes del ejército*, pp. 160–62.

37 Almada, *Diccionario chihuahuenses*, p. 282; Sebastián Guzmán to Ministro de Guerra y Marina, 24 Aug. 1846, García Conde to Juan Almonte, 29 Sep., 1 Nov., 1 Dec.1846, Santa Anna to Almonte, 17 Nov. 1846, Juan Nepomuceno Balboa to José Ignacio Gutiérrez, 10 Dec. 1846, Gutiérrez to Ministro de Guerra y Marina, 14 Dec. 1846, AHDN, Cancelados, Exp. 2–284, II, folios 292, 295, 305–13, 317–18, 329–30, 336–39, 346, 349; Prieto, *Memorias de mis tiempos*, II, 167; Alcaraz, *Apuntes para la historia de la guerra*, pp. 144–45.

38 Almada, *Diccionario sonorenses*, p. 298; Sosa, *Biografías de mexicanos distinguidos*, pp. 400–401.

39 *Periódico Oficial* (Mexico City), 28 Apr. 1849.

40 Salazar Ylarregui, *Datos de los trabajos*, p. 12; *El Monitor Republicano* (Mexico City), 25 Jul. 1849.

41 Salazar Ylarregui, *Datos de los trabajos*, p. 12.

42 Official Journal, pp. 19, 23–31, Bartlett Papers; Salazar Ylarregui, *Datos de los trabajos*, p. 13. [An azimuth line is derived from an angle measured clockwise from a reference meridian].

43 SED 108 (832), pp. 3–4. [Triangulation is a means to determine positions of points trigonometrically to compute horizontal distances.]

44 Salazar Ylarregui, *Datos de los trabajos*, pp. 13–15.

45 Cuevas to García Conde, 2 Mar. 1849, García Conde to Ministro de Relaciones, 16 May 1849, ASRE, Exp. 22, pp. 337–39, 304–305.

46 SED 108 (832), p. 4; Jiménez to Ministro de Relaciones, 24 Jan. 1853, "Límites entre México y los Estados Unidos de A. —Correspondencia relativa a … la línea divisoria… ." Expediente-X/221 (72:73) "852"/24 (Archivo de la Secretaría de Relaciones Exteriores, Mexico City; Hereafter cited as ASRE, Exp. 24), p. 73; Salazar Ylarregui, *Datos de los trabajos*, pp. 17–18.

47 Official Journal, p. 35, Bartlett Papers; Salazar Ylarregui, *Datos de los trabajos*, pp. 17–21; Gray to Weller, 4 Oct. 1849, SED 34 (558), pt. 1: 29–30; García Conde to Ministro de Relaciones, 30 Sep. 1849, ASRE, Exp. 22, p. 320.

48 Official Journal, pp. 37–41, Bartlett Papers; Salazar Ylarregui, *Datos de los trabajos*, p. 21; Weller to Clayton, 3 Nov. 1849, SED 34 (558), pt. 1: 31.

49 Salazar Ylarregui, *Datos de los trabajos*, pp. 21–22; Harry P. Hewitt, "The Mexican Boundary Survey Team: Pedro García Conde in California," *Western Historical Quarterly*, XXI (May, 1990), pp. 182–84.

50 SED 108 (832), p. 5; Salazar Ylarregui, *Datos de los trabajos*, pp. 15, 19; *Alta California* (San Francisco), 10 Dec. 1849.

51 Weller to Clayton, 3 Nov. 1849, SED 34 (558), pt. 1: 31.

52 Salazar Ylarregui, *Datos de los trabajos*, pp. 15–16.

53 Weller to Clayton, 5 Oct. 1849, SED 34 (558), pt. 1: 30–31; SED 108 (832), p. 4; Emory to Whipple, 23 Aug. 1849, Folder 18, Emory Papers.

54 "Journals," 12, 14 Sep. 1849, Amiel Weeks Whipple Papers (Oklahoma State Historical Society, Oklahoma City).

55 William McPherson, ed., *From San Diego to the Colorado in 1849: The Journal and Maps of Cave J. Couts* (Los Angeles: 1932), pp. 11–13, 16, 18; "Journals," 22 Sep. 1849, Whipple Papers.

56 "Journals," 29 Sep., 1 Oct. 1849, ibid.; Salazar Ylarregui, *Datos de los trabajos*, p. 10; McPherson, *From San Diego to the Colorado*, p. . 26–27.

57 "Journals," 2 Oct. 1849, Whipple Papers; Emory to Whipple, 23 Aug. 1849, Folder 18, Emory Papers.

58 Couts to Emory, 19 Oct. 1849, Folder 1, ibid.; "Journals," 13, 14, 15 Oct., 23 Nov. 1849, Whipple Papers.

[59] "Journals," 15, 16 Oct. 1849, ibid.; McPherson, *From San Diego to the Colorado*, pp. 45–46, 54.

[60] "Journals," 19 Oct., 26 Nov. 1849, Whipple Papers.

[61] Salazar Ylarregui, *Datos de los trabajos*, p. 24; García Conde to Ministro de Relaciones, 1 Feb. 1850, ASRE, Exp. 22, pp. 322–25.

[62] "Journals," 29 Nov. 1849, Whipple Papers; Whipple to Salazar Ylarregui, 29 Nov. 1849, Folder 21, Emory Papers; Salazar Ylarregui, *Datos de los trabajos*, pp. 24–25.

[63] "Journals," 30 Nov. 1849, Whipple Papers; Salazar Ylarregui, *Datos de los trabajos*, pp. 25–26; Weller to Clayton, 3 Feb. 1850, SED 34 (558), pt. 1: 2-3; ibid., pp. 37–38; Memoranduum, 7 Jan. 1848, Container 10, Trist Papers.

[64] "Journals," 1 Dec. 1849, Whipple Papers.

[65] Gardner to Charles K. Gardner, 15 Oct. 1849, Gardner Papers.

[66] Salazar Ylarregui, *Datos de los trabajos*, pp. 27, 30, 38; "Diario-Memoria de los trabajos científicos practicados bajo la dirección de Francisco Jiménez…, 1857." (Archivo de la Secretaría de Relaciones Exteriores, Mexico City; Hereafter cited as "Jiménez Memoria"), p. 3; Hewitt, "The Mexican Boundary Survey Team," pp. 187–88.

[67] Official Journal, pp. 43, 47–57, Bartlett Papers; Salazar Ylarregui, *Datos de los trabajos*, p. 30; García Conde to Ministro de Relaciones, 1 Feb. 1850, ASRE, Exp. 22, pp. 322–25.

[68] Weller-García Conde Journal, 29 Jan., 15 Feb. 1850, File 397, Records Relating to the United States-Mexican Border, Record Group 76 (National Archives, Washington, D. C.; Hereafter cited as NA, RG/76); Salazar Ylarregui, *Datos de los trabajos*, pp. 30–31; Gray to Ewing, 20 Feb. 1850, SED 34 (558), pt. 2: 5.

[69] Salazar Ylarregui, *Datos de los trabajos*, pp. 31–34.

[70] Official Journal, pp. 71–73, Bartlett Papers.

[71] Weller to Clayton, 3 Jan, 1850, Clayton to Weller, 20 Jul. 1849, SED 34 (558), pt. 1: 11, 38; Weller to Clayton, 28 Jul. 1849, File 398, NA, RG/76.

[72] Weller to Clayton, 3 Jan. 1850, SED 34 (558), pt. 1: 38.

[73] Weller to Ryan, 26 Aug. 1849, in *Telegraph* (Hamilton), 25 Oct. 1849.

[74] Letcher to Clayton, 8 May 1849, IV, John M. Clayton Papers (Library of Congress, Washington, D. C.).

[75] Clayton to Frémont, 20 Jun. 1849, Clayton to Weller, 26 Jun. 1849, Frémont to Clayton, [?] Aug. 1849, SED 34 (558), pt. 1: 9, 28; *Congressional Globe*, 31st Cong., 2nd sess., 1850, pp. 79–80; Weller to Ewing, 1 Mar. 1850, *Report of the Secretary of the Interior* … , 32nd Cong., 1st sess., 1852, S. Ex. Doc. 119 (Serial 626), pp. 74–75 [Hereafter cited as SED 119 (626)].

[76] Emory to Adjutant General, U. S. Army, 12 Jun. 1849, Folder 2, Emory Papers.

[77] Ewing to Weller, 19 Dec. 1849, SED 34 (558), pt. 1: 15; Weller to Ewing, 1 Mar. 1850, SED 119 (626), pp. 74–75; Ewing to Emory, 8 Jan. 1850, SED 108 (832), p. 8.

[78] Emory to Ewing, 2 Apr. 1850, SED 34 (558), pt. 2: 14.

[79] Emory to Ewing, 20 Aug. 1850, Official Dispatches, No. 17, Bartlett Papers; SED 108 (832), pp. 5–6, 10; *Report of the Secretary of War* … , 32nd Cong., 1st sess., 1852, S. Ex. Doc. 121 (Serial 627), p. 186 [Hereafter cited as SED 121 (627)].

[80] Emory to Ewing, 2 Apr. 1850, SED 34 (558), pt. 2: 16; Emory to Abert, 5 Jan. 1850, File 399, NA, RG/76; Emory to Stuart, 13 Sep. 1851, Folder 3, Emory Papers.

[81] Abert to Emory, 25 May 1850, Folder 15, ibid.

[82] Gray to the Secretary of the Interior, 1 May 1850, File 429, NA, RG/76; Gray to Ewing, 20 Feb., 1 Mar. 1850, SED 34 (558), pt. 2: 5, 11; Emory to Gray, 13 Jun. 1850, Gray to Emory, 1, 15 Jul. 1850, Gray to Ewing, 25 Jul. 1850, SED 119 (626), pp. 76–77, 294–97.

[83] Gardner to Mrs. Charles K. Gardner, 6 Apr. 1849, Gardner to Charles K. Gardner, 20 Apr. 1849, Gardner Papers.

[84] Gardner to Clinton McLean, 23 Jul. 1850, Gardner to Col. and Mrs. Charles K. Gardner, 30 Jun. 1850, ibid.

[85] Emory to Ewing, 1 Mar. 1850, SED 34 (558), pt. 2: 9–10; Alexander Graham to Emory, 23 Oct. 1850, Graham to Gray, 23 Oct. 1850, Official Dispatches, Nos. 22, 24, Bartlett Papers; SED 108 (832), pp. 9–10.

[86] Emory to Ewing, 2 Apr. 1850, SED 34 (558), pt. 2: 14.

[87] Weller-García Conde Journal, 29 Jan., 15 Feb. 1850, Hardcastle-Jiménez Agreement, 23 Feb. 1850, Files 397, 427, NA, RG/76.

[88] Hardcastle to Emory, 3 Jun., 3, 17 Jul. 1851, Folder 31, Emory Papers; "Minutes of Proceedings," 26 May, 14 Jul. 1851, File 396, I, NA, RG/76, pp. 102–105; Ramírez to Ministro de Relaciones, 28 Feb. 1852, ASRE, Exp. 22, pp. 378–84 [The "Minutes of Proceedings" kept by Hardcastle and Ramírez are also included in these documents].

[89] García Conde to Ministro de Relaciones, 24 Jul., 31 Aug., 30 Sep. 1849, 1 Feb. 1850, Ministro de Relaciones to García Conde, 31 Oct. 1849, ASRE, Exp. 22, pp. 306, 311–13, 320–25.

[90] García Conde to Ministro de Relaciones, 1 Feb., 30 Mar. 1850, ASRE, Exp. 22, pp. 322–25, 328–31; Whipple to Emory, 15 Dec. 1849, Emory to Weller, 16 Dec. 1849, SED 34 (558), pt. 1: 33–34, 36.

[91] García Conde to Ministro de Relaciones, 1 Feb. 1850, ASRE, Exp. 22, pp. 322–25; García Conde to Ministro de Relaciones, 6 Oct. 1851, ASRE, Exp. 24, p. 29.

[92] García Conde to Ministro de Relaciones, 24 Feb. 1850, ASRE, Exp. 22, pp. 136–39; Salazar Ylarregui, *Datos de los trabajos*, p. 35.

[93] García Conde to Ministro de Relaciones, 1, 24 Feb., 30 Mar. 1850, ASRE, Exp. 22, pp. 139, 322–25, 328–31.

[94] García Conde to Ministro de Relaciones, 22 Jul., 31 Aug. 1849, Lacunza to García Conde, 28 Aug. 1849, ASRE, Exp. 22, pp. 311–14; Weller to Clayton, 28 Jul. 1849, File 398, NA, RG/76.

[95] ASRE, Exp. 22, pp. 140–47; De la Rosa to Clayton, 20 Apr. 1850, SED 119 (626), pp. 2–4.

[96] Emory to Ewing, 2 Apr. 1850, SED 108 (832), pp. 20–21.

[97] William H. Emory, *Notes on the Survey of the Boundary Line Between Mexico and the United States* (Cincinnati: 1851), p. 4.

[98] Abert to Ewing, 10 Apr. 1850, File 402, NA, RG/76.

El Paso
del Norte

"la Providencia quiso favorecernos esta vez ... "

Pedro García Conde,
Mexican Boundary Commissioner

At the same time that Emory and Gray were stranded in California, John Russell Bartlett was proceeding to El Paso del Norte with members of the new boundary commission he had organized under the Department of the Interior. Bartlett had eagerly sought the position, and later related that while he had always led a sedentary life, he ever yearned to explore unknown regions. Of a scholarly bent, he possessed an abiding interest in the Indians of North America and was particularly pleased to have this opportunity to be thrown amongst them.[1] Yet he was never able to conceive of the Indian as being anything but Rousseau's noble savage. This misconception was to cause his commission considerable loss in time and property. If Bartlett's idealization of the Indian caused him difficulty, his inability to understand the frontiersman and laborers in his expedition troubled him throughout the survey and contributed to the failure of his commission.

Soon after his birth in Providence, Rhode Island, on 23 October 1805, John Russell Bartlett's family moved to Kingston, Upper Canada, where he passed the early years of his life. It was in Kingston that he first became interested in the American Indian. The streets of that city were not strange to Indians from the regions near Lake Huron or Lake Superior. Receiving his education at schools in Kingston, Lowville, New York, and Montreal, Bartlett became an accountant and assisted his father in business in New York and Canada.[2] Bartlett returned to Providence in 1824 to work as a clerk in his uncle's clothing store, and later became a bookkeeper in the Bank of North America.

While Bartlett had prepared to follow his father's career, he also became a skillful artist and draftsman, and developed a love of reading, especially of history and geography.[3] During the years spent in Providence, Bartlett became a member of the Franklin Society and the Rhode Island Historical Society, and was one of the founders of the Providence Athenaeum. Bartlett continued his participation in learned societies after he moved to New York

John Russell Bartlett, Portrait by Augustus de Vaudricourt, Courtesy The John Carter Brown Library at Brown University.

in 1836. There he opened a bookstore, in association with Charles Welford, dealing largely in English and foreign volumes. The firm of Bartlett and Welford was the first to keep a large selection of fine old works in every genre of literature and attracted the leading scholars and literary men of New York and other parts of the country. Fitz-Greene Halleck and James Fenimore Cooper were daily visitors, and, along with others, would at times remain for hours in pleasant conversation.

Bartlett soon became a member and later secretary of the New York Historical Society, whose president was Albert Gallatin, secretary of the treasury in the Jefferson and Madison administrations. Bartlett and Gallatin became fast friends and cooperated in founding the American Ethnological Society. In these two societies, Bartlett spent several rewarding years preparing papers on subjects to his interest, and encouraged the historical and ethnological investigations of others. It was at Bartlett's suggestion that John Lloyd Stephens determined to explore the then unknown past of Yucatán while fulfilling his duties as United States minister to the United Provinces of Central America.

Bartlett had won some literary renown in 1847 with the publication of *Progress of Ethnology*, an account of the scholarship in that field. His *Dictionary of Americanisms*, which ran through several editions in English as well as foreign languages, further enhanced his reputation. Bartlett's association with Gallatin led him to produce *Reminiscences of Albert Gallatin* in 1849, but his renown in scholarly circles and the advantages and opportunities he had won during his fifteen years in New York had not markedly improved his material fortune. He withdrew from bookselling and returned to Providence in 1850.

When Bartlett's friends urged him to seek an appointment in government service, he traveled to Washington in the hope of securing the vacant diplomatic post to Denmark from the newly elected Whig administration.[4] A letter of recommendation from his friend, Albert Gallatin, to John C. Calhoun gained not only the support of the senator from South Carolina, but also that of senators Jefferson Davis of Mississippi and Thomas Hart Benton of Missouri. Bartlett also had the support of Stephen A. Douglas of Illinois, but his Whig connections and powerful Democratic supporters were unable to secure him the post he desired. Just at this moment the position of United States boundary commissioner became vacant, and Bartlett's friend, Senator John H. Clarke of Rhode Island, suggested he apply for the post. Bartlett's appointment encountered little opposition in the Senate, and on 19 June 1850 Secretary of the Interior Thomas Ewing sent Bartlett his commission.[5]

D. C. Goddard, chief clerk of the Department of the Interior, who had temporarily replaced Ewing, instructed Bartlett to proceed to El Paso del Norte by the nearest and most convenient route so as to reach that place by the first Monday of November in compliance with the decision of the Joint Commission. Goddard impressed upon Bartlett the importance of exploring the area near the Río Gila to determine if a feasible route for a railroad could be found which would fulfill the stipulations of the Treaty of Guadalupe Hidalgo.

The department also directed Bartlett to avail himself of every opportunity to acquire information regarding the geography, natural history, and other areas of human knowledge when he could obtain it without retarding the survey.[6] The search for new knowledge would be for Bartlett the most pleasurable part of his task as commissioner. It would give him an opportunity to study the American Indian firsthand, to see new flora and fauna, and to examine the remains of ancient Indian cultures along the Gila. It would also be a major reason for the failure of his commission. Andrew B. Gray was to remain as United States surveyor, while Colonel John B. McClellan of the Topographical Engineers was to serve as chief astronomer in Emory's stead.

On the very day of his appointment, Bartlett sought the advice of Colonel James Duncan Graham in organizing his commission. Graham, one of the most prominent members of the Topographical Engineers, was the most logical choice Bartlett could have made.[7] Apparently eager to be of assistance, Graham answered Bartlett's request the following day with a program consisting of two astronomical parties and three reconnaissance teams, each replete with surveyors, assistant engineers, laborers, cooks, and servants. His program also called for the commissioner and chief astronomer to have a party of like composition, altogether numbering ninety-six men. Ewing approved this program, which became Bartlett's guide in the organization of the commission in New York.[8] The newly appointed commissioner was at once faced with a flood of letters from young men seeking employment, all accompanied by recommendations from powerful men. Inexperienced in dealing with such political pressure, Bartlett yielded, filling positions such as assistant surveyor or chainbearer with men qualified only by their youthful eagerness to traverse unexplored regions.[9] By early July Bartlett was complaining that he had no vacancies left on the commission, yet men were being recommended to him with Ewing's authorization that they be appointed. Bartlett's fear was that the $50,000 Congress had appropriated for the survey would be eaten up by "this large corps of gentlemen chain-bearers...."[10] Bartlett also hired a large number of bootmakers, saddlers, muleteers, carpenters, stonecutters, and other workmen in New York whom he transported to El Paso del Norte, at which point most of their services were unnecessary, including those of the commission's six tailors.[11]

To fill out the expedition, Bartlett appointed his lifelong friend, Dr. Thomas H. Webb, secretary of the commission. Webb would also serve as zoologist and geologist for the scientific section of the commission. The abilities of Dr. John M. Bigelow, the surgeon of the commission who served as botanist, and Augustus de Vaudricourt as artist and draftsman, complemented those of Dr. Webb. Bartlett determined to undertake the ethnological and philological studies himself.[12]

At the urging of Webb, Bartlett chose John C. Cremony, a reporter for the *Boston Herald*, as interpreter. Cremony was an excellent choice. He had previously been in the area to be explored, had served in the Mexican War as an interpreter, and had won high admiration for his varied abilities. Armed with goatee and mustache, the colorful Cremony also sported four Colt revolvers, while a bowie-knife completed the picture of a man hailed as being worth a dozen ordinary men. A man to be trusted, Cremony was skillful, intelligent, well educated, and possessed with a capacity to endure hardship and fatigue.[13]

With an escort of eighty-five men of the Third Infantry under the orders of Lieutenant Colonel Lewis S. Craig, Bartlett's expedition departed New York on 3 August 1850 and reached Indianola, Texas, on the thirty-first.[14] It was an unusual organization that now trooped across the rolling plains of Texas. The assistant surveyors and engineers served as a detachment of cavalry under the command of Lieutenant Isaac G. Strain of the United States Navy, and a rifle corps of laborers under command of Captain Edmund Barry of the army. The men of the rifle corps were ordered to don red flannel shirts, blue pantaloons, and white hats, which they could purchase from the commissary. No such resplendent uniform was required of the gentlemen of the commission, however.

Bartlett's inseparable companion on this trek was his good friend Dr. Webb who bothered himself a great deal about his and Bartlett's personal safety.[15] To ease his mind, it was determined that the commissioner and his secretary would ride in a carriage "well supplied with Colt's and Sharp's rifles, Colt's pistols, a double-barreled shot gun, lots of ammunition, a spyglass, and a number of small but useful tools."[16] So prepared, the United States boundary commissioner was quite ready for whatever the West would offer. Or so it seemed.

The march to El Paso del Norte was beset with near constant bickering, and before reaching that town was cursed with several murders on the part of the commission's unruly teamsters. The bitterest of these crimes was the death of young Edward C. Clarke, assistant quartermaster of the commission and the son of Bartlett's friend Senator Clarke of Rhode Island. The offenders were soon arrested and brought to trial before a jury of local citizens and members of the boundary commission, found guilty, and hanged.[17]

The journey from New York had thus far been anything but harmonious. The laborers justly complained about the provisions provided them, but a greater cause for dissatisfaction was the rate of pay assigned to them. The commissioner had quoted one figure in New York, but when the commission reached El Paso del Norte Bartlett quoted a lower figure. This was necessary to reduce the expenses of the commission, but in doing so Bartlett failed to consider the injustice he was committing.[18] Bartlett further demonstrated his lack of tact by attempting to place the onus for the pay reductions upon Jonathan Chamberlain, the superintendent of the workmen. Chamberlain objected to this and left the commission in disgust and without having been paid.[19]

Similar difficulties led to the recall of Colonel McClellan, who was seriously ill with an inflammation of the eyes during much of the journey to El Paso del Norte. Apparently, Bartlett followed the advice of a young, inexperienced, and troublesome friend, Lieutenant Strain of the navy, on matters of transportation and organization of the commission. Strain, Chamberlain, and McClellan had worked together in New York preparing the equipment of the expedition and advising Bartlett in regard to the hiring of the laborers. Chamberlain was on good terms with Strain and McClellan, but feelings of enmity soon arose between the latter two.

They first disagreed about the type of boat to be used on the river surveys. McClellan thought copper boats, which could be converted to wagons, would be best for the Gila survey.[20] Strain, however, ordered four large collapsible boats of galvanized iron. Weighing 1,000 pounds each, they were too large, too heavy, and required too many men to man them; there is no evidence that any of them was ever employed.[21]

Disagreement between the two men increased on the steamer *Galveston* that conveyed the commission to Indianola, Texas.[22] There the imbroglio erupted before Bartlett when Strain ordered camp to be struck and the march continued, while McClellan countermanded the order. Bartlett had placed Strain in charge of the camp and McClellan in charge of the daily march, and could not understand why a colonel in the army's elite Corps of Topographical Engineers should resent receiving orders from a lieutenant in the navy.[23]

Bartlett had also taken Strain's advice about the surveying instruments he would require for the survey. Having a navy lieutenant procure surveying instruments for the officers of the Topographical Engineers was at best indiscreet, but Strain's insufferable attitude compounded the indiscretion.[24] The squabble ended when Strain resigned from the commission and returned to Washington. The difficulty lay not so much with McClellan or Strain as with Bartlett, who saw McClellan's position as chief astronomer as scientific, not military.[25]

In Washington on 9 October, Strain sent a report to the Department of the Interior charging McClellan with habitual drunkenness, conduct unbecoming an officer and a gentleman, publicly using offensive and disrespectful language to Bartlett, and undermining the discipline of the commission by his example.[26] Alexander Stuart, who had replaced Ewing as secretary of the interior, recalled McClellan on the next day, and directed Bartlett to request the colonel to resign on the score of ill health. He refused, and Bartlett relieved him on charges of *"habitual drunkenness and conduct unbecoming an officer and a gentleman."*[27] McClellan had indeed been seriously ill during most of the journey to El Paso del Norte, and perhaps habitually intoxicated, although the testimony is contradictory on this point. He had, however, questioned Bartlett's ability to perform the duties of commissioner.[28] Bartlett resented any derogation of his authority and with Stuart's aid had McClellan recalled.

The mule train that reached El Paso del Norte on 28 November brought the news of McClellan's recall. At the same time it brought the sad news of the death of Bartlett's daughter, his "darling little Leila;" he wrote in his journal, "I am overwhelmed with grief at the afflicting news and cannot realize it."[29] The following day Bartlett was ill, being a greater distance from his Providence home than miles can measure. Laying his grief aside until perhaps a later and more reflective time, Bartlett wrote to his fellow Whig, Thomas Ewing, that he was greatly relieved by McClellan's removal, and revealed his uneasiness with the Corps of Topographical Engineers when he requested that Ewing send no other to replace the colonel in order to maintain harmony in the commission.[30]

Whipple, whom Bartlett had appointed to replace McClellan, took a rather different view. He now saw himself as chief astronomer and topographical engineer, and felt that all topographical surveys and construction of maps belonged to the Corps.[31] Bartlett disagreed, as he informed Whipple, "You are here as a member of the Astronomical and Topographical Department.... In this Commission you occupy a highly important scientific, and not a military position...."[32] Bartlett could not conceive of Whipple's military rank as having any bearing upon the organization of the survey, while Whipple could not conceive of his rank as being anything but central to the organization of the survey.

While the United States commission was squabbling at El Paso del Norte, the Mexican section was having its own difficulties. On returning from California, the Mexican commission also underwent a reorganization, though not so extensive as that of the United States. Minister of Foreign Relations José María Lacunza was upset with García Conde for returning to Mexico City without permission, but accepted the general's explanation for the commission's inability to continue beyond the junction of the Gila and Colorado. Lacunza also accepted Salazar Ylarregui's resignation as surveyor. He requested the commissioner to suggest a replacement and prepare to meet the United States commission at El Paso del Norte.[33] The general responded that in order to march, a reorganization would be necessary with respect to the personnel of the commission, its finances, the military escort, and lastly, his own instructions.

Since Salazar Ylarregui had left the commission, he proposed Francisco Jiménez, whose abilities were beyond doubt. To fill Jiménez' position as first assistant engineer, García Conde suggested Captain of Engineers Juan Bautista Espejo. Francisco Martínez de Chavero, who had performed yeoman service on the California line, had also resigned. In his place the commissioner suggested his son, Agustín García Conde. He also requested the appointment of lieutenants of engineers Manuel Alemán, and the brothers Agustín and Luis Díaz. Lacunza agreed to the appointment of Jiménez as surveyor as well as to García Conde's other requests, but Salazar Ylarregui soon informed the government of his desire to continue in his former post. He had been in dispute with certain of García Conde's agreements with the United States commissioner on the California line, and may have resigned for this reason. His stated reason, however, was that he expected a completely new commission would be organized. In any case Salazar Ylarregui was reappointed surveyor, while Jiménez continued as first assistant engineer of the commission to which Espejo, Alemán, and the Díaz brothers were added. Felipe de Iturbide remained as interpreter.[34]

As to the budget, García Conde informed the government that he would require 18,000 pesos for transport and purchase of mules and horses, another 17,000 for the wages of ten carpenters, teamsters, and muleteers, and 10,000 pesos for extraordinary expenses. Additionally, 34,882 pesos would be needed to cover the salaries of the members of the commission for a total of 79,882 pesos. General García Conde further requested an escort of twenty-five cavalry, under his orders, to accompany the commission from Mexico City to El Paso del Norte as it would pass through areas made unsafe by the Apache. Minister of war Mariano Arista agreed to an escort, but by no means would he provide the commissioner with twenty-five cavalrymen. Instead he suggested that García Conde secure proper escort from the governor when he reached Chihuahua.[35]

García Conde also informed the minister of foreign relations that he would need new instructions before he departed for El Paso del Norte, especially regarding the southern and western boundaries of New Mexico. He noted that the limits of the northern states had never been fixed and therefore were given to different interpretations. Disturnell's map, he continued, was part of the treaty that the Joint Commission must follow, but it contained a number of serious errors.

Former minister of foreign relations Luis Cuevas had also been aware of the problem. In his original instructions to García Conde he noted the great obscurity as to where the Río Gila struck the western boundary of New Mexico.

Disturnell placed the birth of the Gila at the crest of the Burros Mountains, but if the map proved wrong it was conceivable that no branch of the river would reach the western line of New Mexico. The minister also noted that Disturnell represented the southern boundary of New Mexico as leaving the Río Grande at 32° 30′ north latitude. The result was that the line would be much farther north of El Paso del Norte than it appeared to be on Disturnell's map, whereon the town lay above the thirty-second parallel, when actually it was below that latitude. That was not important, Cuevas went on to say, for the government could never accept the latitude Disturnell gave to the settlement. With regard to El Paso del Norte, all the treaty stated was that the town would remain with Mexico, not that it have the same distance from the southern boundary of New Mexico as shown on Disturnell's map.

After reflecting upon his instructions, García Conde felt there was some difficulty in accepting 32° 30′ as the limit between Chihuahua and New Mexico. On the map that line was no latitude at all, but rather slightly undulating, and as such could not be surveyed. Taking the mean of the line's sinuosities, García Conde found that 32° 22′ was more exact, but placed the line 8′ of latitude farther south than called for in Cuevas' instructions.[36] There the matter rested until García Conde's return to Mexico City after completing his work on the California line. In a memorandum submitted to the minister of foreign relations, García Conde cautioned that the undulating line that served as the southern boundary of New Mexico on Disturnell's map could be considered to be just one league above El Paso del Norte, and that this was what the United States would claim. If that were the case, the point of the settlement would have to be fixed. The western limit of New Mexico was also an undulating line and it would be necessary to adopt the mean for it as well.[37]

After an investigation of the problem, the new minister of foreign relations, José María Lacunza, ordered García Conde to take the latitude that the map gave and refer to no towns. If the United States commissioner did not agree, García Conde was instructed to draw the latitude and leave the United States to trace its line. Under no circumstances was the Mexican commissioner to accept a boundary merely one league north of El Paso del Norte. He also instructed the general to select the mean of the sinuous western line of New Mexico.[38]

Armed with his new instructions, García Conde departed Mexico City on 1 October 1850 for El Paso del Norte on the new and as yet undetermined frontier.[39] Difficulties began as early as the commission's arrival in the city of Durango where the general learned that no one had received orders to provide him with an escort. He plaintively asked the minister of foreign relations how he could continue without any protection for the men under his charge. The government responded to his plea by informing him that the minister of war had ordered the military commander of Chihuahua to provide the commissioner with fifty or sixty men of infantry and cavalry. At length he received an escort of merely fifteen men to accompany the commission through the hostile Indian territory that led to El Paso del Norte. During all the long years of the international boundary survey, the Mexican commission would suffer much delay and frustration due to the lack of an adequate escort.[40] By the twenty-third of November the Mexican Boundary Commission was able to leave Chihuahua City escorted by Colonel Emilio Langberg. Upon reaching El Paso del Norte on 1 December 1850, they were greeted by John Russell Bartlett, who called on the Mexican commissioner in company with Dr. Thomas Webb and other members of the United States section.[41]

During the course of the Joint Commission's discussions that were about to begin, the two commissioners had ample opportunity to form an estimation of one another. Bartlett found García Conde "a very intelligent and gentlemanly man. He is very quiet and I think possesses a good deal of what we call Yankee shrewdness."[42] He considered the general very agreeable and wrote, "I have no fears however of his overreaching me."[43] García Conde, on the other hand, found Bartlett to be, "a clever fellow, but unqualified for the labors that we must perform...."[44] The Joint Commission assembled on the third of December, García Conde and Salazar Ylarregui representing Mexico, and Bartlett, the United States, Gray having not yet arrived. Also present were Felipe de Iturbide, acting as interpreter, and Francisco Jiménez as secretary for the Mexican commission, while Cremony and Dr. Webb occupied the same positions for the United States.

García Conde began the meeting by questioning whether discussion could begin without Gray, the United States surveyor. Bartlett replied that there was no need for delay as there were certain points that only the commissioners could settle before the surveyors' duties began. In any event, Bartlett was prepared to appoint another in Gray's place should circumstances require it, claiming that such action would be in conformity with the power vested in him. García Conde accepted Bartlett's answer, stating that his reason for broaching the subject at the outset was merely to avoid a repetition of the dispute that arose between Gray and Emory during the California survey. Bartlett foresaw no difficulty since the commissioners were superior to other officers of the Joint Commission. García Conde again concurred, and this settled the matter for the moment.[45]

García Conde believed the first act should be to fix the initial point where the Río Grande struck the southern boundary of New Mexico. Bartlett agreed, observing that the Joint Commission should establish the western terminus of the line as well. García Conde related that he had already calculated the initial point on the Río Grande as 32° 22′ north latitude, but Bartlett replied that the astronomers should fix the point according to the treaty map. García Conde then pointed out to Bartlett the errors in Disturnell's map. El Paso del Norte lay in 31° 45′ north latitude, not in 32° 15′ as shown on the map. Further, Disturnell represented the Río Grande as being two degrees of longitude east of its true position on the surface of the earth. To prove his assertion, García Conde produced a map of the State of Chihuahua which he had constructed sixteen years earlier.[46]

Bartlett's opinion was that the commissioners must follow the treaty map regardless of its inaccuracy, and referred to the words in the treaty, which defined the boundary as running along the whole southern limit of New Mexico which runs north of El Paso del Norte. García Conde's position was that the negotiators of the treaty had made reference to El Paso del Norte only to ensure that it remained Mexican and that its mention had nothing whatever to do with the distance of the boundary north of the town. Bartlett was not satisfied that the line must merely run north of the settlement rather than *immediately* north of it as shown on the treaty map. He believed the treaty framers had taken the town as a landmark that the Joint Commission could not ignore. García Conde then pointed out on his manuscript map where he thought the line would be. Bartlett claimed that the line would then be shorter than the southern boundary of New Mexico, and with the matter unsettled, the Joint Commission ended its first meeting.[47]

The Joint Commission met the following day but accomplished nothing as Bartlett reported that, "Our place of meeting was in a room without a fire, and with open windows. We stood around the table with our greatcoats on, shivering for three quarters of an hour, when we adjourned...."[48] Because ice had made the Río Grande impassable, they did not again meet until the ninth of December. Bartlett opened the discussion, proposing that he and García Conde determine the initial point and measure three degrees of longitude west as shown on the treaty map. García Conde could not accept this, because a line so measured would terminate beyond the western boundary of New Mexico and thereby be in violation of the treaty. García Conde then proposed a postponement of discussion until the Joint Commission reached an agreement regarding the initial point. Should the Joint Commission agree to 32° 22′ north latitude as the initial point of the southern boundary of New Mexico, García Conde stated that he would have no objections to its length. Bartlett still believed the line should run immediately north of El Paso del Norte, but was willing to concede the point.

While compromise was within their grasp, discussion continued. García Conde still hoped to fix the initial point on the Río Grande at 32° 22′ north latitude and determine the western end of the line by astronomical observation in order to conform to the treaty map. This would give New Mexico a southern boundary west of the Río Grande approximately one degree of longitude in length. Bartlett meanwhile claimed the entire southern boundary of New Mexico as it appeared on Disturnell's map. This could only be done by fixing the initial point on the Río Grande and measuring three degrees west. At length Bartlett and García Conde resolved that Salazar Ylarregui and Whipple, should determine by astronomical observation where the southern boundary of New Mexico struck the Río Grande as shown on Disturnell's map without reference to El Paso del Norte.

When the Joint Commission met on Christmas Day, the astronomers reported that the initial point on the Río Grande lay in 32° 22′ north latitude and ran three degrees west as measured in conformity with the treaty map. Bartlett stated that this agreed with his opinion. García Conde concurred, proposing that they fix the initial point at 32° 22′ north latitude and run the line three degrees west. Bartlett accepted the proposal. This compromise not only ignored the erroneous positions of El Paso del Norte and the Río Grande on Disturnell's map, it also ignored the true position of El Paso del Norte and the western boundary of New Mexico.[49]

Before Bartlett reached his compromise with García Conde, he asked Lieutenant Whipple for his opinion. Whipple answered that since the treaty framers had not referred to lines of latitude and longitude, the Joint Commission should not refer to those on the map. Whipple also stated that as El Paso del Norte was a point of reference in the treaty, it should not be overlooked, especially as the treaty negotiators intended to represent the distance from the town to the southern boundary of New Mexico on the map. Whipple believed a true construction of the treaty would run the line three degrees west from the Río Grande and then north to the Gila.[50] Interested only in the length of the boundary line, Bartlett believed Whipple's opinion regarding the initial point and the southern boundary of New Mexico "fully coincided with mine...."[51]

General Pedro García Conde had won a great victory. The United States commissioner had agreed to the Mexican interpretation of the treaty line. He now reported to the minister of foreign relations:

> The most vital question and that of greatest interest in the determination of the dividing line between our Republic and that of the United States, is resolved favorably in the interests of the Nation. The boundary is not finally that which Disturnell traced, to the very eaves of El Paso del Norte, leaving this town without the dam of the river whose waters fertilize its farms, and without woods that produce the fire-wood and lumber so necessary for everyday life: it is the parallel of 32° 22′ of latitude, nearly thirty-seven geographic miles

straight north from the town, embracing the dam, woods & the population of La Mesilla which today has more than two thousand inhabitants, and eleven hundred square leagues extending along the entire southern limit of New Mexico, the value of which can not be estimated at less than one-half million pesos. You, more than anyone, know the fears which the resolution of this grave negotiation caused me..., but Providence wishes to favor us this time....[52]

Though not so ecstatic as García Conde over the compromise line, Bartlett was pleased that he had obtained the entire southern boundary of New Mexico including the gold and copper regions at the source of the Gila. He argued that had the terminus of the line been established by an astronomical point as García Conde desired, this would have been lost, "I could not, for a moment, be governed by astronomical points or meridians of longitude in settling the question before us."[53] Bartlett wrote the secretary of the interior, "Gen^L. Conde, who is better acquainted with the country between here & the head of the Gila informs me that the mountains in which that stream takes its rise, abound in the precious metals."[54]

While quite content with the agreement he had reached with García Conde, Bartlett was disturbed by the situation within the United States commission. He found that few of the nineteen assistant surveyors attached to the commission were competent to perform their duties, and informed Whipple he had received orders from the Department of the Interior to reduce their number. Whipple concurred, informing Bartlett that he felt none qualified to perform the work he intended for them.[55] Bartlett painfully compared his corps of assistant surveyors to the small number of engineers under García Conde and Salazar Ylarregui, "I am compelled to confess, that this small number of 10 engineers possess more science than the whole American commission. This I would not say openly, but *it is certainly true.*"[56] García Conde held a similar opinion and informed his government that except for two or three of Bartlett's assistants none understood the first thing about surveying.[57] Whipple believed certain of the assistant surveyors needed only practice and that the real problem was the lack of experienced officers to lead detached parties in the field.[58]

This was indeed the problem. Bartlett lamented to Secretary of the Interior Stuart that Congress had appointed Surveyor Gray and four first assistant surveyors to take charge of parties in the field: Joseph Morehead, John Bull, J. Hamilton Prioleau, and Gray's assistant, Charles Radziminski. Congress also appointed Colonel John B. McClellan chief astronomer and added Captain Edmund Hardcastle and Lieutenant Strain. Only two of these remained. Bartlett had dismissed McClellan; Strain had departed for

Washington; Morehead returned home because of illness; Prioleau was disabled; and Hardcastle was still in California. As to Gray and his assistant, Bartlett had no idea whatever as to their whereabouts. That left him with only Whipple and Bull, which placed serious restrictions on his scale of operations.[59] The disorganization of the United States section was such that its principal draftsman, Augustus de Vaudricourt, who had previously worked in the Bureau of the Corps of Topographical Engineers in Washington, resigned. Placing the onus for the lack of organization on Bartlett, Vaudricourt declared, "It has become a disgrace to be a member of the Commission."[60] Destitute for having received no pay, Vaudricourt easily secured a position on the Mexican commission because he was so fine a draftsman.[61]

García Conde had originally feared that the large corps of men Bartlett brought to El Paso del Norte would delay the work and now saw these fears realized. Upset that the United States surveyor had not yet arrived, he reported to his government that the work advanced as best as possible considering the disorganization he observed in the United States commission.[62] The slow progress of the work resulting from Gray's absence and the disorder in Bartlett's camp put an additional strain on the precarious finances of the Mexican section. García Conde lamented that he had received no money from his government and informed the ministry that he could neither hold the commission together, nor expect the men to work without pay.[63]

In spite of all the problems that bedeviled Bartlett and García Conde at El Paso del Norte, they had reached agreement on the southern boundary of New Mexico, and on 9 January 1851 the Joint Commission directed Salazar Ylarregui and Whipple to determine by astronomical observation where 32° 22′ actually lay on the ground. The two astronomers accomplished this by 4 April and the Joint Commission met on the twenty-fourth at the initial point to ratify their findings. Since Gray had still not arrived, Bartlett suggested that he appoint Whipple surveyor ad interim. García Conde agreed and Whipple "officially" became surveyor. The commissioners and surveyors then signed a document confirming 32° 22′ north latitude as the initial point of the boundary. The Joint Commission marked the spot with a wooden post until a more durable marker became available and the ceremonies fixing the initial point of the southern boundary of New Mexico on the Río Grande came to an end.[64]

García Conde now reported to his government that his negotiations with Bartlett regarding the southern and western limits of New Mexico were concluded with all possible formality. His only concern was the absence of Surveyor Gray and Bartlett's claim to have authority from Washington to appoint another in his place. He emphasized to the minister of foreign relations that the Mexican section had been organized in strictest conformity with the treaty from the very first meeting of the Joint Commission. He did not believe that any question regarding the legitimacy of the boundary could possibly arise.[65]

The following day the Joint Commission met and approved a plan, which Whipple and Salazar Ylarregui had earlier agreed upon, for running the line three degrees west from the initial point. Bartlett then mentioned his intent of establishing a depot at Santa Rita del Cobre. García Conde expressed his intention to do the same, remarking that the next three months were most favorable for fieldwork and freedom from Indian raids.[66] The plan Whipple and Salazar Ylarregui employed in surveying 32° 22′ north latitude was a system of signal flashes checked by triangulation. The two sections operated jointly and alternated with each other in the advance to successive astronomical stations. Actual surveying began on 1 May 1851 with the Mexican commission forming one party under Jiménez, consisting of Agustín García Conde and Manuel Alemán, and another under Salazar Ylarregui with the Díaz brothers assisting, each surveying party having an escort of four to six men.[67]

The two commissions worked together in complete harmony although Whipple, whose only assistant engineer was Moritz von Hippel, was unable to proceed as quickly as the two Mexican surveying parties. The United States section also suffered from short rations, which ultimately caused an outbreak of scurvy, Whipple having to send three men of the escort back to El Paso del Norte with the disease. Two others had deserted, causing him to worry that the remaining five would prove inadequate to fend off an Apache attack.[68] Despite these problems the work continued without incident.

The survey began at astronomical station one, or the initial point of the southern boundary of New Mexico on the Río Grande. Salazar Ylarregui determined the position of station two by means of fifty azimuth observations and successively prolonged the line to astronomical stations three, four, and five. Whipple, who apparently was unable to begin work as soon as the Mexican surveyor, verified Salazar Ylarregui's determination of station two and accepted the observations made at stations three, four, and five by the Mexican party. Now both teams could follow their original plan, alternating in the prolongation of the line to successive astronomical stations. In this way Whipple fixed points at stations six, eight, ten, and eleven, while Salazar Ylarregui determined those at seven and nine. Whipple's efforts to begin work at station twelve were seriously hindered by dense clouds of smoke covering an immense area resulting from fires the Indians set on the prairies.[69]

Meanwhile Bartlett left for Santa Rita del Cobre on 27 April. With a supply of wood for fuel, good grass, and a running stream of pure water, Santa Rita del Cobre made an excellent site for the commission's headquarters. To his delight Bartlett discovered a fort of large size, good soil for agriculture and horticulture, as well as ample work for the botanist. García Conde arrived three days later, but soon moved his camp to the banks of the Río Mimbres where he believed he would find more satisfactory grazing for his animals. Whipple and Salazar Ylarregui were actively progressing the survey of 32° 22′, but García Conde was anxious to begin the Gila survey as well. Bartlett had long since organized his surveying parties, but had no astronomical corps to send with them. In addition to Whipple's party, a second was surveying the Río Grande from the initial point at 32° 22′ to San Elceario. Another was making a survey of the environs of El Paso del Norte, and the commissioner had sent John Bull to conduct a reconnaissance of the country between the Río Grande and the Gila. Bartlett felt he could do nothing more until the arrival of Lieutenant Colonel James Duncan Graham, whom Topographical Bureau chief Abert had detailed to replace McClellan as chief astronomer.

Unable to send any more parties into the field, Bartlett determined to make the most of his time by visiting the frontiers of Sonora to investigate the condition of the wagon road which Colonel Philip St. George Cooke had blazed during the war, and to learn to what extent supplies could be furnished to the commission from the area. Perhaps Bartlett's reconnaissance was justifiable, for by the end of the century United States influence and the number of its citizens in Sonora had become significant. Believers in Manifest Destiny were confident that the state would soon fall to its northern neighbor. At the time, however, this excursion kept Bartlett from his duties from 16 May until 17 June. Soon thereafter, Graham arrived.[70] Bartlett was very pleased when he learned of Graham's appointment and was grateful that the government was "sending me such an accomplished and gentlemanly officer. I anxiously await his arrival."[71]

Colonel Graham was indeed a man of considerable merit. He was born in Prince William County, Virginia, on 4 April 1799. Choosing a military career, he graduated from West Point in 1817 and the following year became first assistant to Major Stephen H. Long on the Yellowstone survey. When the Corps of Topographical Engineers was established in 1838, Graham accepted a commission as major and the next year served as astronomer on the survey of the new boundary with the Republic of Texas. From 1840 to 1843 Graham was one of the commissioners on the survey of the northeastern boundary.[72] Upon completing the maps from that work, Graham served in the Mexican War as a "Special Bearer of Despatches," and then was detailed to work on the resurvey of the Mason–Dixon Line. When Graham received his appointment as chief astronomer on the United States Boundary Commission, he had been in the army for thirty-five years, and all but two of those years as a Topographical Engineer in the Corps. With pride he could boast, "With a single exception, there is not an officer of that corps who has been employed on any of our boundary surveys who is not my pupil."[73]

Like Bartlett, moreover, Graham had a lively interest in intellectual pursuits. The colonel enjoyed opera when time allowed, and while in Mexico took pleasure in that nation's art and architecture. Graham especially delighted in his art collection, and at one point came to own some seventy-three paintings. Later, he was one of the contributors to the First Chicago Art Exposition. In 1840 Graham was elected to the American Philosophical Society. He was also a member of the American Academy of Arts and Sciences, the Academy of National Sciences, and a member of various state historical societies.[74] Colonel Graham does not appear to have been much attracted to politics and seems to have been more interested in his memberships in scholarly societies, providing them with copies of all his survey reports. Graham was an engineer who loved art and architecture, and, when he attended the opera, brought the score so that he could more closely follow the performance. The gentlemanly colonel should have gotten on famously with the scholarly John Russell Bartlett. Yet this was not to be. Rumors of the disorder in Bartlett's commission were already beginning to filter back to Washington. Colonel Abert expressed his alarm when he recommended Graham as chief astronomer, "allow me to say that it will be extremely difficult for any officer to be of much service, if reports are correct of present arrangements of the Commissioner, of numbers and baggage in the field."[75]

When Stuart informed Graham of his appointment, he directed him to investigate the state of the astronomical and surveying instruments before departing. After perusing the correspondence of the boundary commission, Graham discovered that Bartlett had gone to El Paso del Norte with only those instruments Whipple had brought from San Diego, and these he considered inadequate.[76] Most of the commission's instruments were with Hardcastle who was at the time completing the survey of the California line. Graham therefore began to collect instruments that had been used on the survey of the northeastern boundary and to have new instruments made as well. These he shipped to Indianola aboard the schooner *William H. Hazard* on 19 February 1851, four months after his appointment.[77] Graham was also aware that the only topographical engineer at his disposal was Whipple and requested that three more lieutenants of the Corps be detailed to the survey. He intended to fit out two surveying teams, one working west from the initial point, the other down the Río Grande, and believed a minimum of three surveying parties would be required for both divisions. Abert at first had no topographical engineer to spare, but at length detailed lieutenants William Farrar Smith and Nathanial Michler to the boundary commission.[78]

While collecting instruments and engineers in preparation for his departure for the distant frontier, Graham had ample time to acquaint himself with Bartlett's negotiations with García Conde. Graham believed 32° 22′ north

latitude was not the southern boundary of New Mexico as laid down on
Disturnell's map. He informed Secretary Stuart that the line should intersect
the Río Grande that same distance north of El Paso del Norte as appeared on
the treaty map. He requested an interview with Stuart that he might bring to
his attention a manuscript map of the Río Grande from Presidio del Norte to
just north of Doña Ana, which Lieutenant Colonel Joseph E. Johnston had
constructed in 1849 from astronomical observation. This would demonstrate
where Bartlett's line actually fell in relation to El Paso del Norte. Stuart, however, failed to meet with Graham and presumably did not investigate Johnston's
map. Graham then asked to explain his views to Goddard, Stuart's chief clerk,
but he also refused to see him. Graham did present his interpretation of the
line to Stuart's secretary, Briscoe G. Baldwin, who was convinced Graham's
view was correct. Graham soon departed for the frontier believing Stuart was
aware of his opinion regarding Bartlett's compromise with García Conde.[79]

Graham left Washington in precipitate haste on the morning of 2 April
1851, five months after his appointment as chief astronomer. Stuart had
grown impatient with Graham's delay in reporting to Bartlett, and noted his
displeasure to President Fillmore during a cabinet meeting on 1 April. Stuart
and Secretary of War Charles Magill Conrad agreed to recall Graham, but as
the ordinary hours for business had passed the matter was left for the following
day. When Stuart and Conrad learned that Graham had already left, presumably in order to avoid being recalled, they decided that so significant a warning
would cause him to act with greater promptitude in the future and withdrew
the order of recall.[80]

Graham had departed Washington for the plains of Texas by way of the
Ohio and Mississippi rivers to New Orleans, and reached San Antonio, Texas,
on 5 May with his instruments in good condition. There he learned that Gray,
who had been delayed because of illness, was but one day from San Antonio
and decided to wait for him before continuing his journey. Two days after
reaching El Paso del Norte on 24 June, Graham dispatched an express to
Bartlett at Santa Rita del Cobre, informing the commissioner that he would
await his expected arrival. By the same express, Graham ordered Whipple to
return to Frontera, the nearby scientific station. Graham wished to consult
with Whipple because he was the only person familiar with the astronomical
work of the commission and had organized all the surveying parties. Learning
that Whipple had no assistant with the competence to continue the survey of
32° 22′ westward in conjunction with Salazar Ylarregui, he sent a second
dispatch ordering Whipple to suspend the survey until they could confer.[81]

When he received Graham's order, Whipple's party was already in difficulty. On reaching astronomical station twelve, his survey team was crippled
when assistant engineer Moritz von Hippel resigned his post and returned to

El Paso del Norte on account of short rations. Whipple, faced with doing the triangulation himself, requested a meeting with Salazar Ylarregui to explore how they might assist one another in this important task. Clearly, the Mexican party was better prepared on this portion of the survey than that of the United States. Some arrangement was apparently worked out, but now mattered little as Whipple had left the line. Whipple, whose career lay with the army, not Bartlett, had no choice but to obey Graham's order. He informed Bartlett of his action and, since Gray and Graham had at last arrived, that he was resigning as chief astronomer and surveyor.[82]

Bartlett was disturbed at Graham's actions. Eight months had elapsed since the colonel's appointment to the commission and his first act had been to halt the survey. As an added insult Graham had informed Bartlett of all this in a dispatch written in pencil, a discourtesy the commissioner found unacceptable. Graham apologized for having accidentally sent Bartlett a pencil draft instead of the final copy of his dispatch in ink, but the relationship between the two men had been soured sometime before. No member of the Corps of Topographical Engineers could forgive Bartlett's rough removal of Colonel McClellan, and Bartlett had his own suspicions regarding Graham's appointment. Bartlett's close friend, Henry Cheevers Pratt, whom he had appointed to replace Vaudricourt as principal draftsman, informed the commissioner that the "Government are terribly alarmed at the great expense of the Commission, and are hurrying him off to put a stopper on the outlays ..., all this Dear B. is *confidential*...."[83] Perhaps Graham's actions confirmed suspicions Bartlett already held. In any case he informed Graham that he had no intention of returning to El Paso del Norte and requested the chief astronomer to report to Santa Rita del Cobre without delay.[84]

If Bartlett was disturbed at Whipple's departure from the line, García Conde was furious. He had hoped the disorganization he observed in the United States commission in California was the result of the gold fever and would disappear when the Joint Commission reassembled at El Paso del Norte. In this he had been deceived. The general now protested to Bartlett that the work on 32° 22′ had advanced in spite of difficulties posed by the lack of water and the threat of Indian attack when Whipple suddenly left the line. He impressed upon Bartlett the loss of time and money this would cause, especially when the Mexican section's expenses had increased greatly as a result of previous delay on the part of the United States commission, and time for working in the desert was a scarce commodity.

Bartlett considered the survey of 32° 22′ now suspended because he had no experienced engineer with which to replace Whipple. Moreover, the country was devoid of water and grass, and since the surveying party Whipple had abandoned was in a state of disorganization, Bartlett ordered it to Santa Rita del Cobre to recoup.[85] Pedro García Conde, on the other hand, had no intention of suspending the survey and informed Bartlett of his determination to push the line on to the Río Gila. In so doing he was merely following the orders of his government.[86] While the Mexican commission was actively surveying 32° 22′ north latitude, Surveyor Andrew B. Gray and Chief Astronomer James D. Graham were wending their way to Santa Rita del Cobre and a chilly reception from Commissioner Bartlett.

CHAPTER III NOTES

[1]   William Gammel, *Life and Services of the Hon. John Russell Bartlett* (Providence: 1886), pp. 50–51.

[2]   Ibid., pp. 3–4; John Russell Bartlett, "The Autobiography of John Russell Bartlett, 1805–1865," Unpublished Manuscript (The John Carter Brown Library, Brown University), pp. 1–14.

[3]   Robert V. Hine, *Bartlett's West: Drawing the Mexican Boundary* (New Haven: 1968), pp. 26–27; Bartlett, "Autobiography," pp. 15–22.

[4]   Gammell, *Life and Services of John Russell Bartlett*, pp. 4–9; Bartlett, "Autobiography," pp. 23–50.

[5]   William Wallace Smith Bliss to Bartlett, 14 May 1850, Corres., I, Ewing to Bartlett, 19 Jun. 1850, Official Dispatches, No. 1, Bartlett Papers.

[6]   Goddard to Bartlett, 1 Aug. 1850, Official Dispatches, No. 16A, ibid.

[7]   Bartlett to Graham, 19 Jun. 1850, Corres., Graham Papers.

[8]   Graham to Bartlett, 20 Jun. 1850, Corres., I, Bartlett Papers; Bartlett, "Autobiography," pp. 51–56.

[9]   Bartlett to Stuart, 7 Jul. 1850, Bartlett to Whipple, 2 Jan. 1851, SED 119 (626), pp. 39, 427; Bartlett, "Autobiography," p. 53; Corres., I, II, passim, Bartlett Papers.

[10]   Bartlett to Ewing, 8 Jul. 1850, SED 119 (626), p. 129.

[11]   Ibid., p. 7; *Report of the Secretary of the Interior ...*, 33rd Cong., 2nd sess., 1855, S. Ex. Doc. 55 (Serial 752), pp. 2–3 [Hereafter cited as SED 55 (752)]; Bartlett to Ewing, 23 Dec. 1850, LIV, Thomas Ewing Papers (Library of Congress, Washington, D. C.).

[12]   Bartlett, *Personal Narrative*, I, vii–x; Hine, *Bartlett's West*, pp. 14–15.

[13]   Webb to Bartlett, 2, 5 Aug. 1850, Isaac H. Wright to Bartlett, 5 Aug. 1850, Corres., II, Bartlett Papers; John C. Cremony, *Life Among the Apaches* (San Francisco: 1868), p. 75.

[14]   Bartlett, *Personal Narrative*, I, 6; Roger Jones to J. van Horne, 30 Jul. 1850, Official Dispatches, No. 13, Bartlett Papers; Bartlett to Ewing, 20 Jun. 1850, SED 119 (626), p. 128.

[15]   Webb to Bartlett, 2 Aug. 1850, Corres., II, Bartlett Papers; Cremony, *Life Among the Apaches*, pp. 18–19; Bartlett, *Personal Narrative*, I, 19–20, 48; Sworn Testimony of James H. Lusby, SED 60 (620), pp. 29–31.

[16]   Cremony, *Life Among the Apaches*, p. 19.

[17]   Bartlett, *Personal Narrative*, I, 32–36, 113–14, 116, 139–40; "Personal Journal of John Russell Bartlett," p. 65, Bartlett Papers; *Report of the Secretary of the Interior ...*, 32nd Cong., 1st sess., 1852, S. Ex. Doc. 60 (Serial 620), pp. 4–5, 25, 157–64 [Hereafter cited as SED 60 (620)].

18 Bartlett to Prioleau, 6 Jan. 1851, Henry Jacobs to Bartlett, 23 Jul. 1851, SED 119 (626), pp. 43–44, 200; Sworn Testimony of Jonathan Chamberlain, et. al., SED 60 (620), pp. 23–40.

19 Chamberlain to Bartlett, 19 Jan. 1851, Bartlett to Chamberlain, 24 Jan. 1851, Bartlett to The Mechanics of the Boundary Commission, 24 Jan. 1851, Bartlett to Stuart, 11 Feb., 14 Mar., 18 Jun. 1851, SED 119 (626), pp. 49–51, 139–40, 402, 409–10; Whipple to Bartlett, 1 Feb. 1851, Corres., III, Bartlett Papers.

20 Strain to Bartlett, 17 May, 18, 30 Jun., 3, 8 Jul. 1850, Corres., I, ibid.; McClellan to Ewing, 9 Jan. 1850, SED 119 (626), p. 68.

21 Property Return, Jan. 1851, Property Returns, 1848–1856, Box #1, Graham Papers; Graham to Stuart, 20 Apr. 1851, File 431, NA, RG/76.

22 Strain to Bartlett, 17 May 1850, Corres., I, Bartlett Papers; Bigelow to [?], 29 Dec. 1850, Sworn Testimony of Chamberlain, et. al., SED 60 (620), pp. 52–61.

23 "Personal Journal," pp. 5–7, Undated Memorandum, Official Dispatches, Bartlett Papers.

24 Whipple to Graham, 12 Nov. 1850, Corres., Graham Papers.

25 Bartlett to Whipple, 28 Dec. 1850, SED 119 (626), pp. 37–38.

26 Strain to Stuart, 9 Oct. 1850, SED 60 (620), p. 50.

27 Stuart to Bartlett, 10 Oct. 1850, Official Dispatches, No. 20, Bartlett Papers; Stuart to Conrad, 10 Oct. 1850, Stuart to McClellan, 10 Oct. 1850, SED 119 (626), pp. 93–94.

28 Bigelow to [?], 29 Dec. 1850, Sworn Testimony of Chamberlain, et. al., SED 60 (620), pp. 51–63; Whipple to James Myer, 5 Nov. 1850, Whipple to Bartlett, 6 Dec. 1850, Corres., II, "Personal Journal," p. 81, Bartlett Papers.

29 "Personal Journal," p. 69, George F. Bartlett to Bartlett, [n.d.], Corres., XII, Bartlett Papers; Bartlett, Personal Narrative, I, 149, 152.

30 Bartlett to Ewing, 23 Dec. 1850, LIV, Ewing Papers.

31 Whipple to Abert, [?] Dec. 1850, Box 2, Folder 15, Whipple Papers.

32 Bartlett to Whipple, 28 Dec. 1850, Box 2, Folder 3, Whipple Papers; Bartlett to Whipple, 15 Dec. 1850, SED 119 (626), p. 32.

33 Lacunza to García Conde, 13 Jun. 1850, ASRE, Exp. 22, p. 164.

34 García Conde to Ministro de Relaciones, 19 Jun. 1850, Lacunza to García Conde, 22 Jun. 1850, Salazar Ylarregui to Comisión de Relaciones del Senado, 1 Aug. 1850, Arista to Ministro de Relaciones, 31 Aug. 1850, Salazar Ylarregui to Ministro de Relaciones, 1 Sep. 1850, ASRE, Exp. 22, pp. 168, 174, 192–93, 206, 208; AHDN, Cancelados, Exp. 4–6842, folio 7, Exp. 4–3868, folio 116; Salazar Ylarregui, Datos de los trabajos, pp. 24–25, 30–31.

35 García Conde to Ministro de Relaciones, 19 Jun. 1850, Lacunza to Ministro de Guerra, 22 Jun. 1850, Arista to Ministro de Relaciones, ASRE, Exp. 22, pp. 168–70, 175–76.

36 García Conde to Ministro de Relaciones, 16 May 1849, 19 Jun. 1850, Cuevas to García Conde, 2 Mar. 1849, ASRE, Exp. 22, pp. 168–70, 304–305, 337–40.

37 "Puntos sobre ... el límite de Nuevo México ...," García Conde, 15 Jun. 1850, ASRE, Exp. 22, p. 58.

38 "Instrucciones que se dan ... en 15 de junio de 1850," ASRE, Exp. 22, pp. 56–57.

39 El Monitor Republicano (Mexico City), 2 Sep. 1850; Jiménez to García Conde, 16 Feb. 1851, ASRE, Exp. 22, p. 223; "Jiménez Memoria," p. 3.

40 García Conde to Ministro de Relaciones, 24 Oct. 1850, 2 Feb. 1851, Arista to Ministro de Relaciones, 13 Nov. 1850, Lacunza to García Conde, 15 Nov. 1850, ASRE, Exp. 22, pp. 210, 212–13, 219, 223.

41 El Monitor Republicano (Mexico City), 13 Dec. 1850; Bartlett, Personal Narrative, I, 151.

42 Bartlett to Ewing, 23 Dec. 1850, LIV, Ewing Papers.

43 Bartlett to Rusk, 16 Dec. 1850, Thomas Jefferson Rusk Papers (Eugene C. Barker Texas History Center, University of Texas).

44 García Conde to Máximo Yáñez, 11 Mar. 1851, ASRE, Exp. 22, p. 226.

45 Official Journal, pp. 1–3, Bartlett Papers; *Report of the Secretary of the Interior...*, 32nd Cong., 2nd sess., 1853, S. Ex. Doc. 41 (Serial 665), p. 2. [Hereafter cited as SED 41 (665)].

46 Official Journal, pp. 6–7, Bartlett Papers; Lawrence Martin, *Disturnell's Map* (Washington: 1937), pp. 341–45, 349.

47 Official Journal, pp. 6–10, Bartlett Papers; SED 41 (665), p. 2.

48 "Personal Journal," p. 72, Bartlett Papers.

49 Official Journal, pp. 12–37, *ibid.*; SED 41 (665), pp. 2–4.

50 Whipple to Bartlett, 12 Dec. 1850, SED 119 (626), p. 247.

51 Bartlett to Whipple, 30 Dec. 1850, SED 121 (627), p. 246.

52 García Conde to Ministro de Relaciones, 24 Dec. 1850, ASRE, Exp. 24, p. 37.

53 Bartlett to Stuart, 28 Dec. 1850, SED 119 (626), p. 392; "Personal Journal," p. 78, Bartlett Papers; Bartlett to Jefferson Davis, 29 Dec. 1850 in Lynda Lasswell Crist, ed., *The Papers of Jefferson Davis* (Baton Rouge: 1983), IV, 146–48.

54 Bartlett to Ewing, 23 Dec. 1850 [addition dated 29 Dec. 1850], LIV, Ewing Papers.

55 Ibid.; Whipple to Bartlett, 20 Dec. 1850, Box 2, Folder 15, Whipple Papers; Bartlett to Whipple, 2 Jan. 1851, Whipple to Bartlett, 2 Jan. 1851, SED 119 (626), pp. 39–40.

56 Bartlett to Ewing, 23 Dec. 1850, LIV, Ewing Papers; Bartlett to Davis, 29 Dec. 1850, in Crist, *Davis Papers*, IV, 148.

57 García Conde to Yáñez, 11 Mar. 1851, ASRE, Exp. 22, p. 226.

58 Whipple to Bartlett, 25 Apr. 1851, Box 2, Folder 15, Whipple Papers.

59 Bartlett to Stuart, [?] May 1851, SED 119 (626), pp. 407–408.

60 Vaudricourt to Bartlett, 21 Apr. 1851, Folder 33, Emory Papers; Vaudricourt to Bartlett, 2 Apr. 1851, Corres., Graham Papers; Bartlett to Stuart, 18 Jun. 1851, SED 119 (626), p. 410.

61 Gardner to C. K. Gardner, 8 Oct. 1852, Gardner Papers; Graham to Vaudricourt, 21 Aug. 1851, Vaudricourt to Graham, 9 Sep. 1851, Corres., Graham Papers.

62 García Conde to Ministro de Relaciones, 16 Dec. 1850, García Conde to Yáñez, 11 Mar. 1851, Yáñez to García Conde, 11 Apr. 1851, ASRE, Exp. 22, pp. 226–27, 352.

63 "Jiménez Memoria," p. 3; García Conde to Ministro de Relaciones, 2 Apr. 1851, Jiménez to García Conde, 16 Feb. 1851, Espejo to García Conde, 30 Mar. 1851, Yáñez to García Conde, 9 Apr. 1851, Mariano Macedo to García Conde, 11 Jun. 1851, ASRE, Exp. 22, pp. 223, 225, 228–30; *El Siglo XIX* (Mexico City), 11 Mar. 1851.

64 Official Journal, pp. 41, 46, 63–67, Whipple to Bartlett, 29 Mar. 1851, Corres. IV, Bartlett Papers; Bartlett to Whipple, 18 Mar. 1851, Whipple to Bartlett, 4 Apr. 1851, Bartlett to Stuart, 14 Apr. 1851, SED 119 (626), p. 405; Bartlett to Whipple, 24 Apr. 1851, File 424, NA, RG/76; Bartlett, *Personal Narrative*, I, 204–206.

65 García Conde to Ministro de Relaciones, 22 Mar. 1851, ASRE, Exp. 22, p. 233.

66 Official Journal, pp. 68–70, Bartlett Papers.

67 Jiménez to Ministro de Relaciones, 24 Jan. 1853, ASRE, Exp. 24, pp. 73–75; Salazar Ylarregui to Ministro de Relaciones, 18 Jul. 1851, ASRE, Exp. 22, pp. 369–71.

68 Whipple to Craig, 18 Jun. 1851, draft report, [n.d.], Box 2, Folders 4, 16, Whipple Papers.

69 "Ligera relación de los trabajos practicados por la Comisión de Límites Mexicana...," in Comisión Internacional de Límites entre México y los Estados Unidos, *Memoria documentada del juicio de arbitraje del Chamizal* ... (3 vols.; México: 1911), II, 159–61.

70 Bartlett, *Personal Narrative*, I, 177–80, 215, 225–27, 238, 241–99; "Jiménez Memoria," p. 5.

71 Bartlett to Ewing, 23 Dec. 1850, LIV, Ewing Papers.

72 Archibald Hanna Jr., "The General James Duncan Graham Papers," *The Yale University Library Gazette*, XXXIX (Apr., 1965), p. 186; Goetzmann, *Army Exploration*, pp. 11–12.

73 SED 121 (627), p. 64; Receipts, Undated-1852, Box #1, Crawford to Philip F. Thomas, 23 Oct. 1849, Corres., Graham Papers.

74 George Thom to Graham, 22 Oct. 1848, passim, ibid.

75 Abert to Scott, 10 Oct. 1850, File 402, NA, RG/76.

76 Stuart to Graham, 23 Oct. 1850, Stuart to Bartlett, 23 Oct. 1850, SED 119 (626), pp. 96–97; Prioleau to Whipple, 11 Feb. 1851, Bull to Whipple, 17 Jun. 1851, Corres., III, IV, Bartlett Papers.

77 SED 121 (627), pp. 7–9; W. A. Graham to Emory, 23 Oct. 1850, W. A. Graham to Gray, 23 Oct. 1850, Official Dispatches, Nos. 22, 24, Bartlett Papers.

78 Whipple to Bartlett, [n.d.], Corres.-Undated, Graham Papers; Graham to Goddard, 9 Dec. 1850, Graham to Stuart, 4 Jan. 1851, Abert to Conrad, 9 Jan. 1851, Graham to Stuart, 7 Mar. 1851, SED 121 (627), pp. 77–78, 82–85, 102; Abert to Conrad, 11 Dec. 1850, File 402, NA, RG/76.

79 SED 121 (627), pp. 11–13; Baldwin to Graham, 2 Mar. 1851, Corres., Graham Papers.

80 SED 121 (627), p. 21; Stuart to James A. Pearce, 17 Aug. 1852, *Report of the Secretary of the Interior ...*, 33rd Cong., Special sess., 1853, S. Ex. Doc. 6 (Serial 688), pp. 15–16. [Hereafter cited as SED 6 (688)].

81 Graham to Abert, 30 Jun. 1850, Corres., Graham Papers; Graham to Stuart, 10 May 1851, Graham to Bartlett, 26 Jun. 1851, Graham to Whipple, 26, 29 Jun. 1851, SED 121 (627), pp. 14–15, 116–18, 129–30, 138.

82 Whipple to Bartlett, 12 Jun. 1851, Whipple to Salazar Ylarregui, 13, 14, 17 Jun., 3 Jul. 1851, Box 2, Folder 16, Whipple Papers.

83 Pratt to Bartlett, 29 Jan. 1851, Graham to Bartlett, 26, 28 Jun. 1851, Corres., III, IV, Bartlett Papers; Bartlett to Graham, 1 Jul. 1851, Corres., Graham Papers.

84 Bartlett to Graham, 23 Jul. 1851, SED 121 (627), pp. 141–42.

85 García Conde to Ministro de Relaciones, 1 Feb. 1850, ASRE, Exp. 22, pp. 322–25; García Conde to Ministro de Relaciones, 6 Oct. 1851, García Conde to Bartlett, 7 Jul. 1851, Bartlett to García Conde, 11 Jul. 1851, ASRE, Exp. 24, pp. 29–30, 33–34; Bartlett to Stuart, 9 Aug., 6 Oct. 1851, SED 119 (626), pp. 433, 462.

86 García Conde to Bartlett, 18 Jul. 1851, Corres., IV, Bartlett Papers; "Instrucciones que se dan ... en 15 de junio de 1850," ASRE, Exp. 22, p. 56.

CHAPTER IV

SANTA RITA
DEL COBRE

"I advise an immediate suspension of the work upon the line...."

Andrew B. Gray, Surveyor,
United States Commission

Seventeen months after the Joint United States and Mexican Boundary Commission had adjourned in San Diego to reassemble in El Paso del Norte, the long absent Surveyor Gray joined Bartlett at Santa Rita del Cobre on 19 July 1851. He had of course been abandoned in California by the failure of Congress to fund its own boundary commission and provide for the salaries of its members. Yet Lieutenant Whipple grumbled in his journal that Gray had tarried so long in San Diego to attend to his real estate speculations, neglecting his duties as surveyor.[1] Acting Secretary of the Interior William A. Graham had ordered Gray, on 23 October 1850, to proceed in haste to El Paso del Norte by the shortest route through Mexico or along the Gila, and informed him that Commissioner Bartlett had already left San Antonio to meet the Mexican commission on the Río Grande. This dispatch was delayed and Gray did not receive it until he reached Washington via Panama in early December. There he became seriously ill and was only now able to join the commission.[2] Still, his long delay appeared unwarranted.

Andrew Belcher Gray was twenty-nine years old when President Polk appointed him surveyor of the United States Boundary Commission in 1849, bringing to the commission a background of experience and ability. Born on 6 July 1820 in Norfolk, Virginia, where his father, William Gray, served as British consul, young Gray learned engineering and surveying under the direction of astronomer and topographical engineer Andrew Talcott, with whom he conducted the survey of the Mississippi Delta. Then, "seized with the spirit of adventure and enterprise," he spent the years 1839 and 1840 as a midshipman in the Texas Navy, but soon returned to surveying.[3] The decision was apparently well taken, for he was at length appointed surveyor on the Joint Commission which established the boundary between the Republic of Texas and the United States. He later served under the United States War Department in the survey of the Keweenaw Peninsula of Michigan.

Gray returned to Texas when the Mexican War began, and there fought in several Indian skirmishes, displaying the courage he was to possess all his life. Captain Peter Rainsford Brady, who commanded the military escort which accompanied Gray's 1853–1854 survey for the Texas Western Railroad, wrote

Andrew Belcher Gray, Courtesy San Diego Historical Society.

that Gray was "an optimist of the first order and everything was rosy hued to him.... I used to think he was insensible to fear, but he lacked discretion and did not seem to know what danger was."[4] The amiable and even-tempered Gray exhibited the same courage and optimism when he challenged the compromise Bartlett had reached with García Conde.

The day after Gray's arrival, the Joint Commission met and Bartlett introduced him to García Conde as the United States surveyor. Salazar Ylarregui, who was actively running 32° 22′ westward, was absent. Gray desired to examine the proceedings of the Joint Commission before he made a statement regarding his acceptance or disapproval of any actions taken thus far.[5] After a perusal of the Official Journal and maps of the Joint Commission, Gray found little of which he could approve. Gray believed he not only had the right to examine operations of the Joint Commission in his absence, but also the right to revise them. This was in accord with the agreement to adjourn reached in San Diego. Gray first objected to the fixing of a point of latitude since there was no mention of parallels or meridians in the treaty. He particularly objected to the Joint Commission's selection of 32° 22′ north latitude as the initial point of the southern boundary of New Mexico on the Río Grande.

Gray argued that the line must be computed from the true latitude of El Paso del Norte, an actual point on the surface of the earth and mentioned in the treaty. He noted that the distance from the town to the point where the southern limit of New Mexico struck the Río Grande was approximately eight miles as measured by the scale drawn upon Disturnell's map no matter how right or wrong the parallels and meridians upon it appeared to be. As the true latitude of El Paso del Norte by astronomical observation was 31° 45′, the boundary was merely eight miles north, about seven minutes of latitude. Adding that distance to the position of El Paso del Norte, Gray asserted the southern boundary of New Mexico lay in 31° 52′ latitude north.

Gray's argument had no effect on Bartlett who informed the surveyor that his opinion regarding the line remained unaltered. The commissioner did feel that Gray's protest made necessary a suspension of the work on 32° 22′ and therefore the United States section should turn its attention to the riverine survey. Gray was too enthusiastic about his argument against the compromise line of the two commissioners to let the matter rest, and presented Bartlett with further remarks on 31 July. He was now convinced that the southern boundary of New Mexico had never been marked as a parallel and that the point where the line struck the Río Grande made no reference to latitude, but rather to natural fixed points upon the surface of the earth. Gray believed the line crossed the river immediately north of El Paso del Norte as shown on the treaty map. He emphasized that the pass was but a few miles north of the center of the town and was an unchangeable, natural ford, the only one of its kind on the upper Río Grande and hence its name, The Pass of the North.[6] The true initial point, he argued, was thus thirty miles south of 32° 22′, rightfully giving the town of La Mesilla, with "its beautiful and highly cultivated valley, and the rich and fertile bottom-land," to the United States.[7]

Andrew Gray's optimism again emerged as he pointed out to Bartlett that the Joint Commission had not determined the initial point of the southern limit of the territory of New Mexico since the United States surveyor had not been present and had yet to sign the pertinent documents. Gray did not believe Bartlett had any authority to appoint a surveyor ad interim, and therefore saw Whipple's signature as of no consequence.[8] Surveyor Gray's buoyancy sank a bit when he wrote Interior Secretary Stuart a few days later that, "It is a great misfortune that the officer of the topographical engineers put his signature to an agreement with those of the Mexican officers, as the surveyor, thus signing away (if his signature is legal) a large piece of territory belonging to New Mexico...."[9] And so the matter remained unsettled for the moment.

Meanwhile Bartlett had informed García Conde that Gray had protested the Joint Commission's adoption of 32° 22′, and that under the circumstances it was not proper to continue work on the line. Bartlett suggested that the Joint Commission turn its attention to the river surveys. García Conde's immediate response was that the initial point was fixed and that the Mexican section could agree to no other despite Gray's objections. He observed to Bartlett that if the United States commissioner had the authority to appoint Whipple surveyor ad interim, as Bartlett had claimed, there could be no change.[10] García Conde refused to suspend the survey of 32° 22′ on the part of Mexico, and Bartlett could do no more than present his own views regarding the line to Stuart along with Gray's objections.[11] His undoubted frustration over Gray's protest against the compromise he had reached with the Mexican commissioner did not disrupt the most amiable personal feelings that existed among the men of the Joint Commission, but the arrival of Colonel Graham soon transformed Bartlett's troubles into exasperation.[12]

The problems that arose between Bartlett and Colonel Graham were now to paralyze the United States commission. When Stuart informed Graham of his appointment as chief astronomer, he related that his duties were defined in Bartlett's 23 October 1850 instructions and enclosed a copy for Graham's benefit. These instructions referred to Graham as chief astronomer and head of the scientific corps. Stuart directed Bartlett to receive and recognize him in that capacity. He ordered that Graham meet with the Joint Commission and aid Bartlett in arranging operations in the field. Stuart informed the commissioner that he and Graham were to reduce and reorganize the scientific corps together in order to diminish the expenditures of the commission. The secretary recommended that Graham take immediate charge of the scientific corps and that all reports be made to Graham who would in turn report to Bartlett.[13]

Bartlett was very sensitive about his prerogatives as commissioner and could not tolerate any encroachment upon his powers. He was suspicious of Graham's intentions before he reached El Paso del Norte and resented his delay of eight months in joining the commission. Not only did Graham fail to report to Bartlett at Santa Rita del Cobre until the second of August, he had caused further delay by calling Whipple in from the field. Under these circumstances, Graham could not expect a warm reception from Bartlett.

On his arrival Graham requested Bartlett to introduce him officially to the commission as chief astronomer and head of the scientific corps, relating at the same time that he was ready to cooperate with Bartlett in reorganizing the corps. Bartlett refused to grant the request, agreeing merely to introduce Graham as chief astronomer. Graham then demanded that Bartlett officially and publicly read his 23 October 1850 instructions wherein Stuart had defined his position. Bartlett again refused on the ground that portions of those instructions were at variance with the treaty. The difficulty arose over the interpretation of what constituted the scientific corps. Graham saw his title as placing him above everyone from Surveyor Gray down to the last chainbearer. This Bartlett could not accept, claiming that Graham was only in charge of the Topographical Engineers.[14] Earlier Bartlett had placed Lieutenant Whipple in charge of "all of the gentlemen belonging to the scientific corps ...," but could not now permit that of Graham, with whom his relations had become so bitter.[15] He certainly could not recognize Graham's pretended authority over Surveyor Gray. Bartlett refused to cooperate with Graham in reducing and reorganizing the commission, claiming that he had already done this himself. He resented Graham's view that the reorganized commission should be a military one as far as possible in order to increase efficiency and lower expenditures.[16]

Gray wished to be conciliatory, but when Bartlett requested his opinion, the surveyor replied that his powers and duties were sufficiently defined in Article V of the treaty. Gray considered the surveyor to be in charge of all linear surveys, of all parties in the field, and of all lines of the boundary. As his commission from the president and the treaty placed him second only to Bartlett, Gray considered himself responsible only to the commissioner, whether he took the field at the head of a surveying party or not.[17] Bartlett agreed with Gray and claimed that Graham had denounced Gray privately to him in the strongest terms for not obeying the chief astronomer's orders.[18]

Graham also presumed authority over the property and provisions of the commission and brought that issue into the dispute when he refused to issue provisions to Henry C. Pratt and his son John J. Pratt, whom Bartlett had appointed in place of the departed Vaudricourt as principal draftsman and assistant in the corps of engineers, respectively. By an arrangement with Secretary of War Conrad, Stuart had assigned First Lieutenant Otis H. Tillinghast and Second Lieutenant Ambrose Everett Burnside quartermaster and commissary of the commission in order to reduce expenses as much as possible. Bartlett was infuriated when the two lieutenants refused to issue supplies to the Pratts. They also denied provisions to the commission's interpreter, John C. Cremony.[19] Bartlett strongly denied that Graham had any authority over the quartermaster and commissary departments, while Burnside, mindful of his career, refused to recognize any superior other than Graham.[20]

At this juncture in the dispute, Bartlett sent First Assistant Engineer Charles Radziminski to Washington with dispatches informing Stuart of the entire affair. Bartlett had been preparing his side of the argument for several days in apparent collusion with Gray and Radziminski. When Graham learned of Bartlett's intentions, he had no choice but to present his version of the feud to Colonel Abert and others in the capital, intending to send Burnside as his messenger. When the lieutenant informed Bartlett that he would depart for Washington on the morrow, 16 August, the commissioner made a most determined effort to complete his charges against Graham. Bartlett wrote all day and into the evening, finishing his last dispatch at 1:00 A.M., and Radziminski left one-half hour later in company with Edward Barry. Lieutenant Burnside departed later the same day at 3:00 in the afternoon and won the race to Santa Fe, arriving two days before Radziminski. The lieutenant had the good fortune to change mounts at the military posts along the way, a courtesy denied to civilian Radziminski whose horse completely broke down before reaching Santa Fe. He made the rest of the journey on his companion's animal, Barry getting back to Santa Rita del Cobre as best he could.

It did not in fact matter who got to Washington first. The Whig administration was already upset with Graham for his tardy departure for the frontier, and was certain to support its own appointee. Moreover the polished Radziminski was no simple courier, but a respected engineer who easily swayed Whig circles to uphold Commissioner Bartlett in everything.[21] Meanwhile the situation at Santa Rita del Cobre continued. To replace Burnside, Graham, on his own authority, appointed Lieutenant William Farrar Smith acting quartermaster. Bartlett then ordered Smith to turn over all property of the commission to Henry Jacobs.[22] Smith refused, replying that, "With regard to the somewhat long reprimand that you have seen fit to bestow upon me, I have to remark that in the first place you have not the slightest right to reprove any one to whom you cannot give an order...."[23]

Responding to this insult, Bartlett requested Colonel Craig, commander of the escort, to take possession of the property of the commission, but Craig declined to interfere. Later, Craig and Graham called on Bartlett, whereupon Graham stated that the quartermaster would have complied with Bartlett's requisition if he had first presented it to Graham for approval. Bartlett answered that he recognized no one's right to approve his requisitions and this apparently settled the matter, for on the next day, 18 August, Smith called on Bartlett and stated his willingness to fill his order, but this did not bring an end to the bickering.[24]

When Graham requested Bartlett to allow him to peruse the journal of the Joint Commission, Bartlett refused. Graham then reminded Bartlett that by his 23 October 1850 instructions, Graham had a right to a seat on the Joint Commission and that the United States government intended the chief astronomer to be aware of previous agreements. Bartlett replied that Graham's demand was in violation of the treaty.[25] García Conde also refused to recognize Graham's claim to a seat on the Joint Commission, but stated that he would be pleased to consult with the chief astronomer when the occasion arose. When Whipple was acting chief astronomer, García Conde recalled, he was invited to a meeting of the Joint Commission on two such occasions. The Mexican commissioner declared that the treaty recognized only the two commissioners and two surveyors as members of the Joint Commission, and that he could receive no instructions from the United States in regard to that body. Graham believed arrangements could have been made for him to attend the meetings of the Joint Commission without voice or vote, merely for Bartlett's reference, but this would have been against the treaty as Bartlett and García Conde claimed.[26]

Bartlett sent several dispatches to Stuart in which he complained that Graham attempted to assume authority over almost everything, and lamented the continual delay that resulted. Nearly a year had passed since Graham's appointment, and he had yet to enter upon his duties.[27] Graham seemed determined to have things his own way, even at the expense of the international survey itself. In part Graham was acting on his own past experience. His official title on the northeastern boundary survey had been Principal Astronomer and Head of the Scientific Corps, and he appears to have been in charge of all actual fieldwork. The military members of the commission of course stood boldly behind Graham, while the civilians led by Gray and Bartlett stood in opposition to the pretensions of the Corps of Topographical Engineers.[28]

Graham's presumptions were not Bartlett's only problem. A large band of Apaches and Navajos surrounded the United States commission at Santa Rita del Cobre. Bartlett and Webb, who had been enamored of the Indian since their early years, persisted in the belief that, "kind treatment, a rigid adherence to what is right, and a prompt and invariable fulfillment of all promises, would secure the friendship of the Apaches...."[29] While Bartlett practiced this belief, the Apaches, led by Chief Mangas Colorado, relieved the commission of over three hundred mules and horses and a number of cattle. At one point Colonel Lewis Craig and the escort were reduced to pursuing the Indians on foot as the attackers had made off with the cavalry mounts. Lieutenants Whipple and Smith led a separate party of twelve men of the commission, surprised the Apache in the highlands of the Gila, and recovered some of the cattle, but the Indians generally bested the commission and its escort at this game. Interpreter John C. Cremony learned from the Navajo thirteen years later that Apache Chief Mangas Colorado had invited them to join in a general attack in the hope of dispersing the commission's headquarters at Santa Rita del Cobre. While the Apache chief's efforts failed, Indian raiding continued to bedevil the border population into the early twentieth century and cause friction between the governments of both nations.[30]

The continual Indian raids during the month of August and the dispute with Graham not only infuriated Bartlett, but seriously delayed his intended departure for his rendezvous with García Conde on the Gila. With very little settled among them, Commissioner Bartlett, Surveyor Gray, and Chief Astronomer Graham, and all their attendants, numbering upward of seventy men, departed Santa Rita del Cobre on 27 August with a Mexican lancer whom García Conde had provided as a guide. Following Whipple's departure from the line, the general had determined to finish the survey of 32° 22´, and wishing not to be further delayed in doing so, moved his camp several times with the United States commissioner in pursuit of him. Graham felt García Conde was deliberately trying to avoid a meeting with Bartlett until he finished the line, and believed it beneath the commissioner's dignity to chase after him.[31]

To be fair to García Conde, Bartlett had already informed him that he would be unable to meet him at the Gila on time as previously agreed because of stolen horses and the absence of Colonel Craig and the escort who were in pursuit of the Indians.[32] Bartlett had assumed he would reach the Mexican commissioner's camp in three days at most, but at each point he expected to encounter him, found instead a note from the general explaining that he had pushed on because of scarcity of water or fear of Indian attack. The commissioner fully accepted this, but Graham saw it as a ruse, Bartlett's party having no difficulty finding water and the sentinels seeing no sign of Indians.

Bartlett at last caught up with García Conde at his camp twenty miles from the Río San Pedro near the western terminus of 32° 22´ at six o'clock on the fifth of September after eleven hours of traveling without food under a broiling sun. García Conde and his entire commission of some seventy men were encamped near some pools of water in an otherwise dry lakebed with not a shrub in sight and the grass very poor. White sand and bare, cracked clay instead filled the eye. The Mexican commissioner received the members of the party with great courtesy, inviting them into his tent for refreshments.[33] García Conde then began a conversation concerning the line, and related that Salazar Ylarregui had completed the survey of 32° 22′ north latitude through its whole three degrees of longitude.[34]

After Whipple's departure from the line, García Conde had directed Salazar Ylarregui to continue the survey immediately without reaching agreement with any member of the United States commission.[35] The surveyor then continued the prolongation of the line from astronomical station eleven, determining the remaining two-thirds of the southern boundary of New Mexico. The surveying parties aligned stations twelve through seventeen by observing signal flashes of gunpowder at night to fix the longitude of each point. The survey team completed the work with a triangulation from the initial point in order to measure with chain the successive distances of each station along the line. Altogether the Mexican commission placed twelve markers of stone along the parallel of 32° 22′.[36]

While Salazar Ylarregui's two surveying parties carried forward the triangulation, Francisco Jiménez fixed the western terminus of the line near the Río Mimbres by astronomical observation over a period of two months, and at length the true position of the river was also determined.[37] Facing the desert, hostile Indians, scarce water, and short provisions, the Mexican section of the Joint Commission finished the work on 5 September 1851, the very day Bartlett and his entourage entered García Conde's camp.[38]

At a meeting of the Joint Commission on 6 September, Salazar Ylarregui officially reported his completion of the line, asking what the intentions of the United States commission were. Gray replied that, having examined the documents and Official Journal of the commission, he could not sanction the agreement regarding the initial point. He informed García Conde that he had apprised his government of his protest under Article XXI of the Treaty of Guadalupe Hidalgo. The Mexican commissioner replied that Gray's actions did not comply with Article V of the treaty and that the initial point of the southern boundary of New Mexico had been determined and could not be changed. Gray responded that while he did not have authority to alter the line, he could dissent from it.

Bartlett concurred with García Conde and considered the initial point fixed. He proposed the survey of the riverine boundary while he awaited instructions from the United States government and stated that Whipple could retrace 32° 22′ on his return from the Gila survey. García Conde desired that the United States commissioner's statement be recorded in the Official Journal and Bartlett agreed. The Joint Commission then resolved that the surveyors should present a plan for the survey of the western boundary of New Mexico from 32° 22′ north until it intersected the Río Gila. The resolution also provided for the survey of the Gila and the Río Grande. With Surveyor Gray having accepted 32° 22′ north latitude as the starting point for the survey of the western line of New Mexico, the Joint Commission adjourned.[39]

The Joint Commission met again on 7 September and Surveyors Gray and Salazar Ylarregui presented their plans for continuing the survey. Their program was accepted and the commissioners directed them to proceed accordingly. García Conde and Captain Francisco Jiménez were to work with Whipple and Gray on the Gila, while Salazar Ylarregui and Colonel Graham conducted the Río Grande survey. The Joint Commission then passed a resolution that the survey of the Río Grande begin at 32° 22′ latitude north, with no objection from Surveyor Gray, who for the second time in as many days had obliquely accepted the Bartlett-García Conde compromise line.[40] While still encamped near the Río San Pedro, García Conde called upon Colonel Graham at his tent and requested that he order Whipple to complete his survey of 32° 22′ after the Gila survey. Graham's response was that he could do so only if he received a joint resolution from both surveyors and both commissioners.[41] There the matter rested for the moment.

Meanwhile the feud between Graham and Bartlett again broke out regarding the instruments the colonel had so painstakingly collected and brought to the frontier. Earlier Bartlett had requested Graham to present his plan for the survey of the rivers, which made up a great portion of the boundary. Graham did so and Bartlett approved his program. Graham however could not agree that Gray should take charge of the Gila survey while he conducted the work on the Río Grande. Graham felt that would be inconsistent with his instructions. Bartlett, by now tiring of the dispute, informed Gray that according to Stuart's instructions to Graham, the United States commissioner had no control over the instruments and that Gray would have to apply directly to Colonel Graham for those he would need on the Gila.[42] Graham's terse reply to Gray's request was that he considered no additional instruments necessary, nor could he be responsible for Gray's party since it did not report to him. Surveyor Gray of course could not consider himself under the direction of Graham. Bartlett seemed to have abandoned the fight and now borrowed a few instruments from the Mexican commissioner's limited supply in order that the United States surveyor could proceed with the survey of the Río Gila.[43]

The constant dissonance among the members of the United States section was not the only delay facing General García Conde. During his resolute survey of 32° 22′, he had gone through nearly all his provisions. He called on Bartlett on the afternoon of the seventh to inform him of his intention of going to Santa Cruz in Sonora to procure supplies before going on to the Gila. Bartlett's stores were also thin and he was in need of a few mules and horses. García Conde replied that Santa Cruz was a mere twenty-five miles off and invited Bartlett to join him—they would reach the town before nightfall. Finding the idea attractive, Bartlett replied that he would follow the general that afternoon. Graham thought it would be far more practical to send to commission headquarters at Santa Rita del Cobre for supplies, but Bartlett insisted. Besides, the journey would give the United States commissioner an opportunity to restore Inéz González to her rightful home, which in fact was Santa Cruz.

Bartlett had rescued this girl from the ungentlemanly hands of one Peter Blacklaws, a trader who had acquired her from the Apaches among whom she had been a captive.[44] Bartlett believed the girl, "was incurring a great risk, instead of being restored to her parents, of being doomed to lasting vassalage and the loss of her virtue...."[45] Lieutenant Whipple described Inéz as "pretty, modest, ladylike, and interesting."[46] Bartlett and Dr. Webb had made quite a fuss over Inéz, and now looked forward to returning her safely to her native town.

Confident that he would reach Santa Cruz before nightfall, García Conde set off immediately with five men and one wagon to carry back the needed supplies. Bitten by wanderlust, Bartlett eagerly made preparations to follow, expecting the entire expedition to require at most a week. He ordered a wagon and several pack mules to be readied, but a sudden shower and the need to cut the banks of the San Pedro to accommodate the wagon caused a delay of several hours. Including Dr. Webb, George Thurber, interpreter Cremony, the two Pratts, young Inéz, a servant and a cook, one laborer, a teamster and three Mexican *arrieros*, Bartlett's high-spirited troop of fourteen left the camp on the Río San Pedro in the late afternoon. A hard rain now accompanied the party as it followed the trail left by General García Conde through the grasslands of the Sonoran Desert and soon the valley was inundated with a sheet of water. Finding a slight rise on the plain, Bartlett encamped for the night in torrential rain.

Salazar Ylarregui, also on his way to Santa Cruz, joined Bartlett the following morning, and with Webb went ahead to join García Conde. Bartlett continued to follow the trail of the Mexican commissioner the next day until he and Cremony noticed that it turned off in a northwesterly course. As Santa Cruz lay to the south, Bartlett and Cremony reasoned that the general must have mistaken his route and taken the trail that led to Tucson.

Bartlett had gone about eight miles out of his way when he decided to cut south across the open plain in the direction of what he later learned were the Santa Rita Mountains. In so doing Bartlett's party became hopelessly lost. Bartlett spent the next two days fruitlessly attempting to pass around the mountains, but lofty peaks, deep ravines, impenetrable swamps, and viney thickets defeated him. It was now 14 September and the sad troop was short of provisions. Henry Pratt caught a number of trout in the brook where they had camped, and this, along with boiled purslane found in abundance, became their main fare.[47]

Meanwhile those left at the San Pedro site had become concerned for the safety of these sojourners, who by now should have returned. Graham, therefore, left camp on 11 September and went in search of Bartlett, catching up with him on the fifteenth, finding the commissioner, "bewildered & lost in a valley.... Like the lost babes in the woods he did not know which way to go, nor what to do."[48] Graham was also short of provisions, but had killed a bear in his search for Bartlett and for the moment there was an abundance of meat. It would not keep long in the heat, however, and there was no way to preserve it.

By the seventeenth of September the situation had become so desperate that Graham and Bartlett decided to return to the camp on the San Pedro as fast as possible. The next day they struck a tributary of the San Pedro, the Río Babocomori, where two Mexican soldiers bearing a message from García Conde caught up with them. The general had indeed missed the turnoff to Santa Cruz and kept on the main trail to Tubac, some distance north. He and his party—his son Agustín and Captain Jiménez—were without food for five days except for a few peaches found at Tubac and some mesquite beans gathered on the plains. But for these García Conde thought his party would have perished and later related to Colonel Graham that he had twice dismounted from his horse, intending to shoot him, but did not have the heart to do it. The terrain forced the Mexican party to abandon its wagon, and only with much difficulty were they able to cross the mountains and reach Santa Cruz.

Bartlett now determined to make another effort to join García Conde. To this end Cremony volunteered to return to the camp on the San Pedro to inform Whipple and Gray of Bartlett's whereabouts and bring back enough provisions to see the commissioner through to his elusive destination.[49] Cremony returned the following day and reported that all was well at Whipple's camp on the San Pedro. Whipple and Gray had also found themselves running short of provisions and were concerned over the commissioner's unexpected long absence. Gray therefore decided to go in search of Bartlett, Graham, and García Conde on 17 September. On the second day out Gray noticed that the tracks became scattered, and decided to follow those of the Mexican commissioner. Gray reached San Xavier del Bac on the following day where he learned he was but seven miles from Tucson, and proceeded to that point to secure provisions before continuing to Santa Cruz, some ninety miles in the opposite direction.

Now assured of reaching Santa Cruz, Bartlett and Graham struck camp on 22 September, recrossed the Babocomori, and with the assistance of the two Mexican soldiers who had remained to serve as guides, found the passage through the sierra, which brought them into the luxuriant valley in which lay the much sought-after town. As the party continued down the valley the following day, Bartlett met Salazar Ylarregui, who was on his way back to the camp on the Río San Pedro to begin work on the western boundary of New Mexico toward the Gila. He informed the commissioner that he and Dr. Webb in company with García Conde had safely reached Santa Cruz on 14 September. Bartlett was no doubt relieved to learn that his good friend was safe, and certainly pleased that he would at last be able to return Inéz to the security of her home. Before departing camp on the twenty-third, he sent word ahead of her near arrival and now encountered nearly the entire village, the young girls dressed all in white and forming a procession to welcome Inéz.[50]

Bartlett later noted in his journal, "As we drew nearer, Mr. Cremony helped Inéz from the saddle, when in perfect ecstacy she rushed to her mother's arms... The mother could scarcely believe what she saw; and after every embrace and gush of tears, she withdrew her arms to gaze on the face of her child."[51] Inéz had left her home exactly one year earlier for the fair at La Magdalena when Apaches attacked her party and took her captive. Now so happily returned to Santa Cruz, Inéz walked first to the church with her family and friends where they all knelt before the altar giving thanks, and thence at last to her home.[52]

His mission of chivalry now ended, Bartlett ordered the campaign tents pitched just beyond the walls of Santa Cruz, and opened a letter from Dr. Webb written earlier, but only now delivered, "The chief, I may say staple productions of this place are fleas, flies, & mosquitos, hogs, dogs, and children; the first three are now in the height of their glory."[53] After ordering his tents pitched, Graham gave himself a tour of the village which he found very poor and unlikely to yield much in the way of provisions, the people living on a subsistence level and having no surplus to offer.[54]

In the meantime Whipple had been left stranded on the Río San Pedro with provisions very short and unable to begin the Gila survey. Having ample time for reflection, the lieutenant considered Bartlett's prolonged search for a Mexican village nothing but a waste of the commission's time. The only point was to restore Inéz to her home, when Bartlett could more easily have placed her in the charge of the gentlemanly García Conde who was going to Santa Cruz in any case. Whipple mused that the need for provisions was secondary since the commission's supplies were at Santa Rita del Cobre and Frontera. Thus the engineer found himself deserted on the frontier while Bartlett, Gray, Graham, and all their attendants were seeking the home of the captive.[55]

Whipple was perhaps fortunate to have been abandoned on the banks of the San Pedro for when the chief officers of the commission at last reached Santa Cruz, the ongoing feud amongst them nearly broke into violence. Dr. Webb and Colonel Graham got into a vehement argument in Bartlett's presence over the failure of the commissary department to send adequate provisions to Santa Rita del Cobre, which had thrown them into their present fix at Santa Cruz. As Graham had presumed all authority over the commission's supplies, Webb placed the cause of their predicament at the colonel's feet. Graham, who had considered the nearly disastrous excursion into Sonora unnecessary from the beginning, took such great offense to Webb's charge that he challenged the good doctor to a duel. Fortunately good sense prevailed, and Dr. Webb declined the offer.[56] Though trivial, the incident does demonstrate the bitterness between Colonel Graham and Bartlett's loyal attendants.

Despite the hot sun and searing tempers in Santa Cruz, the Joint Commission found an opportunity to meet on 25 September 1851 and decided to work separately on the Gila survey, the Mexican section beginning at its mouth and the United States commission starting at the most approximate junction of the Río Gila and the western boundary of New Mexico. The Joint Commission decided upon this course because the lateness of the season made united work impractical.[57] Salazar Ylarregui had departed Santa Cruz two days before to begin work on the western boundary of New Mexico toward the Gila. Tracing this line was as painful as the work on 32° 22´, being carried across high mountains covered with snow and rough brush in every direction.[58]

Salazar Ylarregui began operations at astronomical station seventeen at the terminus of the southern boundary of New Mexico, which also served as station one of the western line toward the Gila. Using a transit telescope, he ran the line toward station two in the Sierra Florida of the Gila, nearly the halfway point along the line to the river. The surveyor then became ill from the cold mountain air, finding it necessary to return to El Paso del Norte to recover his health. The task of finishing the work now fell to Captain Juan Bautista Espejo. The talented Espejo was a particularly good choice. While a student at the Colegio Militar, he had devoted himself exclusively to the study of engineering and won the prize for architecture. Like many of his fellow graduates of the academy, he had fought during the war, and in the defense of Chapultepec was taken prisoner. In the work on the western line of New Mexico, he was assisted by the two brothers Agustín and Luis Díaz. After Agustín Díaz fixed the longitude of the line at station two, Espejo used a sextant to make observations on the sun to determine the station's latitude. The small surveying party then established a third astronomical station farther along the line in like manner. This done, Espejo marched to the point where the western boundary of New Mexico cut the Río Gila. He was only able to determine the approximate latitude of that point because of the "great and exhausting difficulties ..." which impeded his efforts to achieve the precision he desired.[59] Having completed the survey of the line, Espejo and the Díaz brothers returned to El Paso del Norte to join Salazar Ylarregui in the survey of the Río Grande with Colonel Graham.

Thus the Mexican section had finished the survey of 32° 22′ and the western line of New Mexico north to its intersection with the Gila. As far as García Conde and Salazar Ylarregui were concerned there was no further question as to the validity of the line under the Treaty of Guadalupe Hidalgo. García Conde called on Colonel Graham on 28 September and, after complaining very much about his stomach ills which seem to have resulted from the long search for Santa Cruz, again requested that he send Whipple back to complete the survey of 32° 22′ after the Gila survey, but Graham replied as before that he had no authority to do so. That same day Graham departed Santa Cruz and reached Santa Rita del Cobre on the tenth of October, having been absent forty-four days.[60]

With the departure of Graham and the business of the Joint Commission settled for the moment, General García Conde found time to compose a brief relation of the commission's affairs to his government. He had not gone to Santa Cruz solely to secure provisions, but for the specific purpose of informing the minister of foreign relations of all that was transpiring within the United States commission. He now anguished over the difficulties that the United States section of the Joint Commission brought to the smallest operation, the lentitude of its labors, the total disorganization in which it found itself, and above all the facility with which it broke the agreements of the Joint Commission. These were circumstances from which the Mexican commission could not escape.

García Conde then reviewed the progress of the Joint Commission from its first meeting in California. He reminded the Minister of Foreign Relations that neither Weller, Gray, nor Emory had left the environs of San Diego, of the dissension among the individuals of the commission, of Weller's absences in San Francisco and his intention not to return to the survey, forcing García Conde to agree to adjourn to El Paso del Norte. The commissioner lamented that on reassembling in that town the United States commission was minus its surveyor, but that Bartlett claimed to have authority to appoint someone in Gray's place. Then came the lengthy discussion over 32° 22′ and after five months in El Paso del Norte, the United States surveyor was yet absent so Bartlett named Whipple surveyor ad interim. Bartlett was still not prepared to fix the initial point because astronomical observations had not been made. This delayed the work another month until 23 April; García Conde had been ready on 20 March. When the Joint Commission agreed that Salazar Ylarregui and

Whipple should trace the line, Bartlett again was not prepared to begin, causing a delay of two weeks more.

The commissioner then noted how the work advanced, with difficulties presented by the threat of Indian attack and the scarcity of water all along the line, to astronomical station twelve, when Whipple suddenly left the survey to report to Graham at El Paso del Norte. Thus another month and ten days were lost with the Joint Commission paralyzed at station twelve. The Mexican engineer then noted the arrival of Surveyor Gray, which caused a formal suspension of the work on Bartlett's part, followed by the arrival of Graham at Santa Rita del Cobre, which precipitated the feud among the colonel, Bartlett, and Gray. García Conde found Graham's presumption to a seat on the Joint Commission and his tutorial attitude toward that body insufferable. He pointed out that when he agreed to go on with the Gila survey at Gray's suggestion, there was another two-week delay before Bartlett was able to inform the Mexican commissioner when he could be ready to begin.

García Conde painfully remarked that the work had now gone on for nearly a year, tracing the line, with all the discussions and resolutions in two languages, involving much labor, time, and money, not to mention six months in the perils of the desert. And the Bartlett-Graham-Gray feud grew ever greater. Money was short and the United States desired to spend a whole year making a complete topography of the Río Grande. Commissioner García Conde had originally estimated completing the entire survey from San Diego to Matamoros in two years' time, but the United States commission had wrecked these plans.[61] Despite his frustration, he informed the minister of foreign relations that he expected to return to El Paso del Norte by December or January after finishing the Gila survey, and believed the survey of the Río Grande could be completed by April or May of 1852.[62]

The Mexican government was not pleased when it received García Conde's report of the delay and disruption within the United States commission. His relation seemed to confirm fears that Mexico's envoy at Washington had expressed earlier in the year. Luis de la Rosa had observed to Secretary of State Daniel Webster that if the United States commission had orders to conduct surveys with regard to railways, roads, and canals, and to collect information regarding the flora and fauna of the area through which the boundary ran, the survey could not possibly be completed in five years' time. If the Joint Commission were to confine its labor to the simple duty of fixing the boundary, however, the work could be concluded in nine months. The envoy expressed his country's hope that the United States would more diligently attend to the stipulations in the Treaty of Guadalupe Hidalgo concerning the international survey.[63]

When the concerns of Mexico reached Interior Secretary Stuart, he considered the apprehensions of the Mexican envoy completely unfounded. Stuart emphasized that the department's instructions to Bartlett had been governed by a desire for prompt completion of the survey. The secretary felt the treaty gave the United States liberty to examine the area for a road, canal, or rail transit, and that the commission had been so staffed to complete both the survey and conduct exploration for transit routes efficiently. Stuart stressed that he had urged promptitude upon Bartlett and had informed the commissioner that the scientific work not directly connected with the survey was incidental and was not to be done at the expense of the work on the line. Stuart concluded his response by noting that he was not aware of any delay upon the part of Commissioner John Russell Bartlett.[64]

Stuart could not so easily dismiss the concern of the Mexican government when its envoy related to the Department of State the nature of the problems within the United States commission as expressed in García Conde's dispatch from the town of Santa Cruz, Sonora. José María González de la Vega, chargé d'affaires ad interim of the Mexican legation informed Webster of Mexico's irritation at Surveyor Gray's refusal to sign the documents of the Joint Commission regarding 32° 22′ north latitude. At the same time he observed that the appointment of Whipple as surveyor in Gray's long absence could in no manner give rise to any question as to the legality of the line.

His greater concern at the moment was the disorganization within the United States commission. The chargé held that García Conde had made every effort to remove obstacles from the progress of the Joint Commission, but his efforts were paralyzed by the difficulties with and within the United States section. He pointed to the suspension of the work in California and the consequent delay in reassembling in Chihuahua where new obstructions were brought forth by members of the United States commission, throwing the work into a state of confusion. The continual changes of personnel on the United States commission, the separate localities occupied by the commissioner, surveyor, and chief astronomer could not but impede the progress of the Joint Commission.

González de la Vega particularly protested Colonel Graham's intention to repeat work that had already been concluded. This would certainly add further delay. Mexico's chargé d'affaires declared his government's wish that the United States section of the Joint Commission be placed on a permanent footing. He stated that Bartlett had been pursuing a system of confusion that had resulted in the prostration of the international survey, and emphasized that Mexico had to bear the increased cost due to the continual delays on the part of the United States commission.[65]

Once more Webster turned the matter over to Stuart, who replied that while there had been some delay, much of it was the result of Surveyor Gray's long illness which could not have been foreseen and had made Whipple's appointment as surveyor ad interim necessary.[66] Officially Stuart attempted to gloss over the problems within the United States commission, which had been placed under the aegis of his department, but privately wondered at the course his fellow Whig, John Russell Bartlett, was pursuing. The secretary did not in fact know quite where the United States commissioner could be found at that moment.

Despite the misfortunes and loss of time that Bartlett suffered during his journey to Santa Cruz, he was able to procure 1,500 pounds of flour and pinole, only with García Conde's assistance. Although insufficient, this was soon sent to the surveying parties on the Gila under care of Gray, who departed Santa Cruz on 29 September to rejoin Whipple. Bartlett and his outfit left on the same day, intending to replenish their supplies at La Magdalena, a town some seventy-five miles farther south. The fair of San Francisco was to take place there in a few days, and Bartlett hoped to find everything he needed, particularly mules.

Bartlett reached his destination without incident, took in the fair of San Francisco and acquired the much-needed mules, but again failed to obtain adequate provisions, and so determined to push on to Ures, distant another ninety miles. This was on 6 October. The following day Bartlett fell ill with a fever, and reached Ures after a miserable journey of six days, during which he suffered equally from the midday sun and the cold of the night. Bartlett's illness kept him in Ures until the end of December, with his friend Dr. Webb in faithful attendance, but on the fifteenth of that month Bartlett decided that Webb and the entire party that had accompanied him to Ures should rejoin Gray and Whipple on the Gila. Bartlett intended to follow some weeks later, when he hoped to have fully recovered.[67]

García Conde, who had remained in Santa Cruz, wrote Bartlett that he intended to push on to the Gila to join Captain Francisco Jiménez, but soon fell ill himself and retired to his native Arizpe, Sonora, for a rest.[68] While García Conde and Bartlett were both ill in Sonora, Graham and Salazar Ylarregui were at El Paso del Norte making preparations for the Río Grande survey, and Jiménez, Gray, and Whipple were somewhere along the Gila.

CHAPTER IV NOTES

1 "Journals," 6 Sep. 1851, Whipple Papers.

2 W. A. Graham to Gray, 23 Oct. 1850, SED 55 (752), pp. 3, 35.

3 S. Barron to Commodore Edwin W. Moore, 13 Dec. 1839, Folder 2, Andrew Belcher Gray Papers (Texas State Archives, Austin).

4 L. R. Bailey, ed., *The Gray Report* (Los Angeles: 1963), pp. xi-xii, 225.

5 Official Journal, pp. 72–73, Gray to Bartlett, 24 Jul. 1851, Corres., V, Bartlett Papers.

6 Gray to Bartlett, 25 Jul. 1851, SED 41 (665), pp. 25–32.

7 Gray to Bartlett, 31 Jul. 1851, ibid., p. 32.

8 Ibid.

9 Gray to Stuart, 3 Aug. 1851, SED 119 (626), p. 298.

10 Bartlett to García Conde, 29 Jul. 1851, García Conde to Bartlett, 3 Aug. 1851, ASRE, Exp. 24, pp. 35–36.

11 Bartlett to Stuart, 8 Aug. 1851, SED 119 (626), pp. 145–49.

12 Gray to Stuart, 3 Aug. 1851, SED 55 (752), pp. 36–37.

13 Stuart to Graham, 23 Oct. 1850, SED 119 (626), p. 96; Stuart to Bartlett, 23 Oct. 1850, Official Dispatches, unnumbered, Bartlett Papers; Graham to Stuart, 25 Oct. 1850, Corres., Graham Papers.

14 Official Dispatches, Memo, [n.d.], Bartlett Papers; Graham to Bartlett, 2, 13 Aug. 1851, Bartlett to Graham, 7, 8, 11 Aug. 1851, SED 121 (627), pp. 143, 152–53, 155, 159–60, 162–65.

15 Bartlett to Stuart, 18 Jun. 1851, SED 119 (626), p. 411.

16 "Personal Journal," p. 141, Stuart to Bartlett, 11 Mar. 1851, Official Dispatches, No. 33, Bartlett Papers; Graham to Bartlett, 9 Aug. 1851, SED 121 (627), pp. 23, 48, 157; Bartlett to Whipple, 2 Jan., 10 Apr. 1851, Whipple to Bartlett, 2 Jan. 1851, SED 119 (626), pp. 39–40, 317.

17 Gray to Graham, 7 Aug. 1851, Corres., V, Bartlett Papers; Bartlett to Gray, 7 Aug. 1851, Gray to Bartlett, 9 Aug. 1851, SED 119 (626), pp. 213–14.

18 "Personal Journal," p. 147, Bartlett Papers.

19 Pratt to Bartlett, 28 Jan. 1850, Graham to Bartlett, 8 Aug. 1851, Burnside to Bartlett, 8 Aug. 1851, Cremony to Bartlett, 22 Aug. 1851, Corres., III, V, Stuart to George F. Bartlett, 5 Jun. 1851, Official Dispatches, No. 38, Bartlett Papers.

20 Bartlett to Graham, 14 Aug. 1851, Burnside to Bartlett, 14, 15 Aug. 1851, Bartlett to Stuart, 16 Aug. 1851, SED 119 (626), pp. 220–24, 444–45.

21 Francis C. Kajencki, "Charles Radziminski and the United States-Mexican Boundary Survey," *New Mexico Historical Review*, LXIII (Jul., 1988), pp. 217–19.

22 Bartlett to Smith, 16 Aug. 1851, Bartlett to Stuart, 20 Aug. 1851, SED 119 (626), pp. 445–48.

23 Smith to Bartlett, 21 Aug. 1851, Corres., V, Bartlett Papers.

24 Bartlett to Craig, 16 Aug. 1851, Craig to Bartlett, 16 Aug. 1851, Bartlett to Stuart, 16, 20 Aug. 1851, SED 119 (626), pp. 444–49.

25 Bartlett to Graham, 8 Aug. 1851, SED 121 (627), p. 156.

26 Bartlett to Stuart, 27 Sep. 1851, SED 119 (626), pp. 458–59; Official Journal, pp. 79–80, Bartlett Papers; SED 121 (627), pp. 169–70.

27 Bartlett to Stuart, 9, 15, 21 Aug., 27 Sep. 1851, SED 119 (626), pp. 435–39, 442–43, 449–51, 457, 461.

28 Emory to [J. A. Pearce ?], 15 Jan. 1852, Vaudricourt to Graham, 9 Sep. 1851, Folders 33, 35, Emory Papers; Daniel Webster to Albert Smith, 30 Mar. 1843, Graham to A. W. Longfellow, 22 Jun. 1844, 17 Apr. 1845, Graham to F. T. Lally, 9 Aug. 1844, Unlabeled Corres., Graham Papers.

29 Bartlett, *Personal Narrative*, I, 321–22.

30 Cremony, *Life Among the Apaches*, pp. 51, 84–85, 172; SED 121 (627), pp. 25–26; Bartlett, *Personal Narrative*, I, 348–54; Bartlett to García Conde, 21 Aug. 1851, SED 119 (626), p. 163.

31 SED 121 (627), pp. 26–29; "Journals," 4 Sep. 1851, Whipple Papers; "Notes," Undated, Misc. Papers, Graham Papers; Bartlett, *Personal Narrative*, I, 361.

32 Bartlett to García Conde, 21 Aug. 1851, SED 119 (626), p. 163.

33 Bartlett to Stuart, 27 Sep. 1851, ibid., p. 458; Bartlett, *Personal Narrative*, I, 358–75; SED 121 (627), pp. 28–30.

34 Official Journal, pp. 80–81, Bartlett Papers.

35 Salazar Ylarregui to Ministro de Relaciones, 18 Jul. 1851, ASRE, Exp. 22, p. 56.

36 "Ligera relación," in *Memoria documentada*, II, 160–61.

37 "Jiménez Memoria," p. 5.

38 Jiménez to Ministro de Relaciones, 24 Jan. 1853, ASRE, Exp. 24, p. 75; Official Journal, 6 Sep. 1851, pp. 80–81, Bartlett Papers; SED 121 (627), pp. 30, 60.

39 Official Journal, pp. 81–87, Bartlett Papers.

40 Ibid., pp. 88–91.

41 SED 121 (627), p. 34.

42 Graham to Bartlett, 8 Aug. 1851, ibid., pp. 153, 181–86, 192–93; "Personal Journal," p. 149; Bartlett to Gray, 6 Sep. 1851, SED 6 (688), pp. 34–35.

43 Graham to Gray, 10 Sep. 1851, Gray to Bartlett, 15 Sep. 1851, Bartlett to Gray, 25 Sep. 1851, Graham to Abert, 16 Nov. 1851, SED 119 (626), pp. 265–67, 333.

44 Bartlett to Stuart, 5 Jul. 1851, ibid., pp. 417–19; SED 121 (627), p. 35; Bartlett, *Personal Narrative*, I, 380.

45 Bartlett to Stuart, 5 Jul. 1851, SED 119 (626), p. 418.

46 "Journals," 29 Aug. 1851, Whipple Papers. Perhaps for Bartlett it was a pleasant coincidence that "Inéz" was also the name of the fair captive in his friend James Fenimore Cooper's *The Prairie*, first published in 1827. Surely Bartlett had read and enjoyed it.

47 Bartlett, *Personal Narrative*, I, 380–90; SED 121 (627), p. 41.

48 "Notes," Undated, Misc. Papers, Graham Papers.

49 Bartlett, *Personal Narrative*, I, 399.

50 SED 121 (627), p. 45; Bartlett, *Personal Narrative*, I, 399–402.

51 Ibid., p. 402.

52 Ibid., pp. 403–405; SED 121 (627), p. 45; Gray to Bartlett, 24 Sep. 1851, Corres., V, Bartlett Papers.

53 Webb to Bartlett, 22 Sep. 1851, ibid.

54 SED 121 (627), p. 47.

55 "Journals," 19 Sep. 1851, Whipple Papers.

56 Graham to Webb, 25 Sep. 1851, Webb to Graham, 26 Sep. 1851, Webb to Bartlett, 27 Sep. 1851, SED 6 (688), pp. 88–90; "Personal Journal," pp. 169–71, Bartlett Papers.

57 Official Journal, pp. 93–94, ibid.

58 Jiménez to Ministro de Relaciones, 24 Jan. 1853, ASRE, Exp. 24, p. 75.

59 "Ligera relación," in *Memoria documentada*, p. 161; AHDN, Cancelados, Exp. 4–6842, folios 7, 9, 17, 19, 32, 62.

60 SED 121 (627), pp. 45–48.

61 García Conde to Ministro de Relaciones, 6 Oct. 1851, ASRE, Exp. 24, pp. 29–32.

62 García Conde to Ministro de Relaciones, 6 Oct. 1851, [Separate letter of same date as the above], ASRE, Exp. 22, p. 373.

63 De la Rosa to Webster, 11 Mar. 1851, *Message from the President* ..., 32nd Cong., 1st sess., 1852, S. Ex. Doc. 120 (Serial 627), pp. 1–2.

64 Stuart to Acting Secretary of State William S. Derrick, 5 Apr. 1851, SED 119 (626), pp. 108–10.

65 González de la Vega to Webster, 16 Jan. 1852, González de la Vega to Ministro de Relaciones, 17 Jan. 1852, ASRE, Exp. 24, pp. 40–44.

66 Stuart to Webster, 11 Feb. 1852, Webster to González de la Vega, 16 Feb. 1852, González de la Vega to Ministro de Relaciones, 29 Mar. 1852, ibid., pp. 45–48.

67 Bartlett, *Personal Narrative*, I, 406–50.

68 García Conde to Bartlett, 15, 19 Nov. 1851, Corres., V, Bartlett Papers; Bartlett, *Personal Narrative*, I, 455.

EL RÍO

GILA

"The cascade Grotto is too wildly beautiful to pass unnoticed."

Amiel Weeks Whipple, Lieutenant,
U.S. Topographical Engineers

John Russell Bartlett's jaunt through northwestern Mexico to restore Inéz González to her home not only separated him from his commission for months, but also delayed the beginning of the Gila River survey. Lieutenant Whipple had departed Santa Rita del Cobre with his surveying party on 27 August 1851 along with other members of the United States commission, and was prepared to begin work when the Joint Commission approved the plan for the survey on 7 September at García Conde's camp near the San Pedro. When, one by one, all the principal officers of the Joint Commission discovered an urge to seek out a little town in Sonora, Whipple obediently remained at his camp on the Río San Pedro, where he languished until early October. Normally of a pleasant demeanor, Whipple was at the moment none too happy with his situation. His provisions were so low that on 14 September he noted in his journal that his party's rations would last only until the next day. He was surrounded by hostile Indians and had no escort. His only defense being two rifles and a Colt five-shooter, he wrote, "between the savages & starvation we must run the gauntlet."[1]

At the same time he had deeper concerns during his lonely vigil, for he silently resented Colonel Graham's calling him off the line and Surveyor Gray's protest of 32° 22′. While he had originally observed to Bartlett that the southern boundary of New Mexico should run immediately north of El Paso del Norte as it appeared on Disturnell's map, he made no objection when the two commissioners agreed to a more northerly line. Whipple was at the midpoint of his career with the Corps of Topographical Engineers when Gray's prolonged absence gave him the opportunity to determine 32° 22′ and trace it westward. This was the most important part of the survey and would have been a fine moment for him and most likely have resulted in a promotion. Long before Graham and Gray's arrival he had accepted Bartlett and García Conde's line as correct, and while tracing it westward adopted 32° 22′ as his own. On learning of Gray's protest, he noted, "Genl. [García] Conde is a man of sound sense and not easily humbugged by any such foolish idea."[2]

Whipple incorrectly believed Gray would eventually retract his protest in order to hurry down the Gila to California and his real estate investments in San Diego. He recorded his disappointment that Salazar Ylarregui had completed the line to its western terminus and now would run the line north to the Gila, while he suffered under enforced inactivity. His greatest resentment was toward Colonel Graham, whose assistant he had been on the northeastern boundary survey and for whom he once had great respect.[3] Now he bitterly resented Graham's interference and privately asserted in his journal that Graham wanted only to get him out of the way down the Gila so he could unite with his old friend Salazar Ylarregui to claim the credit for surveying a parallel of latitude and an arc of meridian. In his silent bitterness Whipple was momentarily convinced that Graham's sole object was to prevent him from receiving credit for projecting and tracing 32° 22′, which was half completed when Graham ordered him to suspend operations.[4] The colonel wanted only a "nameless crew …" about him for fame divided was but half won.[5]

In his quiet grumbling Whipple had not been entirely fair to Graham, who informed the lieutenant that he desired that he return from the Gila survey to El Paso del Norte via Mazatlán and promised that if 32° 22′ was to be verified the task would be Whipple's. Should a new parallel be chosen, Graham asserted that it would be only just that Whipple have the honor to trace it. Whipple was not certain of Graham's good intentions and wondered whether the colonel's object was merely to prevent him from returning by way of Panama with Bartlett to the mouth of the Río Grande where he might determine its position before Graham's arrival.[6] Whipple had in fact misjudged Graham's intentions from the beginning, as he would later discover.

Amiel Weeks Whipple was born in Greenwich, Massachusetts, in either October or November of 1816, according to the scant evidence he himself provides, although some sources place the year of his birth as 1818. Thus at either age sixteen or eighteen, while teaching in a district school in Concord, he unsuccessfully applied for an appointment to the United States Military Academy at West Point in 1834. Whipple then enrolled in Amherst College and at length succeeded in obtaining an appointment to West Point in 1837. On graduation in 1841, he ranked fifth in his class, receiving only six demerits in his final year.[7] After various assignments in New England, Whipple served as assistant engineer under Colonel Graham on the northeastern boundary survey from 1844 to 1849. Everyone associated with the United States

Amiel Weeks Whipple, Courtesy San Diego Historical Society.

Boundary Commission found Whipple a fine officer and thorough gentleman. Whipple was tall and slender, boasted the strength of an athlete, and wore his brown hair long, almost over the collar, as did many of his fellow officers serving in the West.

Colonel Graham, who had been his mentor for years, thought highly of Whipple as a man and held his ability as an astronomer in equally high regard. Though Whipple had some difficulty with Bartlett, he got on with the commissioner better than any other member of the Topographical Engineers, and was able to share his intellectual curiosity with him. Both men had an interest in Indian languages and made vocabularies of them. Whipple did a vocabulary of the Yumas and requested Bartlett's opinion of it. While at the junction of the Gila and Colorado in 1849, Whipple spent a part of his spare time on his Yuma vocabulary and delved into the religious beliefs of the Yumas as well. On one occasion Chief Anastasio took up Whipple's prayer book, whereupon the good lieutenant explained what it was and read a portion of it to the chief in French.[8] Whipple, despite his melancholy moment on the Río San Pedro, was anything but a morose figure. Rather, he was a good-natured fellow who obeyed orders, as his dearth of demerits at the academy shows. His even temper enabled him to keep his resentment of Graham to himself, and this would accrue to his merit in the future. He was about to begin the survey of the Gila and enjoy the beauty of the country through which it flowed.

As he departed his encampment on the San Pedro for the Gila on 3 October, Whipple's party consisted of eighteen men with Henry C. Force and Frank Wheaton as first assistant engineers. Bartlett, with Graham's assent, had placed Whipple in charge of the topographical survey of the river, and Gray with a similar outfit in charge of the linear survey. Gray's first assistant engineers were John Bull and J. Hamilton Prioleau.[9] The Joint Commission had agreed that the Mexican section would do the astronomical work of the survey while the United States commission would take the topography of the river. The Joint Commission resolved that Mexico's team begin at the mouth of the Gila and that of the United States at the most approximate junction of the river with the western boundary of New Mexico.[10]

Whipple, who was not particularly fond of Gray, believed the civilian surveyor wished to run the Gila survey himself to the exclusion of the Topographical Engineers. He wrote in his journal, "It is evident to me that the present calm in the American commission precedes a storm. There is to be struggle fiercer than ever before."[11] Neither was he pleased with his present assignment. By a resolution of the Joint Commission he was to fix three points astronomically in longitude and latitude: one where the western boundary of New Mexico struck the Gila; a second at the mouth of the first branch of the Gila; and a third at the mouth of the Río San Pedro. All this was to be done on fourteen-and-a-half days' rations of flour—no sugar, coffee, rice, or pork—only flour and fresh meat. He complained that it would be impossible to do the work properly and determined to work under silent protest. In this mood Whipple reached Salazar Ylarregui's camp at the western terminus of 32° 22′ and was greeted by Lieutenant Agustín Díaz and Captain Juan Espejo. While he verified Salazar Ylarregui's calculations made at the end of the line, Whipple himself made no astronomical observation at that point because Colonel Graham desired that he not do so. He noted how strange it was that the United States section should have prevented him from completing an operation of such interest.[12]

Whipple reached the initial point of the Gila survey northeast of Mount Graham on the evening of 9 October, mounted the transit instrument that night and observed both limbs of the moon for longitude. The topographical survey of the Río Gila began at this point. Andrew Gray, meanwhile, had left Santa Cruz on 29 September and joined Whipple on the Gila on 9 October, beginning his linear survey on the tenth. Both parties labored on short provisions in a hostile environment with the noon temperature ranging from 110° to 116° Fahrenheit in the shade, and ever fearful of hostile Indians. Neither party had an escort. The survey would have to be pushed on to the Pima villages as rapidly as possible.[13]

Gray's party operated in nearly straight lines from camp to camp, at times several miles from the river to which offsets were occasionally measured. Whipple groused that Gray could not know of the minor bends or islands that abound in the river. Whipple proceeded along the river itself, noting every curve and island, measuring width, depth, and position of every channel. To the lieutenant this seemed of the utmost importance to the survey, difficult as it was. The banks of the river were covered with huge cottonwood trees measuring six and eight feet in diameter, and along with willow and mesquite covered the whole valley to the base of Mount Graham. Ducks, geese, quail, raccoon, deer, and bear were abundant. The cottonwoods, thickets of almost impenetrable willows, deep barrancas with perpendicular banks rising ten and twenty feet, high barricades of driftwood, boggy shores, and a deep channel rarely fordable were the obstacles Whipple's party had to overcome.

Perhaps it was such rough going combined with the heat that caused First Assistant Engineer Henry Force to lose his temper with his mule and beat him with the micrometer telescope he was carrying, breaking out the micrometer spider lines. Whipple lamented that he had neither glue nor spider web with which to repair it and wondered how he could get the topography of the river without that particular instrument. Fortunately, after several frustrating attempts, he managed to fix it using the glue from a prepared envelope and single fibers of raw silk. With Mr. Force no doubt more mindful now of his temper, the surveying crew struck the Río San Francisco and camped at that river's mouth on 23 October.[14]

Whipple carried the survey without difficulty below the mouth of the San Francisco as far as the entrance of the canyon of the Pinal Llano Mountains. Into this the party now forced its way, though Indians had told them neither man nor beast could penetrate it. At times wading, at others scaling the sides of the canyon that rose in perpendicular heights to five and even fifteen hundred feet, Whipple progressed the survey some eight or ten miles. Lack of men and provisions prevented him from sending reconnoitering parties ahead.[15] This "terrible cañon ..." forced Whipple to cross and recross the very narrow channel of the river a hundred times in eight miles. He found the high precipices on either side of the river "beautifully worn into curious shapes and often terminated in spires or towers as perfect as if formed by hand of man."[16]

On reaching a gorge where a mountain stream threw itself into the Gila, Whipple's party was forced to abandon its wagon. This occurred at Cañon Springs on 27 October 1851.[17] On returning to camp, Whipple and his party celebrated the desertion of their wagon by opening sherry, sardines, and pickles, each having a share. They then invited Gray and the gentlemen of his party who were encamped nearby to a lunch, "better appreciated among these wild mountain gorges than in the halls of a crowded city."[18] For the remainder of the month of October Whipple's surveying team continued by pack mules over steep mountains, with the scenery becoming ever more intriguing. Whipple found that "The Cascade Grotto is too wildly beautiful to pass unnoticed."[19] The company descended over twelve-hundred feet in an hour and abruptly came upon an Indian garden of maize, beans, melons, and to Whipple's surprise, a field of cotton. A mineral spring delightfully gushed from the mountain, watered the garden, and then coursed through a ravine, skipping from cliff to cliff in lovely cascades until it entered the Río Gila appearing in view some thousand feet below. The scene was replete with a stalactite cave beneath the first waterfall and shrubs blessed with red flowers at the foot of the precipice. There followed a geologic formation filled with petrifications, including the trunk of a large cottonwood tree.

As the river became inaccessible at this point, Whipple hired an Indian guide and reluctantly turned his back to the Gila. Passing through the strongholds of the Pinal Llano Indians, the party again struck the Gila but a scant ten miles down river on 1 November. From that point he surveyed up the river as far as nature would permit, and then continued taking the topography of the river to the mouth of the San Pedro. Here Whipple observed the culminations of the moon for longitude. Since he would be so employed for some time, he sent a party on to the Pima villages to purchase flour.[20] Provisions were now quite low and wolves hovered around camp every night. One saucy wolf attacked Frank Wheaton's mule while he was standing beside it holding its bridle. He and Frederick Schaaf beat the predator away.[21] When Whipple's surveying crew arrived at the Pima villages in December, he was pleased to find Colonel Lewis Craig with an escort of twenty-three men and Captain Edmund Barry with about twenty-eight days' rations.[22]

While at the Pima villages Whipple invited John Cremony to observe an eclipse of the moon. As the astronomer finished setting up his telescope, one of the Pima chiefs joined them and inquired as to the meaning of the engineer's odd activity. Cremony replied that the instrument was a great cannon and that Whipple was destroying the moon. This aroused the Indians who had gathered around, placing Whipple's party in grave danger. Cremony then asked Whipple what to do. In an undertone Whipple asked the interpreter to tell the Pimas that if they would keep quiet and make no hostile move, he would restore the moon as bright as ever. The Indians quietly waited and were greatly relieved when the fullness of the moon reappeared. All the while Whipple continued his observations, writing the results in his notebook, never appearing the least bit ruffled or concerned. His equanimity earned

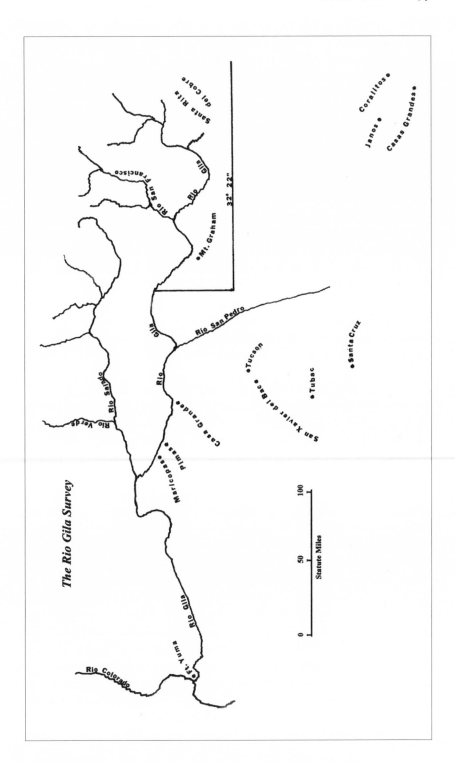

The Rio Gila Survey

him great respect, and the astronomer's influence among the Pimas was suddenly all powerful.[23]

With his eyes much inflamed from observing at night and traveling by day under a brilliant sun, Whipple left the Pima villages and pushed on to the junction of the Río Salado with the Gila. He found the Salado to be a beautiful stream, crystal clear, as large as the Gila, and to his surprise not saline. After carrying the topographical survey to within eighty miles of the confluence of the Gila with the Colorado, the party found its provisions so short that Whipple determined to suspend operations on 14 December and make a quick march to the army post at Camp Yuma. There he could procure adequate supplies and retrace his steps, finishing the work.

Whipple's surveying team set out in good spirits and reached the confluence in four days, on 18 December 1851. There he met Captain Jiménez, Agustín García Conde, and Manuel Alemán of the Mexican section, who informed him that the United States military depot had been abandoned, and that no food could be purchased from the Yuma Indians, who had become quite hostile. It was now impossible for the lieutenant to retrace his steps and finish the topography of the Gila. Whipple found himself confronted with a swiftly flowing Colorado River over one quarter of a mile wide and from fifteen to thirty feet deep. The Yumas, numbering some 1,500, had seized the two flatboats and refused to cross the surveying party. The chiefs then began to harangue the assembled tribe. The faces of the interpreters blanched when they heard that the Yumas intended to kill everyone in Whipple's party by morning. Whipple and Craig then prepared for what promised to be a desperate resistance, throwing up a circular redoubt of wagons and camp equipment. Almost all had a rifle and two pistols and an ample supply of ammunition.

As night grew nearer, Chief Colo Azul approached the breastwork and Whipple, hoping to avoid an uncertain battle, offered the chief two dollars for every man and one dollar for each horse and mule the Yumas carried across the river. Before an answer could be given, Chief Juan Antonio's young daughter walked up to her father, whispering briefly in his ear. This brought to an end Whipple's interview with Colo Azul, as Antonio withdrew a bit to confer with the other chiefs and all the Yumas gazed at the lieutenant. The chiefs then asked Whipple if he were the same man who had come from San Diego two years before and camped on the hill. When the surveyor replied that he was, the girl clasped her father's hand and walked up to Whipple, touched him on the arm and spoke once more to Chief Antonio. It seems Whipple had done her a kindness while he was making his observations at the junction of the Gila and Colorado. She had been suffering from hunger when Whipple beckoned her to his tent and gave her a watermelon and a little mirror. This is what she had whispered to her father. In scarcely an hour the flatboats were ferrying the entire party across the Colorado and the surveyors and soldiers found themselves blessed with friends who did all in their power to ensure the comfort and safety of the men of the Gila survey. Now able to strike posthaste for San Diego, Whipple left a note for Gray's party to follow swiftly.[24] After a hard journey cursed with a sandstorm and little water or food, Whipple camped at San Diego on 8 January 1852. Surveyor Gray and party arrived the same day.[25]

Gray had also been forced to interrupt his linear survey and march to Camp Yuma to secure provisions. By 12 December his outfit had progressed the survey to within sixty miles of the junction of the Gila and Colorado rivers. That portion of the line was fixed and marked, monuments of stone having been erected. Learning that Whipple and Colonel Craig with the escort had decamped immediately for San Diego, Gray's party followed their example, having no trouble with the Yumas whatever. His provisions were now so meager as to admit only of rapid marches to the California coast.[26] Whipple reported to Interior Secretary Stuart that he had heard nothing from Commissioner Bartlett since he left him at the Río San Pedro to go to Santa Cruz. He informed the secretary that he had arrived in San Diego with eighteen men and no authority to discharge them, nor money to pay them. Whipple pledged his own credit for several hundred dollars for their sustenance, but could not do so indefinitely.[27] By 1 February Whipple feared that Bartlett might never appear in San Diego and informed Stuart that he and Colonel Craig had decided to return to the Colorado, complete the Gila survey in ten days' time, and then push on through the hostile Indians to El Paso del Norte as soon as Major Samuel Heintzelman reestablished the military post on the Colorado. In the meantime Whipple and his assistants were actively completing their observations and plotting the notes of the topographical survey.[28]

Lack of wherewithal to complete the Gila survey was not Whipple's only worry. Rumor had it that Colonel Graham had been dismissed as chief astronomer and Major Emory appointed in his stead. Whipple had chaffed under the orders of Emory while working on the California line, and he particularly resented Emory's "jealousy lest some assistant may share in the credit due to the work...."[29] Whipple wrote privately to Graham that should such rumor be true, he wished to be ordered to Washington to complete the work of the Gila survey. He emphatically informed Graham that he would never again serve under the command of Emory if he could avoid it. He intimated to his mentor of many years that he felt he must do something for his country or himself—the years were passing quickly.[30] The possibility of his name being associated with the tracing of the parallel of 32° 22′ and the arc of the meridian that represented the western line of New Mexico now seemed remote. His greatest fears were realized when Stuart denied his request to be returned to Washington and ordered him to remain on the survey under Chief Astronomer Emory.[31]

While the surveying parties waited in their crippled state for Bartlett to reach San Diego, the Mexican section of the Joint Commission managed to complete its portion of the Gila survey. Salazar Ylarregui assigned the Gila survey to Francisco Jiménez, naming as his assistants Agustín García Conde and Manuel Alemán. Another graduate of the Colegio Militar, Alemán was talented and noted for his valor during the war. A man of exemplary military conduct, he had proven himself particularly adept at building fortifications around Mexico City, and was one of the defenders of his beloved academy on the heights of Chapultepec. Salazar Ylarregui now informed Jiménez that, according to a resolution of the Joint Commission, the United States was to take the topography of the river and carry the astronomical work from the most approximate point where the Gila cut the western line of New Mexico to the Pima villages, while Mexico carried the astronomical work from thence to the junction of the Gila and Colorado. He directed Captain Jiménez to adopt measures that would ensure that his marches along the river would be short, following the Río Gila without ever losing sight of it if at all possible. Salazar Ylarregui ordered him to fix each point of his march along the Gila in longitude and latitude, employing as many astronomical observations as needed. He instructed Jiménez to determine the latitude and longitude of the confluence of every river with the Gila north and south. Should the Gila divide into more than one channel, Jiménez was to determine the position of each, especially if the islands so formed were sizeable. Finally, Salazar Ylarregui directed Jiménez to take the topography of the river, even though the Joint Commission had assigned that task to the United States section. Commissioner García Conde had originally intended to accompany Jiménez, but his health would not permit it.[32]

Francisco Jiménez now began a work that was completed only with great difficulty and under the most miserable conditions imaginable during a peregrination of two-and-one-half months along the Río Gila.[33] Jiménez was given a scant 200 pesos for expenses and an escort under his orders commanded by Captain Hilarion García. The party also took along a quantity of trade goods that could be exchanged for provisions at the Pima villages. Jiménez left Santa Cruz, Sonora, on 27 October 1851 with a vague hope of being able to provision his outfit at the Pima villages in the middle of the desert. Captain García's escort consisted of twenty-one vicious and insubordinate men with neither uniforms nor footwear. His sixteen pack mules had no muleteers to tend them and harness that was almost useless. With but four sacks of flour and seventeen head of cattle, provisions were short. Precious also were the three bottles of oil for the lamps as the astronomical work would have to be done at night. Having received no pay for months, all that sustained Captain Jiménez was *"el deseo de cubrir el honor nacional...."*[34]

The surveying crew and escort arrived in Tucson on 1 November after a most painful *jornada*, having lost one mule and three head of cattle to the whims of the desert. Three soldiers had seen fit to desert, and the flour that had been packed in sacks that proved too fragile was lost entirely. In Tucson Jiménez purchased some flour and a few other provisions, and hired five muleteers. At midnight on 2 November he renewed the march to the Gila, but when six more soldiers deserted, reducing the escort to twelve men, he ordered Captain García to return to Tucson to hire four Apaches. He returned two days later and the escort was in this way somewhat strengthened. The march now became increasingly difficult as no water was found during the next two days' journey. The party was halfway to the Gila and neither the men nor the mules had had any water to drink for thirty hours. The mules were in particularly bad shape when Jiménez struck camp on the night of 6 November, forcing him to leave half his cargo behind and continue with only the instruments. The following day the suffering men and animals found a few pools of water, reaching the Pima villages on 8 November. Noting that he was but a few leagues from the confluence of the Río Salado with the Gila, Jiménez continued his march, arriving at the mouth of the tributary on 10 November, where he encamped.

There the engineer was able to hire some Papago Indians to retrieve the cargo abandoned in the desert, but by the sixteenth they had failed to return, forcing Jiménez to purchase provisions from the Pimas. Left with but ten pesos and no supplies, Francisco Jiménez wondered how he could carry on the survey. It could have been no surprise to him when two more soldiers deserted, but fortunately the Papagos returned with the flour and other cargo on 19 November putting his mind somewhat at ease. Meanwhile Jiménez, Alemán, and Agustín García Conde had completed their astronomical observations at the mouth of the Río Salado, and on the twenty-third left that stream and continued their trek along the Gila.

The survey team was able to make about fifteen miles a day despite the miserable condition of the mules. Jiménez observed the heavens each night, but found it necessary to interrupt his progress at Fezatal on 28 November, remaining there until 5 December to rest the mules. With his provisions beginning to run out, Francisco Jiménez decided to make a forced march to the Colorado. The soldiers of the escort were without proper clothing and had no campaign tents to protect them from the winter rain. Jiménez grieved that they had no means of succor in their distress; all were suffering. It was necessary to push on, but the mules were reduced to such a sad few that even though Jiménez had scarcely any provisions and only three boxes of instruments, it was too much for them. No doubt wincing at his own actions, the engineer buried two boxes of instruments and left Fezatal on 6 December 1851.

Making observations at each camp along the way, Jiménez and his party reached the Colorado on 17 December. The only hope the survey team had before them was the United States military post at Yuma, which they found abandoned. Neither were they able to obtain any food from the Indians. Jiménez and Captain García therefore began their return the following day, and met Lieutenant Whipple's party, which they found to be as desperate for provisions as their own.[35] After sharing their tales of misery, the two surveying teams parted company; Whipple pressing on to San Diego and Jiménez retracing his steps up the Río Gila. Losing more mules to the rigors of the march, and not in the finest spirits themselves, the engineers and their escort reached the pueblo of the Maricopas on 29 December. Thanks to the generosity of the Maricopa Indians and the trade goods brought along by Captain Hilarion García, they were able to procure sufficient provisions.

Jiménez and Captain García continued their journey until they arrived at the Pima villages on the last day of December, and established a camp on the left bank of the Gila on 1 January 1852. There Jiménez made his final astronomical observations. Altogether he had made enough observations to fix seventeen points of latitude and longitude on the Río Gila. With his task completed and having fulfilled his instructions, Jiménez struck for Tucson on 7 January. Along the way the Mexican party met that of Dr. Thomas Webb, who was on his way from Santa Cruz to the Gila. Thus Webb had an opportunity to learn that Whipple and Gray were most likely in San Diego, and that he could expect an arduous trip ahead. Jiménez, Alemán, and young García Conde then continued their journey, arriving at Arizpe, Sonora, on 11 February.[36]

In order to cover his drafts upon the government and to enable himself and his assistants to return to El Paso del Norte, Jiménez obtained 3,000 pesos from the governor of Sonora. Part of the debt was due to him as he had used his personal credit to obtain provisions in Tucson on his march to the Gila. It had been a difficult journey for man and beast alike. Of the thirty-one mules with which he had begun the journey in Santa Cruz only thirteen remained.[37] Apparently Captain Jiménez had been a bit too forthright in his reports during the expedition on the Gila, for the minister of foreign relations found one of his letters so disrespectful that he requested the engineer's resignation from the commission. Jiménez responded that if his reports appeared impertinent, the cause was not disrespect toward the government, but rather the harsh conditions in which Jiménez' surveying crew had labored. He informed Salazar Ylarregui that he was willing to serve the Mexican Boundary Commission in any way he could. This attitude proved acceptable and Francisco Jiménez remained on the commission.[38] He would have been difficult to replace.

Three days before Jiménez reached Arizpe and could report that the Mexican section had completed its work on the Río Gila, John Russell Bartlett appeared in San Diego. During his long convalescence of eighty days at Ures, Sonora, Bartlett had occupied himself by making vocabularies of the Yaqui and Opate languages and studying the history and geography of Ures and its environs. Too weak from his long illness to travel overland back to the Gila, Bartlett left Ures on 29 December 1851 for the port of Guaymas intending to reach San Diego by sea. With a fresh wind the schooner *María* set sail for Mazatlán on 4 January with the United States commissioner aboard. Once in that picturesque town, Bartlett learned there was slight chance of his catching a steamer for California, and opted for passage to Acapulco by sail on the *Miguel.* Since the California steamers stopped at Acapulco for coal each week, he reasoned that would be faster than sailing directly for the California coast at that time of the year when northwesterly winds would make for a long voyage upwards of a month.

After brief stops in San Blas and again in Manzanillo, where he found a little time for hunting waterfowl along the shore of the lagoon, Bartlett reached Acapulco at four o'clock in the afternoon of 31 January. Two days later the traveler boarded the crowded mail steamer *Oregon.* This proved an uncomfortable voyage with many of the passengers ill with fever, the only delightful moment being the numerous whales sighted off Cabo San Lucas. After a voyage of 3,300 miles, Bartlett's steamer passed Punta Loma and dropped anchor in the bay of San Diego in the late evening of 8 February 1852. The next day he learned that Whipple and Gray had reached the settlement one month earlier, having had to abandon the survey.[39] He was particularly concerned about his good friend Dr. Webb, who had not been heard from since he and the remainder of Bartlett's entourage had left the commissioner ill at Ures in December 1851.

While Bartlett convalesced at Ures, Webb led the party to San Diego by way of the Pima villages and the Gila. He now began a journey he could scarcely believe and would never forget. His mules, feeble at the outset, were not fit for such a trek. After leaving the Pima villages, the heat and lack of adequate grazing and water began to take their toll. Webb began with twenty-seven mules at Santa Cruz and arrived in San Diego with three. The remainder sank under their burdens in the desert and were abandoned to their fate. They either fell into the hands of Indians or the ravenous hunger of the wolves, which were constantly near. Their howling filled the night sky and their prowling surrounded the camp in broad daylight. The loss of mules forced Webb's party of twelve to sacrifice much of their property. Cooking utensils, campstools, bedding, clothing, books, and other items were abandoned to the endless appetite of the desert. They at last were forced to sacrifice their tents to it as well, and so at the end of the day's march were without protection from the elements, whether rain or sun. At noon the dry, brain-burning heat was too much to withstand, while sunset brought a cold that was equally unbearable; the temperature fluctuating by 60° or 70° Fahrenheit. Eventually most members of the party gave up their riding animals to be employed as pack mules, leaving themselves afoot. In spite of such hardship as well as at least one Indian attack, Webb and his party safely reached the California coast after crossing a land that "in barrenness of verdure, destitution of water, tremendous storms of sand, &c., &c., it is doubtful if any tract of ground can surpass the jornada which we crossed."[40]

Pleased at Webb's safe arrival and having at last rejoined his commission, Bartlett paid off those members of the surveying parties who wished to leave the service, and prepared to journey to San Francisco to refit the commission. He sought to obtain new tents and camp equipment, have the commission's instruments repaired, procure provisions for the return to El Paso del Norte, and negotiate drafts on the government to cover expenditures. Bartlett left for the northern city on the steamer *Sea Bird* on 24 February, arriving three days later in company of Dr. Webb and George Thurber. While awaiting the preparation of the camp equipage, Bartlett determined to visit the geysers and volcanic region of Napa Valley. There Webb collected a few mineral samples and Thurber kept an eye out for any botany of interest, while Bartlett was armed with his sketchbook as he marveled at the columns of steam and fumes of sulphur.

With his business at last concluded, Bartlett and his companions embarked on 14 April for Monterey on the steamer *Ohio*. There he transferred to the United States revenue cutter *Frolic* which would stop at every small port between Monterey and San Diego, giving Bartlett a better chance to explore the coast than had he remained on the steamer, which would not put into the smaller coastal towns. In this manner Bartlett casually wended his way to San Diego, sailing past Punta Loma and into the bay on the evening of 24 April, after an absence of two months.[41]

He soon learned that Secretary Stuart had dismissed Gray as United States surveyor. Gray had already begun the linear survey of the Río Gila when Stuart received Bartlett's account of the surveyor's objections to 32° 22′ as the southern boundary of New Mexico. Mindful of the complaint from the Mexican legation regarding the many delays on the part of the United States commission headed by his fellow Whig John Russell Bartlett, and this being an election year, Stuart saw fit to support the compromise line. He informed Gray on 31 October 1851 that the other members of the Joint Commission were not required to suspend all operations connected with the survey during his absence. As the two commissioners had agreed to the initial point as 32° 22′ latitude north, Stuart directed Gray "to remove the only obstacle which now exists to the completion of this branch of the work by affixing your signature to the requisite papers."[42]

Stuart apparently had second thoughts about Gray's tractability, for on 4 November he addressed another dispatch to Gray, informing him that the president had appointed Major Emory to replace him as surveyor. The secretary instructed Gray to turn over all instruments and materials of the survey to Emory.[43] Gray received neither of these dispatches, which Stuart had directed to El Paso del Norte, but received copies of them on 30 April 1852 while stranded in California without funds for the second time during his stint as United States surveyor. Gray believed Stuart's action unfair, as the 4 November dispatch gave him no opportunity to comply with Stuart's communication of 31 October.[44]

When Gray finally received Stuart's two dispatches, Bartlett requested him once more to sign the documents regarding 32° 22´, but Gray refused on the ground that he was no longer surveyor.[45] Despite their disagreement over the initial point, Gray and Bartlett parted with friendly feelings between them.[46] Bartlett now discharged the men who had been in Gray's outfit and committed the task of completing the linear survey to Lieutenant Whipple. One other change in the commission was the resignation of John Cremony, who had learned from a Washington friend that Bartlett's affairs had created a stir in the Senate. Always the clearheaded thinker, Cremony thought it wise to leave. George Thurber, the commission's botanist, took his place as interpreter.[47] Bartlett had been unable to purchase mules on his excursion to San Francisco, and now required a month to do so in the vicinity of San Diego. This delay gave him an excellent opportunity to visit the Coronado Islands, and later explore the mission of San Luis Rey. With new equipment and fresh animals, the United States section, once more united with its commissioner, departed San Diego on 26 May 1852 to resume the survey of the Gila. The return from San Diego to El Paso del Norte would prove to be an arduous one for all concerned, beset by tragedy, rancor, and dissension. Before the commission crossed the Colorado, Colonel Lewis S. Craig was murdered by two deserters whom he was attempting to coax back into the ranks.[48] Craig had served throughout the war, having been severely wounded at the battle of Churubusco, and was a "most gallant, and universally esteemed ..." officer.[49]

After Craig's death, Lieutenant Whipple assumed command of the escort, which was then on the Colorado. Dissension erupted immediately as Bartlett, who claimed the troops were under his authority alone, held that Whipple was on special assignment to the United States Boundary Commission and had no rights or duties as an officer of the army. When Whipple sternly disagreed, Bartlett threatened to prefer charges against him, and intimated that he would be sustained as he had been in all his controversies with officers of the army.[50]

Bartlett soon informed Stuart that he refused to recognize Whipple as commander of the escort, noting that he saw Whipple as of lower rank. He saw the affair as an attempt by Whipple to subordinate the civil to the military authority. Whipple of course could never accept Bartlett's contention that his detachment to the commission had denuded him of all military rank, duties, and privileges. The lieutenant could only assume Bartlett had sent charges against him to Washington. While he and Bartlett camped near one another during these days, Bartlett chose to mention nothing regarding charges, giving Whipple no opportunity to send countercharges.[51] Bartlett had pursued the same tactic in his controversies with McClellan and Graham. The Topographical Engineers naturally sided with Whipple. Colonel Graham later wrote privately that the lieutenant would have been justified in putting in irons those who sought to meddle with the men in Whipple's command, and that he ought have tied Webb to a wagon tongue and had him whipped.[52] There the matter rested, or rather smoldered.

Meanwhile the surveying party had crossed the Colorado on 12 June and begun the survey, but not before the Indians made off with thirteen mules and three horses, including Bartlett's $300 steed. The crew under Whipple then continued up the Gila, pleased that the mules and horses were not suffering, as Gila grass, salt grass, spear grass, willows, and mesquite beans were plentiful, the animals generally having a choice. The going was not so pleasant for Whipple, however, who complained that Bartlett refused to furnish him with enough men to carry out the manual labor of the surveying party, nor men sufficient to attend to the pack mules. The astronomer was particularly bitter that Bartlett refused him use of the spring wagon for transporting the instruments, declaring that he required it to carry his and Webb's personal baggage. Thus the instruments were carried in a lumber wagon, damaging some of them and destroying others.[53]

Despite the constant bickering between Whipple and Bartlett, both parties reached the Pima villages by early July, and Whipple was able to inform the commissioner on the sixth that the survey of the Río Gila from its junction with the Colorado to the western boundary of New Mexico had been completed.[54] The astronomer himself reached the villages on 10 July and was greeted by many Pima friends who remembered him for having restored the moon. Whipple now grumbled that his movements were dependent upon those of the commissioner, whom he charged was busy selling his trade goods to the Pimas and Maricopas. Bartlett caused further delay by visiting the nearby Casa Grande ruins before beginning the long journey to El Paso del Norte.

The United States commission now retraced Dr. Webb's arduous route by way of Tucson, San Xavier del Bac, and Tubac to Santa Cruz. This was a miserable trip with the party suffering from excessive heat, the thermometer rarely falling below 100° during the day and at times reaching 120°. They labored also through thirty-four days of rain, causing many to be afflicted with fever and ague, while a few cases of scurvy broke out among the escort. Yet the hardest affliction for Bartlett was his astonishment at finding Inéz González at Tubac, living with a certain Captain Gómez who commanded a small detachment there. Bartlett and Webb were convinced after making some inquiries that he had separated Inéz from her parents by skulduggery and was keeping her with him against her wishes. Bartlett was able to speak with Inéz and found her sad, unhappy, and, he believed, under some restraint. The commissioner later wrote a letter to the governor of Sonora on her behalf, but neither saw nor heard of Inéz again.[55] The entire party reached Santa Cruz on 24 July, taking advantage of the blacksmith there to shoe the mules and repair the much-abused wagons. Leaving that familiar settlement, Bartlett and company began a reconnaissance into Chihuahua, which brought them to Janos, Coralitos, and from thence on to El Paso del Norte.[56]

The lieutenant from Massachusetts had perhaps seen enough of the Gila and the desert when he noted in his journal on 9 August at his camp at Coralitos, "Prepared, harnessed & packed for a start. But Mr. Bartlett learning that Casas Grandes were but 20 or 30 miles south determined to visit them; and desired the train to await his return."[57] Bartlett managed to irritate Whipple one last time before reaching El Paso del Norte when he dismissed the lieutenant's muleteer, Guadalupe Medina, who in Whipple's estimation had no equal in tending the mules.[58] Having already lost one mule in a rainstorm, Whipple bemoaned the loss in his journal, "Guadalupe gone to El Paso taking with him 'García,' belle mare greatly to the dissatisfaction of my mules & myself."[59]

When Bartlett and Whipple finally reached El Paso del Norte in mid-August 1852, eleven months had passed since the beginning of the survey of the Gila; the same task had been completed by the Mexican section under Francisco Jiménez in four.[60] The failure of the United States commission to complete the Gila survey in good time lay not with Whipple or Gray, but with Bartlett. The September 1851 parade to Santa Cruz that led to his long illness was unnecessary and left the surveying teams on the river destitute of provisions and without funds when they were forced to interrupt the survey and hurry on to San Diego. The three-and-one-half months Bartlett spent in California before resuming the survey are inexplicable. Neither Whipple nor Gray mentioned any need to refit, and certainly not in distant San Francisco. All that was required were provisions that could have been obtained in a month's time in San Diego. No wonder Lieutenant Whipple had had his fill of Bartlett when he found himself stuck in camp at Coralitos while the commissioner was studying the wonderful ruins at Casas Grandes.

In any case Lieutenant Whipple was pleased to have reached El Paso del Norte and receive letters from home. His arrival also gave him an opportunity to visit his old friend Charles Radziminski, who was carrying forward a portion of the Río Grande survey near San Elceario. He learned that Emory, who had by now replaced Graham as chief astronomer, had originally desired Whipple to join him on the Río Grande, but now sent very different orders.[61] Major Emory directed Whipple to "complete any work that may remain unfinished west of the [Río Grande] del Norte of which you have any knowledge."[62] Lieutenant Whipple, who was as willing as ever to complete 32° 22′ north latitude, replied to Emory that he would run the line west from the Río Grande and then north to the Gila as soon as he could organize a party. Bartlett then requested the astronomer to present a program for completing that line.[63] Whipple complied, and by 1 October 1852 was prepared to depart El Paso del Norte with a party of twenty-one officers and men to begin the survey of the line west and north to the Río Gila. He was pleased to have the escort placed under his command.[64]

Whipple had less difficulty than expected, but found that the triangulation carried west by Assistant Engineer Moritz von Hippel was hastily left without permanent markers from which it could easily be resumed. Therefore Whipple had to begin anew from the initial point on the Río Grande to astronomical station twelve. He reported to Emory at the end of October that, "The weather is cold and we are greatly troubled with storms of wind, hail & rain."[65] As he had feared, Whipple did have trouble with the Indians, but lost neither mules nor horses. He reported that following an attack by the Apaches, he retaliated by invading the Indian camp at night, relieving them of all their horses. Having thus turned the tables on the Apaches, he and his small troop were ambushed on return, but kept all the horses and suffered no casualties. The next day the Apaches sought peace and Whipple returned a portion of their mounts to them, having no trouble after that episode.[66] With the fieldwork of the survey finished, including the topography of the line, Whipple returned to the Río Grande on 1 January 1853. He soon moved to Magoffinsville where he took a small room in James Wiley Magoffin's store to complete the fieldwork.[67]

Lieutenant Whipple of the Topographical Engineers completed the survey of 32° 22′ north latitude and determined the western line of New Mexico to the Gila. Previously, en route to the Gila survey, he had verified the correctness of Salazar Ylarregui's calculations made from astronomical observations at the western terminus of 32° 22′, and the point where the north-south line struck the Gila. His report to Bartlett of 15 May 1852 stating that "the Southern and Western limits of New Mexico may be considered as agreed upon and established," was duly recorded at a meeting of the Joint Commission held on 30 September 1852.[68] At an earlier meeting of the Joint Commission

on 18 September, it was agreed that monuments of iron be placed at the western terminus of 32° 22′, the point where the western line of New Mexico struck
the Gila, and where the road from Janos to Santa Rita del Cobre crossed the
line. It was further agreed that two iron markers were to be placed on the
banks of the Río Grande at El Paso del Norte, Commissioner Bartlett agreeing
to procure the monuments.[69] It appeared, therefore, that Surveyor Gray's cry
of protest against the compromise boundary line Bartlett had agreed to with
García Conde had been lost in the desert wind. No wonder that patriotic
Mexicans would ever claim that 32° 22′ was the correct line of demarcation.
All that now need be done was to complete the survey of the Río Grande.

CHAPTER V NOTES

[1]   "Journals," 14 Sep. 1851, Whipple Papers.

[2]   "Journals," 6 Sep. 1851, ibid.

[3]   Ibid.; Whipple to Graham, 29 Oct. 1850, Corres., Graham Papers.

[4]   "Journals," 6, Sep. 1851, Whipple Papers; Bartlett to Stuart, 27 Sep. 1851, SED 119 (626),
       p. 457.

[5]   "Journals," 7 Sep. 1851, Whipple Papers.

[6]   "Journals," 12 Sep. 1851, ibid.

[7]   Dictionary of American Biography, X, 168; Official Register of the Officers and Cadets of
       the U.S. Military, West Point, New York. June 1841 (New York: 1841).

[8]   Cremony, Life Among the Apaches, p. 98; SED 121 (627), pp. 24, 64; Official Dispatches,
       Memo, [n.d.], Whipple to Bartlett, 9 Jul. 1850, Corres., I, Bartlett Papers; "Journals," 18
       Nov. 1849, Whipple Papers.

[9]   "Journals," 27 Aug. 1851, ibid.; Bartlett, Personal Narrative, II, 347, 356–57; Whipple to
       Graham, 10 Jan. 1852, SED (627), p. 221.

[10]   Salazar Ylarregui to Jiménez, 21 Sep. 1851, "Jiménez Memoria," p. 6; Official Journal,
       pp. 93–94, Bartlett Papers.

[11]   "Journals," 25 Sep. 1851, Whipple Papers.

[12]   "Journals," 30 Sep., 5 Oct. 1851, ibid.

[13]   Whipple to Graham, 10 Jan. 1852, SED 121 (627), p. 221; Gray to Stuart, 10 Jan. 1852,
       File 429, NA, RG/76; File 396, I, ibid., pp. 126–33.

[14]   "Journals," 13, 17, 20, Oct. 1851, Whipple Papers.

[15]   Whipple to Graham, 10 Jan. 1852, SED 121 (627), p. 221.

[16]   "Journals," 25, 27 Oct. 1851, Whipple Papers.

[17]   Whipple to Graham, 10 Jan. 1852, SED 121 (627), p. 222.

[18]   "Journals," 27 Oct. 1851, Whipple Papers.

[19]   Whipple to Graham, 10 Jan. 1852, SED 121 (627), p. 222.

[20]   Ibid.

[21]   "Journals," 29 Nov. 1851, Whipple Papers.

[22]   Whipple to Graham, 10 Jan. 1852, SED 121 (627), p. 222.

23 Cremony, *Life Among the Apaches*, pp. 98–102.

24 "Journals," 16, 18 Dec. 1851, Whipple Papers; Whipple to Graham, 10 Jan. 1852, SED 121 (627), pp. 222–23; "The Boundary Line: Trials and Adventures of the Survey—or as Described by General Frank Wheaton," *Arizona Daily Citizen* (Tucson), 27 Jul. 1895.

25 Whipple to Graham, 10 Jan. 1852, SED 121 (627), p. 223; Gray to Stuart, 10 Jan. 1852, File 429, NA, RG/76; "Journals," 21, 25, 28 Dec. 1851, 8 Jan. 1852, Whipple Papers.

26 Gray to Stuart, 10 Jan. 1852, File 429, NA, RG/76.

27 Whipple to Stuart, 16 Jan. 1852, Box 2, Folder 16, Whipple Papers; Graham to Stuart, 16 Aug. 1851, SED 121 (627), p. 186.

28 Ibid., p. 225; Whipple to Stuart, 1 Feb. 1852, SED 119 (626), p. 85.

29 Whipple to Graham, 29 Oct. 1850, Corres., Graham Papers; Whipple to Stuart, 16 Jan. 1852, Box 2, Folder 16, Whipple Papers.

30 Whipple to Graham, 15 Feb. 1852, Corres., Graham Papers.

31 Stuart to Whipple, 21 Feb. 1852, SED 119 (626), p. 126.

32 Salazar Ylarregui to Jiménez, 21 Sep. 1851, "Jiménez Memoria," pp. 5–6; AHDN, Cancelados, Exp. 5–190, folios 1, 5–7, 13, 15, 17.

33 Jiménez to Ministro de Relaciones, 24 Jan. 1853, ASRE, Exp. 24, p. 75.

34 "Jiménez Memoria," p. 7.

35 Ibid., pp. 7–9; "Journals," 18 Dec. 1851, Whipple Papers.

36 Jiménez to Ministro de Relaciones, 24 Jan. 1853, ASRE, Exp. 24, p. 75; "Jiménez Memoria," p. 9; Bartlett, *Personal Narrative*, II, 252–53.

37 "Jiménez Memoria," 20 Sep. 1852, pp. 10–11.

38 Salazar Ylarregui to Jiménez, 30 Sep., 2 Oct. 1852, Jiménez to Salazar Ylarregui, 1 Oct. 1852, ASRE, Exp. 22, pp. 262–64.

39 Bartlett, *Personal Narrative*, I, 438–505.

40 Webb to Bartlett, 14 Feb. 1852, SED 119 (626), pp. 465–67.

41 Bartlett, *Personal Narrative*, II, 6–85.

42 Stuart to Gray, 31 Oct. 1851, Official Dispatches, No. 48, Bartlett Papers.

43 Stuart to Gray, 4 Nov. 1851, Official Dispatches, No. 50, ibid.

44 Gray to Stuart, 30 Apr. 1852, SED 6 (688), p. 116.

45 Bartlett to Stuart, 30 Apr. 1852, ibid., p. 117.

46 Gray to Bartlett, 30 Apr. 1852, Corres., VI, Bartlett Papers.

47 Bartlett, *Personal Narrative*, I, 505, II, 2–6, 85; Cremony, *Life Among the Apaches*, pp. 129–30; Thurber to Emory, 21 Jul. 1856, File 425, NA, RG/76.

48 Bartlett, *Personal Narrative*, II, 85–91, 111, 137–38.

49 *Alta California* (San Francisco), 20 Jan. 1852.

50 "Journals," Draft-Statement of facts to Dept. of War, [n.d.], 20, 21 Jun. 1852, Whipple Papers.

51 Bartlett to Stuart, 1 Jul. 1852, File 424, NA, RG/76; Whipple to Bartlett, 9 Jul. 1852, Bartlett to Whipple, 9 Jul. 1852, SED 6 (688), pp. 66–67; "Journals," Draft-Statement of facts to Dept. of War, [n.d.], 13 Jul. 1852, Whipple Papers.

52 Graham to Whipple, 16 Sep. 1852, Box 2, Folder 5, ibid.

53 Bartlett, *Personal Narrative*, II, 156; "Journals," 11, 17, 18, 24 Jun., 3 Jul. 1852, Whipple Papers.

54 Official Journal, pp. 136–37, Bartlett Papers; Whipple to Bartlett, 6 Jul. 1852, Box 2, Folder 16, Whipple Papers; Bartlett to Stuart, 9 Jul. 1852, SED 6 (688), p. 138.

55 Bartlett would have been pleased to have known that the story had a happy ending. Inéz bore Captain Gómez two sons and ultimately the couple was married. Gómez later died and Inéz then married the *alcalde* of Santa Cruz, who was a respected man of means. By this marriage she had another boy and a girl. See, Cremony, *Life Among the Apaches*, p. 58.

[56] "Journals," 21 Jun., 8, 10, 11, 12, 24 Jul., 10 Aug. 1852, Whipple Papers; Bartlett, *Personal Narrative*, II, 285, 303, 316–17, 379.

[57] "Journals," 9 Aug. 1852, Whipple Papers.

[58] "Journals," 16 Dec. 1851, 12 Aug. 1852, ibid.

[59] Journals," 13, 14 Aug. 1852, ibid.

[60] Bartlett, *Personal Narrative*, II, 378; "Journals," 18 Aug. 1852, Whipple Papers.

[61] Emory to Whipple, 29 Jan. 1852, File 425, NA, RG/76; "Journals," 18, 25 Aug. 1852, Whipple Papers.

[62] Emory to Whipple, 11 Jun. 1852, Folder 5, Emory Papers; "Journals," 20 Aug. 1852, Whipple Papers.

[63] Bartlett to Whipple, 20 Aug. 1852, SED 6 (688), pp. 71–72; Whipple to Emory, 20 Aug. 1852, Whipple to Bartlett, 21 Aug. 1852, Box 2, Folders, 16, 17, Whipple Papers.

[64] Whipple to Bartlett, 23 Aug. 1852, Whipple to Emory, 1 Oct. 1852, Whipple to Barnard E. Bee, 2 Jan. 1853, Box 2, Folder 16, ibid.; Bartlett to Whipple, 29 Sep. 1852, SED 6 (688), pp. 76–78; Bartlett to Stuart, 12 Feb. 1853, SED 41 (665), pp. 22–23.

[65] Whipple to Emory, 31 Oct. 1852, Folder 44, Emory Papers.

[66] Whipple to Bee, 2 Jan. 1853, Box 2, Folder 16, Whipple Papers.

[67] "Journals," 1, 14, 17 Jan. 1853, ibid.

[68] Official Journal, pp. 128–29, Bartlett Papers; Whipple to Bartlett, 15 May 1852, Box 2, Folder 16, Whipple Papers.

[69] Official Journal, pp. 121–22, Bartlett Papers.

EL RÍO BRAVO

DEL NORTE

*"This Commission is the meanest affair
that was ever got up under the Government."*

George C. Gardner, Assistant Surveyor

After his feud with Commissioner Bartlett had reached fever pitch at Santa Cruz, Colonel James Duncan Graham decamped for El Paso del Norte to begin the survey of the Río Grande. Stopping at Santa Rita del Cobre to order all the commission's property to Frontera, he reached the river on 13 November 1851.[1] On that day Mexican Surveyor José Salazar Ylarregui informed him that he had orders from García Conde to enter into an agreement with Graham for the survey. The Mexican commissioner had observed to Salazar Ylarregui that he could not possibly spend a year and a half to two years taking the topography of the river in its entire course from the initial point to Matamoros, as appeared to be the intention of the United States. He informed the surveyor that his instructions from the minister of foreign relations specifically directed him to fix a number of points of latitude and longitude by astronomical observation on the banks of the river and to determine the deepest channel of the river where there were two or more.[2] García Conde was particularly concerned about any island formed by the river, especially that which contained the settlements of Isleta, San Elceario, and Socorro.[3] The minister of foreign relations shared his uneasiness and had instructed him to take great care in this matter.[4]

Loss of these three towns was also a concern of Mexicans not connected to the government, as well as the inhabitants of the settlements who considered themselves citizens of the state of Chihuahua.[5] The question had been raised at a meeting of the Joint Commission on 20 July 1851 when the United States surveyor asked whether the riverine boundaries changed should the rivers seek a new channel. García Conde expressed his opinion that the boundary would remain the same.[6] Shortly thereafter Bartlett requested Graham to organize the survey of the Río Grande as soon as possible. He too held concern for the island, and observed to Graham that, only a few years before, the deepest channel of the river had run east of the island, but now cut to the west of it. Bartlett feared the river would again change, throwing Isleta, San Elceario, and Socorro into Mexico.[7] García Conde's opinion was dramatically tested a few years after completion of the survey when the Río Grande carved a new channel in 1864, cutting a 630-acre tract of land from Mexico in the vicinity of El Paso del Norte. This became known as the Chamizal, a no-man's-land between the future cities of Ciudad Juárez and El Paso, Texas. The dispute remained a point of friction for a century until 1963 when the territory was returned to Mexico. This was not the only instance in which the shifting river created disputes over territory cut from one side and thrown into another. Of course, García Conde could not have foreseen this.

Now eager to begin work, Graham and Salazar Ylarregui met on 24 November and adopted a detailed plan for the survey. They agreed to run out the course and sinuosities of the river with theodolites, or surveyor's compasses, and make the measurements with chain or with micrometer telescopes. All towns, villages, habitations, and topography near the Río Grande were to be surveyed and laid down on the maps. They agreed to correct the run of the work by astronomical observations for latitude and longitude at suitable stations and to connect such points in longitude with signal flashes when possible. Their plan also provided for the careful survey of all islands and the determination of the river's deepest channel where islands might occur. Should the Río Grande have more than one channel at its mouth, all were to be sounded. Graham and Salazar Ylarregui finally agreed that either party could begin without the other or make a less minute survey than the other, but must authenticate the more detailed effort.[8]

In the meantime Graham had had an opportunity to examine that small portion of the Río Grande from Doña Ana to San Elceario already surveyed, but found the survey notes useless and ordered a resurvey.[9] By mid-November Graham was able to report to Secretary of the Interior Stuart that the surveys of the Gila and Río Grande were progressing as planned. He expected the entire international boundary line would be completed by the end of 1852.[10] This was not to be, however, for dispatches from Bartlett and the protest of the Mexican government had reflected so adversely on Graham's course that Stuart saw fit to dismiss him from his post as chief astronomer on 13 September 1851. Stuart was annoyed at Graham's long delay in joining Bartlett in the field, and displeased that he had abruptly ordered Whipple to El Paso del Norte, causing a suspension of the survey of 32° 22′. The secretary also found Graham's pretensions regarding his rights, powers, and privileges as chief astronomer extraordinary and unacceptable.[11]

Graham received Stuart's order of dismissal on 25 November 1851, the day after his agreement with Salazar Ylarregui for the survey of the Río Grande, and exactly thirteen months after his appointment. When he returned to Washington he received something of a rebuke from Bureau Chief Abert, who observed that the surveyor recognized in the treaty was in charge of all

José Salazar Ylarregui, Courtesy Benson Latin American Collection, University of Texas at Austin.

scientific operations. Abert pointed out that the title of chief astronomer was not known to the treaty and therefore had no force. Graham's error in Abert's eyes was his failure to have himself appointed surveyor before he left the capital for the wilds of Texas. Regarding Graham's long delay in departing for El Paso del Norte, Abert asked his fellow Topographical Engineer why he failed to explain the need to procure sufficient instruments for the survey—a detail to which Bartlett had devoted little attention. Thus Bartlett got his story out first, tarnishing Graham's reputation if not that of the Topographical Engineers. Abert clearly believed Graham had proceeded improperly in his feud with Bartlett.[12]

In the hope of promoting harmony and efficiency in the United States commission, Stuart appointed Major William Emory chief astronomer and ordered him to proceed at once to Texas where the commanding officer would provide him with an escort of dragoons. On reaching commission headquarters he was to deliver Stuart's letter relieving Graham of duty and receive from him all instruments and materials pertaining to the office of chief astronomer.[13] Emory, who was pleased to have been relieved of his assignment to the commission after the survey of the California line, did not look forward to rejoining a mixed commission headed by men who in his opinion were unfit for public office and ignorant of scientific knowledge. Reaching San Antonio after a dreary march across the plains of Texas, Emory wrote, "as I approach the scene of action things look gloomy. I hear of nothing but dissensions, of debts without number, and finally of the loss of most of the means of transportation growing out of the depredations of the Indians."[14]

When he reached El Paso del Norte on 25 November his worst fears were confirmed. The whereabouts of Bartlett were unknown, the commissioner having been last reported en route to Santa Cruz, Sonora. Rumor had it that Bartlett was only interested in writing a book and, fearing he might be relieved before finishing it, had deserted the commission on some pretext.[15] He was equally distressed to find that most of the young men Bartlett had brought to El Paso del Norte knew nothing of surveying and were embroiled in feuds with each other and aligned in hostility toward either Bartlett or Graham.[16] After his experience on the California line, Emory concluded that a well-ordered surveying team should have as few civilian employees and assistants as possible, but Bartlett had arrived the year before with over a hundred, most of them incompetent.[17]

Emory found the situation to be extremely embarrassing. The commission was bereft of money and utterly without credit. Some of the men whom Bartlett had previously discharged could not be paid, and were thus stranded on the frontier. Those still employed could not be paid either and were selling their pay accounts at 50 percent value in order to clothe themselves. Emory's secretary, young George Gardner, summed up the general feeling when he wrote home, "This Commission is the meanest affair that was ever got up under the Government."[18]

Emory lamented that he had no authority to disband the commission, which now fell under his charge due to the prolonged absence of Bartlett. To his further surprise, he found that all that had been accomplished in the past year was the determination of the initial point, a parallel of latitude run fifty-eight miles westward, that two surveying parties were somewhere along the Gila, and that all the previous work on the Río Grande had to be resurveyed. Yet the princely sum of $500,000 had been expended! Demonstrating the energy for which he was then already known, Emory found officers and men who were willing to work on credit, and established observatories at Frontera, San Elceario, and Eagle Pass. Emory's only aid was a loan of money and supplies from James Wiley Magoffin, with whom he had served in the recent war.[19]

At this point Emory received his commission as United States surveyor, which he accepted with the understanding that it did not interfere with his standing in the army.[20] Emory now felt he had authority to assume responsibility for the United States commission, indeed that he must do so or see it disintegrate. He reported that on the line of present operations there was neither civil nor military law and the men of the commission were almost without arms in a hostile land. When Emory at length received authority from Secretary Stuart to reduce the number of employees as he saw fit and full authority over all matters, it was almost too late to salvage the situation.[21] All that maintained the surveying parties was the generosity of Magoffin.

The Department of the Interior was pleased that Emory had transformed a state of chaos into one of activity, but at wits end to understand what Bartlett was doing in San Francisco and via Acapulco at that. Mortified at Bartlett's failures, Stuart desired Emory to do everything necessary to prosecute the work. The major's friends, meanwhile, advised him to hold his temper and be prudent in his decisions, base any changes on the need for economy and avoid Bartlett's affairs at all costs. He had in fact been following a more circumspect course than Graham, who sought to paralyze the commission until he got his own way. Emory rather took the means at hand and pushed the survey to the utmost.[22]

Having found Graham's resurvey of the river from Doña Ana to San Elceario inaccurate, Emory ordered yet another survey. Assistant Surveyor Charles Radziminski now at last made an accurate survey of that portion of the Río Grande.[23] The major did find the plan for the survey of the river that Graham had worked out with Salazar Ylarregui useful and made very few changes. In a meeting with the Mexican surveyor, Emory agreed to divide the work on the Río Grande into six sections: from the initial point of the south-ern boundary of New Mexico on the river to San Ignacio; from thence to Presidio del Norte; from the presidio to the military colony of Agua Verde; from that post to Laredo; from Laredo to Matamoros; and from that town to the mouth of the Río Grande.

In order to save time and avoid difficulties, the first and last portions of the river were to be surveyed in detail by both parties, the second and fourth sections by the United States Boundary Commission; and the third and fifth by the Mexican commission. The two engineers further agreed to establish astronomical stations at either Agua Verde or the mouth of the Río Pecos, Eagle Pass, Laredo, Matamoros, and the mouth of the Rio Grande. Other points were to be determined astronomically as the work demanded.[24] The plan Emory adopted for the survey of the Río Grande was to touch the river at convenient intervals, determine those points astronomically, establish depots for the surveying parties, and connect the intervening spaces by lineal survey. While Emory personally attended to the astronomical points and depots, he placed Lieutenant Nathaniel Michler of the Topographical Corps, and civilian assistants Moritz von Hippel and Marine T. W. Chandler in charge of the actual survey.[25]

Despite the continued absence of John Russell Bartlett, who would not return to the Río Grande for a full year, Emory surmounted all troubles and got the survey under way. In April 1852 the major reported that the Mexican section was organized and prepared to start the survey, but complained that the United States section was without money to progress the work. Nevertheless, Emory was able to continue the survey down river with the means at hand, and by June had reached Presidio del Norte, having completed all astronomical observations and the survey to that point.[26]

The condition of the United States section was indeed desperate. Moritz von Hippel, a German immigrant whose administrative abilities and knowl-edge of surveying Emory held in high regard, bemoaned the forlorn condition in which his surveying party found itself. Von Hippel had carried the survey as far as Presidio del Norte, but reported that nearly every article of clothing and everyone's boots were worn out. The flour brought earlier to Presidio del Norte he found almost unfit for use. The mule trails were so impracticable as to overturn some animals, causing much damage to the equipage. He was 150 miles from any place where his party might refit, and found it impossible to purchase anything but mezcal. In any case von Hippel had no money, and could not continue the survey.[27]

To prevent the breakup of the party, Emory borrowed $250 on his own credit, and sent it to von Hippel that he might push the survey below Presidio del Norte a hundred miles, and return to refit before going on to Eagle Pass.

When von Hippel received the money, he used it to pay off and discharge certain disagreeable members of his party. At this juncture Emory received timely authority to draw upon his government, which enabled him to keep von Hippel's party together, the men not having been paid for almost a year.[28]

A heroic effort to carry the survey forward was now attempted by Assistant Surveyor Marine Tyler Wickham Chandler, who challenged the difficulties of the terrain between Presidio del Norte and Eagle Pass. In 1851 the very capable Colonel Emilio Langberg, inspector of the military colonies in Chihuahua, had led a reconnaissance team along the right bank of the river from San Carlos to Monclova el viejo in the forbidding area of the Big Bend. Langberg had fought in a number of engagements during the war, and had led various campaigns against the Comanches. Despite his years on the northern frontier, Langberg found this expedition on the Río Bravo del Norte an arduous one, his men often without water, the horses without pasture, and the fury of the sun without mercy.[29] Had Chandler access to Langberg's report of the expedition, his surveying party might have been better prepared. Emory did provide Chandler with a map that Langberg had constructed following his expedition, and while inaccurate gave some indication of the rugged land Chandler was about to encounter.[30]

The able Chandler was apparently a great talker for Gardner described him as "a bag of gas, if you give him a chance to explode."[31] Despite his loquacity Chandler was an excellent choice for the task that awaited him in the canyons of the Río Grande.[32] Because of the nature of the terrain Chandler would face, Emory placed his entire escort, under the command of Lieutenant Duff C. Green, at his disposal. After repairing to El Paso del Norte to replenish the commission's exhausted supplies at the presidio, Green was prepared to march, but the river proved unwilling to cooperate. On the eighth and ninth of September 1852, Chandler's party was troubled by a sudden and entirely unexpected rise in the river, which forced him to move his camp for the security of life and property.[33]

Chandler was unable to get under way until 12 September, and found that of his three boats, only one proved seaworthy as he entered Bofecillos Canyon. On the thirteenth he was surprised to see a drastic change in the country through which he now passed. No longer did Chandler witness a broad and fertile valley as he had at the beginning of the survey. The Río Grande soon led him through precipitous rocks and cliffs, which so confined the river as to provide in numerous places only the narrowest shore on which to set up his instruments. Elsewhere a perpendicular wall of rock forced him to project the line from the heights above the river. Immediately upon entering the canyon, the swift current threw one of Chandler's boats into a whirlpool, which held it fast. The boatmen exerted every effort to free the craft safely, but it quickly filled with water before they could draw it to shore. All its cargo was lost, save for a few bits of clothing. The boat itself, once gotten on shore, provided Chandler's small surveying team with the only available shelter from the storm that further insulted them that night. On the following day Chandler and his men shot the rapids and lost both the boats that had been filled with supplies and equipment. "We saw ourselves reduced in an instant to one single bag of flour, water-soaked, & a small bag of beans. A fortunate accident saved a single tin saucepan & bakery pan & these with two buckets were all I had left for twenty men."[34]

Lieutenant Green meanwhile had gotten under way with the escort and pack mules on the thirteenth. Making only three miles that day, he pitched camp with only five of his eighty mules and but two with their loads secure. His men gathered the mules and most of the loading by dark, and got under way again on the fifteenth. While Green attempted to keep close to Chandler, he often had to make a detour of forty miles or more with the escort and pack train to gain but a few miles on the river. At times the mule train was separated from the surveying team for days. When Green reunited with Chandler on 20 September, he found him in the deplorable condition described earlier, "eating his last piece of pork when I came into his camp on the Mexican Side of the Río Grande."[35]

The mountainous terrain forced Green and Chandler to separate once more as the mules found the going impossible. The two parties were reunited at the mouth of Santa Elena Canyon where Chandler was also compelled to abandon the river. Finding a guide who led them around the great canyon, they made a detour of ninety miles to reach the lower end of the canyon but twelve miles downriver. A further march of two days brought Green to the Indian crossing known as the Vado de Fleche and there he crossed to the Texas side of the Río Grande. The lieutenant was able to stay in contact until they reached the old military colony of San Vicente, after which Green found the trail ahead anything but cheering. He had no guide and his advance guard was unable to find a trail of any kind on the left bank of the river. Green therefore crossed once more into Mexico on 26 October.

The following day the escort and pack train were again forced to separate from the surveying party, continuing for two days without being able to find an opening to the river. When Green finally brought his men and mules to the river's edge, he realized it would be impossible to turn the pack train upstream and was more anxious than ever about Chandler, whom he had left two days before. Green sent a search party upriver, but was greatly relieved when Chandler and his assistant, E. A. Phillips, straggled into camp at eleven o'clock that night. Having struck Green's trail, they had walked forty miles in one day without water, and gone seventy-two hours without food. Green now

made a careful reconnaissance downstream and found no point where his pack
train could reach the Río Grande. After three days of hard going, his advance
guard could make but six miles by the river. While the magnificently wild
topography of the Big Bend barred Green's path, Chandler found he could
not continue the survey with the means at his disposal.[36] Chandler's crew had
suffered further overturned boats, loss of food and clothing, and an outbreak
of scurvy so that, "the esprit of the party began to flag...."[37]

With his men exhausted, barefoot, nearly destitute of clothing, having
scarcely any food, his boats leaking so badly as to be useless, Chandler left the

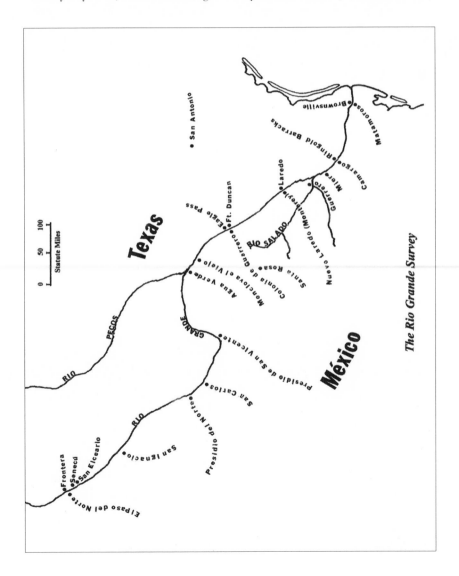

Río Grande on 5 November and suspended the survey.[38] His decision was not that of the fainthearted. Of Chandler Duff Green wrote, "His work ...could not have been more difficult. Natural obstacles almost impassible, and still worse attempts of mutiny, now all are met and overcome, and he only seemed happy when at the camp planning some difficult work for the coming day."[39] Rather than continue to test the temper of the river, Chandler and Green decided to strike overland for Santa Rosa, Coahuila, and from that town for Fort Duncan near Eagle Pass. They made the march to Santa Rosa without incident, their greatest concern being the lack of water.

On 17 November, after a skirmish involving bluster but not battle with a band of Indians, Green reported to the authorities at Santa Rosa in order to explain his presence on Mexican soil. Permission to pass through was easily granted, and the ragged expedition continued the journey to Fort Duncan, reaching that post on 24 November 1852.[40] Arriving ten days before Chandler and Green was Charles Abbott, a laborer on the commission, who with several other men had decided to take the best of the boats and brave the unknown rapids that awaited them downstream. During the exhilarating ten-day trip, Abbott kept notes and made a very rough map of the river which later provided Emory and his engineers with at least a hint of what they would face when they returned to survey the river scientifically. Abbott and his comrades, their clothes in tatters and with little food, challenged the dangerous waters of the Río Grande in an India-rubber boat, and won.[41]

The difficulties between Presidio del Norte and Eagle Pass were indeed so great that Emory turned Lieutenant Nathaniel Michler's surveying team upriver to work toward Chandler's party. Emory had previously placed Michler in charge of that portion of the river between Eagle Pass and Ringgold Barracks. When Michler received Emory's order to turn his party around and push the survey up river, he had completed the work as far as Laredo. By the end of June Michler had begun the survey above Eagle Pass.[42]

In early November 1852, after one year's effort to complete the survey of the Río Grande in the absence of Commissioner Bartlett, Emory suspended the work.[43] The energetic but hot-tempered major now fairly exploded:

> Superadded to the physical obstacles to be overcome, the men
> became almost insubordinate from the long absence of the com-
> missioner from the work, and his unpardonable neglect to furnish
> money for their payment. Some of them had not received any pay
> for eighteen months, and the commissioner was at that moment,
> with an equipage and corps of attendants, visiting the States of
> Chihuahua and Sonora, and the Geysers of California—places
> sufficiently distant from the line.[44]

Emory wrote to Michler that he found Bartlett's activity utterly irresponsible.[45] At Presidio del Norte one of the surveying parties became mutinous from the deferred promises of pay, and on one occasion Emory "was obliged to put down a riot in my camp, single-handed, and at the risk of being shot by an insubordinate fellow, insane from the effects of the intoxicating mezcal."[46]

The continued absence of Bartlett placed the United States section of the Joint Commission in a truly desperate condition. Emory bitterly lamented the situation since he had managed to overcome all difficulties and bring the survey of the Río Grande to a point where its completion by the spring of 1853 was a very reasonable expectation. He had achieved all this without any assistance from Bartlett or so much as one cent of the money appropriated for the survey.[47] Local merchants refused to cash Emory's drafts upon the government, leaving him completely destitute, as he reported to the Department of the Interior, "God knows how the thing has happened, but unless relief is afforded, I stand a chance of seeing the inside of a Texas jail...."[48] At last Emory received word from Bartlett along with two checks amounting to $20,000, but local merchants refused to cash these as they had Emory's. At wit's end, Emory suspended the work on 5 November and retired to Ringgold Barracks to await Bartlett's expected arrival.[49]

The Mexican section of the Joint Commission suffered equally, if not more so from the lack of money, resources, military escort, and an adequate number of engineers to carry on the work. The commission incurred its greatest loss, however, with the death of Pedro García Conde at Arizpe, Sonora, on 19 December 1851. The starving journey to Santa Cruz had brought upon him severe stomach pains that caused him to delay his departure to join Francisco Jiménez on the Gila, and instead seek repose at Arizpe. He had left that frontier outpost as a boy, never returning until now. There he was stricken by a fever and died in the house where he was born forty-seven years earlier.[50] When Salazar Ylarregui informed Emory of the general's death, the major invited all the officers and men of the United States commission to wear crepe on the hilt of their sabres and left arms for thirty days in memory of the Mexican engineer they had all come to respect.[51]

José Salazar Ylarregui now sent Captain Juan Espejo to Mexico City with the sad news and himself awaited further orders at El Paso del Norte. The government responded quickly, appointing him commissioner as well as surveyor.[52] In doing so the government chose wisely, for the new commissioner was widely respected as an engineer in Mexico and knew the area of the international boundary as thoroughly as any of the gentlemen connected with the Joint Commission. The men of the United States section were also pleased with the choice for they had long since come to hold him and his abilities in high regard. Lieutenant Whipple described him as the most persevering, energetic, and talented man he had ever known. The gentlemanly Salazar Ylarregui was moreover an amiable, interesting, and agreeable fellow, easily making friends among the officers of the United States commission.[53] The poetic engineer, who enjoyed the beauty of his country's landscape, would now need all the perseverance he could muster.

Salazar Ylarregui and Emory soon agreed to hold an official meeting to authenticate the work on that portion of the Río Grande thus far surveyed, Emory agreeing to accept the Mexican commissioner's selection of time and place. Salazar Ylarregui, who urgently needed to go to Chihuahua City to get additional funding and arrange other matters for his commission, suggested they meet at Presidio del Norte 1 August next. To this the major agreed, but requested an official meeting immediately that they might arrange to leave a number of assistant engineers behind to finish the survey. Consequently the two surveyors met on 18 April, verified the line from Frontera to the point where the San Antonio road left the Río Grande, and agreed to meet on 1 August at Presidio del Norte to sign the maps from the initial point at 32° 22′ to the presidio. They also arranged to appoint engineers to complete the survey.[54]

In its survey of the Río Grande, the Mexican section had naturally begun with the initial point at 32° 22′ and worked its way down river. Particular attention was given to the position of El Paso del Norte, a task Salazar Ylarregui had placed under the direction of Francisco Jiménez as early as January 1851. Assisted by Juan Espejo, Agustín García Conde, and Manuel Alemán, Jiménez made 100 observations in ten days' time under favorable circumstances, determining the latitude of El Paso del Norte as 31°44′15″54 north.[55]

From the initial point the Mexican commission carried a triangulation connecting several points along the river to the colony of San Ignacio. Following the course and sinuosities of the river as closely as possible, the surveying party made a more detailed survey on the Mexican side of the Río Grande, assuming that the United States team would do likewise on its side. Salazar Ylarregui himself began the survey from the mouth of the old irrigation channel at La Mesilla, but soon turned the task over to Augustus de Vaudricourt, now in the employ of the Mexican Boundary Commission. Vaudricourt carried the effort as far as the little settlement of Los Amoles.[56]

Salazar Ylarregui had meanwhile ordered Agustín Díaz to work from San Ignacio upriver until he met Vaudricourt. While he gave the lieutenant of engineers the task of taking the topography of the river, he instructed him to avoid concerning himself with minutiae that would hinder the work. The commissioner desired that Díaz limit his topography to the range of hills that confined the valley of the river, noting principal towns and roads on both sides of the river, taking particular care to note the course of the river within its banks. Additionally, he ordered Díaz to ascertain the major irrigation channels, arroyos, and the general direction of any line of contiguous or isolated hills and mountain chains that approached Mexico's side of the Río Grande.

Regarding any island Díaz might encounter, and particularly the one that held the settlements of Socorro, Isleta, and San Elceario, he was to mark both channels with great care and take soundings for depth at as many points as possible. To assist Agustín Díaz, Salazar Ylarregui assigned his brother Luis and five laborers with all that was required for two months in the field. The party received no escort and the laborers proved too few for the work, let alone to provide protection from the Indians then raiding in the area.

With all in readiness, Agustín Díaz and his small party marched to San Ignacio, arriving at the colony on 25 March 1852. The following day Díaz reconnoitered the area to determine the most suitable terrain for beginning the survey, and there established his camp. Operations continued smoothly, but by April's end the Río Grande began to flood, making an approach to its banks difficult. There being no safe crossing to work on the other side of the river, Luis Díaz returned to El Paso del Norte to secure a boat to cross the flooded river. He returned on 3 May with an India-rubber boat that Salazar Ylarregui provided until the wooden boat then being constructed in La Mesilla could be completed. This more serviceable craft was unfortunately not finished in time to be of any use to Díaz.

Despite continued flooding that made the work difficult, and some apprehension caused by the appearance of a band of Indians, Díaz' team carried the triangulation onward, but found no island below that which held Socorro, Isleta, and San Elceario. The rubber craft proved very inadequate for the purpose of making soundings, tearing itself three times on the branches of trees being carried down the river by the floodwaters. Toward the end of May daily rains gave the Díaz brothers added bother, but despite the rising waters of the Río Grande and a very careful survey, they saw no rise in the old channel that might have given Mexico claim to that island and its three settlements. In fact the "island" no longer existed, placing the three towns irrevocably in the United States.

By 1 June the river had risen so much as to make passage in the flimsy boat so dangerous that part of Díaz' crew became stranded on the left bank of the river, having to trek to Isleta to effect a crossing. With the boat now unusable, and the edge of the river impossible to approach because of the deeply mired shore, the survey team made a reconnaissance as far as Senecú. Finding it necessary to await the abatement of the flooding, Díaz carried the triangulation eastward in reverse order to his previous surveying station.

The Río Grande continued to rise well into July, hindering the progress of the work, but after 12 July the flooding began to wane. Along with this grant of mercy from the river, Díaz received an additional theodolite from Salazar Ylarregui. Now the Díaz brothers were able to work separately and the survey went rapidly, bringing the triangulation to El Paso del Norte by the end of the month. On 1 August Díaz received instructions from the commissioner, then at Presidio del Norte for his meeting with Emory, to send with all speed maps of the course of the river from Los Amoles to Frontera. This errand he placed in the care of Luis, while he himself completed the topography of the survey to Los Amoles on 9 August 1852. The fieldwork completed, Díaz compared and verified his survey with Vaudricourt's work from the initial point to Los Amoles. In this he was assisted by Manuel Alemán, and all that remained was the completion of the maps of the survey.[57]

Though the Mexican commission was not officially responsible for that portion of the river from San Ignacio to Presidio del Norte, Salazar Ylarregui fully intended to continue the survey to that point and so informed the Joint Commission on 8 October 1852. Evidence that he did so is his letter to Jiménez dated 15 May 1853, in which he related that he had just finished the survey to his position at the presidio. No official report on the commissioner's work from San Ignacio to Presidio del Norte seems to exist, however.[58] In a later effort the Mexican section returned to the river in an attempt to carry the survey as far as Laredo. The party included topographical engineers Manuel Fernández Leal, Miguel Iglesias, and Francisco Herrera, all of whom were products of the Colegio de Minería where Salazar Ylarregui had been professor of geodesy until his appointment to the commission. Work began at Presidio del Norte in January 1855. Although under repeated attack from the Apache and Comanche, with whom they at length made a treaty of peace, the team completed the survey to the old presidio of San Carlos in March. They were now destitute of provisions, and, learning none could be had from Salazar Ylarregui, were forced to abandon the effort to continue.[59]

For the moment, however, the Mexican section had brought the riverine survey downstream only as far as San Ignacio and could proceed no farther. Salazar Ylarregui had received neither money nor escort from his government, and had only carried the line to this point by employing his personal credit, as had García Conde before him. The Mexico City newspaper, *El Siglo XIX*, brought Salazar Ylarregui's patriotic effort to public attention in an editorial, comparing the government's lack of support for the commission to the 17,000 pesos recently appropriated for the removal of the statue of Carlos IV from the Zócalo to the paseo.[60] In a personal and sincere note to Emory, Salazar Ylarregui explained that unless he received more support from Mexico City, he would not be able to move so much as one surveying party into the field.[61] From Presidio del Norte he requested either to be relieved as commissioner and surveyor, or sent additional engineers and money to finish the survey.[62]

The condition of the Mexican section was truly desperate. Agustín García Conde returned to Mexico City to report the deplorable situation of the commission's funds to the government. Added to the great distances being traversed in tracing the line and the absence of regular communication, the complete failure of the government to provide for its commission on the frontier had caused a paralysis of the work. The pay of every member of the commission was in arrears, and that of García Conde by eight months. He did not think he would be able to rejoin the Mexican section and feared he would have to resign his post. Agustín García Conde told the minister of war that his father's dying wish had been that he report the dire financial condition of the commission to the government.[63]

By late September 1852, himself suffering from fevers, Salazar Ylarregui was forced to suspend the survey for lack of funds, engineers, and an adequate escort. He had not been able to bring the survey as far down the river as Presidio del Norte.[64] He privately wrote to Mexican president Mariano Arista that his nation's commission was in a miserable state, having been virtually abandoned on the frontier. Salazar Ylarregui's situation had become so extreme that he could not leave El Paso del Norte himself, let alone send a surveying party into the field. Were it not for the aid of Alejo García Conde and José Merino, respectively administrator and comptroller of the customs house at El Paso del Norte, he and his commission would have been starving. Agustín García Conde later remarked that the work of the commission had been done at great sacrifice, the suffering and hardship had been as difficult as it was dangerous.[65]

Of even greater concern for Salazar Ylarregui had been the disinclination of Emory to honor their agreement to meet at Presidio del Norte and sign the maps of the survey of the river. When the Mexican commissioner arrived at the presidio on 22 July 1852, he informed Emory that he would be pleased to meet at the major's convenience. Emory responded that he could not meet as previously agreed since Bartlett had not yet arrived and he had not had access to the records of the Joint Commission. He also observed that his work was not fully completed, since the maps had yet to be plotted and that could not be done in the field. Moreover the Mexican section had not completed its fieldwork as far as Presidio del Norte. Salazar Ylarregui, on the other hand, believed only the work of one commission need be completed and accepted by the other to be valid. In this he was correct, for according to their official plan of operations, the section of the Río Grande from San Ignacio to Presidio del Norte was the responsibility of the United States surveying party, not that of the Mexican. Therefore, in view of the agreement reached at Frontera on 18 April, he again pressed Emory to meet and sign the maps from the initial point to Presidio del Norte.[66]

At length Emory agreed to meet on 26 August, but refused to sign the map containing the initial point, stating that when he made the Frontera agreement he fully expected Bartlett would have arrived by 1 August. The major's argument was rather weak since he knew that Bartlett was probably on the California coast when the Frontera agreement was reached.[67] A second meeting was held the following day at which Salazar Ylarregui again urged Emory to sign the map which contained the initial point of the southern boundary of New Mexico at 32° 22′ north latitude. In obedience to his instructions from the Secretary of the Interior, Emory at last agreed to sign the map with the following attachment, "The Boundary line as agreed upon by the two Commissioners April 24th 1851."[68]

Emory had put off Salazar Ylarregui as long as he could in the hope of receiving new instructions or even the slightest authority to reopen the discussions regarding the southern limit of New Mexico.[69] One way out of the trap presented by Secretary Stuart's instructions to sign the documents regarding 32° 22′ was for the United States Senate to reject Emory's appointment as surveyor. Emory was concerned that he would not be confirmed unless he resigned his commission in the army, something he had no intention of doing. He wrote privately to Salazar Ylarregui of his anxiety over the issue that he not be disappointed to arrive at Presidio del Norte to find that Emory was no longer surveyor.[70]

There was indeed opposition in the Senate to Emory's confirmation, not because of his rank in the army, but because of his instructions to sign the documents regarding 32° 22′. He was of course eventually confirmed, but did not learn so until weeks after his 27 August meeting with Salazar Ylarregui.[71] One is tempted to wonder if Emory would have been greatly relieved to learn that the Senate had rejected his nomination, providing him with an honest excuse not to sign. Hearing nothing, he followed his instructions and authenticated the line as that of the two commissioners. If the surveyors were without authority on the Joint Commission, the Bartlett-García Conde line was valid. If the authority of the surveyors was equal to that of the commissioners, the compromise line would fall.[72]

Emory's obstinate attitude had not been lost on Salazar Ylarregui. In early November he wrote to President Mariano Arista a letter filled with anxiety and foreboding. He observed that after fixing the initial point of the southern boundary of New Mexico on the Río Grande, Commissioner Bartlett had acted in a contrary manner, and pointed out that some members of the United States Senate held 32° 22′ illegal—that it did not conform to the treaty. While he affirmed that this was simply not true, Salazar Ylarregui emphasized that the Democrats would most likely return to power next March. This party he observed to the president was the greater enemy of Mexico and the party to which many members of the United States commission belonged. These men, no doubt referring to the attitude of Graham and Emory, had been his friends, but recently had acted in a manner that was at the very least intransigent. He urged Arista, therefore, to give him the means to complete the survey before the Democratic Party came to power, and not leave his commission stranded for want of everything at El Paso del Norte.[73]

Unfortunately Arista would not be able to send so much as a peso to the engineer on the frontier because a revolt had broken out calling for Arista's removal and the return of Antonio López de Santa Anna. Echoing Salazar Ylarregui's plea, Mexico's envoy at Washington, Manuel Larráinzar, lamented to Arista that never more than at that time did Mexico need healing; the questions pending with the United States were a danger demanding firm and concentrated effort by the government. Just when speed, strength, and an abundance of funds were needed, revolt came to weaken the nation. The great question, he pressed upon Arista, was the boundary survey.[74]

With both sections of the Joint Boundary Commission having suspended operations, Salazar Ylarregui stranded and ill at El Paso del Norte, and Major Emory stalled at Ringgold Barracks, the long-absent Commissioner Bartlett was wending his way to meet Emory by a rather circuitous route. Having gotten Whipple off to complete the survey of 32° 22´, Bartlett intended to join Emory at Eagle Pass, taking the San Antonio road. He was unfortunately delayed by the lack of an escort, or so he later explained. The twenty-four men at Fort Fillmore would be scarcely adequate for Whipple's escort in the heart of Apache country, and Bartlett had heard the Comanches had become a danger on the San Antonio road.

When Bartlett reached El Paso del Norte on 17 August 1852, he found Lieutenant Duff Green preparing to depart for Presidio del Norte with the supplies Emory had requested him to procure for Chandler's party. Bartlett informed Green of Colonel Craig's death, which made him commander of the escort, and requested the lieutenant to attend him to Eagle Pass. Green, who had promised Emory that he would return to Presidio del Norte with all due haste and provide Chandler's crew with an escort, refused to accompany Bartlett. Green did not feel that Bartlett needed to send all twenty-four troops with Whipple; he could have kept a small detachment with himself and easily proceeded along the San Antonio road as he always traveled with a large number of teamsters and employees about him. Had he not journeyed up the Río Gila and across the desert through the heart of Apache country with but five soldiers? Moreover, Green felt the San Antonio road was quite safe, pointing out that Emory had traveled to Presidio del Norte with no escort whatever. In refusing to escort Bartlett, Green believed he was following Colonel Craig's original orders to let nothing hinder the operations of the surveying parties in the field. In short he considered his duty to assist Chandler greater than the United States commissioner's request for an escort. Equally important, Major Emory had promised Green that he would do all he could to see to his promotion if Chandler's effort proved successful.[75]

Bartlett, who was always vigilant that the military authority not supersede the civilian, seems to have made no objection whatever to Green's refusal to accompany him. The truth of the matter is that Bartlett was not concerned for his safety on the San Antonio road. He had been making inquiries about the route through Chihuahua, and eagerly accepted Colonel Emilio Langberg's offer to escort him by way of Chihuahua City. This route would take the United States boundary commissioner to Camargo on the Río Grande via Chihuahua and through the states of Durango, Coahuila, Nuevo León, and Tamaulipas. It promised to be an enjoyable and exciting little trip. Before his departure he wrote to Emory that he thought he would meet the major at Camargo, but was not at all certain precisely where he would reach the Río Grande. It was well that Green did not wait for Bartlett as the commissioner spent a full seven weeks at El Paso del Norte. He employed this time purchasing new wagons, repairing others, and seeing to the refitting of the harness, tents, and other equipment of his party. The mules also needed time to be made fit for the journey ahead.[76] When Emory learned of Bartlett's intentions, he found them incomprehensible. The surveyor considered the commissioner's junket through the wilds of Chihuahua with Langberg irresponsible since the Indian threat was more dangerous on the Mexican side of the river. Emory noted that two wagon trains had taken the San Antonio road since Bartlett's arrival at El Paso del Norte and wondered why the commissioner did not avail himself of their protection.[77]

While the San Antonio road was not quite as safe as Green and Emory inferred, the journey through Chihuahua proved even more dangerous. Despite efforts of the national government and the northern states to defend against Indian attacks on the northern frontier, President José Joaquín de Herrera lamented before the Congreso General that these depredations were "una de las mayores calamidades de la República."[78] Bartlett and his entourage left El Paso del Norte on 8 October, but before reaching Chihuahua City were forced to fight off an attack by some forty Indians. After an arduous trip of nearly two and one half months, during which wagon tongues were snapped off and wheels crushed by the hazards of the road, Bartlett reached Mier on the Río Grande in December 1852. The following day he continued on to Camargo some miles distant and crossed the river to meet Emory at Ringgold Barracks.[79]

Surveyor Emory, who had been waiting in frustration for Bartlett to appear, now informed the commissioner that work on the river had ceased on 5 November for want of funds. Bartlett also learned that the United States Congress, concerned that the Bartlett-García Conde line might be a departure from the treaty, had suspended the appropriation for the survey. Stuart informed Bartlett in a dispatch dated 15 October 1852 that the work on the river could continue if he had the means to keep his surveying parties in the field.[80]

Emory of course had no means to resume the survey and Bartlett had scarcely money enough to get himself and other members of the commission to Washington: It was impossible to go on. He therefore ordered the chiefs of all surveying parties to proceed to Washington and report to him with their field notes.[81] The major had received Stuart's dispatch on the morning of 11 November. While he waited until Bartlett's arrival to order the Río Grande surveying parties to Washington, he immediately ordered Whipple to cease operations on 32° 22′. [82] His hopes of interrupting Whipple's survey failed, for the lieutenant had returned to El Paso del Norte after completing the survey of the southern and western limits of New Mexico on 1 January 1853, and did not receive Emory's order until 4 February. He had been plotting his work but quickly disbanded his party and repaired to Washington.[83]

Bartlett now considered how best to dispose of the commission's property and requested Emory's advice on the matter. Emory insisted that Bartlett assume all responsibility for discharging the employees of the commission and paying its debts since, in Emory's opinion, Bartlett's long absence had brought about the deranged state of affairs in which they all found themselves.[84] Acting on Emory's recommendation, Bartlett divided what money he had among the officers of the commission to cover their expenses home. It was enough for only about half of them. As the surveying parties of the United States Boundary Commission broke up and decamped for Washington, John Russell Bartlett may have sensed that he would never return to the Río Grande. Indeed, he believed it had been the intention of the United States Congress to break up the international survey; in this he was correct.[85]

CHAPTER VI NOTES

1 SED 121 (627), pp. 47, 60.

2 García Conde to Salazar Ylarregui, 30 Sep. 1851, in Salazar Ylarregui to Graham, 13 Nov. 1851, Corres., Graham Papers.

3 "Puntos sobre los cuales pide instrucciones ...," ASRE, Exp. 22, p. 58.

4 "Instrucciones que se dan ...en 15 de junio de 1850," ibid., pp. 56–57.

5 El Siglo XIX (Mexico City), 14, 25 Feb. 1849, 6 May 1850; Jesús José Sánchez and Bartolo Madrid to the Governor of Chihuahua, 6 May 1850, José C. Muñoz and Luis Rubio to the Governor of Chihuahua, 11 Apr. 1850, "Valle de "La Mesilla ...," Legajo 1–2-566 (I) (Archivo de la Secretaría de Relaciones Exteriores, Mexico City; Hereafter cited as, ASRE, Leg. 1–2-566 (I)).

6 Official Journal, p. 76, Bartlett Papers.

7 Bartlett to Graham, 23 Aug. 1851, SED 121 (627), pp. 186–87.

8 For the text of the plan see, File 431, NA, RG/76.

9 Whipple to Prioleau, 14 Feb. 1851, Corres. III, Bartlett Papers; SED 121 (627), pp. 19–20; von Hippel to Graham, 20 Aug. 1851, Corres., Graham Papers.

10 Graham to Stuart, 16 Nov. 1851, SED 121 (627), pp. 203–204; Graham to Abert, 16 Nov. 1851, SED 119 (626), p. 470.

11 Stuart to Graham, 13 Sep. 1851, Corres., Graham Papers; Stuart to Conrad, 11 Sep. 1851, SED 121 (627), pp. 240–41; Stuart to Pearce, 17 Aug. 1852, SED 6 (688), pp. 16–18.

12 Graham to Stuart, 10 Dec. 1851, Abert to Graham, 3 Mar. 1852, SED 121 (627), pp. 219, 239–40; Abert to Graham, 28 Sep. 1851, Abert to Conrad, 30 Oct. 1851, 29 Oct. 1852, Corres., Graham Papers; Gardner to Sarah Gardner, 27 Nov. 1851, Gardner Papers.

13 Stuart to Emory, 13 Sep. 1851, Stuart to Graham, 13 Sep. 1851, Official Dispatches, Nos. 44, 45, Bartlett Papers.

14 Emory to Joseph Henry [draft], 13 Oct. 1851, Folder 33, Emory Papers; SED 108 (832), pp. 10–11.

15 Jacobs to Emory, 30 Nov. 1851, Jacobs to Tillinghast, 2 Dec. 1851, Emory to Stuart, 8 Dec. 1851, SED 119 (626), pp. 79–82; Gardner to Sarah Gardner, 27 Nov. 1851, Gardner Papers.

16 SED 121 (627), p. 52; Gardner to C. K. Gardner, 11 Jan. 1852, Gardner Papers.

17 SED 108 (832), pp. 10–11; Graham to Abert, 16 Nov. 1851, Bartlett to Whipple, 10 Apr. 1851, SED 119 (626), pp. 317, 334; García Conde to Yáñez, 11 Mar. 1851, ASRE, Exp. 22, p. 226.

18 Gardner to C. K. Gardner [?], 27 Mar. 1852, Gardner Papers; Emory to Stuart, 11 Mar. 1852, SED 6 (688), pp. 103–104.

19 SED 108 (832), p. 11; Emory to Stuart, 20 Jan., 18 Apr. 1852, File 425, NA, RG/76.

20 Emory to Stuart, 22 Jan. 1852, SED 119 (626), p. 472; Stuart to Emory, 4 Nov. 1852, Official Dispatches, No. 51, Bartlett Papers; Emory to Stuart, 1 Feb. 1852, Folder 36, Emory Papers.

21 Emory to Stuart, 8 Feb. 1852, SED 119 (626), p. 483; Emory to Stuart, 11 Mar. 1852, Stuart to Emory, 12 Jun. 1852, SED 6 (688), pp. 4–5, 103–104.

22 Pearce to Emory, 20 Nov. 1850, Emory to Pearce, 15 Jan. 1852, Hardcastle to Emory, 12 Mar. 1852, Chandler to Emory, 17 Mar. 1852, Goddard to Emory, 8 Apr. 1852, Miles to Emory, 26 May 1852, Bache to Emory, 1 Sep. 1852, Folders 27, 35, 37, 38, 39, 43, Emory Papers; Gardner to C. K. Gardner, 16 May 1852, Gardner Papers.

23 Emory to Bartlett, 14 Feb. 1853, SED 6 (688), p. 3; Radziminski to Emory, 6 Jun. 1852, Folder 5, Emory Papers.

24 File 396, NA, RG/76, I, 115–16.

25 SED 108 (832), p. 12; Emory to Magoffin, 29 Dec. 1851, Folder 34, Emory Papers.

26 Emory to Stuart, 12 Apr. 1852, File 425, NA, RG/76; Emory to Stuart, 10 Jun. 1852, Folder 5, Emory Papers; Gardner to C. K. Gardner, 20 Jun. 1852, Gardner Papers.

27 "Recommendation for Moritz von Hippel," [?] Jan. 1856, Folder 83, Emory Papers; von Hippel to Emory, 15 May 1852, File 400, NA, RG/76.

28 Emory to von Hippel, 26 May 1852, von Hippel to Emory, 4 Jun. 1852, Emory to Stuart, 23 Jul. 1852, Folder 5, Emory Papers.

29 Emilio Langberg, "Itinerario de la Espedición de San Carlos á Monclova el viejo hecha por el Coronel D. Emilio Langberg ...en el año de 1851." (Beinecke Library, Yale University), pp. 4, 12, 15; AHDN, Cancelados, Exp. XI/111/2–400, II, folios 1, 2, 9, 25, 34, 40, 42. For an interesting note on Langberg see, Bob Cunningham and Harry P. Hewitt, "A 'Lovely Land Full of Roses and Thorns': Emil Langberg and Mexico, 1835–1866," *Southwestern Historical Quarterly*, XCVIII (Jan., 1995).

30 Ronnie C. Tyler, *The Big Bend: A History of the Last Texas Frontier* (Washington, DC: 1975), p. 82.

31 Gardner to C. K. Gardner, 6 Feb. 1852, Gardner Papers.

32 Tyler, *The Big Bend*, pp. 82–97; Ronnie C. Tyler, ed.,"Exploring the Rio Grande: Lt. Duff C. Green's Report of 1852," *Arizona and the West*, X (Spring, 1968), p. 58.

33 Ibid., pp. 51, 53; Chandler to Emory, 1 Dec. 1852, Folder 46, Emory Papers; SED 108 (832), pp. 80–85.

34 Chandler to Emory, 1 Dec. 1852, Folder 46, Emory Papers.

35 Tyler, "Exploring the Rio Grande," pp. 54, 58.

36 Chandler to Emory, 4 Nov. 1852, Folder 6, Emory Papers; Tyler, "Exploring the Rio Grande," pp. 55–58.

37 Chandler to Emory, 1 Dec. 1852, Folder 46, Emory Papers.

38 *Ibid.*

39 Tyler, "Exploring the Rio Grande," p. 58.

40 *Ibid.*, pp. 58–60.

41 William H. Goetzmann, "Science Explores the Big Bend: 1852–1853," *Password*, III (Apr., 1958), pp. 62, 65–66.

42 Emory to Michler, 11 Dec. 1851, Folder 34, Michler to Emory, 28 Jun. 1852, Emory to Stuart, 23 Jul. 1852, Folder 5, Emory Papers; Emory to Bartlett, 18 Sep. 1852, SED 6 (688), p. 46.

43 Emory to Bartlett, 30 Oct. 1852, SED 108 (832), p. 13.

44 Ibid., p. 12.

45 Emory to Michler, 26 Oct. 1852, Folder 6, Emory Papers.

46 SED 108 (832), p. 12.

47 Emory to Stuart, 30 Nov. 1852, File 425, NA, RG/76.

48 Emory to George Whiting, 15 Oct. 1852, Folder 6, Emory Papers.

49 Emory to Bartlett, 30 Oct. 1852, SED 6 (688), pp. 46–47; SED 108 (832), p. 15.

50 Bartlett, *Personal Narrative*, I, 455–56.

51 Salazar Ylarregui to Emory, 19 Jan. 1852, Circular, 20 Jan. 1852, Folders 3, 35, Emory Papers.

52 Salazar Ylarregui to Bartlett, 6 Feb. 1852, Corres. VI, Bartlett Papers; Salazar Ylarregui to Emory, 11 Mar. 1852, File 425, NA, RG/76.

53 Bartlett to Ewing, 23 Dec. 1850, LIV, Ewing Papers; Whipple to Bartlett, 23 Aug. 1852, Corres. VI, Bartlett Papers; "Journals," 25 Sep. 1851, Whipple Papers.

54 Salazar Ylarregui to Emory, 27, 30 Mar., 17 Apr. 1852, Emory to Salazar Ylarregui, 27, 30 Mar., 17 Apr. 1852, "Minutes of a meeting of the Surveyors, Frontera, 18 Apr. 1852," Folder 4, Emory Papers.

55 "Jiménez Memoria," pp. 3–4; Emory to Salazar Ylarregui, 17 Apr. 1852, Folder 4, Emory Papers.

56 "Ligera relación," in *Memoria documentada*, II, 162; Harry P. Hewitt, "The Mexican Commission and Its Survey of the Rio Grande River Boundary, 1850–1854," *Southwestern Historical Quarterly*, XCIV (Apr., 1991), pp. 566–69.

57 "Memoria de D. Agustín Díaz," in *Memoria documentada*, II, 195–213.

58 "Ligera relación," in ibid., 162; Salazar Ylarregui to Jiménez, 15 May 1853, in "Jiménez Memoria," p. 34; Hewitt, "The Mexican Commission," pp. 571–72.

59 Manuel Orozco y Berra, *Apuntes para la historia de la geografía en México* (México: 1881), pp. 463, 465; Santiago Ramírez, *Datos para la historia del Colegio de Minería recogidos y compilados bajo la forma de efemérides* (México: 1890), pp. 362–63, 370, 384, 389, 396; Juan López de Escalera, *Diccionario biográfico y de historia de México* (México: 1964), p. 348; Paula Rebert, "Mapping the United States-Mexico Boundary, 1849–1857" (Ph.D. diss., University of Wisconsin, 1994), pp. 270, 277–78.

60 *El Siglo XIX* (Mexico City), 29 May 1852.

61 Salazar Ylarregui to Emory, 28 Feb. 1852, Folder 36, Emory Papers.

62 Salazar Ylarregui to Ministro de Relaciones, 11 Aug. 1852, ASRE, Exp. 22, pp. 245–47.

63 [?] Ramírez to Ministro de Guerra y Marina, 16 Jul. 1852, J. Miguel Arroyo to Ministro de Guerra y Marina, 21 Dec. 1852, AHDN, Cancelados, Exp. 5–2470, folios 63–64, 70.

64 Salazar Ylarregui to Ministro de Relaciones, 4, 22 Sep., 2 Oct. 1852, Anaya to Ministro de Relaciones, 21 Oct. 1852, ASRE, Exp. 22, pp. 252–53, 260–61, 397–98, 400.

65 Salazar Ylarregui to Arista, 1 Nov. 1852, "Comisión Límites," Legajo 17–11–118 (Archivo de la Secretaría de Relaciones Exteriores, Mexico City; Hereafter cited as ASRE, Leg. 17–11–118); García Conde to Ignacio de Mora y Villamil, 29 Sep. 1853, AHDN, Cancelados, Exp. 5–2470, folio 78.

66 Salazar Ylarregui to Emory, 22 Jul., 14, 18, 21 Aug. 1852, Emory to Salazar Ylarregui, 11, 13, 15, 17, 20 Aug. 1852, Folders 5, 41, Emory Papers.

67 "Minutes of the Joint Commission," 26 Aug. 1852, Presidio del Norte, File 425, NA, RG/76; Emory to Jacobs, 5 Feb. 1852, ibid.

68 "Minutes of the Joint Commission," 27 Aug. 1852, ibid.

69 Emory to Volney Howard, 7 Nov. 1852, Folder 6, Emory Papers.

70 Stuart to Emory, 4 Nov. 1851, Official Dispatches, No. 51, Bartlett Papers; Emory to Stuart, 1 Feb. 1852, Emory to Salazar Ylarregui, 11 Jun. 1852, Folders 36, 40, Emory Papers.

71 Howard to Emory, 12 Apr. 1852, Bache to Emory, 1 Sep. 1852, Hardcastle to Emory, 10 Sep. 1852, Folders 5, 43, ibid.

72 Emory to Howard, 7 Nov. 1852, Folder 6, ibid.

73 Salazar Ylarregui to Arista, 1 Nov. 1852, "Comisión Límites," ASRE, Leg. 17–11–118.

74 Larráinzar to Arista, 6 Nov. 1852, ibid.

75 Bartlett, *Personal Narrative*, II, 396; Tyler, "Exploring the Rio Grande," pp. 51–53; Emory to Green, 30 Aug. 1852, Folder 42, Emory Papers.

76 Bartlett, *Personal Narrative*, II, 397; Tyler, "Exploring the Rio Grande," p. 52; Bartlett to Emory, 5 Oct. 1852, SED 6 (688), p. 76.

77 Emory to Stuart, 30 Oct. 1852, ibid., pp. 168–69; Emory to Michler, 26 Oct. 1852, Folder 6, Emory Papers.

78 "Discurso del Presidente José Joaquín de Herrera en la apertura de sesiones el 1, I, 1850," AGN. Gob., Sec. s/s, C: 371-E.6, C: 365-E.17.

79 Bartlett, *Personal Narrative*, II, 396–512.

80 Emory to Bartlett, 30 Oct. 1852, SED 108 (832), p. 13; Stuart to Bartlett, 15 Oct. 1852, Official Dispatches, No. 54, Bartlett Papers.

81 Bartlett to Stuart, 12 Feb. 1853, SED 41 (665), p. 22.

82 Emory to Stuart, 30 Nov. 1852, File 425, NA, RG/76; Emory to Whipple, 11 Nov. 1852, SED 6 (688), p. 48.

83 "Journals," 4 Feb. 1853, Circular, Whipple to Campbell, Wheaton, Garner, and White, 5 Feb. 1853, Whipple to Emory, 15 Apr. 1853, Box 2, Folder 16, Whipple Papers.

84 Bartlett to Emory, 21 Dec. 1852, Emory to Bartlett, 22 Dec. 1852, Emory to Tansill, 7 Jan. 1853, Folders 6, 47, Emory Papers; Bartlett to Emory, 23 Dec. 1852, SED 6 (688), p. 80.

85 Bartlett, *Personal Narrative*, II, 517–19.

LA BOCA
DEL RÍO

*"No puede U. formarse una idea de los trabajos
que he pasado y estoy pasando..."*

José Salazar Ylarregui, Mexican Commissioner

Though he had braved the deserts of Sonora and the danger of the Comanche, none of Commissioner Bartlett's adventures proved so perilous as the political web into which his travels had led him. For the poison that had paralyzed Weller on the California line now completely infected him as well. Although the play of political intrigue has long been suspected of having a major role in crippling the United States Boundary Commission, the story, to be told fully, must begin with the 1848 election in Ohio, before the commission's formation. In that election the Whigs were desperate, fearing a coalition of Free-Soilers, including Free-Soil Whigs and Democrats, which would do great damage to the party.[1] The vast territory acquired from Mexico made the United States a continental nation, but placed a great strain upon the sinews that held it together. The great question was whether slavery would be extended into the new territory or be limited to its present expanse. In 1848 neither Democrats nor Whigs took a definite position on the subject, but rather attempted to appeal to moderates in both the South and the North. This led to much division within the two major parties and greatly strengthened the appeal of the Free-Soil Party for those voters who wanted to take a firm stand on the issue. In Ohio the race for the governorship was a hard-fought and bitter battle between Seabury Ford, a Whig tinctured with abolitionism, and John B. Weller, the popular Democrat who would soon become the United States boundary commissioner. The Free-Soil Party chose not to field a candidate, which heightened the contest between Ford and Weller for the gubernatorial vote of the third-party members. The election was to be a close one and in the minds of some Whigs in doubt until Election Day itself.[2] Thomas Ewing, the

Ohio Whig who would later dismiss Weller, believed the gubernatorial election would indicate the outcome of the 1848 presidential race. John M. Clayton of Delaware concurred that Ohio was critical if the Whigs were to win.[3]

The Whigs had reason to be concerned. Weller was a young, successful politician and appears to have been exceptionally gifted. Moreover, having commanded the First Ohio Regiment of Volunteers at Monterrey during the war, the former lieutenant colonel could campaign as a war hero.[4] The campaign began on a lively note, but by midsummer had turned into a slanderous attack upon Weller.[5] Assailing Weller's record as a public servant and soldier in Mexico, the pro-Whig *Ohio State Journal* of Columbus charged that he was "reserved and haughty in his demeanor, and anything but a favorite of the people—a demagogue of the most unmitigated character."[6] Taking unusual delight in belittling Weller's part in the battle of Monterrey, the *Hamilton Intelligencer* mocked the colonel as a "bloviating, windy demagogue."[7]

Much more damaging than this typical campaign-opponent baiting was an allegation of embezzlement. Weller had recently been one of the commissioners of the Butler County, Ohio, Surplus Revenue Fund. The commissioners were empowered to loan surplus revenues to citizens of the county in order to earn interest. After collecting the principal and interest from a first set of loans, the commissioners decided to offer another round of loans, but found no takers. Saddled with unsought-after money and believing they were required to make interest on the Surplus Revenue Fund, the commissioners saw fit to loan the money to themselves. Weller borrowed $11,000 and, when charged with malfeasance in office, claimed he had done nothing wrong.[8] The Whig press in Ohio had a field day with the story, especially after Weller refused to turn over the records of the Surplus Revenue Fund to Butler County authorities. In response, county officials filed a suit against him.[9] Since he had secured the loan with real estate in Butler County, Weller probably had no intention of embezzling the $11,000. Yet he had certainly acted improperly, since Ohio law explicitly stated that the surplus revenues should not be reloaned, but paid into the state treasury.[10] Nonetheless, these charges hurt Weller's campaign and would dog his future role as United States boundary commissioner, severely hindering the survey under his charge.

In his quest for the governorship, Weller made a powerful appeal to the Free-Soil vote, which terrified the Whigs, who had dominated Ohio since 1836, but now felt their power ebb.[11] The situation was considered serious enough for William Henry Seward of New York to make a speaking tour of Ohio and for Truman Smith, chairman of the National Executive Committee, to beseech Ohio Whigs to avoid the Free-Soil controversy altogether.[12] On Election Day Ford won the governorship by a mere 345 votes. Though Weller carried Butler County by 1,435 votes, the embezzlement controversy probably defeated him. The pro-Whig *Hamilton Intelligencer*, referring to Weller as "The Gallant Defaulter ...," had intoned the cry of fraud in every issue of the paper.[13] Yet if enough Free-Soil Whigs voted for Ford to ensure his victory, too few of them voted for Taylor. Sentiment against the extension of slavery ran high in Ohio among Whigs and Democrats alike. Indeed, Martin Van Buren, the Free-Soil candidate for the presidency, polled some 35,000 votes in Ohio. Since most of the Free-Soil vote in Ohio had formerly been Whig, Van Buren's candidacy threw the victory in that state to the Democratic nominee, Lewis Cass.[14] Clearly the Free-Soil deserters would have to be won back to the fold; a cabinet post would be reserved for Ohio.[15]

Morose as they were over their situation in Ohio, the Whigs still had the satisfaction of Taylor's victory in the nation and the pleasure of forming a Whig cabinet. One cabinet post in particular would have a direct bearing on the boundary survey; Thomas Ewing of Ohio, Weller's greatest political enemy, became secretary of the newly created Department of the Interior. The victorious Whigs felt some need to placate Ewing, an active supporter of Taylor, especially since the defection of Free-Soil Whigs in Ohio had undermined Whig control of the state legislature and had thereby destroyed his chances of winning a vacant seat in the United States Senate.[16]

After entering the cabinet, Ewing remained concerned about the desertion of the Free-Soil Whigs in Ohio, which had been so harmful in the recent elections and which threatened to be more so in the upcoming 1850 hustings.[17] Weller's June 1849 dismissal from the boundary commission and his expected return to Ohio might enable him to play a major role in the new coalition between Free-Soilers and Democrats in that state. Weller was still quite popular in Ohio, and in the next Democratic National Convention would receive the vote of the entire Ohio delegation on the ballot for vice president. But if charges of embezzlement had done much to cause Weller to lose the governorship in 1848, similar allegations against him as boundary commissioner might ruin his political future. Weller later accused Ewing of doing just that. Charges that Weller had misused boundary commission funds appeared in the Whig press of Ohio in August 1849 and reached California in September.[18] Since the charges against Weller were made after his removal from the survey, the possibility of partisan politics must not be ignored.

Another means of ruining Weller's career in Ohio would be to prevent his return. Ewing's friend and fellow Whig John M. Clayton had already seen to this. While the boundary survey was still under the aegis of the Department of State, Secretary Clayton declined to pay any of Weller's drafts upon the department until his vouchers arrived in Washington and his accounts were brought up to date. This was rather unreasonable, considering the great distance and difficulty of transportation and communication between

Washington and California at that time. Whatever Clayton's intentions, his decision on this matter paralyzed Weller in California.[19] Since the sheriff of Butler County, Ohio, had sold Weller's property to pay his debts before Weller's appointment as boundary commissioner, there was perhaps little chance that Weller's personal finances would enable him to return to Ohio to resume his political career.[20] For the moment, then, Weller's financial troubles forced him to remain in California.

After learning that Weller did not intend to return to Ohio, Ewing, so Weller claimed, spread scandal in California.[21] Allegations of Weller's misuse of boundary commission funds were circulating in California as early as September 1849, and continued to do so throughout the following year. According to Weller, Ewing had intimated that Weller intended to misappropriate some $25,000 drawn upon the government.[22] Writing some years later, Emory looked back upon the work on the California line with bitterness. He confirmed that the government had used Weller cruelly by protesting his drafts and repudiating his disbursements to the extent that Weller found "himself denounced as a defaulter; when, at that very time, as the settlement of his accounts afterwards showed, he was in advance to the government."[23]

Weller had in any case opted to remain in California and pursue a career in law and politics. As the popular choice of the Democrats, he was elected to the United States Senate in January 1852.[24] In that forum he encountered his political enemy face to face. Within a year after dismissing Weller, Ewing resigned from the cabinet and accepted an appointment to a vacant United States Senate seat from Governor Ford.[25] Soon after Ewing's arrival on Capitol Hill, Lewis Cass of Michigan asked the former secretary of the interior if Weller would have been removed from the office of boundary commissioner if he had been a Whig. Senator Ewing replied that the Democrats had appointed Weller in December 1848 after the Whigs had won the presidency, thus depriving them of the fruits of victory. Ewing went on to explain that had Weller been a Whig, he would have recommended his dismissal because Weller failed to render his accounts according to the rules of the Department of State as instructed, and hence the refusal of Clayton to accept Weller's drafts upon the department.

Senator William M. Gwin, Democrat from California, defended Weller by asserting that Weller had visited Taylor in Cincinnati before leaving for the Pacific coast to inquire whether he would be retained as boundary commissioner after the new Whig administration took office. The president-elect intimated that Weller would be continued at his post, and, satisfied with this response, the commissioner departed for California. Gwin further noted that the accounting officers of the government had accepted Weller's account without question, clearing the former commissioner of all charges of malfeasance.[26] In fact, Weller's original instructions provided him with rather broad powers because he would be so very distant from the settled portions of the country.[27]

Gwin charged that Weller had been removed for political reasons. The letter of 26 June 1849, by which Clayton informed Weller of his removal, was to have been delivered by John C. Frémont after the latter entered upon his duties as boundary commissioner. Appointing Frémont, a Democrat, would relieve Clayton from the odium of replacing Weller with a Whig and perhaps derail Frémont's bid for a Senate seat from California. Frémont of course preferred the Senate and kept his appointment as United States boundary commissioner in his pocket until the Senate slot was assured. Since Frémont never took up his duties as commissioner, Gwin argued, Weller could not have received official notice of his dismissal.[28] Knowledge of all this, Gwin asserted, reached Washington in late 1849 when Congress was in session. The administration to its dismay, found Weller still in office. There was but one way to remove him and that was to nominate his successor and let the Senate act upon it. But Weller had friends in the Senate who would ask the cause of his removal. Gwin charged that the Whigs hoped to be relieved of the odium of Weller's dismissal by starving him out. They would fail to act on the salaries of the commissioner and surveyor, and then, by refusing to accept Weller's drafts upon the government, destroy his credit in California.[29]

While Ewing was under fire, John B. Weller took his seat as senator from the new state of California. When Weller arrived on the Senate floor in early 1852, he of course concurred with all that his colleague from California had charged. Weller was by this time very bitter toward Ewing in particular and the Whigs in general. Taking the offensive, Weller seemed determined to get at Ewing by destroying the credibility of a man he had never met: the man who had replaced him as boundary commissioner, John Russell Bartlett. Weller now successfully called for resolutions requesting that the secretary of the interior submit to the Senate all information concerning the boundary survey from its inception and that the secretary of war inform the Senate of any charges against Bartlett.[30]

Bartlett had endured the difficulties of the boundary commission with a cheerful resilience if not always with efficiency, but the labyrinth of Washington proved more difficult for him to negotiate than the deserts of Sonora. A factor that had plagued Bartlett during the survey was the constant bickering between civilian and military members of the commission. Bartlett himself was involved in disputes, major as well as minor, with every military officer in the party. His bitter dispute with Colonel John McClellan had led to the latter's dismissal for intemperance. While McClellan may well have been intoxicated during much of the journey to El Paso del Norte and had often referred to Bartlett as a "d—d Yankee bookseller," one must note that Bartlett was unable to appreciate the sensitivity of a situation in which a colonel in the elite Corps of Topographical Engineers found himself under the orders of a civilian quartermaster.[31]

Urged on by Colonel James D. Graham, who hated Bartlett, and to preserve his honor, McClellan preferred serious charges against the commissioner. He accused Bartlett of using government transportation for private purposes; of incompetence in the direction of nearly all affairs of the commission to the neglect of the health, safety, and well-being of its members; and of misman-agement of the public trust and funds in his care.[32] Particularly odious was "the boot, shoe, blanket, & beads trade" that Bartlett and his brother carried on at El Paso del Norte and Santa Rita del Cobre at a time when employees of the commission were in extreme want of clothing and footwear.[33] The charges McClellan brought against Bartlett were largely true. Their importance here lies in the fact that they discredited Bartlett and delayed appropriations des-perately needed by the commission involved in the survey on the unsettled frontier. Chandler wrote to Emory from Washington that his father, with great effort, had guided the current deficiency bill through the House without a remark against the commission, and that it would have passed the Senate had not Weller arrived and stirred up a hornets' nest.[34]

Weller now eagerly chaired a select committee of investigation. Among the committee members was Senator Thomas Jefferson Rusk of Texas, who had taken a lively interest in the boundary survey from the outset. Rusk's primary concern was the dream of a transcontinental railroad that he hoped would be built through Texas. Rusk had been in close contact with Surveyor Gray, his fellow Texas Democrat, who informed him that the Bartlett-García Conde line was thirty miles too far north and would surely lose the rail route. Embittered by his dismissal, Gray called the boundary a "Texas line," and was adamant that Texas be represented on the survey team.[35] Rusk could not agree more, writing to Jefferson Davis of Mississippi that the southern route would be less expensive to build and of greater commercial value than either a northern or middle rail route. Rusk had no difficulty in accepting Gray's opinion that construction of a railroad from the Río Grande to the Gila through the disputed area and beyond to the Pacific was perfectly feasible. Rusk was prepared to do everything in his power to bring the rail route as far south as possible.[36]

With Bartlett already discredited by Weller's attack, Senator Rusk turned the attention of the Senate from the question of Bartlett's competence to the accuracy of 32° 22′ north latitude. There was growing belief in Congress that the compromise line was in violation of the treaty. The senators and represen-tatives from Texas were concerned that Bartlett's compromise with García Conde might have lost the rail route that they believed the southern boundary of New Mexico, as represented on Disturnell's map, would provide.[37] Senator

Rusk protested to President Fillmore on 28 June 1852 that Bartlett and García Conde's line was too far north, did not comply with Article V of the treaty, and would surely lose the best route for a railroad to the Pacific.[38] Believing the initial point of the boundary on the Río Grande to be in error, Rusk stated before the Senate, "I do not intend to vote another dollar to this boundary commission—so far from it, I mean to resist the appropriation of any more money until we have some assurance that the treaty of Guadalupe Hidalgo, and not the negotiations between the Commissioners, is to settle the initial point of the line upon the Río Grande."[39] Rusk, along with other southerners, was convinced that Bartlett had agreed to 32° 22′ as the southern boundary of New Mexico in order to defeat any proposal for a southern rail route to the Pacific.[40]

Reporting to the president on 24 July, Stuart supported the Bartlett-García Conde line. The secretary believed that the initial point had been fixed and that he had the authority to order Gray to sign the requisite documents. Stuart stated that all the instructions from the Departments of State and Interior had been addressed to the commissioner, "as he alone is recognized as possessed of diplomatic or judicial powers. The surveyor is regarded as simply a ministerial officer, appointed to execute the decisions of the joint commission."[41] Stuart did not believe the surveyors could overrule the commissioners and stated that the surveyors' signatures were not to indicate their approval of the principles settled by the two commissioners, but to attest to the authenticity of the documents.

Defending the initial point itself, Stuart stated that had Bartlett insisted on the line being the same distance from El Paso del Norte as it is shown on the map, he might not have obtained the full three degrees of longitude west from the Río Grande as the southern boundary of New Mexico. He might also have lost the gold and copper mines and a greater area lost to Mexico than that supposed to have been lost by 32° 22′. It was true that the United States would have lost the mines and a greater portion of territory to Mexico only if Stuart compared the compromise line to García Conde's original boundary proposal. Stuart's defense of 32° 22′ was invalid, however, if he compared it to 31° 52′, the line Gray claimed as the correct boundary. Finally, Stuart believed the United States could not repudiate the initial point without violating the treaty.[42] Two days later, Stuart added that the commissioners had always met apart from the surveyors and that if the surveyors did have equal powers with the commissioners, then the decision of the majority of the Joint Commission should be binding on the whole.[43]

Led by James M. Mason of Virginia, the Senate Foreign Relations Committee found itself in agreement with Rusk and Gray. They believed the line should run immediately above El Paso del Norte as shown on Disturnell's map and expressed concern over the possible loss of a rail route. Mason could not accept Stuart's opinion that the commissioners alone had the power to determine where the boundary would run to the exclusion of the surveyors' opinion. He also disagreed with Stuart's grant of diplomatic powers to the commissioners. Mason believed that the commissioners and surveyors were equals and held power jointly. The senator repudiated Stuart's opinion that a majority decision within the Joint Commission was binding on the whole. Such an interpretation would place the rights of the United States at the mercy of Mexico. Finally, the committee declared Bartlett's compromise a departure from the treaty.[44]

Mason soon undercut Bartlett's commission, then in the field, by offering an amendment to the appropriations bill before the Senate, which contained a provision of $120,000 for the boundary survey. Mason's proviso declared:

> That no part of this appropriation shall be used or expended
> until it shall be made satisfactorily to appear to the President of the
> United States, that the southern boundary of New Mexico is not
> established by the Commissioner and Surveyor of the United States
> further north of the town called Paso than the same is laid down on
> Disturnell's map which is attached to the treaty.[45]

The intention of the senator from Virginia was clear. As he himself put it, "The object of this amendment is to break down that commission where it stands unless this line is re-formed."[46] The amendment passed, and President Fillmore concluded that the appropriation could not be used to complete the survey. This was the unpleasant news that reached Bartlett at Ringgold Barracks, Texas, on 20 December 1852. The survey was suspended, the field abandoned by the entire United States commission.[47]

Mexican envoy Manuel Larráinzar, who had been watching events in Washington closely, was aghast to report to his government that the United States Congress had suspended the survey. He gave his opinion that this was tantamount to suspending the treaty, and warned that this action threatened the Bartlett-García Conde line already agreed upon. Larráinzar further pointed out that the Whig administration had accepted Bartlett's appointment of Whipple as surveyor ad interim, and therefore the line was valid. That administration's days were numbered, however, and it was with equal concern that Larráinzar informed the government of the move in Congress to release funds for the survey of the Río Grande, but for no other part of the line.[48] It had become evident to those in the Senate who opposed Bartlett's line that it was unnecessary to suspend operations on the riverine portion of the boundary. At Secretary Stuart's suggestion, therefore, Senator Mason submitted a bill to free the appropriation for the survey of the Río Grande below El Paso del Norte. The bill easily passed, and the United States Boundary Commission was given new life.[49]

The United States section of the Joint Commission was then reorganized and General Robert Blair Campbell of Alabama was appointed commissioner. Emory continued as chief astronomer and surveyor and was in actual direction of the survey, while Campbell simply presided over Major Emory and his assistants.[50] To survey the three leagues from the mouth of the Río Grande into the Gulf of Mexico as required by the treaty, Campbell entered into a $1,000 contract with Professor Alexander D. Bache, superintendent of the United States Coast and Geodetic Survey. The Coast Survey already possessed the ships and engineers necessary for the task, which would thereby be completed with less expense. The actual hydrography of the three leagues was carried out under the direction of Lieutenant John Wilkinson of the Coast Survey commanding the surveying schooner *Morris*. Wilkinson's only difficulty was the unseaworthiness of the *Morris*, which had been damaged in a hurricane at Galveston on 2 May. Under arrangement with Emory, Wilkinson completed operations on 20 August 1853.[51]

Emory also faced rough weather when he sailed from New Orleans in May 1853 in the miserable steamer *Comanche*, suffering a near disaster in a storm off the coast of Texas, and was relieved to be safely ashore with his instruments.[52] The parties of the reorganized commission took the field on 21 April 1853. Emory posted Lieutenant Michler with Assistant Surveyors Edward Ingraham and E. A. Phillips with a strong party to finish the work above Eagle Pass, while Emory himself marched to the lower Río Grande with two parties and the astronomical instruments, establishing an observatory at Ringgold Barracks. Charles Radziminski and assistants Thomas W. Jones and James H. Houston surveyed the river from that point to its mouth and Arthur Schott, aided by Malcolm Seaton and John E. Weiss, surveyed that part of the Río Grande from Laredo to Ringgold Barracks. Emory ordered a second astronomical observatory to be established at the mouth of the Río Grande under the direction of Assistant Surveyor George C. Gardner. The major himself made the observations for latitude, while Gardner observed for longitude.[53]

After organizing his party at San Antonio, Michler took the well-used road to El Paso del Norte as far as Pecos Springs, where he left the road and struck directly for the Río Grande. Nature made his course toward the Chisos Mountains difficult and circuitous, the country being cut up by deep chasms and cliffs, which seemed to appear at his feet out of nowhere. The sharp igneous stones that paved his course made the trip especially painful for the animals as well. On leaving King's Springs he changed to a southeasterly course, until he struck one of the Indian trails. Michler found that, "It was a

dreary sight to look upon the dull, wide waste around us; its parched barrenness, combined with the influence of a scorching July sun, was enough to
madden the brain."[54]

The nearer the river, the rougher the terrain became, with deep ravines
and arroyos making the progress of the wagons slow. When Michler reached
the river at Lipan Crossing about forty miles down river from the point where
Chandler had been forced to suspend the survey the year before, he found it
a near impossibility to approach the river for the first twenty miles of the
survey because its course was so tortuous. Michler described the river as
forcing "its way through a deep cañon nearly twenty miles in length, its banks
being composed of high perpendicular masses of solid rock, resembling more
the work of art than of nature."[55]

His party was forced to make detours of twenty-five to thirty miles in
order to advance the work a few hundred feet. Since conducting the survey on
land proved difficult unless attended by great delay, Michler decided to carry
on the effort in the bed of the river, using the boats constructed in San Antonio
for that very purpose. Having been built from green wood, these craft were
barely seaworthy, and were now so warped as to present a less than nautical
appearance. Hemmed in by the walls of rock, the party at times traveled for
miles without being able to find a place to land. Michler found that the only
practical means of surveying the river was to allow the boats to drop down the
channel, taking the direction of the courses and timing the passage from bend
to bend. To make certain of his work, Michler observed the heavens every
night for time and latitude. Not knowing what lay before them, Michler's party
lived these days in a continual excitement as the swift current swept their
unseaworthy craft through rapids of white water and dangerous rocks.
Helplessly trapped in the narrow canyon with its fortress like walls, reaching,
it seemed, ever upward to the sky, they at times did not find enough space to
plant a foot let alone a shore upon which to pull their boats. So they dashed
blindly on in constant apprehension of destruction to the watercraft and their
own peril of drowning.

A near disaster visited the party the first day they took to the boats. When
scarcely under way the river quickly narrowed to twenty-five feet so the oars-
men could touch both walls of the channel with their oars. Immediately before
them an immense rock divided the river leaving a narrow rapid over large
rocks. The two skiffs shot the white water safely, but the flatboat was dashed
upon the rocks breaking into splinters, endangering lives and provisions both.
Only the expert swimming and quick thinking of two Mexican boatmen saved
the unwieldy craft.[56] And yet, surpassing all difficulties, Lieutenant Michler
and his party completed the survey from Boquillas Canyon where Chandler
left off the previous year to the mouth of the Río Pecos.[57]

Meanwhile Assistant Surveyor Arthur Schott completed the survey of that portion of the river between Laredo and Ringgold Barracks without incident, and then aided Charles Radziminski in the survey to the mouth of the Río Grande. Here the United States section faced difficulties equal to those experienced by Michler's team. Bad weather followed Radziminski during the course of his work, three floods swamping the area while northers made for a number of cold, rainy days. "And mosquitos! They are of the size of Buffalo bulls, and there are hives or herds of them in every square foot of the ground."[58]

A tragedy visited Radziminski's party when a squall on the lower Río Grande caused his boat to capsize, spilling men, supplies, and instruments into the river. Young Thomas Jones, son of General Walter Jones, tried to swim ashore, but drowned in the storm-swept waters. Radziminski himself nearly drowned as well, but a Mexican employee of the commission pulled him onto the overturned boat, saving his life.[59] More serious was the yellow fever that raged among Radziminski's and Schott's parties. Radziminski was prostrated by the fever and Schott lost three men to it. Schott further reported a general disintegration taking place among the laborers in his surveying party caused by drunkenness and disorderly conduct. He discharged them without being able to recruit others in their stead, and was thus forced to continue the work with only five men and three boatmen.[60]

The Mexican section of the Joint Commission had also been able to renew its efforts, though attended by equal hardship. From his exile at El Paso del Norte, Salazar Ylarregui wrote a friend that it would be impossible to understand the difficulties he had suffered and was yet suffering. The escort had deserted him, absconding with pack mules, saddle horses, campaign tents, and other items. He found himself in the predicament of traveling alone through completely unknown parts, expecting to fall into the hands of the barbarous Indians at any moment. It saddened him to find himself without the ability to take so much as one step toward fulfilling the obligations of his office. The bank draft for 3,000 pesos against the customs house in El Paso del Norte could not be cashed because of the disorder found at that port of entry.[61]

While abandoned with no funds, men, or escort in El Paso del Norte, Salazar Ylarregui had directed First Assistant Surveyor Francisco Jiménez to begin work on the Laredo-Matamoros stretch of the Río Grande. Captain Jiménez and Lieutenant Alemán were to do the astronomical work while Agustín and Luis Díaz, working independently of Jiménez, were to begin the topography at the mouth of the Río Grande and work upriver until they should meet Salazar Ylarregui. The Mexican commissioner ordered Jiménez to Mexico City to refit his surveying party, purchase additional instruments, and proceed to Matamoros. In Mexico City Jiménez received 4,200 pesos for the survey, a sum he considered very inadequate. At his request the government ordered that he be provided with an additional 2,000 pesos from the Veracruz customs house.

By 10 February 1853, Jiménez, surveyors Manuel Alemán and Agustín Díaz and interpreter Felipe de Iturbide left Mexico City by coach, arriving in Veracruz on the thirteenth. Owing to the extraordinary circumstances in that city, which was awaiting the arrival of Antonio López de Santa Anna, Jiménez had some difficulty in obtaining the 2,000 pesos from the customs house. He at length received the money on 15 February, just one hour before the packet ship left for New Orleans. Unfortunately the accomplished Lieutenant Luis Díaz, making a more careful and much slower journey with the instruments, had yet to arrive. Jiménez directed Lieutenant Agustín Díaz to await his brother's arrival, while the main party took the packet to New Orleans. By mid-March the Díaz brothers were able to rejoin the other members of Jiménez' team, delayed in New Orleans awaiting the only steamer to Matamoros, which sailed but once a month. The reunited Mexican section departed New Orleans on 25 March and four days later arrived with all instruments at Matamoros, just one month before the return of the United States commission to the survey.[62]

Jiménez suffered from insufficient funds and inadequate military escort for the remaining months of the Río Grande survey. These resources the central government had allotted him from the Matamoros customs house, but they were rarely forthcoming in good time. Jiménez found the situation particularly embarrassing after Major Emory and the United States section arrived in Brownsville on 21 May 1853, equipped with everything in abundance.[63] Agustín Díaz, now a captain, wrote to General Adrian Wool, lamenting that he had received no pay, credit, or other resources with which to carry on the topographic survey, and requested Wool to convey this situation to the minister of war that at least someone in the government know of the commission's plight. At length Jiménez was provided with sufficient funds to continue the work after a frustrating delay of three months. Nevertheless, Jiménez had managed to complete construction of an astronomical observatory at Matamoros, calibrate his instruments, and begin nightly observations of the heavens with Assistant Surveyor Manuel Alemán. These observations were conducted in late June, and Jiménez made preparations to proceed to the mouth of the Río Grande.[64]

Mexican commissioner Salazar Ylarregui had instructed Jiménez to observe for the length of an entire lunation at only three points—the river's mouth, Matamoros, and the Colonia de Monterey opposite Laredo. He believed Jiménez should be able to complete the survey from Laredo to the mouth of the river by the end of September. Salazar Ylarregui lamented to

Jiménez that he had suffered greatly as a result of the political turbulence then troubling the nation, and as a consequence had not received so much as a peso from his government since Jiménez had left El Paso del Norte. Informing Jiménez that he had now completed the survey as far as Presidio del Norte, Salazar Ylarregui doubted that he would be able to effect a timely arrival in Monterey, and feared he would not be able to reach any farther than Guerrero, opposite Fort Duncan, no matter how vigorously he pushed the survey. Therefore he ordered Jiménez to continue on to the Colonia de Guerrero after carrying his survey to Laredo.

Jiménez, however, did not think it possible to conform to the commissioner's instructions because of the terrain below Laredo, explaining that it would take much longer than Salazar Ylarregui's estimate. Moreover, the instructions regarding the use of signal fires would prove impractical since there were no prominent points between Matamoros and the mouth of the river. In any case Jiménez never received an answer from the Mexican commissioner and had to rely on his own judgment for the remainder of the survey. After determining the initial point of the survey at the mouth of the Río Grande, and erecting temporary monuments, Jiménez proposed to proceed to Nuevo Laredo where he would be in a good position to push the survey up river. According to his plan, Captain Jiménez marched to the river's mouth on 12 July 1853, and began his astronomical observations to determine longitude and latitude, while Agustín Díaz mapped the topography of the river.[65]

While the Mexican section was at work at the mouth of the Río Grande, Charles Radziminski of the United States team was working his way downriver. The two commissions had agreed to work independently on the difficult portions of the river and Jiménez now felt it necessary to confer with Surveyor Emory. Salazar Ylarregui in his original instructions to Jiménez had authorized him to treat with whomever the United States commissioner might appoint in determining the deepest channel at the mouth of the Río Grande and in placing of suitable monuments. Proper documents were to be prepared in Spanish and English and signed by both engineers in accordance with a resolution of the Joint Commission dated 8 October 1852.[66]

Therefore, when Emory first reached Brownsville, in May 1853, Jiménez and interpreter Iturbide paid the major a visit to inform him of his instructions and ask whom the United States commissioner had appointed to work with him. Jiménez found Emory's answer ambiguous and was surprised to learn that the United States surveyor had no intention of recognizing the resolution of the Joint Commission under the pretext that he had not been present when that resolution was passed. Emory observed that since neither commission had brought the survey down the river as far as Matamoros, it would be premature to detach a surveying party to the mouth of the Río Grande. The testy major added that he did not think that the appointment of the engineer in question was necessarily the obligation of the United States commissioner rather than that of the United States surveyor.

When Emory asked Jiménez how far downriver Salazar Ylarregui had brought his survey, the captain replied that he did not know since he had received no communication from the Mexican commissioner in quite some time. Emory then prepared a rough draft of the minutes of their meeting and proposed that both affix their signatures thereto, giving the impression of compliance with the Joint Commission. Jiménez refused to sign the memorandum. He believed Emory was attempting to avoid any recognition of the resolution of the Joint Commission while Bartlett had been commissioner because of the opposition to the Bartlett-García Conde line in the United States Senate. The following day, 23 May, Jiménez officially requested in writing to know whom the United States commissioner had designated to work with him in determining the deepest channel at the river's mouth and in placing the monuments in accord with the 8 October 1852 resolution of the Joint Commission. Emory's answer was the same as in their conversation of the day before, adding that his own best information was that the Mexican commission had not yet brought the survey down to Presidio del Norte.[67]

Salazar Ylarregui had in fact completed the survey to the presidio by 15 May, but Jiménez would not receive this information until 21 June. In any case Emory's excuses were rather weak since the program for the survey of the Río Grande had divided the river into segments. There was no reason the section from Matamoros to the river's mouth could not be done before the portion from Laredo to Matamoros, or any other segment for that matter. Emory's disinclination to comply with the Mexican engineer's request was nothing more than a desire to avoid giving legitimacy to the actions of John Russell Bartlett and 32° 22′ north latitude. Jiménez, receiving no cooperation from Emory, put the matter to rest for the moment.

After Captain Jiménez completed his astronomical observations at the mouth of the river and Agustín Díaz the topography, he again found it necessary to confer with the obstinate major. Emory now appointed Radziminski to survey the river from Brownsville to Barita and to agree with Jiménez on the line that would constitute the boundary. Emory himself would agree with Jiménez on fixing the deepest channel of the river's mouth and in determining the placement of monuments. Jiménez was eager to work with Emory, but informed the major that he hoped to begin his survey toward Laredo by 10 August.[68] In this he was to be disappointed, for it was not until the seventeenth that Emory and Jiménez agreed to place a monument on the United States side of the boundary 450 feet from the center of the channel measured in the meridian, and another on the Mexican side 1,560 feet from the center of the channel in the same meridian. Since the United States section had not yet mapped the topography of the river's mouth, Emory agreed to use the topography already completed by Agustín Díaz. Neither commission had found islands in the river below Matamoros, Jiménez and Radziminski having little difficulty fixing that portion of the riverine boundary.[69]

While Emory and Jiménez pushed the survey ahead with the vigor and energy for which they were both well known, it had not been done without another headstrong clash over the 8 October 1852 resolution of the Joint Commission. When Commissioner Robert Campbell arrived at the mouth of the river, he held a conference with Emory and Jiménez on 10 August 1853. In the discussion concerning the placement of the monuments, Jiménez observed the need to obey the resolution of the Joint Commission by preparing the proper document in Spanish and English duly signed on the part of both sections. Campbell replied that he had never seen this resolution, a response that seemed strange to Jiménez.[70]

A few days later Jiménez sent Emory a note requesting him to sign an enclosed document, in Spanish and English, stating where the monuments were to be placed marking the terminus of the boundary at the river's mouth in accord with the Joint Commission's 8 October 1852 resolution. Emory replied that his communication to Jiménez of 16 August regarding the monuments was officially binding as if jointly signed by both engineers and that no other document was needed. Regarding the 8 October resolution, Emory stated that he was then and presently a member of the Joint Commission, was at that time on the line and could have been summoned to attend the meeting in question. He was not, however, informed of the meeting, had never been furnished a copy of the proceedings of the Joint Commission, and therefore refused to acknowledge it. Jiménez decided to extricate himself from this vicious circle of official notes and acquiesce to Emory's obstinacy, but with the understanding that he, himself, had not deviated from the resolution of the Joint Commission.[71]

When he sent copies of his correspondence with Jiménez to Commissioner Campbell, Emory observed that it "appears to have no other object than to get me to acknowledge the acts of Mr. Bartlett and Mr. Salazar as those of the Joint Commission."[72] Emory and Campbell may indeed have feared that to recognize Commissioners Bartlett and Salazar Ylarregui as solely constituting the Joint Commission would be to recognize Commissioners Bartlett and García Conde in the same manner. If the surveyors were not members of the Joint Commission, their signatures would have no authority and 32° 22′ north latitude was legal, fixed, and run. Emory was opposed to this line. As Jiménez surmised, it was ridiculous for Campbell and Emory to assert that they had never seen the Official Journal of the Joint Commission. When the secretary of the interior informed Bartlett of his replacement, he ordered him to turn all materials of the United States commission over to Campbell.[73] It would be absurd to think Campbell and Emory had not at least perused the official proceedings of the commission. Having successfully avoided recognizing the acts of the Joint Commission, Major Emory returned to Washington and reported that all the fieldwork of the United States commission on the river had been completed from Frontera to the mouth of the Río Grande.[74]

Jiménez was no doubt relieved to be free from his squabble with Emory, but found the work of his surveying party increasingly difficult as he turned upriver from Matamoros. On 29 August he requested from the frontier garrison an escort of twenty-five men provisioned for three months, the time he believed necessary to determine the astronomical points along the river between Matamoros and Nuevo Laredo. On departure, however, his escort consisted of merely six men and one sergeant, and when he reached Camargo on 16 September he received a new escort of only twelve men. After two days of rest, Jiménez left Camargo and reached Guerrero on 19 September where he found Agustín Díaz in need of pay and provisions for his party then carrying forth the topography of the river.[75]

Leaving Guerrero, Jiménez found the road very bad, the wagon carrying the instruments tipping over several times. Arriving in the Colonia de Nuevo Laredo on 25 September, Jiménez found the military settlement reduced to four or five families since the troops that formed the colony had left, the few remaining souls living in constant fear of Indian attack. On the following day the commission's escort departed. Jiménez provides neither the reason for its departure nor its destination, but in any case was left with only an unnamed teamster and Lieutenant Alemán to begin the astronomical observations on 3 October. By the time his astronomical work at Nuevo Laredo was completed, he had as yet received no word of instruction from Salazar Ylarregui, or reply to his letter of 23 June. Jiménez therefore decided to leave Nuevo Laredo on 25 October with the objective of determining some points along the river according to the plan he had earlier proposed. It was a difficult trip, with the road so rough that several of his delicate instruments were ruined.

When a broken axle caused some delay because of the difficulty in finding wood with which to replace it, Jiménez took the opportunity to determine the position of Guerrero. On 2 November, the wagon now repaired, but lamenting that his only good barometer was broken, he pushed on to the confluence of the Río Salado with the Río Grande and observed for longitude and latitude until 14 November. No other astronomical points were determined because of rain and by 24 November Jiménez and his small party had returned to Camargo, where he learned the sad news that the commission's interpreter, Felipe de Iturbide, had died of yellow fever, then raging on the lower Río Grande.

Once more short of funds, because of the greatly diminished income of the customs house at Matamoros, and lacking an escort, Captain Jiménez and Lieutenant Alemán reached that port at the mouth of the river on Christmas Day 1853. Though bad weather continued to hinder his efforts, observations were made at several points between Camargo and Matamoros. Having received no word from Salazar Ylarregui, Jiménez decided to leave Agustín Díaz to finish the topography of the river, while he and Alemán returned to Mexico City. Díaz continued taking the topography of the Río Grande for another seven months after Jiménez and Alemán's departure, and on very little money. During this time his brother Luis was stricken with an inflammation of the eyes and, failing to receive timely treatment, his illness became chronic. Jiménez and Alemán departed Matamoros on 7 January 1854 and, traveling by way of Ciudad Victoria and San Luis Potosí, arrived in Mexico City on 20 February. There they made the calculations for the many astronomical points observed along the Río Grande, their work now complete.[76]

Meanwhile Salazar Ylarregui had also returned to the capital and informed the minister of foreign relations that the survey of the river from Nuevo Laredo to its mouth was finished.[77] The Mexican commission had now completed its fieldwork from San Diego on the Pacific Ocean to the initial point of the southern boundary of New Mexico on the Río Grande. Along the river itself, the commission had completed its survey from 32° 22′ to Presidio del Norte, and from Nuevo Laredo to its mouth. The Mexican commission later carried the survey between the Presidio and San Carlos, but was unable to complete the survey from thence to Laredo, and no report appears to exist indicating that such an attempt was undertaken. Proof that this portion of the river was surveyed only by the United States team lies in the cartographic record.[78] This did not matter, however, since Salazar Ylarregui and Emory had at the beginning of the riverine survey agreed to accept each other's work if need be.

The Mexican Boundary Commission could therefore consider the survey completed along the entire boundary and was prepared to erect proper monuments where none had yet been placed. To this end Salazar Ylarregui had earlier ordered Ricardo Ramírez to remain at El Paso del Norte and oversee the placing of monuments on 32° 22′ and the western line of New Mexico toward the Río Gila. He directed Ramírez to work in conjunction with whomever the United States appointed for the same purpose in accordance with the resolutions of the Joint Commission. Salazar Ylarregui enjoined Ramírez to remain at El Paso del Norte even though no United States engineer arrived.[79] None ever did, for the Joint Commission was now just as frozen as the Río Grande had been on the day Bartlett and García Conde reached their fateful compromise. Nor could the river's survey ever be considered finished, as the Río Grande irritatingly shifted its channel from time to time transferring land from one nation to another. This led the United States and Mexico to create an International Boundary Commission in 1889 for the purpose of settling such disputes. Hundreds of acres of land have experienced a change in sovereignty in this way.

CHAPTER VII NOTES

1   E. N. Lile to Ewing, 6 Apr. 1848, LI, Ewing Papers; Price, "The Election of 1848," p. 244.

2   Albert T. Burnely to John J. Crittenden, 18 Oct. 1848, Truman Smith to Crittenden, 3 Oct. 1848, Joseph Vance to Crittenden, 24 Oct. 1848, XII, John J. Crittenden Papers (Library of Congress, Washington, D. C.); Peter Hitchcock to Ewing, 22 Jul. 1848, LI, Ewing Papers.

3   Ewing to Crittenden, 6 Oct. 1848, Clayton to Crittenden, 12 Oct. 1848, XII, Crittenden Papers; Francis P. Weisenburger, *The Passing of the Frontier* (Columbus: 1941), p. 468.

4   Price, "The Election of 1848," pp. 270–72; *Plain Dealer* (Cleveland), 3 Feb. 1848; Bartlow, *History of Butler County*, pp. 914–16.

5   *Daily Enquirer* (Cincinnati), 31 Jan. 1848.

6   *Ohio State Journal* (Columbus), 17 Apr. 1848.

7   *Intelligencer* (Hamilton), 10 Feb. 1848.

8   *Daily Enquirer* (Cincinnati), 21 Sep. 1848; *Gazette* (Lancaster), 21 Jul., 11 Aug., 1 Sep. 1848; *Telegraph* (Hamilton), 21, 28 Sep. 1848; *Intelligencer* (Hamilton), 27 Jul., 10 Aug. 1848.

9   *Herald* (Cleveland), 20 Jul., 1, 8, 19 Sep. 1848; *Ohio State Journal* (Columbus), 10, 17 Jul., 19, 26 Aug. 1848; *Gazette* (Lancaster), 6 Oct. 1848; *Intelligencer* (Hamilton), 24 Aug., 21 Sep. 1848.

10 *Ohio Statutes*, XLIII, 69, 72, XLIV, 121.

11 Price, "The Election of 1848," pp. 244, 271–72; *Plain Dealer* (Cleveland), 27 Sep. 1848; *Ohio State Journal* (Columbus), 19 Aug. 1848.

12 Price, "The Election of 1848," pp. 290–93; Edgar A. Holt, "Party Politics in Ohio 1848–1850," *Ohio Archaeological and Historical Quarterly*, XXXVIII (Apr. 1928), pp. 305–306, 316–18; Weisenburger, *The Passing of the Frontier*, p. 468; Frederick J. Blue, *The Free Soilers: Third Party Politics, 1848–54* (Urbana: 1973), p. 115.

13 *Intelligencer* (Hamilton), 24 Aug. 1848; *Daily Enquirer* (Cincinnati), 12, 17 Oct. 1848; Bartlow, *History of Butler County*, p. 915; William Bebb to Mother, 21 Nov. 1848, William Bebb Papers (King Library, Miami University).

14 Vance to Crittenden, 13 Nov. 1848, XII, Crittenden Papers; Holman Hamilton, *Zachary Taylor, Soldier in the White House* (New York: 1951), II, 110, 132–33; Brainerd Dyer, *Zachary Taylor* (Baton Rouge: 1946), pp. 290, 300; Holt, "Party Politics in Ohio," pp. 306–307, 316; Blue, *The Free Soilers*, p. 143; Allan Nevins, *Ordeal of the Union* (2 vols.; New York: 1947), I, 215–16.

15 Weisenburger, *The Passing of the Frontier*, pp. 468–70.

16 Bebb to Crittenden, 24 Nov. 1848, XII, Crittenden Papers; Bebb to Mother, 19 Jan. 1849,
    Bebb Papers; Roy Franklin Nichols, *The Democratic Machine, 1850–1854* (New York: 1967),
    p. 24. Long a prominent Ohio Whig, Ewing was a prime target of the Democrats and espe-
    cially Weller during and after the 1848 campaign. See *Telegraph* (Hamilton), 15 Nov. 1849,
    10 Oct. 1850; *Herald* (Cleveland), 19 Sep., 4 Oct. 1848; *Plain Dealer* (Cleveland), 27 Jun.,
    29 Aug. 1849; "Diaries," 7 Dec. 1849, LXXXV, William L. Marcy Papers (Library of
    Congress, Washington, D. C.); Price, "The Election of 1848," p. 304; Francis Preston Blair
    to Martin Van Buren, 10 Jun. 1849, LVI, Martin Van Buren Papers (Library of Congress,
    Washington, D. C.).

17 William Dennison Jr. to Ewing, 14 May, 6 Oct. 1849, A. F. Perry to Ewing, 7 Dec. 1850, John
    Greiner to Ewing, 24 Dec. 1850, LIII, LIV, Ewing Papers; *Herald* (Cleveland), 15 Dec. 1849.

18 *Congressional Globe*, 32nd Cong., 1st sess., 1852, XXV, App., p. 797–98; *Herald*
    (Cleveland), 13, 15 Aug. 1849.

19 Clayton to Weller, 20 Jul. 1849, Weller to Clayton, 3 Jan. 1850, SED 34 (558), pt. 1: 11,
    38; Emory to Ewing, 2 Apr. 1850, ibid., pt. 2: 14.

20 *Ohio State Journal* (Columbus), 2 Oct. 1848.

21 *Congressional Globe*, 32nd Cong., 1st sess., 1852, XXV, App., p. 797; *Alta California* (San
    Francisco), 6, 11, 13 Jun. 1850; SED 108 (832), p. 5.

22 *Congressional Globe*, 32nd Cong., 1st sess., 1852, XXV, App. p. 798; Weller to Ewing, 1 Mar.
    1850, SED 119 (626), pp. 74–76.

23 SED 108 (832), p. 5.

24 Hubert Howe Bancroft, *History of California* (7 vols.; San Francisco: 1884–1890), VI,
    659, 663.

25 Paul Ingersoll Miller, "Thomas Ewing, Last of the Whigs" (Ph.D. diss., The Ohio State
    University, 1933), pp. 232–34; Fillmore to Ewing, 20 Jul. 1850, Ellen Boyle Ewing
    Sherman to Hannah Harris Ewing, 1 Aug. 1850, LIV, X, Ewing Papers.

26 *Congressional Globe*, 31st Cong., 2nd sess., 1850, XXIII, pp. 41, 80–81.

27 Buchanan to Weller, 24 Jan. 1849, SED 34 (558). pt. 1: 2.

28 *Congressional Globe*, 31st Cong., 2nd sess., 1850, XXIII, pp. 79–80; Clayton to Frémont,
    20 Jun. 1849, SED 34 (558), pt. 1: 9.

29 *Congressional Globe*, 31st Cong., 2nd sess., 1850, XXIII, pp. 80–82.

30 *Congressional Globe*, 32nd Cong., 1st sess., 1852, XXV, App., pp. 797–99; ibid., XXIV,
    pt. 1: 814.

31 Thurber and Cremony to Bartlett, 8 Jul. 1851, in *Congressional Globe*, 32nd Cong., 1st
    sess., 1852, XXV, App., p. 854.

32 SED 60 (620), pp. 2–5, 10–17, 23–63.

33 Graham to Whipple, 16 Sep. 1852, Box 2, Folder 5, Whipple Papers; Bigelow to Ewing, 12
    Feb., 12 Jun. 1851, LV, Ewing Papers; Malcolm Seaton, et. al., to Graham, 18 Jul. 1851,
    Corres., Graham Papers.

34 Chandler to Emory, 28 Apr. 1852, Folder 38, Emory Papers.

35 Gray to Rusk, 1 May 1852, Rusk Papers; *Congressional Globe*, 32nd Cong., 2nd sess.,
    1853, XXVI, pt. 1: 43.

36 SED 55 (752), pp. 27–29, 31–33; Rusk to William H. Cushney, 27 Oct. 1849, Rusk to
    Jefferson Davis, 21 Apr. 1853, Rusk Papers.

37 Rusk, Howard, Sam Houston and David Kaufman to Stuart, 20 Jan. 1851, Official
    Dispatches, No. 26, Bartlett Papers.

38 Rusk, Howard, Houston and Richardson Scurry to Fillmore, 28 Jun. 1852, SED 6 (688),
    pp. 141–43.

39 *Congressional Globe*, 32nd Cong., 1st sess., 1852, XXIV, pt. 2: 1,660.

40 Russell, *Improvement of Communication*, p. 137.

41 Stuart to Fillmore, 24 Jul. 1852, SED 6 (688), pp. 8–10.

42 *Message from the President of the United States* ..., 32nd Cong., 1st sess., 1852, S. Ex. Doc. 131 (627), pp. 1–3. [Hereafter cited as SED 131 (Serial 627)].

43 Stuart to Fillmore, 26 Jul. 1852, SED 6 (688), p. 1,013.

44 *Report of the Committee on Foreign Relations* ..., 32nd Cong., 1st sess., 1852, S. Rep. 345 (Serial 631), pp. 2–7.

45 *Congressional Globe*, 32nd Cong., 1st sess., 1852, XXIV, pt. 3: 2,402.

46 Ibid.

47 Stuart to Bartlett, 15 Oct. 1852, Official Dispatches, No. 54, Bartlett Papers.

48 Larráinzar to Ministro de Relaciones, 29 Oct., 26 Nov., 18 Dec. 1852, ASRE, Exp. 24, pp. 1–21, 41–69, 77–79, 80–83.

49 *National Intelligencer* (Washington), 16 Oct. 1852; *Congressional Globe*, 32nd Cong., 2nd sess., 1853, pp. 58, 88, 204, 221, 881, 1,045.

50 SED 108 (832), p. 15.

51 Campbell to McClelland, 22 Aug. 1853, File 426, NA, RG/76; *Report of the Superintendent of the Coast Survey* ..., 33rd Cong., 1st sess., 1854, S. Ex. Doc. 14 (Serial 704), pp. 74–76.

52 SED 108 (832), pp. 53–54.

53 Emory to McClelland, 8 Oct. 1853, Emory to Schott, 19 Apr. 1853, Folders 7, 50, Emory Papers; Emory to McClelland, 16 Mar. 1854, File 426, NA, RG/76.

54 SED 108 (832), p. 75.

55 Ibid., p. 76.

56 Ibid., pp. 77–80.

57 Michler to Emory, 19 Aug. 1853, Folder 54, Emory Papers.

58 Radziminski to Emory, 29 Oct. 1853, Folder 7, ibid.

59 Gardner to Sarah Gardner, 30 Jul. 1853, Gardner Papers; Radziminski to Emory, 23, 24 Jul. 1853, Folder 53, Emory Papers.

60 Schott to Emory, 7 Nov. 1853, Radziminski to Emory, 8, 28 Nov. 1853, Folder 57, ibid.

61 *El Siglo XIX* (Mexico City), 3 Apr. 1853 [Letter date is 9 Feb. 1853].

62 "Jiménez Memoria," pp. 14, 16–18, 20–23; AHDN, Cancelados, Exp. 7–5835, folios 9, 13, 17; Sosa, *Biografías de mexicanos distinguidos*, pp. 526–27.

63 Jiménez to Cruzado, 30 Mar. 1853, Cruzado to Jiménez, 30 Mar., 9 May, 15 Jun. 1853, Jiménez to Ministro de Relaciones, 11 Apr., 18 Jun., 24 Mar. 1853, Alamán to Jiménez, 18, 23, 25 May 1853, Jiménez to Administrador de la Aduana, 7 May, 15 Jun. 1853, Jiménez to Cruz, 1 May 1853, all in "Jiménez Memoria," pp. 24–26, 29–33.

64 Woll to Ministro de Guerra y Marina, 3 May 1854, AHDN, Cancelados, Exp. XI/111/4–8954, folios 6, 8; "Jiménez Memoria," pp. 28, 34.

65 Salazar Ylarregui to Jiménez, 15 May 1853, ibid., pp. 34–38. See also "Mapa de la Frontera de la República Mexicana con los Estados Unidos del Norte ..., 1848," in Ministerio de Guerra y Marina, *Colonias militares. Proyecto para su establecimiento en las fronteras de oriente y occidente de la república* (México: 1848).

66 Salazar Ylarregui to Jiménez, 31 Oct. 1852, "Jiménez Memoria," pp. 17–18; Official Journal, 8 Oct. 1852, Bartlett Papers.

67 Jiménez to Emory, 23 May 1853, Emory to Jiménez, 23 May 1853, "Jiménez Memoria," pp. 30–31, 80–81.

68 Emory to Jiménez, 29 Jul. 1853, Folder 7, Emory Papers; Jiménez to Emory, 31 Jul. 1853, "Jiménez Memoria," p. 81.

69 Emory to Jiménez, 16 Aug. 1853, Folder 54, Emory Papers; Emory to Jiménez, 17 Aug. 1853, Radziminski to Jiménez, 14 Nov. 1853, Jiménez to Radziminski, 21 Nov. 1853, "Jiménez Memoria," pp. 38, 82, 84–85.

70 Ibid., pp. 37–38.

71 Jiménez to Emory, 17, 18 Aug. 1853, Emory to Jiménez, 16, 17 Aug. 1853, Folder 54, Emory Papers; "Jiménez Memoria," pp. 39, 82–83.

72 Emory to Campbell, [31?] Aug. 1853, Folder 54, Emory Papers.

73 McClelland to Bartlett, 17 Mar. 1853, Official Dispatches, No. 57, Bartlett Papers.

74 Emory to Abert, 10 Jan. 1854, Folder 7, Emory Papers. For a different view of Emory's attitude, see Hewitt, "The Mexican Commission," pp. 574–76.

75 Jiménez to Ministro de Relaciones, 9 Sep. 1853, Manuel Díez de Bonilla to Jiménez, 6 Oct. 1853, "Jiménez Memoria," pp. 39–41.

76 Ibid., pp. 41–47.

77 Salazar Ylarregui to Ministro de Relaciones, 24 Feb. 1854, ASRE, Exp. 22, p. 283.

78 Paula Rebert, *La Gran Línea: Mapping the United States-Mexico Boundary, 1849–1857* (Austin: 2001), p. 157.

79 Salazar Ylarregui to Ministro de Relaciones, 3 Apr. 1853, ASRE, Exp. 24.

DOÑA ANA

"No doubt now remains, on my mind, that this
quondam Boundary Commissioner, is both Fool & Knave....

William Carr Lane, Governor, New Mexico Territory

What broke the stalemate over the southern boundary of New Mexico was the precipitate declaration of territorial governor William Carr Lane that the disputed area rightfully belonged to the United States. Appointed governor in the summer of 1852, Lane was known only as the genial first mayor of the city of St. Louis, and a man with something of a penchant for adventure. Born in Pennsylvania on 2 December 1789, Lane attended Jefferson College in Chambersburg, later continuing his education at Dickinson College. After studying medicine in Louisville, Kentucky, he was caught up in the frontier war fever of 1813 and for a time served under then Major Zachary Taylor as surgeon's mate at Fort Harrison in Indiana. With the War of 1812 ended, Lane pursued his medical career at the University of Pennsylvania, but failed to complete his degree. Once more placing himself in the service of his country, Lane spent part of 1816 and much of 1817 in the capacity of army surgeon at various posts along the upper Mississippi. Leaving the army a second time, he moved to Vincennes, Indiana, where he received his diploma by examination from the state medical board.

Apparently nostalgic for the life of the camp, the young doctor briefly toyed with the idea of going off to join the liberating army of Simón Bolívar in Venezuela. If not sober reflection, then certainly his marriage to Mary Ewing of Vincennes caused him to rethink his future. Following another brief stint as army surgeon on the upper Mississippi, he settled in St. Louis to practice medicine in 1819.

William Carr Lane was a tall, energetic man who loved people and public affairs, an extrovert whose reddish-brown hair hinted at his occasional flights of temper. Elected mayor of St. Louis in 1823, he served six consecutive one-year terms before retiring to his medical practice. While still mayor he found

William Carr Lane, Courtesy Palace of the Governors (MNM/DCA) Neg. No. 9999.

time to serve in the state legislature in 1826 and for the years 1830–1832. A zealous and incorruptible public servant, he was prevailed upon to return to the mayor's office in 1838 and 1839.

Though a slaveholding Whig and Southern sympathizer, Lane does not appear to have formed an opinion regarding the Bartlett-García Conde compromise line that threatened to block a southern railroad to the Pacific until after becoming governor of New Mexico. Lane was sixty-six years old, but in excellent and robust health when he left St. Louis for the wilds of New Mexico Territory, arriving at the capital on 9 September 1852.[1] In his inaugural address to the people of Santa Fe and early correspondence as governor, he did not refer to the boundary question at all. Lane seemed more concerned about humane treatment of the Indians and the organization of the territorial administration, a difficult task since the governor had no revenue at his disposal.[2] A minor complaint was the Governor's Palace which he found to be "a mud-house whitewashed, inside and outside, one story high, with a plaza in front, & a flat roof, of earth—with apartments oddly arranged, rudely furnished & badly ventilated. Fortunately the air is very pure...."[3]

While at first seemingly uninterested in the disputed southern boundary of the territory, Governor Lane later related that when he departed for Santa Fe in late July 1852, Richard H. Weightman, the territorial delegate for New Mexico, urged him to claim jurisdiction over La Mesilla and take possession of it by force of arms if necessary. Lane at first refused to consider such action, but changed his mind on the subject when he learned, in February 1853, that the United States Senate had suspended the survey the previous August.[4] Writing to his wife, Lane hinted at the plan that was now coursing through his mind, "be not surprised if I should take possession of the disputed Territory..., be assured, that if duty calls upon me, to occupy & protect this country, provisionally, until the line shall be definitely established, I will do it."[5]

Governor Lane soon made good his word, creating quite a stir at Doña Ana on 13 March 1853 when he issued a proclamation claiming jurisdiction over the disputed Mesilla Valley. Lane justified his action by declaring that the area had been a part of New Mexico from 1824 to 1851 and Chihuahua had no right to annex the area because the Joint Commission had not determined the boundary.[6] He sent a copy of his rather lengthy proclamation to Governor Ángel Trías of Chihuahua, but before Trías could reply, Antonio Jaques and Tomás Zuloaga, commissioners for the state of Chihuahua whom Trías had ordered to the scene, organized a force of volunteers to resist Lane's threatened occupation of La Mesilla. The commissioners also directed a letter to Lane on 19 March, repudiating his declaration. Lane responded that the United States Senate's rejection of 32° 22′ alone justified his action, and that the absence of instructions from Washington in no way invalidated his claim to La Mesilla.[7]

When Governor Trías replied to Lane's proclamation on 28 March, he refuted each point of the statement and claimed that Mexico had in her favor possession of the area from time immemorial and had occupied the valley in plain sight of the authorities of the United States who, he noted, were not used to remaining silent when their rights were threatened. Trías claimed that the boundary upon which the Joint Commission had agreed gave the area to

Ángel Trías, Courtesy Benson Latin American Collection, University of Texas at Austin.

Mexico. Finally, Trías reminded Lane that in threatening to occupy La Mesilla by force, he was in violation of Article XXI of the Treaty of Guadalupe Hidalgo, which provided for the pacific settlement of differences between the two nations.[8]

Trías charged that Lane's proclamation was a practical declaration of war without the consent or knowledge of Washington. One of the wealthiest and most powerful men of Chihuahua and lord of the princely Hacienda Encinillas, Ángel Trías was born in 1809. He had received an excellent education, had traveled widely in Europe and the United States, and was fluent in several languages including flawless English. Governor Trías was as comfortable in polite European society as he was on his vast landed estate and was easily the intellectual match of the doctor from St. Louis. Trías had spent his entire life in government and military service, currently serving his fourth term as governor of Chihuahua. He had fought in the war against the United States at the battle of Sacramento near Chihuahua City and later with Santa Anna at Cerro Gordo, rising to the rank of brigadier general. Always ready to defend his country, Trías' patriotism equaled his hatred of North Americans.[9] *El Siglo XIX* noted that the general had fired the last shot in the recent war with the United States and wondered if he would fire the first shot in the next. The paper was referring to the skirmish Trías fought at Santa Cruz de Rosales, some forty miles southeast of Chihuahua City just one month after Nicholas Trist had put his signature to the Treaty of Guadalupe Hidalgo. In an editorial the Mexico City newspaper reasoned that Lane's conduct was not justifiable and that law would decide the issue, not another war that the nation could ill afford.[10]

In addition to refuting the governor of New Mexico, Trías sent a special courier with Lane's proclamation and news of the situation in La Mesilla to Mexico City. Trías declared that he was prepared to march his troops to Mesilla to protect the inhabitants who were legal citizens of Chihuahua, and related his fears that a force from New Mexico would soon attempt to take possession of the disputed area.[11] This news reached Minister of Foreign Relations José Miguel Arroyo on 8 April. That afternoon he related the threatening situation in Chihuahua to Alfred Conkling, the United States envoy to Mexico.[12] Arroyo noted that Lane claimed an area that had always been in the possession of Mexico and within the boundary that the Joint Commission had established. From the reports he had received, Arroyo related to Conkling, it appeared that Lane was gathering troops to occupy the area. He strongly protested Lane's unilateral conduct, which was risking war between the two nations. In order to avoid conflict, Arroyo requested Conkling to send a note to Lane.[13]

While Conkling responded to Arroyo's note by protesting what he considered Trías' own unilateral action in Chihuahua, he agreed to send a note to Lane because of the extreme gravity of the situation. Conkling informed Lane of Arroyo's protest and of his own opinion that there was no need for the measures Lane was taking. While Congress had attached a proviso to the appropriations bill that suspended the survey, the secretary of state had instructed Conkling to explain to Mexico that the difficulty would be solved at the next session of Congress. Beyond this, Conkling related to Lane that he knew of no other act on the part of the United States regarding the disputed initial point. Conkling also informed Lane that he had no right to exercise any authority over the disputed area and that existing possession should be left undisturbed until an agreement was reached between the two governments.[14]

Secretary of State William L. Marcy of the recently installed Democratic administration did not entirely approve of Conkling's actions. Marcy had little doubt that La Mesilla was a part of New Mexico, that the treaty had given the area to the United States, and that nothing had occurred since to transfer it to Chihuahua. Marcy's view was that the disputed area should remain in its present condition until an amicable arrangement settled the problem. He stated that the United States had no intention of deviating from this course and that Mexico had given no notice that she intended to assume jurisdiction over the area. Marcy believed that Lane was justified in claiming the disputed area as a part of New Mexico, and in denying that the acts of the Joint Commission had in any way effected a transfer of the area to Chihuahua. Marcy could not approve Lane's "proceeding to enter the territory and hold it by force of arms ...," and instructed Conkling to assure the government of Mexico that the United States wished to have the area remain as it was until the Joint Commission or future negotiation solved the difficulty.[15]

Marcy noted that it was quite unusual, if not irregular, for Conkling to have written an official communication to Lane without having received instructions to that effect. The secretary stated that this might not have been the subject of his disapproval if Conkling had not assumed an attitude that could impair the claim of the United States to the disputed territory. Marcy observed that Arroyo was careful in his note to Conkling to avoid pretending that La Mesilla was not a part of New Mexico when the treaty was framed. Nor did he assert that it was a part of Chihuahua until the commissioners chose 32° 22′ as the boundary. Marcy stated that Conkling's letter implied that the disputed area was a part of Chihuahua.[16] Conkling had related to Lane that Arroyo had protested Lane's actions taken "for the purpose of acquiring possession of a portion of territory formerly, and, as Mr. Arroyo insists, still forming a part of the State of Chihuahua."[17] Marcy observed that if the disputed territory was indeed formerly a part of Chihuahua, the United States had no claim to it. But Arroyo had not said this; Conkling had. Marcy then directed Conkling to explain to Arroyo that he had not been relating to Lane his position regarding the disputed area, but that of Mexico.[18]

Conkling's note to Lane did perhaps cause the governor of New Mexico to reconsider his stance. More importantly, Governor Trías had taken measures to resist any possible occupation of La Mesilla and soon reached El Paso del Norte with 750 soldiers, Emilio Langberg serving as second in command. He was later reinforced with 500 troops and four pieces of artillery arriving from Zacatecas.[19] This left Lane quite alone, for Colonel Edwin Vose Sumner, military commander of the Department of New Mexico, refused to enforce Lane's proclamation with United States troops. Sumner of course had no orders from his superiors to do any such thing. While Lane later claimed to have had the support of New Mexican and Texan volunteers "who were importunate in their demands that I should take the country, and restore our citizens to their rights of person and property in this district ...," he decided that it would be best not to attempt a forcible seizure of the territory, and therefore placed the matter before the president.[20] The most prominent and wealthy citizen living across the river from El Paso del Norte, James Wiley Magoffin, reported that when Lane reached Doña Ana and issued his proclamation, he received no support from the citizenry and had no military force to back up his warlike words. Finding so little support from the people he had come to protect, Lane simply returned to Santa Fe.[21]

In an interview with Santa Anna, who had returned to the presidency of Mexico, Conkling gave his opinion that the United States government would probably not condone Governor Lane's actions.[22] This seemed to be the case when President Franklin Pierce replaced Lane with David Meriwether. The Mexico City newspaper *La Crónica* viewed Lane's removal as a rebuke for his bellicose actions and as official support for the commissioners' line of 32° 22′, but the fear of war was still in the air.[23] Manuel Larráinzar, Mexico's envoy in Washington, had been expressing his concern that Mexico might lose the Mesilla Valley, which he considered very important to the economy of El Paso del Norte.[24]

These fears were supported when Brevet Brigadier General John Garland superseded Colonel Sumner as the military commander of New Mexico. In discussing Garland's appointment, some portions of the United States press assumed an extremely bellicose attitude toward Mexico.[25] The *Washington Union* saw the dispute over the boundary line and Lane's actions as an opportunity to "extend the area of freedom."[26] Despite the official opinion that Marcy had instructed Conkling to relay to the Mexican government, and Lane's removal from office, such warlike talk in United States newspapers did not allow Mexico to rest at ease. Manuel Díez de Bonilla, who had become minister of foreign relations, believed General Garland was marching to New Mexico with a sizeable number of troops. The dispatch that Larráinzar had sent on 22 June merely confirmed Díez de Bonilla's fears.[27]

While Mexico had very good reason to fear an outbreak of war over the boundary dispute, the official press declared that there should have been no dispute in the first place. Agreeing with Bartlett's interpretation of the boundary line, the *Diario Oficial* correctly pointed out that Stuart had recognized his acts as official. Since Emory had later, on Stuart's orders, signed the documents relating to the initial point, the paper considered the matter settled.[28] The perceived threat of war reached its height during August and September of 1853. *El Universal* reported on 17 August that fighting had broken out between the forces of Garland and Trías.[29] The *Diario Oficial*, however, refuted this assertion on 9 September, reporting that the frontier remained peaceful.[30] There was still a great degree of uncertainty in Mexico as to the intentions of the United States when Joaquín J. de Castillo, Mexico's consul at Brownsville, Texas, reported his belief that United States troops would soon invade Mexico.[31] Mexico was certainly attuned to the voice of Manifest Destiny as she had been from the beginning of her relations with the United States and had to take Lane's proclamation seriously. Later attempts, both rhetorical and physical, to overpower Yucatán, Sonora, and Baja California would continue to be an irritant between the two nations through the end of the century and into the next.

In any case Governor William Carr Lane's pugnacious proclamation in the little town of Doña Ana had focused the attention of both governments on the propriety of commissioners Bartlett and García Conde's selection of 32° 22′ north latitude as the southern boundary of New Mexico. Former surveyor Andrew Gray had for some time been arguing powerfully that this line was incorrect. The heart of the controversy was the interpretation of the treaty map. Gray had long held that the error in Disturnell's map lay not in the position of El Paso del Norte, but rather in the incorrect representation of the parallels on the map. Had these parallels represented the true latitude given them on the map with regard to the placement of the towns on the Río Grande, Gray affirmed that Bartlett's line would be the same as his own. He reasoned that Mexico made the retention of El Paso del Norte a sine qua non, and that while the United States wished to obtain the settlement Buchanan was willing to give it up. In this condition of things, the negotiators, Gray became convinced, agreed to disregard all parallels and take the line marked on Disturnell's map in order to ensure that El Paso del Norte remained Mexican.[32]

According to Bartlett, the Río Grande was actually about two degrees of longitude farther west on the surface of the earth than it appeared to be on the treaty map. This would give a line one degree or sixty miles in length for the southern boundary of New Mexico, while its length as described in the treaty and represented on the map was nearly 176 miles. García Conde realized that Bartlett would not accept this, so Gray claimed, and did not press the error in Mexico's favor because his compromise with Bartlett had already gained the Mesilla Valley, the great pass of the Sierra Madre and some 6,000 square miles of territory. Gray argued that García Conde's agreement to measure the line three degrees west from the initial point was easy after Bartlett's agreement to 32° 22´.[33]

Gray also refuted Bartlett's contention that no law existed that defined the northern boundary of Chihuahua as running a few miles north of El Paso del Norte. There was indeed such a law of 27 July 1824, which stated that the northern limit of Chihuahua began on the Río Grande at "the point or town called Paso del Norte, on the one side, with the jurisdiction it has always possessed, and the hacienda of the Río Florido on the side of Durango with its respective appurtenances."[34] The jurisdiction of El Paso del Norte, Gray maintained, had always extended to and included the *acequia*, or irrigation canal, about eight miles north of the central plaza and was so represented on Disturnell's map. Gray pointed out that during the discussions of the Joint Commission, García Conde made no reference to this law.[35] Gray believed the true latitude of the southern boundary of New Mexico had to be computed from the true latitude of El Paso del Norte, a fixed point on the surface of the earth and mentioned in the treaty.[36] Gray held that the only proper way to determine the boundary would be to measure seven minutes north from the center of El Paso del Norte.

Bartlett argued that the line had always been north of 32° 22´, and cited several authorities to sustain his argument in the report he presented to the secretary of the interior. José Agustín de Escudero placed the northern boundary of Chihuahua in 32° 50´ north latitude.[37] In his statistical survey of Chihuahua, García Conde described the northern line as being in 32° 57´ 43˝ north latitude.[38] Bartlett also referred to two maps of Mexico that represented the southern boundary of New Mexico as 32° 22´ or north of that line.[39] While in Chihuahua, Bartlett found in the office of Governor José Cordero what he considered the most important evidence in support of 32° 22´. This was a large manuscript map of Chihuahua that García Conde had drawn. The state of Chihuahua had organized a geological, topographical, and statistical survey in 1833 and placed García Conde in charge. In addition to the survey, García Conde constructed a map that represented the northern boundary of Chihuahua intersecting the Río Grande at 32° 35´ north latitude and after running west to the Río Mimbres continuing northward as far as the Mogollon Mountains in latitude 32° 57´ 43˝. Bartlett directed Charles Radziminski to make a copy of this map, which Governor Cordero then certified.[40]

Bartlett also found support for this line in the constitution of the state of Chihuahua, wherein the boundaries are the same as those on García Conde's

1834 map and his statistical survey.[41] Bartlett considered García Conde's map, statistical survey, and the constitution of Chihuahua as definitive proof that 32° 22′ was correct. By adhering to Disturnell's map, Bartlett insisted, the United States had gained nearly 6,000 square miles of territory, including the Santa Rita copper mines, the Río Mimbres, and the Mogollon Mountains, all of which García Conde's 1834 map and survey placed within the confines of Chihuahua.[42]

Gray maintained that García Conde's map of Chihuahua carried no weight at all in a discussion of the boundary line, since the treaty did not refer to it and because it was an instrument of the state of Chihuahua and the government of Mexico had never sanctioned it. The limits on García Conde's map, Gray believed, merely expressed the boundaries Chihuahua wished to possess.[43] Both Gray and Bartlett held that his line alone contained the key to a rail route to the Pacific.[44]

After Lane's proclamation at Doña Ana, Gray reiterated to Secretary of State Marcy that Bartlett and García Conde's compromise line had been agreed to illegally, and that he, when United States surveyor, had not committed the nation to 32° 22′ as the new boundary. Gray held that the Whig administration had supported that line only to defend a partisan appointee—that Stuart had ordered Gray to authenticate the line only to save Bartlett. From the beginning of the controversy, Gray had maintained that Bartlett had no authority to appoint Whipple temporary surveyor. He held that all four members of the Joint Commission had to sign all maps, charts and plans for surveys in order to make such acts a part of the treaty. The treaty, Gray believed, did not assign diplomatic powers to the Joint Commission, but merely ministerial powers. Nor did the treaty make a distinction between the powers, duties, rights, and privileges of the commissioners and those of the surveyors.[45]

Whipple had given his opinion on the subject before Bartlett had reached his compromise with García Conde, reasoning that since the treaty had not defined the line in terms of latitude and longitude, the Joint Commission should not follow them on the map, as that would frustrate the intentions of the treaty framers. Since El Paso del Norte had been mentioned in the treaty, Whipple emphasized that it should not be overlooked and that the distance of the line north of the town was that represented on the map.[46] It is difficult to see how Bartlett could think that Whipple supported his decision to compromise with García Conde on 32° 22′.

Colonel Graham expressed the opinion that if Bartlett had followed Whipple's advice, the boundary would lie in 31° 52′ as Gray insisted. Graham was aware of the compromise line before he departed Washington to take up his duties as chief astronomer. He was also aware of the concern of the senators and representatives of Texas regarding the boundary and its effect upon obtaining a rail route to the Pacific.[47] Graham informed Stuart that he would not put up his instruments on that line, but Stuart turned a deaf ear.[48]

Convinced of his own opinion, Graham set out for El Paso del Norte determined to disrupt the survey at all costs. His first act was to pull Whipple from the active survey of 32° 22′ and then refuse to provide the United States commissioner with the instruments he had so carefully brought to Santa Rita del Cobre. His higgling feud with Bartlett over his prerogatives as chief astronomer and head of the scientific corps damaged Graham's reputation for a time, but at the moment provided a wonderfully thick smoke screen for his real intentions. He later wrote:

> The very object ... in refusing Mr. Bartlett a control over the instruments was to hold a check over him & [García] Condé [sic] in their partnership operations of running the lines as General [García] Condé [sic] pleased, & without any attention whatever to the just rights of the United States. Mr. Bartlett throws the responsibility of stopping the survey along the false parallel of 32° 22′ on Colonel Graham.—*Granted.*[49]

After his dismissal and return to Washington, Graham wrote Whipple his belief that the government would repudiate Bartlett's line; that the country would never be satisfied with it, as he informed the lieutenant on first reaching El Paso del Norte. He advised Whipple to have no more to do with the survey of 32° 22′. "Whipple, my friend, I tell you that if you do otherwise it will injure you in the estimation of the country."[50] Before he received Graham's letter, Whipple had completed the survey of the southern boundary of New Mexico as well as the north-south line to the Gila.[51] That this was done, and under Emory's orders at that, seems to have been ignored by everyone at the time and ever since.

Graham agreed with Gray that García Conde had deceived Bartlett by failing to inform him of the 27 July 1824 act of the Mexican Congress fixing the boundaries of the state of Chihuahua and consequently the southern boundary of New Mexico. Graham was convinced that García Conde had at once perceived Bartlett as a weak and vain man, and instead of enlightening Bartlett as to the true position of the boundary, flattered him into believing they were ambassadors with power to negotiate an international boundary. Graham insisted that once García Conde had convinced Bartlett of this, the bookseller from Rhode Island was in his power and he twisted him around his finger like a piece of pack thread. While General Pedro García Conde demonstrated his superiority over Bartlett, he practiced an unwarranted fraud upon

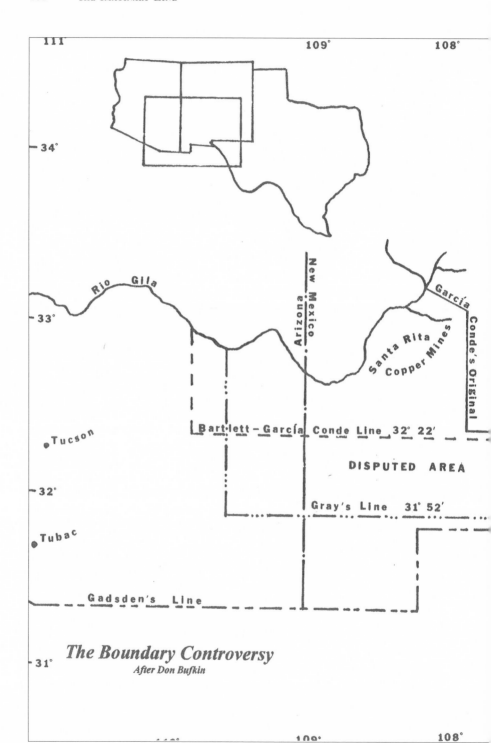

The Boundary Controversy
After Don Bufkin

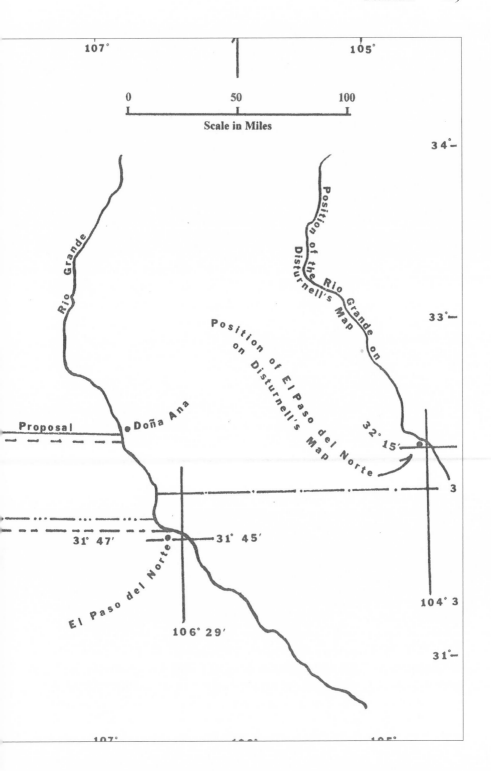

him by concealing from him the northern boundary of Chihuahua according to the act of 27 July 1824. Or so Graham thought.

Graham was convinced that Mexico would be compelled to give up its claim to 32° 22′. William Carr Lane had already been inaugurated governor in Santa Fe when Graham wrote, "I presume the civil authority of New Mexico will not henceforth permit the exercise of Mexican jurisdiction beyond a line more than eight miles north of the plaza or church of El Paso."[52] Had Graham informed Lane of his opinion regarding the southern boundary of New Mexico? Since both men were in Washington at the time of Lane's appointment as territorial governor it is quite likely, but there is no evidence that the former mayor of St. Louis and the topographical engineer from Virginia ever met. Graham did send Lane a copy of his official report on the survey, but that had been ordered to be printed on 31 August 1852, some six weeks after Lane's departure from Washington. There is no proof that Lane received the report before he issued his troublesome proclamation. Some time after his posturing at Doña Ana, Lane wrote Graham thanking him for the report and emphasized, "The U. S. owes Mr. Gray & yourself, a debt of gratitude, for the stand you have both taken against great odds."[53] Graham ever felt that it had been his duty to stop the survey of 32° 22′ north latitude, and instead of being disgraced for pulling Whipple off the line found it the proudest act of his life.[54]

Major William Emory took a different view. He early feared there was little hope that the Mexican commission would retreat from the Bartlett-García Conde line. Mexico, he believed, would certainly retreat no farther than Gray's line, but in fairness to Bartlett, Emory was convinced that neither line would provide a rail route to the Pacific. He considered this the result of Gray and Graham's ignorance of the topography west of 110° longitude. Gray's line would strike the Gila east of Mount Graham; the canyon of the river that formed a barrier to a railroad was west of that point. Emory also noted that Gray and Graham wrongly assumed the commissioners had no power to negotiate, but were bound literally to the treaty map. "The truth is they did not know what they wanted and made the fight in the dark."[55]

Not long before Lane's appointment as governor of New Mexico, Emory expressed a deeper fear that the United States was irrevocably committed to 32° 22′. He noted that President Fillmore and Secretary of the Interior Stuart had accepted that line in an official report. Commissioner Bartlett had accepted the initial point of 32° 22′ on the Río Grande, a stone monument had been erected at the spot, and the Mexican commission had surveyed the line west and north to the Gila. Emory further believed that Gray had unwittingly accepted Bartlett's line when he agreed to begin the survey of the Río Grande at the point designated by the commissioners who of course selected 32° 22′.

When Bartlett directed Colonel Graham to begin at that point, he agreed, in effect recognizing the Bartlett-García Conde line. It appeared to Emory then, that the president, the secretary of the interior and the United States commissioner, surveyor, and chief astronomer had committed the government to 32° 22′ north latitude as the southern boundary of New Mexico.[56] Whipple, moreover, had surveyed the entire length of 32° 22′ as well as the western line of New Mexico to its intersection with the Gila.

Emory had also authenticated the line with his signature as ordered by Stuart, but only as the line agreed upon by the two commissioners. He was convinced that he had not committed the United States to that line, but believed that only a new treaty could throw it farther south. His great concern was the railroad.[57] Without such communication along its southern border, the United States would be unable to maintain the military posts along the frontier required to stem the Indian raids upon the northern states of Mexico as required by the Treaty of Guadalupe Hidalgo.[58] A transcontinental railroad was of course of much greater significance for the United States than a mere means to restrain Indian depredations. Whether built in the North or South, a railroad was essential to tie the newly won territory on the Pacific to the rest of the nation. It was indeed a vital concern as Emory freely admitted. "The road is the great object: the land is not worth a chew of tobacco. It really seems to me the only way left now to get the road, is to take it, and the justification will be in the necessity of the case which requires us to have a continuous line of military posts along our frontier."[59]

From the moment he learned of Bartlett's compromise, Emory hoped for some means to reverse that decision, becoming convinced that only the negotiation of a new treaty could provide the desperately needed railroad. He certainly had not expected the opportunity that the public-spirited governor of New Mexico now provided. William Carr Lane had acted solely to protect the interests of the people of New Mexico. There is no evidence in his public or private correspondence that the challenge issued at Doña Ana was a Washington intrigue to reopen the question of the line, or that Lane was anyone's cat's-paw. Yet in precipitating the Mesilla conflict and bringing on a threat of war, Governor Lane had opened the way for the Gadsden Treaty.

CHAPTER VIII NOTES

1 Walter B. Stevens, *St. Louis, The Fourth City, 1764–1911* (3 vols.; St. Louis: 1911), I, 91–93; David H. Armstrong to Lane, 16 Mar. 1853, Lane to Lyman Trumbull, 24 Feb. 1859, and passim, William Carr Lane Papers (Missouri Historical Society, St. Louis); *Intelligencer* (St. Louis), 6 Mar. 1857; William G. B. Carson, "William Carr Lane Diary," *New Mexico Historical Review*, XXXIX (Jul., 1964), pp. 181–87; Ralph E. Twitchell, "Historical Sketch of Governor William Carr Lane," *Historical Society of New Mexico*, No. 4, Santa Fe, 1917, pp. 5–9.

2 "Inaugural Address of Governor William Carr Lane," 13 Sep. 1852, Lane Papers.

3 Lane to William Glasgow, 26 Sep. 1852, ibid.

4 Lane to J. L. Taylor, 23 Jan. 1854, *Report of the Committee on Territories … ,* 33rd Cong., 1st sess., 1854, H. Rep. 81 (Serial 742), pp. 1–2 [Hereafter cited as HR 81 (742)]; Thornton Grinsby to Lane, 27 Aug. 1852, Lane Papers; Lane to Darby, 1 Dec. 1852, John Fletcher Darby Papers (Missouri Historical Society, St. Louis).

5 Lane to Mary Ewing Lane, 15 Feb. 1853, Lane Papers.

6 Lane to Taylor, 23 Jan. 1854, HR 81 (742), pp. 1–2. For the text of the proclamation see Twitchell, "Historical Sketch," pp. 18–20, or *El Centinela* (Chihuahua City), 29 Mar. 1853, or *El Siglo XIX* (Mexico City), 10 Apr. 1853.

7 Lane to Jaques and Zuloaga, 23 Mar. 1853, in *Weekly Gazette* (Santa Fe), 14 May 1853, in Lane Papers; *El Siglo XIX* (Mexico City), 13 May 1853; Florence C. and Robert H. Lister, *Chihuahua, Storehouse of Storms* (Albuquerque: 1966), p. 138.

8 Lane to Trías, 13 Mar. 1853, Trías to Lane, 28 Mar. 1853, in *El Centinela* (Chihuahua City), 29 Mar. 1853; *El Siglo XIX* (Mexico City), 10 Apr., 13 May 1853.

9 Almada, *Diccionario de historia, geografía y biografía chihuahuenses*, pp. 714–15; *El Monitor Republicano* (Mexico City), 10 Feb. 1849; Lister, *Chihuahua*, p. 117; Josiah Gregg, *Commerce of the Prairies* (Norman: 1954), pp. 306–307; Alcaraz, *Apuntes para la historia de la guerra entre México y los Estados Unidos*, pp. 139–50.

10 *El Siglo XIX* (Mexico City), 27 Apr., 5 Jun. 1853; Lister, *Chihuahua*, p. 132; Smith, *The War with Mexico*, II, 166; Alcaraz, *Apuntes para la guerra entre México y los Estados Unidos*, pp. 397–401.

11 Trías to Arroyo, 28, 29 Mar. 1853, ASRE, Leg. 1–2-566 (I).

12 Conkling to Marcy, No. 31, 9 Apr. 1853, Despatches from United States Ministers to Mexico to the Department of State, Record Group 59 (National Archives, Washington, D. C.; Hereafter cited as Despatches, NA, RG/59).

13 Arroyo to Conkling, 8 Apr. 1853, ibid.

14 Conkling to Arroyo, 9 Apr. 1853, ASRE, Leg. 1–2-566 (I); Conkling to Marcy, No. 31, 9 Apr. 1853, Conkling to Lane, 8 Apr. 1853, Despatches, NA, RG/59.

15 Marcy to Conkling, No. 20, 18 May 1853, Diplomatic Instructions of the Department of State, Record Group 59 (National Archives, Washington, D. C.; Hereafter cited as Instructions, NA, RG/59).

16 Ibid.

17 Conkling to Lane, 8 Apr. 1853, Despatches, NA, RG/59.

18 Marcy to Conkling, No. 20, 18 May 1853, Instructions, NA, RG/59.

19 Magoffin to Bartlett, 24 Apr. 1853, Corres., VII, Bartlett Papers; *El Siglo XIX* (Mexico City), 27 Apr. 1853; David R. Diffenderfer to the Secretary of State, 23 Mar., 14 Apr. 1853, Despatches from United States Consuls in Ciudad Juárez (El Paso del Norte), 1850–1906, Record Group 59 (National Archives, Washington, D. C.); AHDN, Cancelados, Exp. XI/111/2–400, II, folio 283.

20 Lane to Taylor, 23 Jan. 1854, HR 81 (742), p. 2.

21 Magoffin to Bartlett, 24 Apr. 1853, Corres., VII, Bartlett Papers; Magoffin to Emory, 24 Apr. 1853, Folder 7, Emory Papers.

22 Conkling to Marcy, No. 35, 3 May 1853, Despatches, NA, RG/59.

23 *La Crónica* (Mexico City), 8 Jun. 1853.

24 Larráinzar to Ministro de Relaciones, 13 Sep. 1852, 26 Apr. 1853, Larráinzar to Marcy, 26 Apr. 1853, ASRE, Leg. 1–2-566 (I).

25 *National Intelligencer* (Washington), 22 Jun. 1853; *Courier and Enquirer* (New York), 8 Jun. 1853.

26 *Union* (Washington), 7 Jul. 1853.

27 Díez de Bonilla to Larráinzar, 4, 9 Jul. 1853, Larráinzar to Díez de Bonilla, 22 Jun. 1853, ASRE, Leg. 1–2-566 (I).

28 *Diario Oficial del Gobierno de la República Mejicana* (Mexico City), 24, 25 Jul. 1853.

29 *El Universal* (Mexico City), 17 Aug. 1853.

30 *Diario Oficial* (Mexico City), 9 Sep. 1853.

31 De Castillo to Díez de Bonilla, 27 Aug. 1853, ASRE, Leg. 1–2-566 (I).

32 SED 55 (752), pp. 7–9; Gray to Stuart, 3 Aug. 1851, SED 119 (626), pp. 298–99.

33 SED 55 (752), pp. 7–9.

34 Dublán y Lozano, eds., *Legislación mexicana*, I, 710.

35 SED 55 (752), pp. 24–26; Official Journal, passim, Bartlett Papers.

36 SED 55 (752), pp. 6–7; Gray to Bartlett, 25 Jul. 1851, SED 41 (665), p. 27.

37 José Agustín de Escudero, *Noticias estadísticas del estado de Chihuahua* (México: 1834), p. 8.

38 García Conde, *Ensayo estadístico*, p. 167.

39 "Mapa de los Estados Unidos Mexicanos, arreglado a la distribución que en diversas decretas ha hecho del territorio el congreso general Mejicano," and "Carta geográfica general de la República Mexicana, formada en el año 1845." (Map Division, Library of Congress, Washington, D.C.).

40 Bartlett, *Personal Narrative*, II, 429–30; SED 41 (665), p. 8. The map is entitled "Carta geográfica del Estado de Chihuahua," a copy of the pertinent portion is in ibid., Map No. 4.

41 Bartlett, *Personal Narrative*, II, 430.

42 SED 41 (665), pp. 8–11.

43 SED 55 (752), pp. 25–26.

44 Bartlett to Stuart, 27 Sep. 1851, SED 119 (626), p. 459; SED 41 (665), pp. 18–21; SED 55 (752), pp. 27–33.

45 Gray to Marcy, 27 Apr. 1853, XXXV, Marcy Papers; Gray to Bartlett, 9 Aug. 1851, Corres., V, Bartlett Papers; SED 55 (752), pp. 3, 14–17, 20–35; SED 131 (627), pp. 2–3.

46 Whipple to Bartlett, 12 Dec. 1850, Bartlett to Whipple, 30 Dec. 1850, SED 119 (626), pp. 247–48.

47 Briscoe G. Baldwin to Graham, 2 Mar. 1851, Corres., Graham Papers; Rusk, Howard, Houston, and Kaufman to Stuart, 20 Jan. 1851, Stuart to Graham, 23 Jan. 1851, Graham to Stuart, 26 Jan. 1851, Misc. Papers-1824–1852, ibid.

48 "Speech of Hon. Volney E. Howard, of Texas, on the Mexican Boundary Question," 6 Jul. 1852. House of Rep., Washington: Printed at the *Congressional Globe* office, 1852.

49 "Notes," pp. 22–23, Undated, Misc. Papers, Graham Papers. [Graham's emphasis].

50 Graham to Whipple, 16 Sep. 1852, Box 2, Folder 5, Whipple Papers.

51 Emory to Whipple, 11 Jun. 1852, Folder 5, Emory Papers; "Journals," 20 Aug. 1852, Whipple Papers.

52 Graham to Whipple, 16 Sep. 1852, Box 2, Folder 5, ibid.

53 Lane to Graham, 16 Jul. 1853, Corres., Graham Papers.

54 Graham to John Nick Watkins, 15 Jul. 1854, File 431, NA, RG/76; Graham to Whipple, 16 Sep. 1852, Box 2, Folder 5, Whipple Papers.

55 Emory to Howard, 18 Dec. 1851, Folder 3, Emory Papers.

56 Emory to Howard, 1 Jun. 1852, Folder 40, ibid.; SED 131 (627), pp. 1–4; Bartlett to
    Graham, 9 Sep. 1851, Graham to Charles Wright, 8 Nov. 1851, Graham to Salazar
    Ylarregui, 12 Nov. 1851, SED 121 (627), pp. 195–99.

57 Emory to Howard, 18 Dec. 1851, 1 Jun., 7 Nov. 1852, Emory to Mason, 16 Feb., 21 Apr.
    1853, Folders 3, 40, 6, 48, 50, Emory Papers; Emory to Stuart, 1 Oct. 1852, SED 108
    (832), p. 20.

58 Abert to Emory, 12 Jul. 1853, Emory to Abert, 11 Aug. 1853, Folder 7, Emory Papers; SED
    108 (832), pp. 17, 20, 41, 45.

59 Emory to Howard, 7 Nov. 1852, Folder 6, Emory Papers.

EL VALLE

DE LA MESILLA

*"Parece pues muy dudoso que la cuestión
de la Mesilla se arregle pacíficamente...."*

**El Marqués de la Ribera,
Spanish Ambassador to Mexico**

In the first weeks of March 1853 there occurred three events that would give
the United States the opportunity to renegotiate the southern boundary of New
Mexico. The Democratic Party, many of whose members adamantly opposed
the Bartlett-García Conde line, returned to power in Washington, Governor
Lane issued his provocative proclamation, and Antonio López de Santa Anna
began his final and most maladroit dictatorship. These events and Mexico's
political instability ultimately gave the Mesilla Valley to the United States.

In an effort to establish a stable, authoritarian government, Mexican
conservatives, allied with a portion of the army and the church, overthrew
the faltering administration of President Mariano Arista in January 1853.
The Spanish ambassador to Mexico, Juan Antoine y Zayas, reported that the
Arista government had been steadily sinking into administrative anarchy
and could not possibly deal with the problems on the Río Grande. He and
his colleagues from France and England believed that only these three maritime
powers could sustain Mexico's independence and save it from absorption into
the United States.[1] Learning that the Congress had been broken up by soldiers
with swords drawn, he wrote of the situation in Mexico City, "It is a chaos so
obscure as to permit no manner of foresight or divination regarding the fate of
this unfortunate country."[2]

Yet despite the ambassador's pessimism a government was taking form.
Under the leadership of the able Lucas Alamán the conservatives planned a
brief dictatorship as a prelude to monarchy. The only man possessing the fire
suitable for the post was the political weathercock Santa Anna, presently

exiled to Venezuela. Elected president with dictatorial powers for one year on 17 March, he eagerly accepted the challenge, making his way to Veracruz via Havana.[3]

In that busy port the returning hero chanced to meet Spain's new ambassador to Mexico, the Marqués de la Ribera, the two men traveling together to Veracruz on the *Southampton*. During this leisurely cruise the new president of Mexico outlined his proposed foreign policy. His first objective, he informed Ribera, was to send diplomatic representatives to Madrid, Paris, London, and Berlin to impress upon those European nations that it would not be in their commercial interests for the United States to seize any more Mexican territory. He observed to Ribera that at the moment Mexico's military forces could not have resisted an invasion of any kind. The army had fallen into such extreme indiscipline as to have become a nullity. Therefore his second objective was to procure in France and Switzerland, but principally in Spain, a number of military officers and men, including sergeants, to assist in reorganizing the Mexican army and give it discipline. His third objective was to seek a military alliance with Spain and perhaps other European powers. The ebullient dictator saw United States aggression toward Mexico and Cuba as one and the same question, making Spain his country's natural ally.[4] Finally, Santa Anna spoke to Ribera of plans for a monarchy, but the Spanish ambassador was unable to determine precisely the president's ultimate objective.[5]

After Santa Anna reached Mexico City and took formal possession of office on 20 April 1853, the Marqués de la Ribera offered his estimation of the new government. He found Minister of Foreign Relations Lucas Alamán an able and brilliant man, an honor to his country and fortunately the head of the cabinet. Teodosio Lares, minister of justice, was also a competent man, Ribera believed, but he viewed Treasury Minister Antonio Haro y Tamáriz and Minister of War José María Tornel as less brilliant, though able enough. The new government began work energetically, with everyone expecting Alamán to dominate the administration. Haro y Tamáriz happily began a program of reform that insisted upon economy and an end to corruption. The government's financial credit improved somewhat, and the plan to establish a bank seemed to be a step in the right direction.[6] All restraining influence upon the dictator was soon lost, however, when the scholarly Alamán suddenly died in June 1853 and the prominent Tornel followed him to the grave in September.[7] The cabinet, now sadly weakened, saw Santa Anna turning to his old tricks and old cronies, but was too cowed to resist the dictator and the sycophants who quickly closed in upon the government. Only Haro y Tamáriz had the courage to resign openly and publish an attack upon the financial abuses now plaguing the treasury department.[8] The tether was cut; Santa Anna was free.

While he quickly forgot about the honest, conservative government Lucas Alamán had hoped to establish, Santa Anna continued to follow the general objectives he had outlined to the Marqués de la Ribera on the *Southampton*. He managed to increase the size of the army to 70,000 men and recruited a number of professional military men from Spain and elsewhere to give it strength and discipline.[9] To buttress Mexico's foreign policy, Santa Anna proposed the assembling of a congress composed of all the Hispanic-American nations and the forging of an alliance among them. Ambassador Ribera was correct in his belief that nothing would come of the idea, but Santa Anna's proposed Hispano-Mexican alliance, strengthened by the adherence of France and England, held out some possibilities. Before his death Lucas Alamán had directed Mexico's envoy to Spain, Buenaventura Vivó, to seek just such an agreement.[10]

In a conversation with Ribera, Santa Anna declared he favored Spain's retention of Cuba, and suggested a mutual defensive alliance against United States aggression. While Spain's foreign office found the Mexican president's concern over Cuba interesting, the question of an alliance was a matter that called for caution.[11] Ribera did not think an alliance with Mexico would be in Spain's best interest.[12] The ministry of foreign affairs had no wish to mingle in Mexican affairs, nor to forge an alliance with Mexico when weak. That would only increase Spain's problems with the United States over Cuba.[13]

Despite these problems Madrid was interested in Santa Anna's plans for reorganizing his army and was willing to aid indirectly, but not directly because of Mexico's weakness and the political situation in Spain.[14] The Madrid government at that moment was itself going through a crisis that ultimately led to the Spanish Revolution of 1854.[15] Nevertheless, the minister of foreign relations expressed to Ribera that Spain was very interested in Santa Anna's proposed Hispano-Mexican alliance. Ribera, who was never very enthusiastic about such an arrangement, reported in August 1853 that Santa Anna's government was weakening and that the dictator no longer had the prestige he enjoyed when he landed in Veracruz the previous April.[16]

By the beginning of 1854 Ambassador Vivó had made little progress toward the defensive alliance, commenting on Spain's preoccupation with internal affairs and the Near Eastern question, which threatened a European war.[17] Mexico's minister in London, Joaquín de Castilla y Lanzas, agreed with Vivó's belief that the war threatened by the recent events in the Near East made conclusion of an alliance unlikely. He further noted that while England wanted friendly relations with Mexico, that power desired even more friendly relations with the United States. France would make no move without England, and Spain, he thought, was only interested in European affairs.[18]

By the spring Buenaventura Vivó was more emphatic in his belief that England would not even provide Mexico with moral assistance because her sympathies and interests lay with the United States. While France had more sympathy with Mexico, Napoleon III would expect some compensation for any sacrifices France might make on Mexico's behalf. Spain meanwhile was not very independent in her external actions; without France, Spain would not act.

Then there was the Near Eastern question, which festered into the Crimean War in March 1854 as France and England declared war on Russia. Even if the proposed Hispano-Mexican alliance became a fact, Vivó mused, it would alarm the United States and provide a motive for further aggression. The Spanish government, he stressed, was well disposed toward Mexico, but this did not translate into ships, men, and cannons. His last dejected remark concerned Spain's foreign minister, Angel Calderón de la Barca, with his long residence in Washington, and his Irish-American wife.[19] In spite of these arguments Santa Anna's government ordered Vivó to continue seeking the desired alliance.[20] There the matter rested for the moment.

Buenaventura Vivó's appraisal of his negotiations was made more ominous by a report from Ricardo Ramírez, who was at El Paso del Norte vainly awaiting the arrival of the United States engineer with whom he was to erect monuments along the southern and western boundaries of New Mexico. Ramírez reported that a number of local figures were plotting to annex El Paso del Norte to the United States. He believed the leaders of the annexationist group were Juan José Sánchez, the local *jefe político*, and Guadalupe Miranda, Mexican consul at Franklin across the river. Salazar Ylarregui contended that Ramírez's charges regarding the two men were true.

Minister of Foreign Relations Manuel Díez de Bonilla, who had entered that post on Lucas Alamán's death, informed Governor Ángel Trías of the plot and asked him to investigate the matter. The governor of Chihuahua claimed that Sánchez and Miranda had been falsely accused, and that all the rumor of annexation was the work of their enemies who opposed Santa Anna. These, Trías claimed, were Alejo García Conde and José Merino, respectively administrator and accountant of the customshouse at El Paso del Norte. They had refused to adhere to the plan returning Santa Anna to power and had accordingly lost their posts. Merino then transferred a large sum of money from the customshouse at El Paso del Norte to Franklin, and with Alejo García Conde and the priest Ramón Ortiz suborned the local detachment of troops in order to incite revolt against the new government.[21]

It was no secret that Alejo García Conde and his now deceased brother, the former Mexican boundary commissioner, had long been enemies of Santa Anna, but there does not seem to have been a serious annexationist plot at El Paso del Norte. Yet such rumors began as early as May 1853 and persisted through February 1854.[22] Strengthening these rumors was the general grumbling among the population of La Mesilla because of the failure of the Mexican

Colonization Commission, created by the government after the war, to provide for the protection and assistance of New Mexican immigrants returning from the lost territory. Antonio Jaques and Tomás Zuloaga, commissioners for the state of Chihuahua, reported that the blame lay with Ramón Ortiz, head of the colonization commission and an opponent of the government.[23]

The situation on the frontier appeared to be growing more dangerous, and Santa Anna's project for a Spanish alliance was not progressing smoothly. The probability that Mexico would be able to maintain its stance regarding 32° 22′ north latitude and retain the Mesilla Valley seemed to lessen each month as Santa Anna's government either struggled with or ignored ever-pressing problems. The army had not been substantially strengthened, and that was his only support—as long as he could pay its generals. His project for a bank failed because the church refused to invest its wealth in the enterprise. The country suffered relentless Indian attacks on the frontier, and the liberals were ready to follow any general or governor who raised the cry of revolt. Thoughtful conservatives were gradually putting some distance between themselves and Santa Anna. His government's greatest problem was its lack of adequate revenue.[24]

The Marqués de la Ribera did not believe that Mexico would be able to support the Bartlett-García Conde line much longer. He reported to Madrid that persons who had read García Conde's correspondence informed him that the former boundary commissioner had perpetrated a fraud upon Bartlett, and the Mexican government had tacitly acquiesced in the happy result. He further informed the foreign ministry that the United States had entirely changed its posture toward the question. Ribera did not believe it possible to settle the question of La Mesilla peacefully. Rather, he expected the matter to be settled by force of arms or another cession of Mexican territory. He later informed his government that the Prussian ambassador, Baron von Richthofen, had expressed his conviction that war between Mexico and the United States was inevitable.[25]

Despite Mexico's justifiable fears regarding another onslaught of Manifest Destiny, there was in fact no real threat of war between the United States and Mexico, for Secretary of State William L. Marcy had already determined to resolve the dispute by negotiation. Marcy thought it well to replace Alfred Conkling, the United States minister to Mexico, whom he perhaps felt had been compromised by the events following Governor Lane's action at Doña Ana. The post now fell to James Gadsden, a railroad entrepreneur from South Carolina who immediately accepted the mission and reported to Washington for instructions.

Marcy held the opinion that the Joint United States and Mexican Boundary Commission had not determined the southern line of New Mexico according to the treaty since Surveyor Gray had not signed the pertinent documents. He considered the Joint Commission independent of both governments and its unanimous decision binding upon each party. The secretary urged Gadsden to impress upon Mexico that the line had not been established under the Treaty of Guadalupe Hidalgo. He stressed that former Governor Lane's bellicose pronouncement had not been approved, and that the United States had no intention of taking military possession of the disputed area, which he believed ought to be left in its present status until the solution of the controversy.

Secretary Marcy then turned his attention to the matter of a railroad. The treaty had provided for a road along either bank of the Gila River to the extent of one marine league. It was now known, he informed Gadsden, that it would be difficult to construct a railroad within the space provided by the treaty, but that a feasible route existed farther south of the river. Secretary Marcy believed the advantages of this railroad to Mexico would be such that it would readily agree to a cession of the required land. While it was difficult to determine how much territory would be needed without a survey, he thought the railroad should touch the Gulf of California.

Marcy then suggested to Gadsden a line beginning on the Río Grande eight miles north of El Paso del Norte and running a considerable distance beyond the western line of New Mexico, thence south about thirty minutes of latitude, and again west to the Gulf. Should Mexico find so large a cession unacceptable, Marcy suggested a line from the same point on the Río Grande continuing westward until it struck the Río San Pedro, and down that stream to its junction with the Gila. Marcy believed there would be a good route north of such a line. Should either line be acceptable to Mexico, efforts would be made to obtain certain knowledge as to the practicality of a rail route within the area.

The secretary directed Gadsden to approach the Mexican government on this subject as soon as possible. If the envoy found Mexico disposed to treat for a new line, Gadsden was instructed not to press a discussion of the United States' position regarding the Bartlett-García Conde line once having stated it. Marcy believed the expedient way to dispose of the question was to merge it with the negotiations for an entirely new boundary. He noted that it might be proper to provide for the settlement of all claims of United States citizens against Mexico as well as the claims of Mexican citizens against the United States under Article XI of the Treaty of Guadalupe Hidalgo, which required the United States to prevent Indian depredations against Mexico emanating from north of the boundary. He instructed Gadsden to secure a final settlement of these claims and a release from Article XI.[26]

Gadsden was from an old and respected family in Charleston, South Carolina. Following graduation from Yale College in 1806, he pursued a career variously as a merchant, military engineer, Florida planter, and politician. He gained some diplomatic experience when he negotiated the treaty with the Seminole Indians that opened northern Florida for settlement. Finding agriculture little to his liking and having no success in Florida's political life, Gadsden returned to Charleston in 1839 after the outbreak of the Seminole War of 1835–1844. Once back in his native South Carolina he entered commerce and soon became president of the Louisville, Charleston, and Cincinnati Railroad.

Gadsden had for some time been interested in linking Charleston with the West, but the company's problems and the financial panic of 1837 forced the enterprise to scale down its ambitions. By 1840 the company was known merely as the South Carolina Railroad. Nevertheless Gadsden continued to promote his project for a southern railroad linking Charleston with the Pacific. At the Memphis Commercial Convention of 1845 he urged the building of such a line and held out the route along the Gila River as the shortest and most economical route available. Gadsden's grand idea did not pay dividends, however, and in 1850 the stockholders voted him out of the presidency of the company. He was still the leading promoter of a southern rail route in 1853 when Secretary Marcy appointed him envoy to Mexico.[27]

Armed with his instructions and a map of the disputed area constructed by Andrew Gray, Colonel James Gadsden arrived at Veracruz in early August 1853. Once in the capital, the new United States envoy found Foreign Minister Manuel Díez de Bonilla a bit tedious, and his concern over courtesy and etiquette ridiculous. Gadsden could not abide all the ceremony and display connected with Santa Anna's government and could not appreciate Díez de Bonilla's pique when he failed to address the president as "His Most Serene Highness," the un-republican title that Santa Anna had recently adopted. While Gadsden suffered from his own form of pomposity and would barely be able to establish a working relationship with the foreign minister, the Marqués de la Ribera agreed with Gadsden that Díez de Bonilla reduced everything to the personal.[28]

Gadsden found Santa Anna's government one of usurpation resting solely upon the army. He believed the arrest and banishment of Santa Anna's opponents merely gave publicity to the dictator's fears; he was alienating his supporters while cultivating no other party. Above all Santa Anna's government needed money. Gadsden believed the only difficulty in the negotiations for another cession of territory would be the consideration to be paid. As his need for money became greater, Santa Anna's repugnance to an alteration of the boundary lessened, but he feared it would bring about a revolt that would topple his government.

Therefore Gadsden confidently requested new instructions as to whether he should treat for two or five of Mexico's frontier states, and inquired if the president of the United States had a contingency fund of some $10 million upon which he might draw to secure a quick purchase of territory if granted the opportunity. Calling for a naval force in the Gulf of Mexico and on the Pacific coast to balance the United States troops on the border, Gadsden advised showing Mexico the sword on all occasions, though covered by the olive branch.[29] He could not have been more blunt when he wrote to Marcy, "This is a Government of Plunder & necessity—we can rely on no other influences but on an appeal to both—we can afford to be liberal in our offerings to the first—but the acceptance depends on our not losing sight of the last...."[30]

Despite his dislike for the government with which he was to treat, Gadsden was making progress toward settling the boundary controversy. In an interview with Santa Anna on 25 September, the two men agreed that the disputed territory should remain in its present condition, free from military occupation on the part of both powers. Orders to that effect were to be sent to the appropriate frontier commanders. Santa Anna further agreed to begin negotiations for a new boundary in order to reconcile the conflicting interpretations of the Treaty of Guadalupe Hidalgo. Gadsden later informed Díez de Bonilla that the United States sought a desert and mountain boundary that would require the purchase of two or more of Mexico's northern states.[31] Such a boundary, Marcy believed, would be the best assurance against the possibility of future conflict between the two nations, but less than a century later that very boundary proved to be the beginning of conflict.

Díez de Bonilla at first refused to relinquish the Mesilla Valley and adhered only to the literal sense of Article V of the treaty; that his government could accept no agreement that implied otherwise. Santa Anna was now too desperate for money to spend much time posturing, and on 30 November Díez de Bonilla confidentially informed Gadsden that José Salazar Ylarregui, José Mariano Monterde, and the foreign minister himself would begin negotiations.[32]

Manuel Díez de Bonilla had been an extreme democrat in his youth, serving as the secretary of the York Rite Masonic Lodge, which the United States' first envoy to Mexico, Joel Poinsett, had organized. He played a principal part in the barracks revolt of the Acordada de México in 1828, which led to the sacking of the famous market known as the Parián, causing the ruin and death of many merchants, citizens, and foreigners alike.[33] He soon turned to conservatism, however, serving as Mexico's minister to the United Provinces of Central America and Colombia, and then briefly as minister of foreign relations. Along with his role as a prominent conservative, Díez de Bonilla was for many years the secretary of the Art Academy of San Carlos, and took pride in his extensive and select scientific library. After holding a variety of civic and honorary posts, he returned to the ministry of foreign relations.[34]

General José Mariano Monterde, after serving in the war for independence, became the *jefe político* and military commander of California, later representing both Californias in the national congress. In 1842 Monterde was appointed governor of Chihuahua where he founded a normal school, opened a music school, and established a military academy. He was also responsible for the construction of Chihuahua City's first theater, and found time to visit the ruins of Casas Grandes and write an essay on this intriguing archaeological site. Along with fighting the Apache, he organized an expedition to defend New Mexico from the Texas-Santa Fe expedition in 1844, assisting in giving the coup de grâce to the invaders, the desert plains already having done their work.[35]

Leaving the governorship, he was appointed director of the Colegio Militar in 1846, and led the defense of Chapultepec Castle, the military academy's home, during the war with the United States. In this most heroic moment of the war, Monterde was wounded and taken prisoner, but with the return of peace in 1848, resumed the headship of the academy. A longtime member of the Sección de Geografía y Estadística in the army, he was associated with the construction of the Carta General de la República. All his life a conservative, Monterde's many years of service on the northern frontier, especially in Chihuahua, made him a natural choice to assist in negotiating a new boundary line.[36] Salazar Ylarregui of course knew the area better than anyone, and along with Monterde would provide an invaluable source of information upon which the foreign minister could draw. Nevertheless, Díez de Bonilla himself carried the brunt of the negotiation with Gadsden.

While Gadsden had been fencing with Díez de Bonilla, Secretary of State Marcy sent him new instructions to be relayed to the United States minister verbally by special messenger Christopher L. Ward. Marcy had directed Ward to commit these instructions to memory and carry no written material concerning them on his secret mission. The secretary reasoned that should these instructions become known to persons other than Santa Anna and his most trusted advisers, the promise of reaching a favorable agreement regarding the boundary would not be fulfilled. Marcy thought that since the situation in Mexico was critical and Santa Anna would need ready money to maintain his position, a liberal cession might be had. At the same time, however, should such negotiations become public, that fact would not only defeat the negotiations, but also overthrow Santa Anna, whose unlimited powers would then be circumscribed and the desired cession unobtainable. It was imperative, therefore, that Ward carry no written instructions of which he might be despoiled en route to Mexico.

Gadsden's new instructions suggested several proposals for a new boundary that variously threw the entire Río Grande Valley, Baja California, and a vast territory into the United States for which he was empowered to pay up to $50 million. If none of Marcy's more exuberant proposals was acceptable to Mexico, Gadsden was to seek an alteration of the line that would give the United States a rail route to the Pacific. Marcy thought a line on the thirty-second parallel to the Gulf of California would provide a suitable railway, but would not be a good boundary.

It was imperative therefore that Gadsden obtain a release from Article XI of the Treaty of Guadalupe Hidalgo which charged the United States to prevent Indian spoliation against the northern states of Mexico. For this and a settlement of all claims against the United States, Gadsden was authorized to pay up to $15 million. The secretary further informed Gadsden that he was vested with discretionary power to modify any of the boundary proposals. One of the modifications Marcy suggested was to deflect the line from the 111th meridian so as to run directly to the mouth of the Gila. This would secure an uninhabited boundary, but would give the line an awkward contour and deprive the United States of a port on the Gulf of California. Marcy did not believe Mexico's internal condition would permit a protracted negotiation and therefore urged Gadsden not to complicate discussion with matters other than the boundary and the reciprocal adjustment of claims.[37]

With his new instructions, Gadsden met with Díez de Bonilla, Salazar Ylarregui, and Monterde at the Palacio Nacional on 10 December and exchanged credentials. Gadsden then presented his treaty proposal. Throughout December the Mexican negotiators consistently refused to alienate Baja California or the Río Grande Valley. Díez de Bonilla informed Gadsden that he was authorized to discuss an alteration of the boundary only to provide the United States with an adequate rail route. The foreign minister then proposed a line following that of the treaty of 1848 between the two Californias to the Río Colorado, and down its deepest channel to a point two marine leagues from the northernmost part of the Gulf of California. The line was to continue directly to the intersection of the 111th meridian and the thirty-first parallel, thence directly to the Río Grande at 31° 47′ 30″ north latitude, following the deepest channel of the river to the Gulf of Mexico. El Paso del Norte and the entire Gulf of California were to remain with Mexico.

This proposal was acceptable to Gadsden on the condition that Lake Guzmán fell within the United States, and that the line ran far enough south of the lake to provide a route for a railroad. Díez de Bonilla agreed. The negotiators further agreed that all the stipulations of the Treaty of Guadalupe Hidalgo would be extended to the citizens and property of the ceded territory. To delineate the new boundary, each nation was to appoint one commissioner to meet at El Paso del Norte three months after the exchange of ratifications. Gadsden had originally suggested that each government name three boundary commissioners to survey the new line, but drawing on past experience Díez de Bonilla wisely held that a single commissioner for each nation would promote greater harmony. Gadsden then insisted that there should be at least an independent arbitrator attached to the Joint Commission to settle any disputes that might arise during the tracing of the line. When Díez de Bonilla observed that no controversy could emerge since the new boundary consisted solely of mathematical lines, Gadsden acquiesced.[38]

Gadsden then proposed the revocation of Article XI, explaining that the United States had complied with its stipulations as far as practical, but had never given the article the interpretation Mexico had placed upon it; that it was impossible to distinguish upon which side of the border Indian depredations had originated. In truth the United States' efforts to prevent Indian incursions upon the northern states of Mexico had been completely inadequate. At no time following the Treaty of Guadalupe Hidalgo did Congress appropriate sufficient funds for the number of cavalry needed to meet Washington's obligations under Article XI.

When the United States agreed to this article, the government knew nothing of the nature or numbers of the Indians it had willingly agreed to restrain, nor the cost of doing so. The indemnity to be paid Mexico for the devastation caused by these Indian raids threatened to become an enormous drain on the treasury. It was imperative that the United States be free of this burden. To settle all claims of United States citizens against Mexico, release from Article XI, and the cession of territory, Gadsden and Díez de Bonilla agreed that the United States would pay $20 million. On 30 December 1853 the negotiators on the part of the United States and Mexico signed the treaty draft, which was to remain secret until ratified by the United States.[39]

President Pierce received the treaty on 19 January and after discussing its provisions with the cabinet, sent it to the Senate. After much discussion during secret executive sessions, the Senate demanded all correspondence and documents regarding the negotiations. The major difficulties the treaty faced in the Senate were the opposition of the antislavery faction and a smaller group that demanded a larger cession of territory including access to the Gulf of California. While efforts to increase the territory to be ceded and obtain a port on the Gulf were defeated, the Senate reduced the consideration to $7 million. Unable to agree on other portions of the treaty, the Senate voted against ratification on 17 April 1854.[40]

Senator Thomas Jefferson Rusk of Texas, ever vigilant in his quest to win a southern railway to the Pacific, had already prepared a fallback position on the amount of territory to be purchased from Mexico. Three days earlier he had asked Major Emory if a line beginning on the Río Grande at 31° 47′ north latitude, running west 100 miles, thence south twenty miles, and again west to the 111° of longitude, and from that point in a straight line to the Colorado River twenty miles south of its junction with the Río Gila would provide a route to the California coast. Rusk was interested in a railroad, not territory.[41]

From a report requested of Lieutenant Whipple exactly one year before, Emory had a ready answer. Whipple believed he possessed satisfactory data, including barometric heights and topographical sketches to show that a route existed between the Río Grande and the San Pedro and westward around the bases of mountains and over plains to the vicinity of Tucson, then directly to the Pima villages on the Gila. Emory was therefore able to answer the senator with conviction that such a boundary would provide a route to the Pacific.[42]

The Senate voted to reconsider the treaty on 18 April. After approving an amendment to increase the compensation to $10 million, and another regarding a transit concession across the Isthmus of Tehuantepec, the Senate voted to ratify the treaty on 25 April by a vote of thirty-three to twelve. The Senate had also amended the article concerning the boundary that now began on the Río Grande at 31° 47′ north latitude, ran west for 100 miles, then south to the parallel of 31° 20′, and west again to the 111th meridian, and from that point directly to the Río Colorado twenty miles south of its junction with the Gila.[43]

United States minister to Mexico James Gadsden was upset with the amended treaty. He considered that it lacked reciprocity and could only be repugnant to Mexico. His greatest objection was that it reopened many issues of which the original treaty had in his opinion disposed. He felt the amended treaty was being imposed upon the government of Mexico, which would be justified in rejecting it.[44] Marcy also regretted that the treaty as it emerged from the Senate failed to provide for the adjustment of the claims of United States citizens against Mexico. He further agreed that the line of the original treaty was preferable to that selected by the Senate. Marcy did not, however, believe the treaty lacked reciprocity, nor was it being imposed upon Mexico. That nation was free either to accept or reject the treaty. He noted the considerable effort to defeat the treaty in and out of the Senate, but emphasized that nothing better for Mexico could be obtained. He impressed upon Gadsden that neither additional amendments nor a different treaty could be passed through the Senate should Santa Anna reject it.[45]

Santa Anna and Díez de Bonilla agreed with Gadsden that the treaty was not reciprocal, but rather onerous and offensive to the weaker contracting party, and complained of its failure to adjust the issues between the two countries. While there were rumors that Santa Anna had decided to reject the treaty, he was unable to do so because of the penury of his government and his failing position in Mexico. He therefore gave his envoy in Washington, Juan Almonte, full powers to accept it.[46]

Though eternally condemned for selling part of the national patrimony, Santa Anna had little choice but to accept the treaty. His government was living hand to mouth for lack of adequate revenue and his efforts to increase the size and efficiency of the army had been only partly successful. He could not have resisted United States power if hostilities had broken out.[47] While he needed money, Santa Anna had to take the possibility of United States aggression seriously. The United States was reinforcing its military position on the border and had increased the size of the army during the past year.[48]

Of equal concern were the recurring filibustering expeditions against Mexico's northern states and the apparent inability of the United States to prevent them. While they came to nothing in the end, and in retrospect are often reminiscent of scenes from Gilbert and Sullivan, the Mexican government could not ignore William Walker's attempted seizure of Sonora and Baja California in November 1853, when Gadsden's negotiations were just getting under way.[49] Mexico's minister to Spain, Buenaventura Vivó, believed Santa Anna had every reason to fear another war with the United States.[50] Santa Anna's fears regarding war seemed justified, as concern over United States aggression was not entirely abated by the treaty.

A few days after the exchange of ratifications, a similar expedition of some fifty North Americans landed on Arenas Island in the Gulf of Campeche in July 1854, ostensibly to extract guano. For this purpose they brought along 100 guns and three twelve-pounders.[51] While the warship *Iturbide* with sufficient force to apprehend the *"ladrones de guano"* and seize their arms soon left Veracruz, Mexico could not help but be concerned.[52] This also brought back to memory earlier threats to Yucatán and Baja California.[53] As though intending to stir troubled waters, Gadsden, in a conversation with the Marqués de la Ribera in late December 1854, remarked that he expected Mexico's northern states would ultimately fall to the United States, and that a proper boundary would run from Tampico to Mazatlán and include those two ports.[54]

War threat or no, Santa Anna could expect no help from the European powers. Buenaventura Vivó had had no success in securing for Mexico an alliance with Spain supported by France and England. Spain in fact seemed more disturbed with Santa Anna's government than desirous of an alliance with it. Though Spain had earlier acquiesced in Santa Anna's request to recruit in Spain, Ribera, who yet remained in Mexico, protested the enlistment of Spanish officers, sergeants, and corporals to serve in the Mexican army. Santa Anna's recruitment methods in Havana ignored the fact that the men had not received discharge papers or passports and therefore were considered deserters from Spain's military forces.[55] Nor did they have any formal written contract with the Mexican government. Ambassador Lozano y Armenta feared that the introduction of Spanish officers into Mexico's military establishment could only arouse hostility toward Spaniards generally. Worse yet, they might end up participating in the country's numerous barracks revolts.[56] Another difficulty was Santa Anna's navigation act of January 1854, which threatened Spain's commerce by calling for a 50 percent tariff on nations that did not treat Mexican ships with reciprocity.[57] After prolonged bickering between Díez de Bonilla and the Spanish envoy, Santa Anna suspended the irksome navigation act, but the damage to Hispano-Mexican relations had been done.[58]

Despite the growing friction between the two countries, Santa Anna's program for Mexico's regeneration had not changed. In a four-hour-long conference with Lozano y Armenta a few days after he had instructed Almonte to accept the amended treaty, he again espoused his belief that, while he needed to rebuild the army, only a monarchy could save Mexico from the United States. He impressed upon Lozano y Armenta his fear that a United States invasion was imminent, that Mexico and Spain had a common enemy, the United States, and informed the ambassador of his instructions to Buenaventura Vivó to work for a defensive alliance.[59]

The outbreak of the Crimean War and Spain's internal disorders of course obviated the success of such negotiations. Spain was more interested in settling the debt question against Mexico and may well have used the negotiations for an alliance as a means to that end.[60] In his eagerness to obtain his alliance, Santa Anna agreed to a claims convention that was decidedly favorable to Spain in November 1853, when he was just beginning his talks with Gadsden. The agreement broke down a little more than a year later, and ultimately left Mexico's relations with Spain in a shambles.[61] The foreign ministry in Madrid did not think a Mexican monarchy possible, and did not believe the situation in Mexico lent itself to fulfilling Santa Anna's dream of an alliance with Spain. The fleet was needed to protect Cuba, and the Spanish economy would not permit costly and doubtful enterprises. The final word from Madrid was that such an alliance would be nothing but a burden for Spain and to the advantage of neither nation.[62]

Though Santa Anna's project for an alliance failed, it could not but cause some concern on the part of the United States.[63] Gadsden's dispatches were filled with rumors of European intervention in Mexican affairs, and consistently in favor of the liberal leadership of the Revolution of Ayutla, which had erupted in March 1854.[64] It seems clear then, that if Santa Anna desired to remain in power, he had no alternative but to accept the treaty. Yet in the end the $10 million from the sale of La Mesilla was not enough to save Santa Anna's government. Indeed, the Gadsden Treaty gave much needed ammunition to the leaders of Ayutla who brought about the dictator's downfall a little more than a year after the exchange of ratifications at the Mexican legation in Washington. By that time the new Joint United States and Mexican Boundary

Commission had nearly finished running the survey of the new line through some of the most inhospitable terrain it had yet faced. Gadsden and Díez de Bonilla were correct in their objection to the amended treaty's failure to settle all outstanding issues between the two countries, but that was a goal perhaps unreachable at the time and remains beyond grasp to the present day.

CHAPTER IX NOTES

[1] Antoine y Zayas to Primer Secretario de Estado y del Despacho, 30 Sep., 2 Oct., 3 Nov. 1852, 2 Jan. 1853, "Correspondencia con Embajadas y Legaciones," Legajo 1652 (Archivo del Ministerio de Asuntos Exteriores, Madrid; Hereafter cited as AMAE, Leg. 1652).

[2] Antoine y Zayas to Primer Secretario de Estado y del Despacho, 1 Feb., 3 Mar. 1853, ibid.

[3] Clyde G. Bushnell, "The Military and Political Career of Juan Alvarez, 1790–1867," (Ph.D. diss., The University of Texas, 1958), p. 246.

[4] Ribera to Primer Secretario de Estado y del Despacho, 30 Apr. 1853, AMAE, Leg. 1652.

[5] Real Orden No. 391 anexa al Despacho No. 5 to Ribera, 21 Jun. 1853, "Correspondencia del Ministro de España en México (Marqués de la Ribera), con el Primer Secretario de Estado y del Despacho Español ...1853–54," Legajo 6–18–76 (Archivo de la Secretaría de Relaciones Exteriores, Mexico City; Hereafter cited as ASRE, Leg. 6–18–76).

[6] Ribera to Primer Secretario de Estado y del Despacho, 28 Apr., 1 May 1853, AMAE, Leg. 1652.

[7] Wilfrid Hardy Callcott, *Santa Anna, the Story of an Enigma Who Once Was Mexico* (Hamden: 1964), pp. 286–88; Gadsden to Marcy, 18 Sep. 1853, Despatches, NA, RG/59.

[8] Callcott, *Santa Anna*, pp. 287–94.

[9] Dexter Perkins, *The Monroe Doctrine, 1826–1867* (Baltimore: 1933), p. 326.

[10] Ribera to Primer Secretario de Estado, 23 Jun. 1853, AMAE, Leg. 1652; Buenaventura Vivó, *Memorias de Buenaventura Vivó, ministro de Méjico en España durante los años 1853, 1854 y 1855* (Madrid: 1856), pp. 3, 53–54.

[11] Ribera to Primer Secretario de Estado, 26, 28 Jul. 1853, Angel Calderón de la Barca to Ribera, 23 Sep., 28 Dec. 1853, ASRE, Leg. 6–18–76.

[12] Ribera to Primer Secretario de Estado y del Despacho, 30 Apr. 1853, AMAE, Leg. 1652.

[13] Ministerio de Asuntos Exteriores to Ribera, 2 Jun. 1853, ibid; Gadsden to Marcy, 2 Sep. 1854, Despatches, NA, RG/59.

[14] Ministro de Asuntos Exteriores to Ribera, 6 Aug. 1853, [Cipher], AMAE, Leg. 1652

[15] Raymond Carr, *Spain, 1808–1939* (London: 1966), pp. 243–51.

[16] Ministro de Asuntos Exteriores to Ribera, 26 Aug. 1853, Ribera to Primer Secretario de Estado y del Despacho, 31 Aug. 1853, AMAE, Leg. 1652.

[17] Vivó to Ministro de Relaciones, 21, 23 Jan. 1854, "Instrucciones giradas a nuestros Ministros en Inglaterra, Francia y España ...," Legajo 6–1-8 (Archivo de la Secretaría de Relaciones Exteriores, Mexico City; Hereafter cited as ASRE, Leg. 6–1-8); Vivó, *Memorias*, pp. 85–87.

[18] Castillo y Lanzas to Ministro de Relaciones, 20 Jan. 1854, ASRE, Leg. 6–1-8.

[19] Vivó to Ministro de Relaciones, 23 Apr. 1854, ibid.

[20] Vivó, *Memorias*, pp. 88–89.

[21]   Ramírez to [?], 24 Sep. 1853, Salazar Ylarregui to Ministro de Relaciones, 5 Nov. 1853, Díez de Bonilla to Trías, 18 Nov. 1853, Trías to Ministro de Relaciones, 15 Dec. 1853, all in "Ricardo Ramírez ..., las tendencias antipatrióticas de algunos mexicanos vecinos del Paso del Norte...." 1853–54, Legajo 1–5-916 (Archivo de la Secretaría de Relaciones Exteriores, Mexico City; Hereafter cited as ASRE, Leg. 1–5-916).

[22]   *El Siglo XIX* (Mexico City), 11 May 1853; passim, ASRE, Leg. 1–5-916.

[23]   Trías to Ministro de Relaciones, 30 Jun. 1849, passim, "El Gobernador de Chihuahua se refiere a la traslación de familias mexicanas de Nuevo México...." 1849, Legajo 2–13-2971 (Archivo de la Secretaría de Relaciones Exteriores, Mexico City); Jaques and Zuloaga to Trías, 1 Mar. 1853, ASRE, Leg. 1–5-916; AGN, Gob., Sec. s/s, C: 347-E.3.

[24]   Ribera to Primer Secretario de Estado y del Despacho, 1, 31 Aug. 1853, AMAE, Leg. 1652; Callcott, *Santa Anna*, p. 294; Gadsden to Marcy, 5 Sep. 1853, Despatches, NA, RG/59.

[25]   Ribera to Primer Secretario de Estado, 2 Jul., 30 Sep., 2 Nov. 1853, AMAE, Leg. 1652.

[26]   Marcy to Gadsden, 12, 24 May, 15 Jul. 1853, Instructions, NA, RG/59.

[27]   Paul Neff Garber, *The Gadsden Treaty* (Gloucester: 1959), pp. 74–79; James Gadsden, "Commercial Spirit at the South," *De Bow's Commercial Review*, Old Series, II (Sep., 1846), p. 132.

[28]   Gadsden to Marcy, 4 Aug., 3 Oct. 1853, Despatches, NA, RG/59; Ribera to Primer Secretario de Estado y del Despacho, 2 Mar. 1854, ASRE, Leg. 6–18-76.

[29]   Gadsden to Marcy, 17 Aug., 5, 18 Sep., 3 Oct. 1853, Despatches, NA, RG/59; Antoine y Zayas to Primer Secretario de Estado y del Despacho, 5 Dec. 1855, "Correspondencia con Embajadas y Legaciones," Legajo 1653 (Archivo del Ministerio de Asuntos Exteriores, Madrid).

[30]   Gadsden to Marcy, 18 Oct. 1853, Despatches, NA, RG/59.

[31]   Gadsden to Marcy, 3 Oct. 1853, ibid. The correspondence between Gadsden and Díez de Bonilla is also found in "Valle de La Mesilla"—Segunda Parte, Legajo 1–2-566 (II), (Archivo de la Secretaría de Relaciones Exteriores, Mexico City).

[32]   Gadsden to Marcy, 3, 21 Nov., 4 Dec. 1853, Despatches, NA, RG/59; Díez de Bonilla to Ministro de Guerra y Marina, 6 Dec. 1853, AHDN, Cancelados, Exp. 2–852, II, folio 297.

[33]   *Diccionario Porrúa*, I, 16; Ribera to Primer Secretario de Estado y del Despacho, 2 Mar. 1854, ASRE, Leg. 6–18-76.

[34]   *Diccionario Porrúa*, I, 653.

[35]   Carreño, *Jefes del ejército*, pp. 225–27; Sosa, *Biografías de mexicanos distinguidos*, pp. 663–66; Santa Anna to Monterde, 18 Jul. 1843, José María Tornel to Monterde, 19 Jul. 1843, AHDN, Cancelados, Exp. 2–852, I, folios 90, 225–26, 228–29; Ralph Emerson Twitchell, *The Leading Facts of New Mexican History* (Cedar Rapids: 1912), II, 82, 89.

[36]   AHDN, Cancelados, Exp. 2–852, I, folios 9, 41, 49, 68, 180, 203; *Diccionario Porrúa*, II, 1,394–95; Juan López de Escalera, *Diccionario biográfico y de historia de México* (México: 1964), pp. 722–23; Smith, *The War with Mexico*, II, 411.

[37]   Marcy to Ward, [Cipher], 22 Oct. 1853, Despatches, NA, RG/76; Ward to Marcy, 31 Oct. 1853, Ward to Gadsden, 14 Nov. 1853, Despatches from Special Agents of the Department of State, XIX, NA, RG/59; Marcy to Gadsden, 22 Oct. 1853, Diplomatic Instructions of the Department of State, Special Missions, III, NA, RG/59; Marcy to Gadsden, 6 Jan. 1854, Instructions, NA, RG/59.

[38]   Alberto María Carreño, *La diplomacia extraordinaria entre México y Estados Unidos 1789–1947*, (México: 1961), II, 93.

[39]   "Notes of Diplomatic Conferences for the adjustment of the various issues between the U. States and Mexico," 10, 16, 22, 23, 24, 30 Dec. 1853, Despatches, NA, RG/59; J. Fred Rippy, "The Indians of the Southwest in the Diplomacy of the United States and Mexico, 1848–1853," *Hispanic American Historical Review*, II (Aug., 1919), pp. 373, 377–79, 392–96. For the text of the treaty as concluded, see *Message from the President of the United States ...*, 33rd Cong., 1st sess., 1854, H. Ex. Doc. 109 (Serial 726), pp. 2–5 [Hereafter cited as HED 109 (762)].

[40] Garber, *The Gadsden Treaty*, pp. 115–26.

[41] Rusk to Emory, 14 Apr. 1854, Folder 7, Emory Papers; Gadsden to Rusk, 5 Oct. 1853, Davis to Rusk, 8 Nov. 1853, Gray to Rusk, [n. d.], Rusk Papers.

[42] Emory to Whipple, 19 Apr. 1853, Whipple to Emory, 19 Apr. 1853, Emory to Abert, 20 Apr. 1853, Emory to Rusk, 15 Apr. 1854, Folders 50, 7, Emory Papers.

[43] Garber, *The Gadsden Treaty*, pp. 126–31. For the text of the amended treaty, see Bevans, *Treaties and Other International Agreements*, IX, 813. On the Tehuantepec issue, see J. Fred Rippy, "Diplomacy of the United States and Mexico Regarding the Isthmus of Tehuantepec, 1848–1860," *Mississippi Valley Historical Review*, II (Mar., 1920), pp. 503–31.

[44] Gadsden to Marcy, 9, 17 Jun. 1854, 5 Jan. 1855, Despatches, NA, RG/59.

[45] Marcy to John S. Cripps, 6 May 1854, Marcy to Gadsden, 11 May, 13 Oct. 1854, Instructions, NA, RG/59.

[46] Gadsden to Marcy, 9 Jun. 1854, with enclosure of Díez de Bonilla to Gadsden, 8 Jun. 1854, Despatches, NA, RG/59; Lozano y Armenta to Primer Secretario de Estado y del Despacho, 30 May 1854, AMAE, Leg. 1652; HED 109 (726) p. 1.

[47] Francisco Bulnes, *Juárez y las revoluciones de Ayutla y de reforma* (México: 1905), pp. 118–22; Richard A. Johnson, *The Mexican Revolution of Ayutla, 1854–1855* (Rock Island: 1939), pp. 35–37; Callcott, *Santa Anna*, pp. 294–96; Ann Fears Crawford, ed., *The Eagle: The Autobiography of Santa Anna* (Austin: 1988), pp. 143–48; Decreto del Presidente Ignacio Comonfort, 10 Jan. 1856, AGN, Gob., Legajo 1041 (1), Caja 1, Exp. 1.

[48] Emory Upton, *The Military Policy of the United States* (New York: 1968), p. 223.

[49] Gadsden to Marcy, 31 Aug., 18 Nov. 1853, Despatches, NA, RG/59; De la Rosa to Crittenden, 23 Oct. 1851, De la Rosa to Webster, 13 Nov. 1851, Almonte to Marcy, 21 Dec. 1853, 22 May, 19 Oct. 1854, Notes from the Mexican Legation in the United States to the Department of State, 1821–1906, Record Group 59 (National Archives, Washington, D. C.); Santiago Vidaurri to Ministro de Gobernación, 14 Sep., 6 Nov. 1853, Manuel María Gándara to Ministro de Gobernación, 11 Nov. 1853, AGN, Gob., Sec. s/s, C: 419-E. 8, 12, 13, Legajo 251, Caja 1, Exp. 1; J. Fred Rippy, "Anglo-American Filibusters and the Gadsden Treaty," *Hispanic American Historical Review*, V (May, 1922), p. 169.

[50] Vivó to Ministro de Relaciones, 21 Jan. 1854, ASRE, Leg. 6–1-8.

[51] "Memorandum," 23 Sep. 1851, with Despatch 242, Lozano y Armenta to Díez de Bonilla, 7 Jul. 1854, "Memorandum" of Mariano Díaz, 11 Jul. 1854, Lozano y Armenta to Primer Secretario de Estado y del Despacho, 25 Oct. 1854, all in "Política: Méjico-1836–1856," Legajo 2545 (Archivo del Ministerio de Asuntos Exteriores, Madrid; Hereafter cited as AMAE, Leg. 2545); José López de Bustamante to Primer Secretario de Estado y del Despacho, 1 Nov. 1853, AMAE, Leg. 1652.

[52] Díez de Bonilla to Lozano y Armenta, 8 Jul. 1854, AMAE, Leg. 2545.

[53] Ministro de Relaciones to Ministro de Guerra y Marina, 11 Jul. 1850, José María Moreno to Ministro de Relaciones, 24, 31 Jan. 1852, AGN. Gob., Sec. s/s, C: 383-E. 15, C: 404-E. 10.

[54] Ribera to Primer Secretario de Estado y del Despacho, 22 Dec. 1854, AMAE, Leg. 1652.

[55] Ribera to Primer Secretario de Estado y del Despacho, 30 Aug. 1853, AMAE, Leg. 2545.

[56] Legación de España en Méjico to Vice Cónsul de España en Mazatlán, 1 Nov. 1852, Lozano y Armenta to Primer Secretario de Estado y del Despacho, 28 Sep. 1854, Mariano Díaz to Ministro de Asuntos Exteriores, 2 Dec. 1854, ibid.

[57] Ribera to Primer Secretario de Estado y del Despacho, 28 Feb. 1854 and passim, ibid.

[58] Richard A. Johnson, "Spanish-Mexican Diplomatic Relations, 1853–1855," *Hispanic American Historical Review*, XXI (Nov., 1941), p. 571.

[59] Lozano y Armenta to Primer Secretario de Estado y del Despacho, 1 Jul. 1854 [Cipher], AMAE, Leg. 1652.

[60] Johnson, "Spanish-Mexican Diplomatic Relations," p. 573; Vivó to Ministro de Relaciones, 21 Jan. 1854, ASRE, Leg. 6–1-8; Lorenzo Carrera, Manuel Gargollo, Bernardo Copca, *España y Méjico en el asunto de la convención española* (Madrid: 1855), pp. 32–34.

[61] Johnson, "Spanish-Mexican Diplomatic Relations," pp. 564–72.

[62] Ministro de Asuntos Exteriores to Lozano y Armenta, 21, 22 Sep. 1854, AMAE, Leg. 1652.

[63] Gadsden to Marcy, 18 Oct. 1853, Despatches, NA, RG/59; Johnson, "Spanish-Mexican Diplomatic Relations," pp. 572–73.

[64] Gadsden to Marcy, 19 Feb., 18 May 1855, Despatches, NA, RG/59.

 QUITOVAQUITA

"A dull, wide waste lies before you ...,
The eye may watch in vain for the flight of a bird...."

Nathaniel Michler, Lieutenant,
U.S. Topographical Engineers

The man most eager to draw this imaginary line through the desert was Major William Emory, who had called for a boundary south of the thirty-second parallel since his rapid reconnaissance of the area during the war. He now enlisted the support of Senator Rusk of Texas who vigorously placed Emory's cause before President Pierce. Secretary of War Jefferson Davis, who was pleased with Emory's efforts in favor of a southern rail route, also pressed for Emory's appointment, which encountered little opposition in the Senate.[1] To avoid the paralysis of the previous Joint Commission, the treaty provided for each nation to appoint one commissioner to direct the survey.[2] Thus on 15 August 1854, Emory received his appointment not only as commissioner but as chief astronomer and surveyor as well. Secretary of the Interior McClelland informed him that he was to be guided by the previous commissioners' instructions from the Departments of State and Interior. The secretary further instructed him to enter into an agreement with the Mexican commissioner to send a surveying team to the Pacific coast to work eastward, while the main party carried the survey westward from El Paso del Norte.[3]

After accepting the appointment with the understanding that it would not affect his commission in the army, Emory quickly facilitated such an arrangement.[4] Lieutenant Nathaniel Michler of the Topographical Engineers sailed with a surveying party for San Diego, California, and from there marched to the Colorado where he was to meet Captain Francisco Jiménez and his Mexican team. Because of the treaty's late ratification, the need to organize the commission, and the difficulties of the topography to be traversed, Emory found it impossible to reach El Paso del Norte by 30 September as required. To fulfill the dictates of the treaty, Emory sent the reliable Frank Wheaton ahead posthaste with a letter to Mexican commissioner Salazar Ylarregui urging him to begin operations without him so that there might be no delay.[5] Wheaton reached El Paso del Norte on the morning of 19 September, but by 22 October had received no word of the Mexican commission or even its whereabouts.[6] Not until early November was Wheaton able to report to Emory the expected arrival of the Mexican commissioner.[7]

Emory meanwhile began to organize the new commission under his charge. All the astronomical and surveying instruments, equipment, and provisions were gathered and shipped from New York. Recalling Bartlett's problems with the Indians, he purchased fifty rifles and 5,000 rounds of ammunition for the commission's protection.[8] Applying his usual energy to the task, Emory got his entire commission to Indianola by 25 September, although not without serious difficulties. Yellow fever raged in epidemic form along the Gulf coast of Texas. Moritz von Hippel, whom Emory was glad to have returned to the commission as first assistant surveyor, reported that six persons in his Galveston hotel were sick of "this dreadful maladie."[9] Several men of the United States commission were stricken with the infirmity, while an outbreak of smallpox also visited the region.[10] As Emory's party was crossing the Gulf, a great storm lashed Matagorda Bay from 17–19 September, leveling the town of Matagorda and inundating much of the surrounding country. The storm caused a delay of one month in starting the journey to San Antonio, but Emory was so thankful at having suffered no damage to the equipment and stores of the commission, "that every other adverse circumstance seemed trifling."[11]

After procuring a sufficient number of mules and enlisting teamsters to drive them, Emory departed Indianola for San Antonio on 26 October. The United States commission consisted of men trusted and well seasoned for the work. Along with von Hippel were Charles Radziminski serving as Emory's secretary, Lieutenant Charles Turnbull of the Topographical Engineers, the able Marine Chandler as a general topographical assistant, and J. H. Clark as first assistant astronomer. Other assistants were Charles Weiss, James Houston, and Hugh Campbell, all of whom had previous service with the boundary survey. There was also the usual number of teamsters, cooks, laborers, and servants, altogether about one hundred men. Captain Edmund K. Smith and a company of the Seventh Infantry served as escort. The journey proved slow because the heavy rains of the storm had made the roads impassable in some stretches, but aside from this irritant it was uneventful, save for the dismissal of several teamsters who were unashamedly drunk at every opportunity.[12] As it was, Emory did not reach El Paso del Norte until 29 November 1854.[13]

Mexican commissioner Salazar Ylarregui also had difficulties in reaching El Paso del Norte in good time to abide by the demands of the treaty. The news Frank Wheaton received from Chihuahua was not very hopeful. The rumors he relayed to Emory were that Santa Anna's government had spent the entire $7 million thus far received from the sale of the Mesilla strip and was directing all its energies toward the liberal revolutionaries of Ayutla, with no money left for the survey.[14] Salazar Ylarregui did indeed have difficulty in obtaining money enough to begin the survey and would be continually plagued by the lack of support for the commission under his direction. He had been unable to leave Mexico City until 14 September, as he had not received the appropriation for the survey until the previous day.[15] The Mexican commission reached Chihuahua City on 20 October and after a few days' rest took the line of march for El Paso del Norte. Arriving on 5 November, he explained to Wheaton that he was prepared to begin the survey, but preferred to await Emory, by which time he expected his more accurate instruments to have arrived.[16] When Emory arrived a full three weeks later, he received a warm welcome from his friend, José Salazar Ylarregui, with whom he had worked so closely over the past several years.[17] Although neither commissioner had been able to arrive on time, they were now prepared to proceed westward with the survey while Lieutenant Michler and Captain Jiménez worked eastward from the Colorado.

Salazar Ylarregui and Emory met formally on 4 December, exchanged credentials and organized the Joint Commission to run the new boundary.[18] The Gadsden Treaty provided a line that began on the Río Grande at:

> The point where the parallel of 31° 47′ north latitude crosses the same, thence due west one hundred miles, thence south to the parallel of 31° 20′ north latitude, thence along the said parallel of 31° 20′ to the 111th meridian of longitude west of Greenwich, thence in a straight line to a point on the Colorado river twenty english [*sic*] miles below the junction of the Gila and Colorado rivers, thence up the middle of the said river Colorado until it intersects the present line between the United States and Mexico.[19]

It was first agreed to determine the initial point on the Río Grande. After making the necessary observations, the commissioners met on 9 January 1855 and ascertained that the difference in their individual calculations for the parallel of 31° 47′ was 84/100 of one second. It was mutually agreed to take the mean as 31° 47′.

Having determined the direction of the line westward, the Joint Commission met at El Paso del Norte on 12 January 1855 and resolved to place one monument of dressed stone as near the river as the terrain would permit, and another of dressed stone at the extremity of 31° 47′. The two commissioners also agreed to place a pyramid of rough stone and mortar where the line struck the nearest range of hills, and a second where the road from El Paso del Norte struck the new boundary. They further decided that Salazar Ylarregui would oversee the erection of the three monuments near the river. Several other pyramids of rough stone and mortar were to be erected at appropriate points along the line, assuming sufficient water and stone were available. The Joint Commission then met on 31 January and laid the corner stone of the first monument.[20] Meanwhile the monument Bartlett had erected at 32° 22′ had been destroyed. Colonel Miles reported to Emory from Fort Fillmore that it had taken three men three days to destroy "this piece of folly."[21]

Emory had already sent his entire astronomical team to the end of the 100 mile line and intended to move his camp to the north-south line between 31° 47′ and 31° 20′ as soon as possible, but was now confronted with the inability of the Mexican commissioner to undertake his half of the survey. Aside from Michler's party at the junction of the Gila and Colorado rivers, Emory then had on the line one astronomical party from which two parties could easily be formed, two surveying teams, and an escort of sixty soldiers. At the same time Salazar Ylarregui had but one party with an escort of thirty troops.[22] This appeared a bit strange since Secretary McClelland had on two occasions impressed upon Emory the Mexican government's desire for a timely completion of the work. The distressed situation of Santa Anna's government, which was but a few months from collapse, no doubt precluded any meaningful support from reaching the Mexican commission.[23]

While Emory understood this, he had received far more interesting information from the New York shipping firm of Howland and Aspinwall. Its owners, William E. Howland and William H. Aspinwall, privately informed him that Mexico City had urged haste upon Salazar Ylarregui and desired all possible cooperation on the part of Emory and the United States government. In their letter of 21 December from New York, Howland and Aspinwall pointed out that the United States enjoyed an advantage in Mexico's urgency and consequent inclination to waive any discussion of doubtful questions regarding the running and marking of the line. The two men suggested that McClelland could not mention this in his official correspondence, but they had been given an intimation that the Department of the Interior wished Emory not to lose sight of this advantage.[24] Before Emory could possibly have received this information, he made an official demand of Salazar Ylarregui on 22 January that he put on the line a force equal to that of the United States commission, at the same time noting the urgings of the Mexican minister in Washington for greater speed on Emory's part. While Salazar Ylarregui sent

Emory's entreaty on to Mexico City, he replied that he did not have at that time the means to adhere to the United States commissioner's request.[25]

When the Joint Commission again met on 26 January, Emory stated his intention to proceed westward with the survey in early February. Salazar Ylarregui rejoined that he would be unable to move so soon for lack of an adequate escort, but would follow as quickly as possible. Emory then noted that the treaty required the presence of both commissioners at the establishment of astronomical points along the line, and should any accident prevent a subsequent verification of Emory's survey by the Mexican section, the United States commission's astronomical observations might be questioned and Emory's work, done at great cost, go for naught. The two commissioners therefore agreed that Emory should pursue the line westward and that Salazar Ylarregui would join him later. If the Mexican commissioner could not be present at astronomical stations along the line, delay was to be avoided by Salazar Ylarregui agreeing beforehand to adopt any points Emory were to establish.[26] Emory had thereby anticipated the private wishes of McClelland, and so the advantage was gained. In frustration, Emory wrote to the secretary of the interior, "The Mexican Commissioner himself is eminently qualified to perform his duties, but he seems to be left with means wholly insufficient."[27]

The major's experience assured him that the survey from the Río Grande to the junction of the Gila with the Colorado ran through territory that would not only become increasingly difficult, but dangerous as well. While occupied with the survey of the Río Grande in early 1852 he had sent George Clinton Gardner with ten men to reconnoiter the area around Lake Guzmán. Emory knew of the desolation stretching before him and the scarcity of water his surveying parties might face. He therefore ordered that no person not in the service and pay of the commission was to accompany it westward. He also feared the lure of the gold fields and the disruption it might cause as the commission neared California; he needed no tagalongs.[28]

Nevertheless, by the beginning of April Major Emory was able to report that the work went well and rapidly; that 31° 47′ north latitude was completely surveyed as well as the north-south line to 31° 20′, upon which work had also begun. He had established an astronomical station at Carrizalillo Springs to the north of the hills of the same name and the water nearest the end of the 100-mile line. The surveying party extended the boundary from that point in both directions; westward to the end of the 100-mile line, and eastward until it met the parallel projected from the Río Grande. The United States section then erected a second observatory at Espia on the Río Janos a few miles east of the meridian connecting 31° 47′ and 31° 20′. Water was then found at Ojo del Perro near the corner of the north-south line and 31° 20′ and Emory moved the Espia observatory to that more convenient location.

Monument No. 40 as repaired in 1892 (stone), view to the west, at the intersection of the parallel and meridian near Carrizalillo Spring, erected by Salazar Ylarregui. Photographed by D. R. Payne, 1893-94. Reproduced by J. Robert Willingham of Southeast Missouri State University, from Report of the Boundary Commission upon the Survey and Re-marking of the Boundary between the United States and Mexico..., Album, 55th Cong., 2nd sess., 1898, S. Ex. Doc. 247 (Ser.3613).

The team of engineers erected a new astronomical station at San Luis Springs some thirty miles west of the initial point of 31° 20′, and two additional observatories at San Bernardino Springs and north of Santa Cruz in order to complete the line. The nearest water at the intersection of that line with the 111th meridian was at Ojo de los Nogales where Emory placed his last astronomical observatory. Emory's party mounted both the transit and zenith instruments and after 120 observations over two lunations determined its longitude and latitude, and then transferred its longitude by direct measurement and triangulation to the intersection of the 111th meridian with 31° 20′ latitude north. Emory was now ready to run the azimuth line to the Colorado.[29]

Still, he had no word from Salazar Ylarregui, the Mexican commission having not left El Paso del Norte.[30] Emory was naturally upset therefore to read in the *Picayune* that the United States commission was beset by delays when in fact he had received no material aid from the Mexican commissioner. Yet he was continually being urged to hasten the running of the line.[31] The support Salazar Ylarregui received from his government was entirely inadequate and to sadden his desperate situation further, Indians made off with his party's entire stock of animals at dawn on 1 May.[32] At the moment the

Mexican commissioner was "entirely without means."[33] By the end of April Salazar Ylarregui's situation seems to have improved a bit, for he wrote Emory that the three monuments left in his charge were finished and that as soon as he replaced the stolen mules he would march. The Mexican commissioner even expended some of his own money to feed the escort.[34]

Shortly after Emory had completed the survey of 31° 20′ to its intersection with the 111th meridian, he was astonished to learn that Salazar Ylarregui had been arrested by the Mexican government and carried off to Chihuahua a prisoner. The question now was whether the United States commission could complete the survey without him.[35] Noting the state of confusion in Mexico at this time, Secretary of the Interior McClelland wondered if the 26 January agreement gave Emory enough authority to complete the field work in Salazar Ylarregui's absence. In any case, he ordered Emory to proceed at his discretion, allowing no delay to the work whether the Mexican commissioner returned to the line or not.[36]

It seems Salazar Ylarregui had sent a dispatch or two bemoaning his miserable sojourn on the frontier that the touchy minister of foreign relations, Díez de Bonilla, found disrespectful and this had provoked his arrest. It was obvious to everyone who knew of his plight that Salazar Ylarregui had done all in his power to carry the survey forward, even to the point of borrowing money on his personal credit to keep his commission together. Juan Almonte, Mexico's envoy in Washington, urged Díez de Bonilla to retain the engineer at his post because of his prestige and the confidence he enjoyed with everyone in the United States commission. Santa Anna therefore agreed to reinstate him on the condition that he retract his disrespectful communications to the government. Altogether Salazar Ylarregui had endured one month of imprisonment and humiliation at the hands of the dying dictatorship in Mexico City. Needless to say, his commission accomplished nothing during this time.[37]

Despite the treatment he had suffered from his own government, Salazar Ylarregui, now returned to El Paso del Norte, made plans to reorganize his commission and complete the survey from the Río Grande to the 111° of longitude. Yet this would take time and delay the completion of the survey his government was so eager to conclude. He therefore agreed to accept the United States commissioner's running of the line to the intersection of 31° 20′ north latitude with the 111th meridian.[38] To this point Emory had carried the survey alone from the initial point on the Río Grande. In addition to his frustration over the Mexican commissioner's inability to make half the survey, Emory was deeply concerned about the surveying party under the command of Lieutenant Michler, who was to bring the survey from the Colorado to the junction of 31° 20′ with longitude 111° west of Greenwich. The line now ran through the dangerous Camino del Diablo of the Sonoran Desert, where the low elevation of the land combined with its scant cloud cover seemed to turn the land into an inferno. With temperatures that might soar to 120° Fahrenheit and water a scarce commodity all along the route and completely absent in some areas, the climate was to be feared more than the Apache. Emory was very much aware of the harshness of the region toward man and beast; his concern for Michler was genuine. Emory had had no news of Michler, his party, or his progress since leaving Washington, and feared that some accident had befallen him.[39] Indeed, Michler and Captain Francisco Jiménez had confronted such difficulties that they were forced to abandon the survey in the Sonoran Desert before its completion.

In accordance with the original agreement of the Joint Commission to conduct operations from both ends of the line, Salazar Ylarregui ordered Jiménez to proceed to the junction of the Gila and Colorado by way of San Blas and thence to Guaymas by ship. From that point Jiménez was to march to the Colorado, the military governor of Sonora having been given orders to provide him with an adequate escort, supplies, and funds in stages along the route. Additionally, the commissioner had given him 3,500 pesos and promised to send more to Sonora later.[40] To assist Jiménez, Salazar Ylarregui appointed Manuel Alemán and the two brothers, Agustín and Luis Díaz. Both products of the Colegio Militar, the Díaz brothers demonstrated an early aptitude for engineering, assisting General José Mariano Monterde in preparing the defense of Chapultepec during the war. Agustín was noted for his tenacity, intelligence, and technical ability, and proved to be an excellent addition to the commission, while the talented Luis was an especially adept draftsman known for his ability to construct maps.[41]

Leaving Mexico City on 9 October 1854 with a very inadequate escort, Jiménez and his surveying party reached San Blas on the Pacific coast at midnight on 17 November. Securing passage for his entire party, he sailed from San Blas six days later, and put into port at Guaymas on 22 December, "after making the most dangerous voyage one can imagine...."[42] Jiménez there requested from the military governor of Sonora a well-provisioned escort of forty infantry and twenty dragoons from the military colonies who knew the frontier. He further requested that Captain Hilarion García and Lieutenant Manuel Romero be assigned as officers since they knew the area well. Captain García had served with Jiménez earlier on the Guadalupe Hidalgo line, but was unfortunately at that moment at Tucson. Despite his request the engineer was to suffer his constant complaint of an inadequate and poorly provisioned escort. This, he reported remorsefully, caused delay in the work during the entire course of the survey.[43]

The surveying section then left Guaymas with the escort on 15 January 1855, arriving three days later in Hermosillo, where he remained until the

Francisco Jiménez, Courtesy Benson Latin American Collection, University of Texas at Austin.

twenty-third to repair the wagons. On that morning Jiménez pushed on to Villa del Altar with an escort of only ten men, arriving on the twenty-ninth, and having made astronomical observations all along the road from Guaymas. There he found no escort at all until 4 February, when thirty men arrived provisioned only with three measures of flour for each soldier. In frustration, Jiménez wrote military governor Domingo de Arellano that his survey team could not make the *jornada* to the Río Colorado with such a poorly supplied escort, expressing his fear that the men would die of hunger.[44]

Jiménez was particularly disgusted to read in *Nacional de Ures*, the official newspaper of Sonora, that General Arellano, with much sacrifice on his part, had gathered an escort of forty men, provisioned with everything needed for three months in the field.[45] Jiménez found this completely at variance with reality, and wrote to the government requesting new orders for Arellano.[46] At length the escort was decently provided for and with Captain García and Lieutenant Romero, both having joined him while in Villa del Altar, Jiménez struck for the Río Colorado on 5 March. Unfortunately, he had been forced to leave the gravely ill Luis Díaz at Villa del Altar. Díaz was suffering from the same painful inflammation of the eyes that had disabled him on the lower Río Grande in 1853. It was feared that if he did not receive proper medical attention the excellent draftsman might lose the sight in both his eyes.[47]

Following Jiménez' departure from Villa del Altar, the escort diminished daily through desertion and was ultimately reduced to thirteen men. The last group to desert even took their officers' saddle horses. This proved to be a miserable journey without vegetation or water for the animals. The horses looked like skeletons and were so tired the men had to lead them. Jiménez reported that his section reached the Colorado on the night of 23 March "in complete disorder and without any desire other than to drink water."[48] The problems attending the military escort had caused a great loss of time, and had crippled the effort of the Mexican section more than Jiménez at the moment realized. After resting the animals and men for two days, the Mexican survey team made contact with the United States section on the afternoon of 28 March, and learned that Lieutenant Michler had arrived on 9 December 1854, already having spent four months on the work.[49]

The agreeable Nathaniel Michler of the Topographical Engineers was in command of the survey from the junction of the Gila and Colorado rivers eastward to a point where he would link up with Major Emory, who was simultaneously pushing the line westward from El Paso del Norte.[50] Michler reached Fort Yuma on the Colorado in good order, and by early 1855 had two surveying parties in the field. One, under the able artist and surveyor Arthur Schott and his assistant, E. A. Phillips, was conducting an accurate survey of that portion of the Colorado, which was to serve as part of the boundary.[51] Meanwhile a second party under Michler carried the triangulation of the straight line twenty miles below the junction of the Gila and Colorado. Michler did not follow Emory's instructions precisely, but described a radius of twenty miles using the point of the Gila-Colorado junction as its center. The radius' intersection with the Colorado was the initial point of the new line. Emory later reported that this method was more in conformity with the treaty and considered any territory won or lost worthless.[52]

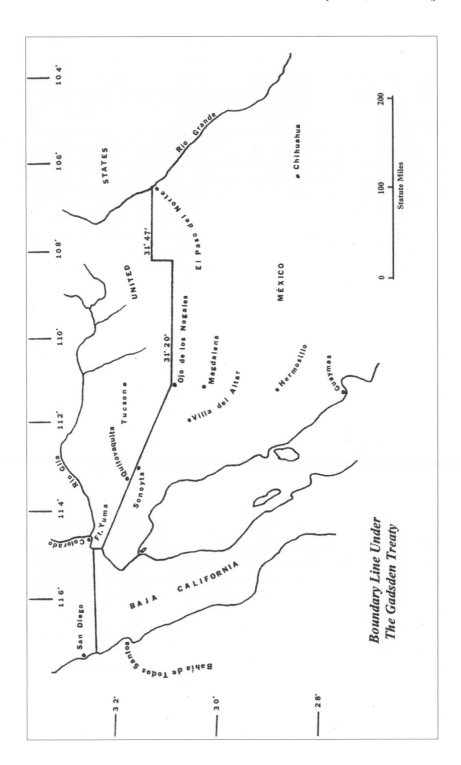

Boundary Line Under
The Gadsden Treaty

Michler and his assistant, John O'Donoghue, made astronomical and meteorological observations each day, and began construction of a general topographical map of the area along the Río Colorado. The nature of the country was a major cause of delay. Michler particularly bemoaned the heavy sand desert over which the triangulation was to run and the dense growth of timber in the river bottom. The river's banks seemed choked with large cottonwood trees and varieties of thickly growing willow, while near the river impenetrable swatches of arrow-wood and greasewood abounded with mesquite trees flourishing a bit farther out. Michler reported that, in order to be able to use his theodolite, he had been forced to cut lines some two miles in length through the worst of it and that sand and dust storms raged for days, during which time no instrument could be used. Then, as though the fates were against him, a sudden freshet from the Río Gila flooded the entire area just when Michler was ready to complete the determination of the initial point of the boundary on the Colorado. His field observatory was inundated, and the instruments saved only by wading and swimming nearly two miles to dry ground. The water rose ever so slowly, but at 2:00 A.M. on 20 March it forced Michler to move his camp to higher ground. This of course prevented any approach to the initial point for many days. When the water abated, Michler began to observe at the river's edge near the initial point, and was thus engaged when Captain Jiménez arrived on 28 March.[53]

Jiménez was surprised to learn that all Lieutenant Michler had left to do was trace the azimuth from the initial point on the Río Colorado to its intersection with the 111th meridian at 31° 20′ north latitude. From the time he had reached Villa del Altar, the captain had known Michler was working on the Colorado and had assumed his work would be quite advanced, but he had never guessed that Michler had no instructions to work jointly with the Mexican section of the Joint Commission. Jiménez therefore sought a conference with the lieutenant on 29 March. At the very least he had to satisfy his conscience that the initial point was correct.[54]

Michler related the work completed thus far and that the survey team under his direction had already suffered long delay in the prosecution of the work. He explained that he could not consent to remain long enough to enable the Mexican section to repeat the work. Michler further noted the urgings of haste that the Mexican legation in Washington had presented to the Department of State. A third difficulty was the scarcity of water in the area through which the azimuth line would pass, compelling completion of the work in the ensuing four or five weeks.[55] Jiménez' instructions, however, were to work in conjunction with the United States section and fix the initial point astronomically by two months of observation.[56] Michler and Jiménez at length agreed that the Mexican party would observe for ten nights for the latitude of the initial point as determined by Michler's triangulation, and that the results would be mutually agreed upon. Michler offered to assist with the signal flashes to determine longitude, and both men expressed an eagerness for a swift prosecution of the work.[57]

Jiménez and Alemán obtained a sufficient number of observations by sacrificing whole nights' sleep to obtain latitude, making sixty such observations between 2 and 7 April. Because of the thick woods and the recent flood, their camp was established some two miles from the observatory on the bank of the Colorado. They were only able to approach the river on a path through the woods, continually interrupted by a waterlogged marsh over which they threw tree trunks in order to form primitive bridges. During the six or seven hours spent each night at the observatory, Jiménez and Alemán suffered so many bites from the excessive number of insects of all descriptions that Jiménez later referred to the experience as a virtual martyrdom.

Despite such inconveniences, Jiménez informed Michler on 8 April that the latitude of the initial point was determined to their mutual satisfaction, and on the twelfth marched to the confluence of the Gila and Colorado to do the signal fires. Michler suggested that once the longitude was established they begin immediately to trace the azimuth line, since the season for finding water in the desert was growing short. Jiménez agreed, and despite some cloudiness, enough observations were made to determine longitude and the two parties returned to camp on the nineteenth to finish their calculations. The following day Jiménez presented his results to Michler, who found them accurate. After Michler and Jiménez had completed all their computations, they met on 20 April and signed an agreement establishing the initial point of the azimuth line on the Colorado at latitude 32° 29′ 44″.45 north, and at longitude 114° 48′ 44″.53 west of Greenwich. It not being possible to erect a monument at the initial point itself, in the middle of the river, the first monument was placed 3,164.84 feet distant in the direction of the azimuth line. They then adopted a plan to trace that line to the 111th meridian.[58]

While Jiménez and Alemán had been thus employed, Agustín Díaz had begun to trace the topography of the river boundary from the confluence of the Gila and Colorado to the initial point of the azimuth line.[59] Díaz later wrote that it was useless to exaggerate the obstacles under which he struggled along the Río Colorado, including the molestation from the innumerable insects in the woods below the confluence of the two rivers. With his small force of four soldiers and no other engineer to assist him, Díaz completed the triangulation of the riverine boundary. Michler found the difference between Díaz' work and his own extremely small considering the difficulty of the terrain for such exacting work.[60]

Before Díaz had finished, Jiménez and Michler attempted to push the line eastward by means of triangulation. The decisive factor was the entire absence of water along the line of march. Distant some forty-five miles over a desert plain were the Tinajas Altas, natural water encasements near the southern end of the Gila Mountains which filled during the rainy season and saved many a traveler's life. The first part of the journey passed over deep white sand so heavy that it was difficult for a wagon to cross even by doubling teams so as to have twelve mules to the wagon. A few miles beyond the first uncertain cachement of water were the Tinajas del Tule located in the Tule mountains. Beyond this were two even more uncertain sources of water: one in an arroyo where some slightly brackish water could be obtained by digging, and farther on at some pools that held water during the rains. The only dependable source of water was near Quitovaquita, some 125 miles from the initial point on the Colorado, where the excellent Agua Dulce Springs flowed during most of the year. About thirteen miles beyond Quitovaquita water was to be had at Sonoyta, but from there to the initial point of the azimuth line on the Colorado stretched a desert where scarcely a blade of grass was to be found and the bleached bones of animals marked the way. Michler could not imagine a more dreary, tiresome, and sterile country. "The burnt lime-like appearance of the soil is ever before you; the very stones look like the scoriae of a furnace; there is no grass, and but a sickly vegetation, more unpleasant to the sight than the barren earth itself...."[61]

Michler and Jiménez began the prolongation immediately and sent out reconnaissance parties to scout along the line for water. Only dribbles were found at the Tinajas Altas, the parties encountering excessive heat and a complete lack of water from the Colorado to Quitovaquita. Michler made a shorter reconnaissance himself and easily concluded that it would be impossible to advance the line. In an addendum to their 26 April agreement, Michler and Jiménez agreed to suspend the work and march via the Gila to the intersection of the parallel of 31° 20′ with the 111th meridian, and trace the line from that point back to the Colorado.[62]

Jiménez later complained bitterly that if he had received an adequate escort in good time, there would have been no such delay, but the orders of the government to so provide him had not been obeyed. Both survey teams now struck for Tucson on 1 May, Jiménez leaving Agustín Díaz to finish his work on the Colorado. The animals of both parties were so weakened as to make the trip up the Gila sufficiently miserable. Michler and Jiménez reached Tucson on 5 June while Díaz arrived on the ninth in a state as wretched as everyone else.[63]

While Lieutenant Michler and Captain Jiménez were struggling up the Gila toward Tucson, Major Emory had as yet received no word from Michler since the United States commission left Washington one year before. From his camp near Santa Cruz, he sent an express to Michler with orders to report his progress and estimate when he would reach the 111th meridian. Emory thought some accident had befallen Michler, and now prepared another surveying party to carry on the work.[64] But on 18 May 1855 Emory at last received a dispatch from Michler dated 13 December 1854 by way of Washington and El Paso del Norte and learned from a traveler that Michler had returned to the Colorado for lack of water. In a tone of chastisement, Emory found it inexplicable that Michler had not anticipated his arrival at the intersection of the parallel of 31° 20′ with the 111th meridian and forwarded the longitude and latitude of the new initial point on the Río Colorado, that Emory might determine the azimuth and begin work on the line westwardly. He now ordered Michler to do so forthwith.[65]

While he awaited Michler, Emory reported to the secretary of the interior that Captain Jiménez had arrived at Ojo de los Nogales on 19 June with a well-equipped and well-organized party, prepared to run the azimuth line.[66] In spite of this praise from Emory, Jiménez continued to lament the condition of his escort, which had been filled out at Tucson, but with eleven of the men who had deserted along the road to the Río Colorado.[67]

Major Emory invited Captain Jiménez to a conference on 21 June and informed him that the Mexican commissioner had not been able to undertake half the joint survey and had agreed to adopt any points determined by himself. Emory explained that the line was completed to the intersection of 31°20′ with 111° longitude and that a monument had been erected at that point. In view of the desire of both governments for speed, Emory suggested that they unite their parties and push the line to the Colorado with as much dispatch as possible. Jiménez remarked that he would have preferred to expend two months in observation to satisfy himself of the correctness of the point, dividing any difference in the results independently obtained by both sections of the Joint Commission. Emory then asked Jiménez if he thought he, Emory, was capable of practicing a deception upon him. Jiménez responded that no person would carry out a fraud upon his own reputation and declared his certitude that the major's results were exact.[68]

It would have been well for Jiménez to have conducted independent observations to establish this important point on the line for Emory had made an error in longitude. While the miscalculation was acceptable considering the surveying methods of the time, it placed the monument marking the intersection of 31° 20′ with the 111th meridian four-and-a-half miles too far west of its true location. This error was discovered in the 1891 to 1896 resurvey of the line, resulting in a loss of territory for Mexico amounting to 290 square miles.[69]

Emory then suggested Jiménez examine the "Official Journal of the Joint Commission" and furnished him with a copy of the 26 January 1855 agreement between himself and Salazar Ylarregui. This convinced Jiménez that the line had indeed been determined. Emory then invited the captain to inspect the instruments with which the observations had been made and which were still in place. Jiménez did so, accepting the results.[70] In turn Emory accepted the agreement of 26 April 1855 between Jiménez and Michler. It was also resolved that Jiménez would determine a central point on the line near Quitovaquita as a check upon its tracing and that Emory would accept the results. Finally, the two engineers agreed that the surveying parties would take the topography near the line, erecting monuments where the line crossed a road, mine, or body of water. Should either party break down in the field, the other was not to suspend or delay operations in consequence of such accident.[71]

In conformance with this convention, Jiménez detailed Agustín Díaz to trace the line with Michler, while he and Manuel Alemán marched to Quitovaquita, arriving on 21 July 1855 in the company of a portion of the United States team. Finding little water or grass on the way, the trip proved torturous for the mules, while one wagon broke down and had to be left in the desert, Jiménez purchasing a replacement from the United States Commission. On 22 July Jiménez established his field observatory, and after numerous observations had determined the point by 10 August. Díaz and Michler had reached Quitovaquita three days earlier after a difficult survey.[72]

The method of running the line toward the Colorado from Ojo de los Nogales resulted from a proposal Agustín Díaz made to Michler. That was a system of triangulation in which two angles of each triangle were to be measured without leaving the line. This permitted both teams to undertake an equal part of the survey and progress the work as rapidly as possible. Michler would do the angles north of the line and Díaz, those to the south of it. More than this plus the topography of the line could not be expected. Michler agreed to this proposal with the stipulation that all the angles of each station be taken by the same individual, alternating from station to station, and that the zenith of each principal point be well marked in relation to prominent features of the adjacent topography. Díaz' plan, thus amended, was adopted.[73]

Díaz considered the area between Ojo de los Nogales and Sonoyta quite dangerous because of the large number of Indians who traversed it, but he took an escort of only Lieutenant Romero, a sergeant, and two soldiers, since the scarcity of water did not permit any additional men. He left the twelve remaining troops of his escort at Ojo de los Nogales to guard the animals and provisions. Despite the very real Indian danger, Michler also operated with a party as small as possible because of the water situation. Díaz and Michler continually had difficulty finding sufficient water near the line, the bleached earth and the temperature that daily reached 110° Fahrenheit, making the work arduous at best. Arthur Schott bemoaned that he often found himself deprived of the simplest and most primitive comforts while working on the line.

Fortunately some relief from the lack of an adequate water supply and the intense heat was provided when it rained on the fourteenth. The day produced a violent storm of wind, rain, and hail, which caught both survey teams by surprise. Díaz' campaign tents were leveled by the wind and the arroyo, in which Michler's team had encamped, filled so suddenly that the party had no time to remove their camp to high ground. Consequently, food supplies, barrels, and surveying instruments were dragged through the arroyo by the swiftly running current.

Despite the damage done Michler's party, this and the lighter showers that followed in the days ahead seemed to assure them that sufficient water would be found near the line. Rain proved a mixed blessing three days later when Díaz and Schott went to the Sierra Verde to obtain a better idea of the direction of the azimuth line. Another unexpected storm forced them to spend the entire day and following night in watch, and since they had intended only a short reconnaissance, without food. The next morning they accomplished their original mission and returned to camp. Díaz and Michler then pushed on to the Sierra de la Unión, finding no water along the route, but search parties that Díaz had sent out separately did succeed in finding a little. On 29 July they were absolutely desperate for water, but found a few pools the next day at a deserted Papago Indian village.

As if the anxiety for water was not bothersome enough, the numerous rattlesnakes drawn toward the glow of each night's campfire made restful sleep difficult. By 3 August both teams reached Sonoyta and remained there the following day to procure supplies. Both parties had spent many days without meat and their supply of grain for the animals was giving out; the unhappy mules were weak from the scarcity of water and pasture. All, man and beast, had suffered in the work. Agustín Díaz found Sonoyta very pleasing and it pained him to leave it the next day, but the grass was insufficient for the mules and prices for provisions were exorbitant, having been brought there solely to sell to the boundary commission. On 7 August Díaz and Michler reached Quitovaquita, the line having been run and monuments fixed to that place.[74]

Spending little time in Quitovaquita, both survey teams marched some twenty-one miles farther on where they camped without water in the Tule desert. On this part of the line it had rained very little; the last permanent spring, Agua Dulce near Quitovaquita, was 125 miles from the Colorado, and from Agua Dulce to the Sierra del Tule, where the next monument was to be placed, about fifty-five miles, the entire distance was a sand desert with no pasture. Therefore, Captain Díaz took special precautions so as to avoid any mishap. He took only three men, two mules, each carrying two barrels of water, the instruments, and provisions. He also advised Lieutenant Manuel

Romero that should he lack sufficient water to return, he was to light fires in the mountains at an agreed-upon hour so that Romero could effect a rescue.

When they reached Tule on 11 August, it rained a little, providing water for five or six days, not counting the barrels, but by the sixteenth, the water at Tule had given out. A search yielded none at all and both parties fixed the last points of the international boundary on short water. The heat had become so unbearable that the parties were forced to operate at night using signal fires. The points fixed at Tinajas del Tule and the Tinajas Altas were quite troublesome. Their summits were so peaked as to make it difficult to find sufficient space to put up an instrument. The men who determined these points had to sit up all night because there was not room enough for them to lie down. On the twentieth of August 1855 Díaz and Michler returned to Sonoyta, the men exhausted, and the animals of both commissions weak and almost useless. Jiménez then suggested to Michler that both sections of the Joint Commission retire to Magdalena, which had a good climate and good pasture for the animals, and make their calculations there. Michler agreeing, the two teams struck camp on the twenty-fifth. Passing through Villa del Altar where Jiménez picked up Luis Díaz, now fully recovered, they reached their destination on 4 September 1855.[75]

While the work at Magdalena progressed quietly, Commissioners Emory and Salazar Ylarregui had already completed their labors at El Paso del Norte. At its meeting on 16 August the Joint Commission examined all the documents, astronomical observations, and maps of the line. They found everything in order and agreed to adopt without condition all monuments, observations, and astronomical points completed by each section of the Joint Commission whether done by the commissioners themselves or their assistants. They further decided that Salazar Ylarregui would erect a monument of dressed stone at the intersection of parallel 31° 47′ with the north-south line. Due to the lack of water at the time he finished his astronomical observations, Emory had only been able to place a rough mound at that point. Emory also agreed that the Mexican commissioner could erect a monument where he felt necessary at any other point along the line in the course of his proposed survey of the new boundary during the current rainy season. The commissioners then stipulated that the line was now surveyed and marked as far as the 111th meridian. They also declared the line would be considered surveyed and fixed from that point to the Colorado River as soon as they received notification of such from Michler and Jiménez. Lastly, the two commissioners resolved to meet in Washington on the first day of April 1856 to complete and sign the finished maps of the entire boundary from the mouth of the Río Grande to the Pacific Ocean.[76]

In the pleasant town of Magdalena, meanwhile, the Díaz brothers worked on the calculations for the maps with Arthur Schott and Lieutenant Michler, while Jiménez did the computations for the observations made at Quitovaquita. By the end of September 1855 the field maps of the line were completed.[77] The fieldwork of the new international boundary between Mexico and the United States, from the Río Grande to the Colorado, was now completed, both sections of the Joint Commission separately repairing to Washington and Mexico City.[78]

Michler enjoyed the homeward journey through the rich valleys of Sonora's Tierra Caliente; through Imuris, San Ignacio, and Cocospera with their lovely irrigated fields of grain and sugarcane, and the gardens blessed with fruit of all varieties imaginable.[79] Jiménez had a more difficult time getting home than Michler because he lacked the necessary funds to pay his party's bills incurred at Magdalena and elsewhere along the line. In early June when he learned from Emory that Salazar Ylarregui had been hauled off to prison, he had but twenty-eight pesos with which to keep his party together. By the beginning of October his survey team was in a miserable condition, Agustín Díaz was gravely ill, and the military governor of Sonora was able to provide only 1,000 pesos to assist him. This was neither enough to settle his accounts nor tend to Díaz, but on 15 November he finally received the 3,350 pesos he was to have received six months earlier. At last he was able to settle his accounts and three days later took the line of march for Mexico City, which he reached by way of the now familiar, though no less troublesome, route through Hermosillo and Guaymas on 16 February 1856. There he turned over all the instruments and documents in his charge to Salazar Ylarregui.[80]

The Mexican commissioner, in the meantime, had not been idle. Following his 16 August meeting with Emory, Salazar Ylarregui was able to reorganize his commission for the survey of the line between the Río Grande and the 111° of longitude near Los Nogales. With engineers Ignacio Molina and Antonio Contreras, an escort of twenty-five men, and all the necessary equipment and provisions, he reached Ojo de Carrizalillo on 6 September 1855 to begin the survey of 31° 47´. While Salazar Ylarregui carried a triangulation from that spring toward the end of the 100-mile line, Molina, at the head of another team, ran the survey eastward to the Río Grande. A graduate of Chapultepec, the valorous Molina was an excellent choice to lead the party as he was especially adept at mathematics and astronomy, having received his engineering degree from the Colegio de Minería. Contreras, though not yet a graduate, had also studied at the Colegio de Minería. The Mexican section completed its efforts along this portion of the new boundary on 15 December. A third team under the direction of Manuel Fernández Leal and Francisco Herrera, also topographical engineers from the Colegio de Minería, extended the triangulation from the end of the 100-mile line along the meridian that connected it with latitude 31° 20´. The commission opted not to carry a triangulation along this section of the new boundary to its intersection with the 111th meridian, Salazar Ylarregui and engineer Miguel Iglesias choosing to make several astronomical observations along the line instead.

During the entire survey the Mexican commission suffered from the usual threat of Indian attack, losing a number of horses and mules to the Apache on one occasion. The scarcity of water was naturally a constant problem in the desert, but the government's failure to provide adequate provision for its surveying team was inexcusable. At times the men of the commission had only the luck of the hunt to sustain them. These difficulties caused several men of the escort to desert, so that Salazar Ylarregui was sometimes reduced to searching for water or a new camp with only two soldiers as escort. Despite all the obstacles thrown before them the engineers of the Mexican commission completed their task, and while Salazar Ylarregui's official acceptance of Emory's previous survey in a sense made their effort moot, they nonetheless bestowed honor upon their country.[81]

All was now made ready for the journey to Washington, but delay continued to haunt the Mexican commission as the upset condition of the country again brought on financial constraints. At length Salazar Ylarregui, with Jiménez and Alemán who were to complete all the calculations resulting from the survey, along with Molina and Luis Díaz, both of whom were excellent draftsmen, reached Washington at the end of June 1856.[82] The Joint Commission met at nine o'clock on the morning of the twenty-fifth of that month to organize its work on the maps of the boundary and begin the comparison of the hundreds of calculations taken at the several astronomical stations along the line.[83] Work then progressed smoothly over the next fourteen months while both commissions diligently constructed the maps that would serve as the culmination of their work and in themselves would prove a remarkable achievement. For Salazar Ylarregui and his fellow engineers, however, it was not to be accomplished without the dire financial straits that had dogged their every step since the first meeting of the Joint Commission in San Diego, California, in July 1849. By February 1857 a complete lack of funds forced the Mexican commissioner to write privately and desperately to Emory asking for a loan of $1,500.[84]

Emory, on his own initiative and unbeknownst to Salazar Ylarregui, wrote to the secretary of the interior that Mexico's unstable condition had prevented them from receiving any support, leaving them in a truly deplorable state. Emory felt that the cordial relations between the two commissions enabled him to know of their difficulties and to sympathize with their plight. He suggested that a sufficient sum of money from the surplus that would be remaining from the boundary survey appropriation be made available to relieve the immediate needs of Salazar Ylarregui and allow him to send home those of his engineers whose task had been completed. The major further noted that the timely completion of the survey was in large measure due to the gentlemanly good sense of the Mexican commissioner, who never himself placed impediments in the path of a vigorous completion of the survey. Emory's plea evoked a favorable response, and Salazar Ylarregui soon requested and received a loan of $10,000 from the funds of the office of the United States Boundary Commission.[85] Of this amount the Mexican commissioner used but $6,000 to cover his expenses, and seemingly received a belated remittance from Mexico City that enabled him to repay the loan in full by the end of September.[86]

Meanwhile the labors of the Joint Commission were coming to fruition. The two commissioners met on 21 September 1857 to make a comparison of the maps of the entire boundary from San Diego to the mouth of the Río Grande and affix their signatures. The Joint Commission met one last time in the office of the United States Boundary Commission on 30 September 1857, found their work complete, and adjourned, *sine die*.[87] Emory then turned over all maps, astronomical observations, and computations of the survey along with his report and the "Official Journal of the Joint Commission" to the secretary of the interior.[88] Nevertheless, he was to continue his general supervision of the completion and publication of his report as well as the scientific reports resulting from the painstaking efforts of all those who had served on the United States Boundary Commission.[89]

After returning to Mexico City, Salazar Ylarregui presented to the minister of foreign relations all the documents of the commission, including the fifty-eight maps constructed in Washington. These consisted of fifty-four detailed maps of the line and four general maps. He also turned over the results of all the astronomical and topographical work, a copy of the original acts of the Joint Commission and all the reports of the engineers who had so diligently served with him during the years of work on the survey. Foreign Minister Luis Cuevas complimented Salazar Ylarregui on his great scientific and patriotic work, but regrettably informed him that the government was unable to pay all the salaries of the officers of the boundary commission at that moment.[90] Surely, José Salazar Ylarregui, who had suffered every imaginable insult and form of abuse from the government he so faithfully served, must have smiled wryly at his reward.

A great work had been completed. During the many difficult months in the desert, both sections of the Joint Commission had worked in a spirit of harmony and cooperation. Captain Jiménez later wrote:

> In all the time during the scientific work performed in union
> with Sr. Michler, the best harmony reigned among all the individuals

of both sections and among the officers of both escorts; the harmony contributed in a most efficacious manner to the happy conclusion of the work, because we aided each other mutually in all the obstacles that we had to suffer.[91]

Agustín Díaz concurred in giving great merit to the harmony that existed between the Mexican and the United States survey teams.[92] This feeling of congeniality is also found in Lieutenant Nathaniel Michler who related to Emory, "I take great pleasure in reporting to the commissioner the very agreeable relations, both official and social, which constantly existed during a difficult work, with those gentlemen of the Mexican Commission with whom we were so long and intimately associated."[93]

The Joint Commission had labored for nearly a year to trace the new international boundary through difficult terrain in an equally harsh climate. This caused delays for which neither survey team could adequately plan. The Joint Commission had no control over the hurricane that lashed the Texas coast or the sand storms that blasted the Sonoran Desert. One can certainly not question the stamina and competence of the men who made up the two surveying teams. Emory and Michler, Salazar Ylarregui and Jiménez, were all engineers of first quality. Their assistants, Agustín Díaz and Manuel Alemán, Arthur Schott and Moritz von Hippel, and all the others, were equally able.

Both sections of the Joint Commission did have difficulties with the escort, but while this does not seem to have caused much trouble for Emory's commission, it crippled Salazar Ylarregui's. Francisco Jiménez lost a full seven weeks en route to the Colorado because of the failure of the military governor of Sonora to carry out the instructions of the central government to provide him with a properly provisioned escort—lost time that he sorely lamented upon reaching Lieutenant Michler's camp on the Río Colorado. While their escort was truly inadequate, Jiménez and Agustín Díaz had only praise for its officers, Hilarion García and Manuel Romero, who were of invaluable assistance in the labors of the commission.[94] Nevertheless, Captain Jiménez was able to carry on the survey jointly with Michler, if indeed in haste. In addition to Díaz' topographical work along the Colorado and Jiménez' determination of the initial point of that end of the line, Díaz provided the plan for running the triangulation from the Colorado to the intersection of the 111th meridian with latitude 31° 20´ north. It should also be noted that Jiménez made all the astronomical observations at Quitovaquita, which Emory readily accepted with complete confidence in their accuracy.

Salazar Ylarregui, on the other hand, was scarcely provided with an escort at all. Nor was he given sufficient funds to enable him to make the survey jointly with Emory. How cruel it must have been for him to sit idly by in virtual imprisonment at El Paso del Norte, not to mention his actual incarceration in Chihuahua City. He did of course work jointly with Emory in determining the initial point of the new boundary on the Río Grande, and singly supervised the erection of the three most important monuments in the vicinity of the river. He also erected a monument of dressed stone at the extremity of 31° 47′ along with three other monuments during his later survey of the line following his last meeting with Emory at El Paso del Norte. In spite of the almost complete lack of support from its government, the Mexican commission did survey the entire new boundary under the Gadsden Treaty, a fact for which it has received little credit. There is no question then, that the Mexican commission played an important role in the survey of the new international boundary. The gentlemen of the United States commission, amply supplied with everything necessary to run the survey, also found the work and the privations that went with it a continual torment. The labors of the men of both commissions were most certainly patriotic, and indeed heroic.

CHAPTER X NOTES

1   Pearce to Emory, 4 [Aug.] 1854, Folder 66, Emory Papers.
2   Bevans, *Treaties and Other International Agreements*, IX, 813.
3   McClelland to Emory, 15 Aug. 1854, File 401, NA, RG/76.
4   Emory to González de la Vega, 19 Aug. 1854, Folder 67, Emory Papers; Emory to McClelland, 16 Aug. 1854, File 399, NA, RG/76.
5   SED 108 (832), p. 23; Emory to Salazar Ylarregui, [?] Aug. 1854, File 399, NA, RG/76.
6   Emory to Salazar Ylarregui, [11 Aug. 1854], Wheaton to Emory, 27 Aug., 1, 20 Sep., 10 Oct. 1854, Folders 66, 67, 68, 69, Emory Papers; Wheaton to Emory, 22 Oct. 1854, File 401, NA, RG/76.
7   Wheaton to Emory, 9 Nov. 1854, Folder 70, Emory Papers; Wheaton to Emory, 2 Nov. 1854, File 401, NA, RG/76.
8   SED 108 (832), p. 23; Emory to Davis, 14 Aug. 1854, Ordnance Office to Emory, 14 Aug. 1854, Folder 66, Emory Papers.
9   Von Hippel to Emory, 12 Sep. 1854, Folder 68, ibid.
10 SED 108 (832), p. 23; Emory to McClelland, 19 Jan. 1855, File 425, NA, RG/76.
11 SED 108 (832), p. 23.
12 Ibid., pp. 23–24; Radziminski to Emory, 17 Oct. 1854, Emory to Radziminski, 19 Oct. 1854, Folder 69, Emory Papers.
13 Emory to Salazar Ylarregui, 30 Nov. 1854, File 399, NA, RG/76.
14 Wheaton to Emory, 22 Oct. 1854, Folder 69, Emory Papers.
15 Wheaton to Emory, 9 Nov. 1854, File 401, NA, RG/76.

16 *El Omnibus* (Mexico City), 5 Dec. 1854; Wheaton to Emory, 2 Nov. 1854, Folder 70, Emory Papers; Wheaton to Emory, 9 Nov. 1854, File 401, NA, RG/76.

17 Salazar Ylarregui to Emory, 2 Dec. 1854, Folder 71, Emory Papers.

18 "Official Journal of the Joint Commission," File 396, II, NA, RG/76.

19 Bevans, *Treaties and Other International Agreements*, IX, 813.

20 Official Journal, File 396, II, NA, RG/76.

21 Miles to Emory, 2 Jan. 1855, File 401, ibid.; R. V. Bonneau to Emory, Folder 71, Emory Papers.

22 Emory to McClelland, 8, 19 Jan. 1855, File 399, NA, RG/76.

23 McClelland to Emory, 27 Nov. 1854, Folder 70, Emory Papers; McClelland to Emory, 20 Dec. 1854, File 401, NA, RG/76; Callcott, *Santa Anna*, pp. 305–15.

24 Howland and Aspinwall to Emory, 21 Dec. 1854, File 401, NA, RG/76; *Cyclopaedia of American Biography*, 8:47, 25:258.

25 Emory to Salazar Ylarregui, 22 Jan. 1855, Salazar Ylarregui to Emory, 23 Jan. 1855, File 425, NA, RG/76.

26 Official Journal, File 396, II, ibid.; "Jiménez Memoria," 26 Jan. 1855, pp. 92–95.

27 Emory to McClelland, 27 Jan. 1855, File 399, NA, RG/76.

28 Gardner to Alida Gardner, 8 May 1852, Gardner Papers; Emory to L. H. Hastings, 13 Jan. 1855, Folder 72, Emory Papers.

29 SED 108 (832), pp. 30–31.

30 Emory to McClelland, 23 Mar., 5 Apr. 1855, File 399, NA, RG/76.

31 *Picayune* (New Orleans), 8 Jan. 1855; Emory to Editor, *Picayune*, 8 Apr. 1855, Emory to Gadsden, 18 May 1855, File 399, NA, RG/76; Emory to McClelland, 23 Mar. 1855, Folder 74, Emory Papers.

32 *El Omnibus* (Mexico City), 9 Apr. 1855; Emory to Whiting, 5 Jul. 1855, File 425, NA, RG/76.

33 David R. Diffenderfer to Emory, 23 Apr. 1855, Folder 75, Emory Papers.

34 Salazar Ylarregui to Emory, 23 Apr. 1855, ibid.; Emory to Whiting, 5 Jul. 1855, File 425, NA, RG/76.

35 Emory to McClelland, 19 Jun., 9 Aug. 1855, File 399, ibid.

36 Johnson, *The Mexican Revolution of Ayutla*, pp. 100–12; McClelland to Emory, 25 Sep. 1855, File 401, NA, RG/76.

37 *El Omnibus* (Mexico City), 22 Jun. 1855; Carreño, *México y los Estados Unidos*, pp. 282–84.

38 Emory to McClelland, 18 Aug. 1855, File 425, NA, RG/76.

39 Emory to McClelland, 8 Jan., 23 Mar., 5 Apr., 1855, Emory to Michler, 10 May 1855, File 399, ibid.

40 Salazar Ylarregui to Jiménez, 12 Sep. 1854, "Jiménez Memoria," pp. 48–49.

41 AHDN, Cancelados, Exp. 7–5835, folios 3, 4, 9, 13, 17, 34, 51, Exp. 4–8954, folios 1, 4, 7, 11, 14, 21; Miguel A. Sánchez Lamego, "Agustín Díaz, ilustre cartógrafo mexicano," *Historia Mexicana*, XXIV (abr.-jun., 1975), pp. 557–60.

42 "Jiménez Memoria," pp. 51–52.

43 Jiménez to Comandante General, Sonora, 26 Dec. 1854, Domingo de Arellano to Jiménez, 27 Dec. 1854, ibid., pp. 53–54.

44 Jiménez to Arellano, 6 Feb. 1855, ibid., pp. 55–57.

45 *Nacional de Ures* (Ures, Sonora), 19 Jan. 1855.

46 Jiménez to Ministro de Relaciones, 6 Feb. 1855, "Jiménez Memoria," pp. 55, 57–58.

47 Arellano to Jiménez, 14 Feb. 1855, Jiménez to Arellano, 5 Mar. 1855, ibid., pp. 57, 59; AHDN, Cancelados, Exp. 7–5835, folio 80.

48 "Jiménez Memoria," p. 60.

49 Ibid.

50 Emory to Michler, 29 Aug. 1854, File 425, NA, RG/76; Gardner to Alida Gardner, 16 Oct. 1852, Gardner Papers.

51 Michler to Emory, 13 Dec. 1854, 12 Feb., 20 May 1855, Files 400, 401, NA, RG/76; SED 108 (832), pp. 105, 112–13.

52 Emory to McClelland, 18 Aug. 1855, File 399, NA, RG/76.

53 Michler to Emory, 13 Dec. 1854, 12 Feb., 20 May 1855, Files 400, 401, ibid.; "Report of Lieut. Michler," in SED 108 (832), p. 113.

54 "Jiménez Memoria," p. 60.

55 Michler to Jiménez, 2 Apr. 1855, File 401, NA, RG/76.

56 "Jiménez Memoria," p. 61.

57 Michler to Jiménez, 2 Apr. 1855, File 401, NA, RG/76; Jiménez to Michler, 6 Apr. 1855, "Jiménez Memoria," pp. 86–87; "Report of Lieut. Michler," in SED 108 (832), p. 113.

58 "Jiménez Memoria," pp. 61–66, 88–91, 392–93; Michler to Emory, 20 May 1855, File 401, NA, RG/76; SED 108 (832), p. 114.

59 "Jiménez Memoria," pp. 61–62.

60 "Memoria sobre los trabajos topográficos que de orden del 1er Ingo de la comisión D. Franco Jiménez practicó el 2° Ingo de la misma D. Agustín Díaz ...Año de 1855," in "Jiménez Memoria," [Hereafter cited as "Díaz Memoria"], pp. 101, 104; Michler to Jiménez, 22 Jun. 1855, ibid., pp. 94–95.

61 "Report of Lieut. Michler," in SED 108 (832), pp. 114–15.

62 Michler to Emory, 20 May 1855, File 401, NA, RG/76; "Jiménez Memoria," pp. 66–67, 88–91; "Report of Lieut. Michler," in SED 108 (832), pp. 115–16.

63 "Jiménez Memoria," pp. 67, 70–71; Michler to Emory, 20 May 1855, File 401, NA, RG/76.

64 Emory to Michler, 10 May 1855, File 425, ibid.; Emory to von Hippel, 15 May 1855, Folder 76, Emory Papers.

65 Emory to Michler, 18 May 1855, File 399, NA, RG/76.

66 Emory to McClelland, 20 Jun. 1855, File 465, ibid.

67 "Jiménez Memoria," pp. 70–71.

68 Ibid., pp. 71–73, 92–93.

69 Joseph Richard Werne, "Redrawing the Southwestern Boundary, 1891–1896," *Southwestern Historical Quarterly*, CIV (July, 2000), p. 11.

70 Official Journal, File 396, II, NA, RG/76.

71 "Jiménez Memoria," pp. 73, 92–93; Official Journal, File 396, II, NA, RG/76.

72 "Jiménez Memoria," p. 73.

73 "Díaz Memoria," pp. 101, 105.

74 "Jiménez Memoria," p. 73; "Díaz Memoria," pp. 106–109; "Report of Lieut. Michler," in SED 108 (832), pp. 119–22; Schott to Engelmann, [?] Dec. 1855, Folder 1, Engelmann Papers.

75 "Jiménez Memoria," pp. 73–74; "Díaz Memoria," pp. 109–110, 123–24, 135.

76 SED 108 (832), p. 33.

77 Michler to Salazar Ylarregui, 14 Oct. 1855, Michler to Emory, 14 Oct. 1855, File 401, NA, RG/76; "Jiménez Memoria," pp. 74–75.

78 Salazar Ylarregui to Ministro de Relaciones, 15 Oct. 1855, File 401, NA, RG/76; Emory to McClelland, 28 Dec. 1855, Folder 82, Emory Papers; "Jiménez Memoria," p. 79.

79 "Lieut. Michler's Report," in SED 108 (832), p. 124.

80 "Jiménez Memoria," pp. 71–72, 75–79.

81 Orozco y Berra, *Apuntes para la historia de la geografía*, pp. 469–82; AHDN, Cancelados, Exp. 717788, folios 20, 23, 27, 37, 62; López de Escalera, *Diccionario biográfico*, pp. 348, 716; Ramírez, *Datos para la historia del Colegio de Minería*, pp. 395–96, 401–402, 404; Rebert, "Mapping the United States-Mexico Boundary," pp. 332–34.

82 Salazar Ylarregui to Emory, 2 May 1856, Folder 87, Emory Papers; "Jiménez Memoria," pp. 79, 441; Manuel de Sandoval to Director General de Ingenieros, 2 May 1856, AHDN, Cancelados, Exp. 717788, folios 37, 70, Ignacio de Mora y Villamil to Ministro de Guerra y Marina, 4 Nov. 1857, Exp. 7-5835, folio 82.

83 Official Journal, File 396, II, NA, RG/76.

84 Salazar Ylarregui to Emory, 19 Feb. 1857, Folder 96, Emory Papers.

85 Emory to Jacob Thompson, 7 May, 6 Jun. 1857, Salazar Ylarregui to Thompson, 20 May 1857, File 399, NA, RG/76; Thompson to Emory, 29 Jun. 1857, Folder 100, Emory Papers.

86 Emory to Michler, 1 Jul. 1857, Emory to Thompson, 29 Sep., 1 Oct. 1857, Michler to Emory, 30 Sep. 1857, Files 399, 400, NA, RG/76; Carreño, *México y los Estados Unidos*, pp. 284-85.

87 Official Journal, File 396, II, NA, RG/76.

88 Emory to McClelland, 29 Jul. 1856, Folder 89, Emory Papers; Emory to Thompson, 28 Sep., 1 Oct. 1857, File 399, NA, RG/76. The maps are located in the Cartographic and Architectural Section, Record Group 76, National Archives, Washington, D.C.

89 Thompson to Emory, 19 Oct. 1857, Folder 104, Emory Papers.

90 Salazar Ylarregui to Ministro de Relaciones, 26 Feb. 1858, Cuevas to Salazar Ylarregui, 10 Mar. 1858, ASRE, Exp. 22, pp. 41-43. The maps are located in the Mapoteca Manuel Orozco y Berra, Mexico City.

91 "Jiménez Memoria," p. 75.

92 "Díaz Memoria," p. 110.

93 "Report of Lieut. Michler," in SED 108 (832), p. 124.

94 "Jiménez Memoria," p. 75; "Díaz Memoria," p. 110.

CONCLUSION

"I have seen rather too much service to be an Asst.

to any man that has not a pair of Epaulettes on his shoulders

and who does not rank me in the Army."

William Hemsley Emory, U.S. Commissioner

The driving force behind the boundary controversy was the United States' need for a transcontinental railroad, but the question lies before us, where should the southern boundary of New Mexico have been drawn? Was Bartlett's compromise with García Conde based upon false assumptions, or were Gray and the Topographical Engineers right all along? Months before any surveyor placed his instruments at the initial point of the line on the Río Grande, García Conde had unraveled the problem. The Treaty of Guadalupe Hidalgo and Disturnell's wretched map were only clear on the placement of El Paso del Norte within Mexico. To the horror of the Mexican government, García Conde pointed out that the boundary was a matter of interpretation; that a line merely eight miles north of the town was as tenable as his own, which threw the boundary farther north by some thirty-seven miles.

Foreign Minister Luis Cuevas, who had been one of the Mexican treaty commissioners, could not accept García Conde's discovery. Cuevas insisted the sinuous line on Disturnell's map was 32° 30′, García Conde's straightening of that line to make it 32° 22′ being of minor importance. Cuevas was certain the line would be farther north of El Paso del Norte than it appeared to be on Disturnell's map.[1] The treaty negotiators had in fact never discussed the distance from the town to the line, their only concern being El Paso del Norte's inclusion within Mexico.[2] There was, then, never any doubt in the minds of the Mexican treaty commissioners as to where the southern boundary of New Mexico fell.

Nor was there doubt in the mind of the United States treaty negotiator. Nicholas Trist held that there was never any question regarding the line; the only question was among the several officers of the United States Boundary Commission. He maintained that Surveyor Gray's only task was to determine the initial point of the boundary and then trace it upon the ground, insisting that Gray had no more right than a chainbearer to discuss the issue with Bartlett. Trist found all the historical and geographical arguments of Bartlett, Gray, Graham, and Emory irrelevant. The treaty, he asserted, demonstrated exactly where the boundary lay: north of El Paso del Norte. It was precisely for that reason that Disturnell's map had been attached to the treaty. Its only relevant features were the latitude of the southern boundary of New Mexico and the longitude of the territory's western line.

Trist believed the task of the Joint Commission was simply to follow the river until it struck the southern limit of New Mexico as it appeared on the map, no matter the Río Grande's actual position on the surface of the earth. The inaccuracy of the map was of no importance. Trist could not fathom why the enemies of 32° 22′ held the distance from El Paso del Norte to the southern boundary of New Mexico on Disturnell's map to be true when everything else on it was so obviously inaccurate. He found Gray's insistence on measuring the distance from El Paso del Norte a departure from the treaty, and believed that the Joint Commission need only determine 32° 22′ on the ground. Trist asked how any dispute could have arisen, and could not comprehend Bartlett's compromise with García Conde. Seeing the agreement of the two commissioners as a deviation from the treaty, Trist asked which line was the boundary, that of Bartlett and García Conde, or that of the Treaty of Guadalupe Hidalgo? Finally, Trist declared that the parenthetical words in the treaty regarding the southern boundary of New Mexico, "(which runs north of the town called <u>Paso</u>)," were thrown in at his own suggestion because good faith on his part and on his government's part demanded it.[3]

Nicholas Trist was not entirely correct in his insistence that the treaty was precise in its description of the boundary. To everyone but the treaty negotiators, the line was sufficiently vague as to give rise to different interpretations, as García Conde quickly discovered. This obscurity permitted one to take 32° 22′ as laid down on Disturnell's map and so mark it upon the earth. Or, one could take the position of El Paso del Norte as it appeared on the map and measure the distance from that point, as it appears on the earth, to the southern limit of New Mexico, which would place the line some thirty-seven miles farther south.

The ambiguity of the document also caused the treaty commissioners to agree to begin the survey on the Pacific coast and work eastward. When high labor and freight costs and continual delays on the part of the United States section shifted the survey from California to El Paso del Norte, the original intent of the treaty framers was frustrated. And no wonder; it was a violation of the Treaty of Guadalupe Hidalgo that obligated the Joint Commission to begin at the initial point on the Pacific and survey the line without interruption eastward to the Gulf of Mexico. This would lead the Joint Commission up the Gila until it struck the western line of New Mexico as it appeared on Disturnell's map, thence south to the southern line of New Mexico precisely in 32° 22′ north latitude.

The position of El Paso del Norte would then not have been a factor and no argument could have arisen. But beginning at the initial point on the Río Grande brought forth the question of El Paso del Norte's true position, and this made it possible to alter the original intent of the treaty negotiators. If one follows the reasoning of Trist, the correct line according to the treaty was neither Bartlett's nor Gray's, but Pedro García Conde's original proposal.

The Mexican commissioner knew the area through which the southern boundary of New Mexico would run better than anyone else. Understanding fully the differing interpretations one could assign to that vague line on Disturnell's map, Bartlett was for him the perfect choice as United States commissioner. This literary man from Providence cared next to nothing about a southern railroad. Bartlett was on a lark, but García Conde had a cause. With a little compromise on García Conde's part, he got Bartlett to accept Mexico's interpretation of that sinuous line on the map.

At the first meeting of the Joint Commission in El Paso del Norte, García Conde held that the town's true position was much farther south than represented on Disturnell's map. He then produced a map of Chihuahua he had constructed in 1834 on which El Paso del Norte lay in 31° 45′ north latitude, its actual position.[4] García Conde was stationed at El Paso del Norte from 1833 to 1834 and again from 1835 to 1838, the very time he was constructing his map of Chihuahua. This was certainly ample time to fix the latitude of that point with his instruments. Indeed, he had ample time to determine the town's latitude the evening before the Joint Commission's first meeting. All he needed to do was to observe the heavens on a single night to ascertain a close approximation of the settlement's latitude.

It is quite possible that García Conde knew all along where the town lay at least with regard to latitude if not longitude. Did treaty commissioners Couto, Cuevas, and Atristáin consult with him when they insisted upon El Paso del Norte remaining in Mexico? As a member of the 1847 Querétaro Congress, García Conde was certainly available for an interview.[5] If they had done so, why would they not have chosen a parallel of latitude to ensure the town's retention instead of the line on Disturnell's irksome map? García Conde's Chihuahua map was in manuscript form only. Perhaps the only copy was the one Bartlett later found in Governor Cordero's office in Chihuahua City. While it may seem odd that García Conde would not have a copy of this map among his personal papers, without such a copy he could not demonstrate El Paso del Norte's position to the treaty framers. Nor is it likely that García Conde could have remembered the town's exact latitude after a lapse of thirteen years. It is only known that he had his map with him at the first meeting of the Joint Commission in El Paso del Norte. Did he retrieve it in Chihuahua City en route?

Then there is García Conde's *Ensayo estadístico* of Chihuahua, done in 1836 and published in 1842, which discusses everything from the population of the smallest village to the agricultural production of the largest hacienda in every region of the state. He failed, nonetheless, to include the latitude or longitude of so much as one fixed point in all of Chihuahua.[6] Precise location of towns does not seem to have been within the scope of his statistical essay. How unfortunate for the treaty framers as well as those who would now get at the truth of the matter. The least bit of uncertainty would have prevented Couto and his colleagues from relying on García Conde's knowledge about so critical a point in the treaty. Perhaps they had no recourse except to fall back on Disturnell's map.

It is also well to remember that the negotiations were held in great secrecy; only a handful of men knew anything of the actual discussions. There is no hard evidence that Couto or anyone else consulted García Conde until after his appointment as Mexican boundary commissioner. The true latitude of El Paso del Norte is mentioned by no one, neither Couto nor Cuevas, nor Trist nor Emory, until García Conde pointed it out to Bartlett on his manuscript map of Chihuahua.

Despite the errors in Disturnell's map, which were brought to Buchanan's attention before the United States commission was even formed, the treaty map itself was not the cause of the controversy, but rather its excuse.[7] What caused the dispute was United States partisan politics that led to the penury of Weller's commission in California and the forced shift of the Joint Commission's work from San Diego to El Paso del Norte. Once there it was easy to "torture" the treaty as Emory had suggested and throw the line farther south in an effort to obtain the rail route so important to the United States.

It was Emory who first understood the nature of the topography along the thirty-second parallel and the Gila Valley and how it might accommodate a rail route to the Pacific. He had discovered this during his war reconnaissance of the area and had urged his government on more than one occasion of the necessity of gaining both banks of the Gila and preferably 32° latitude as the boundary. Buchanan, however, did not make that line a sine qua non of the treaty and Trist ultimately came to conclude that Mexico would not sign a treaty based on that parallel.[8] Despite Emory's hopes of torturing the treaty to place the line as far south as possible, this was not attainable, for in his view neither Bartlett's nor Gray's line would secure a rail route. The only recourse was to negotiate a new boundary.[9]

The way toward a new treaty began when Gray protested 32° 22′, but it was Graham who purposely scuttled its survey by calling Whipple off the line and then refusing to give out any of the instruments he had so meticulously gathered on the East Coast. The waters had now become so muddied that it would have been nearly impossible to have resolved the controversy without resorting to a new treaty. The boundary survey then had reached an impasse that was ultimately broken by New Mexico's governor, William Carr Lane, whose precipitous action opened the road toward a peaceful resolution to the conflict.

It was here that Mexico's political instability played a decisive role. With the overthrow of the honest government of Mariano Arista, the United States had to deal only with the dictatorship of Santa Anna, not an unruly congress. Moreover, Santa Anna's government was in trouble, and as Gadsden correctly saw, only money could save it. Thus the purchase of the Mesilla Valley, ignoring all arguments in favor of Gray's line or that of Bartlett and García Conde, at length settled the boundary controversy.

Aside from the boundary question itself, what helped to turn the survey into a nightmare for nearly all concerned was the inability of John Russell Bartlett to focus his attention upon the duties of the commissioner. Except for his friends, nearly everyone considered him unequal to the task, including García Conde. Bartlett, the intellectual dilettante, was a failure as boundary commissioner for the same reason his bookstore failed. He was a poor administrator who would rather discuss books than sell them. In the same vein he could not bear to be in the new territory and fail to learn all that he could about the terrain, flora, fauna, and the Indians, tirelessly constructing vocabularies of their languages. Surely the survey would take care of itself while he studied Rousseau's noble savage. Bartlett's endless travels that took him to far-away Acapulco and San Francisco would be inexplicable if it were not understood then as now that he was writing a grand travelogue after the manner of his friend John Lloyd Stephens. The resulting waste of time and expense had a profound impact on the work of the United States commission and affected the Mexican section as well. One wonders if Bartlett had received the diplomatic post to Denmark, would he have ended up in Vladivostok?

One of Bartlett's greater difficulties was his inability to get along with the officers of the Topographical Engineers. Throughout his tenure as commissioner, he refused to recognize any "military" responsibility, duty, or authority of the Topographical Engineers assigned to the United States commission. In his eyes they were simply surveyors and astronomers under his direction and responsible to him alone. He could not comprehend that this attitude would offend that prideful corps. Yet one cannot lay all the blame for this military-civilian feud at the feet of John Russell Bartlett. The Topographical Engineers were an elite corps with pedigrees, connected to famous and powerful people, prima donnas all. They were jealous of each other's accomplishments and quick to challenge subordinate and superior alike. Could Bartlett really have worked smoothly with them?

It was perhaps unwise for the Polk administration to have created a mixed commission in the first place. Here the fault lies with Polk himself. Ever wary of prominent military men, his first inclination was to appoint the man most qualified to serve as United States commissioner, Major Emory. While Polk had chosen correctly, his distrustful nature caused him to stipulate that Emory resign his commission in the army—a most unreasonable demand to which the major could not accede. Then to compound matters, the administration created the superfluous post of chief astronomer, that Emory might yet be attached to the commission. And so the mixed commission was born and this almost guaranteed conflict. The government's confusing and contradictory instructions to Bartlett and Graham merely threw oil on already troubled waters.

Colonel Abert put the problem clearly when he noted that, if the surveyor were to be a civilian, all his assistants should be civilians. A mixed commission, he emphasized, could not work together harmoniously, but would lead to continual bickering, misunderstanding, and delay.[10] Events, of course, proved Abert correct, but never more so than when Emory became the United States commissioner in charge of surveying the Gadsden Line. The energy and efficiency then brought to the work was sorely wanted from the beginning of the commission's labors in 1849. Hindsight suggests the entire survey should have been placed under the Topographical Engineers at the start—from commissioner to lowly chainbearer.

The government's greater fault was to leave its commission without adequate funds and escort on the untamed frontier. While one can understand the Whig administration's effort to sabotage John B. Weller by failing to provide him the wherewithal to do the work of the survey, that same administration refused to honor the drafts of its own appointee and fellow Whig. Bartlett's spendthrift course was troublesome to be sure, but he was not entirely to blame. Perhaps the root of the problem was that so few in Washington had an appreciation for the difficulties of terrain and climate in the area of the survey. Most of the work had to be done in areas so remote from settled regions that provisioning several surveying parties was no simple matter. Of those hamlets along the line, most had little to sell and some nothing at all.

The Mexican commission suffered under even greater difficulties, not the least of which was the nation's political instability and the lamentable condition of its treasury. While García Conde began his efforts in San Diego with a fairly well-equipped commission, the problems facing the Mexican section became increasingly desperate until Salazar Ylarregui found himself stranded at El Paso del Norte without so much as a peso at his disposal. Captain Francisco Jiménez discoursed in his final report that it had been difficult to carry out his instructions exactly because he never had a sufficient number of engineers at his disposal, nor adequate supplies or escort in a desert country traversed by savage Indians. The only favorable circumstance at hand was the exceptional quality of those few scientific officers he did have.[11] Indeed, Jiménez' experience reflected that of the Mexican commission as a whole, for its greatest asset was the high quality of its members, not the least of whom was its first commissioner, Pedro García Conde. Beyond all the burdens placed upon him, he was in control of his commission in a way that Weller and certainly Bartlett could never have been.

Until recently there has been little focus on the efforts of the Mexican commission, giving the casual impression that the international survey was largely the work of the United States section of the Joint Commission. In part this is understandable since the papers of the Mexican Boundary Commission have been made available only in the past few years. This impression, however, is also due to the opinion Emory presented in his final report on the survey. Emory was loath to share the credit for the work with his fellow Topographical Engineers, let alone the Mexican surveyors who worked with him. Giving scant credit to the Mexican team, he wrote, "I looked for little or no aid from the Mexican commission, for although composed of well educated and scientific men, their instruments were radically defective. Our determinations, after being re-observed and re-computed by the Mexican commission, were received by them without correction."[12] It has been ably demonstrated that this was simply not the case.[13] While Salazar Ylarregui bemoaned the condition of his instruments in California, he later arrived at El Paso del Norte with an entirely new set.[14] Both sections of the Joint Commission suffered injury to their instruments resulting from the rigors of the work and the difficulties of transport over terrain that would make any surveyor fear for the safety of the delicate tools of his trade. There was in fact much friendly borrowing of instruments on the part of both teams.[15]

Although it is true that the United States section was at times working in advance of the Mexican commission, most obviously on the Gadsden survey, the opposite was sometimes the case. One need only point to García Conde's lament over the endless delays of the United States commission in California, and the seeming lack of desire on the part of Weller, Gray, and Emory to depart

San Diego for the mouth of the Gila. This of course paled in comparison to his experience with Bartlett. There is also Whipple's complaint that he could not carry forward the survey of the southern boundary of New Mexico as rapidly as Salazar Ylarregui because he had only one assistant and inadequate instruments.

As to Emory's charge that the Mexican engineers simply accepted the observations and calculations of the United States surveyors without correction, the reverse was also true. Michler found no more discrepancy between his work and that of Jiménez on the Colorado than Radziminski did with Agustín Díaz on the lower Río Grande. Emory himself accepted Díaz' topography of the river without question. The fact is, as Emory well knew, in surveying there are always errors. A survey can be precise, but never exact. The object of the surveyor is to minimize such errors. The discrepancies between the two surveying teams were always minute.

The Mexican commission did accomplish a great deal. Its achievement included the survey of the California line, the Gila, the Bartlett-García Conde line, and those portions of the Río Grande assigned to it by agreement with the United States commission, as well as portions not assigned to it. The Mexican section surveyed the entire Gadsden line, although completing the segment from the Río Grande to the 111th meridian near Los Nogales somewhat belatedly. It is perhaps time to give the engineers of the Mexican Boundary Commission just recognition for their honest efforts.

It is indeed fitting to honor the labors of all the men of the Joint Commission, whose task took them into unexplored deserts, down enchanted valleys, and over crashing rapids. One can only admire their perseverance in the face of scant provisions and little water, broken instruments and smashed wagon wheels, and all the while bedeviled by hostile Indians, wolves, and government neglect. Yet they overcame all obstacles thrown in their path. That their great work was completed over terrain they found arduous makes their achievement the more remarkable and surely of epic quality.

While the engineers of both sections were glad at long last to leave their difficult work on the survey behind them, and while the line was completed to the satisfaction of both governments, the new boundary did not allow the two nations to go their separate ways. Rather it held them together, at first lightly, but then ever more closely. One border problem that neither the Treaty of Guadalupe Hidalgo nor the Gadsden Purchase was able to solve was the intermittent Indian raids along the new international line. These had plagued northern Mexicans to such an extent before the war that the area was becoming depopulated, as Mexican settlers departed for safe haven to the south. Members of both sections of the Joint Commission noted the deserted presidios along the border and were in constant danger of attack themselves. The United

States had little success in preventing these raids into Mexico despite its obligation to do so under the treaty of 1848, and quickly sought release from this duty in the negotiations leading to the Gadsden Treaty. The Indians of course recognized no border, crossing the boundary and raiding at will into the later years of the nineteenth century.

Equally disturbing were the filibustering raids that fell upon the northern tier of states as well as Yucatán. The notorious raid of William Walker was the most remarkable, but there were several others that posed equal danger. This was Manifest Destiny at its worst and was of great concern for Mexico.[16] There were quieter attempts as well. In 1883 the Mexican consul in Tucson drew to the government's attention the growing influence of the North American colony in Sonora, reinforced by the nearness of the Southern Pacific Railroad and New York capital. Hermosillo had a population of 16,000 at the time, of which eight hundred to a thousand were citizens of the United States. A particular threat was the Sonora Land and Mining Company with plans to settle thousands of North Americans in Sonora along the Yaqui River within easy reach of Arizona and the Southern Pacific Railroad. General Bernardo Reyes, the Mexican military commander in the region, saw this as a grave danger as the colonists' loyalty would remain with the United States. Reyes called the scheme another "Texas" in the making.[17] In the end the colonization project came to naught, but the threat was perceived as quite real to Mexican patriots at the time.

As ranches were established and mines discovered, economic activity along the border increased and the population began to grow at numerous points along the border, but the Joint Commission had erected only fifty-three monuments along the international line between the Río Grande and the Pacific Ocean, leaving considerable doubt as to where it actually ran. This was certainly the case along the Arizona-Sonora border where the original monuments were nothing more than conical piles of stones, some as far apart from one another as eighty miles and in one instance over a hundred. At length this forced a resurvey of the boundary from 1891 to 1896, which discovered a number of errors in the original survey, leaving Mexico with a net loss of territory of approximately 320 square miles. Considering the extreme conditions under which the 1849–1857 commission labored, and the more accurate surveying methods of the 1891–1896 commission, such errors were considered acceptable. While Manifest Destiny played no role in this newly discovered loss for Mexico, the beast was not dead. Any attempt to rectify the boundary would fuel the desire of the citizens of Arizona for an outlet on the Gulf of California, leaving Baja California cut off from the rest of Mexico. The issue was laid to rest in 1898 as the United States turned its attention to Cuba, and the Porfiriato thought it best to let sleeping dogs lie.[18]

With the beginning of the Mexican Revolution of 1910 the focus of both nations on the border became more intense. Along with military disturbances that disrupted the peace among urban settlements, thousands of Mexicans sought to escape the fury of the great rebellion by crossing the border. Many remained after the violence subsided, adding to the Mexican population that had been there since the days of the boundary survey. One island of peace during the revolution was Baja California Norte, whose governor kept the revolution at bay, paid his small army in gold double eagles, and ruled the territory as his own fiefdom. His attitude led many north of the border to hope, and many south of the border to fear, that the peninsula would yet fall to Manifest Destiny's hunger. During this time economic and social life on both sides of the California line became increasingly intertwined. At one point some citizens of Calexico, California, sent their children to the high school across the line in Mexicali because it was considered the better facility.[19]

The era of the Mexican Revolution and World War I exerted a profound influence on northward migration. Mexicans fled the violence of the revolution while economic growth in the United States during the war was an equally powerful draw, providing employment for the new arrivals. Mexico's northern railroads, although built for the convenience of United States economic interests, aided the northward flow. Not all the emigrants were displaced indigent peasants. Many were of the professional class who settled in the cities of the Southwest, or were members of Mexico's upper classes who simply wished to flee the revolution or had ended up on the losing side of the political struggle.[20]

While migration northward to Mexico's border cities and across the line into the United States' own Southwest did not abate with the end of the revolution, World War II gave it dramatic impetus. The economic boom and the employment created by the war led to the establishment of the Bracero Program that legally brought hundreds of thousands of Mexican farm laborers into the United States. Many of course remained, their families joined them, and the growing colony became a magnet for thousands of others hoping to improve their lives *al norte*. Agriculture north of the border easily became dependent upon an endless supply of cheap labor and continued to lobby for a loose immigration policy after the war. Thus the Bracero Program began a massive migration, creating a new economic and social organism that was transnational in nature, and could not be separated by a boundary line drawn in the desert sands.[21]

Mexican emigration to the United States remains one of the most pressing issues between the two countries, acting as a safety valve for Mexico and satiating the needs of agriculture and industry in the United States for inexpensive labor. In the early presidencies of George W. Bush and Vicente Fox, it appeared that a fundamental area of agreement had been reached on immigration. There appeared to be an understanding of the policies to pursue: an expanded temporary worker program; the need to raise undocumented workers currently in the United States to legal status; enhanced border security; serious action against migrant traffickers—the infamous *coyotes*; and meaningful investment in those areas of Mexico that supply the most migrants. Negotiations appeared to move swiftly, but Fox wanted too much too quickly and the Bush administration was not prepared to risk loss within its political base by rapidly seeking an all-inclusive policy on immigration. The events of 11 September 2001 gave Bush excellent cover from which to drop the entire effort, while the United States' view of foreigners and its open borders turned decidedly sour.[22]

Narcotics remains a critical issue between the United States and Mexico, and as long as the enormous market in illegal drugs north of the border remains unchecked, the traffickers will find a way through that porous border to fill the demand. Narcotics trafficking has created considerable social costs, with organized crime in control of the deadly business, and sometimes in control of certain portions of various Mexican states, making them off limits to law enforcement. The corruption of local officials and the undermining of government institutions threatens the security of the Mexican state, while drug trafficking has become a social cancer in the border region on both sides of the line. The cooperation and mutual trust needed to combat the drug lords will be difficult to achieve.[23]

The economies of Mexico and the United States have been intertwined from the days of the Santa Fe Trail, and became increasingly so by 1900, with the border especially involved in the economic life of both nations. After World War II economic integration grew rapidly until Mexico became the third-largest trading partner of the United States. A part of this growth was due to the *maquiladora* program, which permitted assembly plants in border cities to import components from the United States and ship the finished product back across the border for sale. The program became an important element in Mexico's hope of enticing foreign capital to invest in the nation's industry. By 1995 the *maquiladora* program amounted to nearly 70 percent of Mexico's trade surplus with its northern neighbor.[24]

Beginning in the 1980s, Mexico made a concerted effort to privatize industry, lower tariffs, encourage foreign investment, and depart from what had amounted to noncompetitive capitalism. It was in this context that the North American Free Trade Agreement (NAFTA) was born in 1993. Since then Mexico has become the United States' second-largest trading partner, and this has impacted the border region significantly. Electric grids and natural gas pipelines now bind the two nations together. By the end of 2001 Mexico was supplying 200 megawatts of energy to California each day, and the nation became the most important export market for California and Texas. NAFTA intensified the integration of the economies on both sides of the international boundary.[25]

While the two border economies have become increasingly interdependent, many difficult problems remain. A solution to migration awaits the political will to address it; Mexico's claim to its fair share of the waters of the Río Grande and the Colorado remains to be fulfilled; environmental issues need to be targeted; and narcotics trafficking endures as an open wound for both nations. The border does not divide these problems into two parts, but rather molds them into one. The people of the sister cities and adjacent states along the international boundary perhaps understand this better than Washington or Mexico City. Civic and intellectual efforts at cooperation abound at all levels. Local officials have found solutions to problems affecting populations on both sides of the line, the governors of the border states meet frequently to further such cooperation, and the universities of both border regions have articulated cooperative agreements.[26]

When the engineers of the Joint United States and Mexican Boundary Commission first set up their instruments in 1849, they were beginning the survey of an international boundary that ran through a land that was for the most part uninhabited and unknown. Today the border region has become home to millions of people, an ever-expanding and vibrant economic power that can no longer be divided by an imaginary line.

CHAPTER XI NOTES

1   Cuevas to García Conde, 2 Mar. 1849, ASRE, Exp. 22, pp. 337–40.

2   Couto, Cuevas, Atristáin to De la Rosa, 16 Jan. 1848, ASRE, Exp. 21, p. 23; "Exposición de motivos …," in *Algunos documentos*, pp. 148–54.

3   Trist to the Editors of the New York *Evening Post*, [n.d.], Draft letter in two parts, Container 11, Trist Papers. Trist's draft, or another version of it, was discovered a number of years ago, see Goetzmann, *Army Exploration*, pp. 189–90.

4   Official Journal, pp. 7–8, Bartlett Papers. A true copy of the relevant portion of García Conde's map may be found in SED 41 (665), following p. 32.

5   Sosa, *Biografías de mexicanos distinguidos*, p. 240–41.

6   Pedro García Conde, *Ensayo estadístico sobre el Estado de Chihuahua* (Chihuahua: 1842).

7   Robert Greenhow to Buchanan, 14 Mar. 1848, Series I, Buchanan Papers.

8   Buchanan to Trist, 13, 19 Jul. 1847, Trist to Buchanan, 6 Dec. 1847, Containers 9, 10, Trist Papers.

9   Emory to Howard, 18 Dec. 1851, 1 Jun., 7 Nov. 1852, Folders 3, 40, 6, Emory Papers.

10   Abert to Conrad, 30 Oct. 1851, File E-402, NA, RG/76.

11   Jiménez to Salazar Ylarregui, 3 Sep. 1857, "Jiménez Memoria," p. 1.

12   SED 108 (832), p. 5.

13   Hewitt, "The Mexican Commission," pp. 555–80; Hewitt, "The Mexican Boundary Survey Team," pp. 171–96.

14   Jiménez to Salazar Ylarregui, 3 Sep. 1857, Jiménez Memoria, p. 3; Salazar Ylarregui to Secretaría de Relaciones, 7 Aug. 1854, Salazar Ilarregui, José.—Que informe donde se encuentran los instrumentos que recibió la Comisión de Límites…," Legajo 40–16–138 (Archivo de la Secretaría de Relaciones Exteriores, Mexico City).

15   Emory to Salazar Ylarregui, 17 Apr. 1852, Salazar Ylarregui to Emory, 7 Apr. 1852, Folders 4, 38, Emory Papers.

16   Joseph A. Stout, *Schemers & Dreamers: Filibustering in Mexico, 1848–1921* (Fort Worth: 2002), pp. 14–37.

17   M. Lomelí to Ministro de Relaciones, 23 Feb. 1883, Plutarco Oruelas to Ministro de Relaciones, 3 Feb. 1880, M. Fernández to Ministro de Relaciones, 31 Jan. 1888, Bernardo Reyes to Ministro de Guerra, 27 May 1881, ASRE, Legajos 15–1–74, 44–12–62.

18   Joseph Richard Werne, "Redrawing the Southwestern Boundary, 1891–1896," pp. 1–20.

19   Eric Michael Schantz, "All Night at the Owl: The Social and Political Relations of Mexicali's Red-Light District, 1913–1925," *Journal of the Southwest*, XLIII (Winter, 2001), pp. 557–61; Joseph Richard Werne, "Esteban Cantú y la soberanía mexicana en Baja California," *Historia Mexicana*, XXX (jul.-sep., 1980), pp.1–32.

20   David E. Lorey, *The U.S.-Mexican Border in the Twentieth Century* (Wilmington:1999), p. 69.

21   Ibid., pp. 90, 119–121, 139; Thomas Torrans, *Forging the Tortilla Curtain: Cultural Drift and Change Along the United States-Mexico Border From the Spanish Era to the Present* (Fort Worth: 2000), pp. 317–18.

22   Jeffrey Davidow, *The U.S. and Mexico: The Bear and the Porcupine* (Princeton: 2004), pp. 230, 238; Robert S. Laiken, "With a Friend Like Fox," *Foreign Affairs*, LXXX (Sep.-Oct., 2001), p. 99; Jorge G. Castañeda, "The Forgotten Relationship," *Foreign Affairs*, LXXXII (May-Jun., 2003), pp. 68, 70–71.

23   Lorey, *The U.S.-Mexican Border*, p. 161; Davidow, *The U.S. and Mexico*, p. 95; Torrans, *Forging the Tortilla Curtain*, p. 322.

24   Lorey, *The U.S.-Mexican Border*, pp. 105–109.

25   Laiken, "With a Friend Like Fox," pp. 100–101; Lorey, *The U.S.-Mexican Border*, pp.

170–73; Robert A, Pastor, "North America's Second Decade," *Foreign Affairs*, LXXXIII (Jan.-Feb., 2004), pp. 124–27, 129.

[26] Lorey, *The U.S.-Mexican Border*, 114, 178–79; Laiken, "With a Friend Like Fox," p. 101; Torrans, *Forging the Tortilla Curtain*, p. 21

BIBLIOGRAPHICAL ESSAY

The several controversies surrounding the United States and Mexican boundary survey and the many years required to complete it generated a large body of material in manuscript and printed form. The sources reviewed in this essay are arranged in order of their importance within each section as far as possible. While all manuscript materials are discussed, newspapers and printed works of minor importance appear only in the notes for the sake of brevity.

MANUSCRIPTS

A most important body of information is included in the Records Relating to the Southern Boundary of the United States: United States-Mexican Border, Record Group 76, National Archives, Washington, DC. They consist of the official journals of the Joint Commission from its first meeting in San Diego until its adjournment in 1857, as well as reports from various surveying parties. There is also a sizeable correspondence among Weller, Emory, and other members of the United States Commission. The original drawings made for the botany portion of the commission's final report are a delightful inclusion: They are truly superb.

Of equal importance are the Diplomatic Instructions of the Department of State, and the Despatches from United States Ministers to Mexico, Record Group 59, National Archives, Washington, DC, which contain the diplomatic correspondence generated by the boundary survey. Also in Record Group 59 are the Despatches from Special Agents of the Department of State, and Special Missions, which deal with the negotiations for the Gadsden Treaty. In the same record group are the Notes from the Mexican Legation in the United States to the Department of State, in which are found the concerns of the Mexican government about the survey.

Complementing the above material is that in the Archivo de la Secretaría de Relaciones Exteriores [ASRE] in Mexico City. Of most value is the "Diario-Memoria" of Francisco Jiménez, who played an important part in the survey, not the least of which was his report to Salazar Ylarregui in which Jiménez details much of the Mexican commission's efforts. Also in the ASRE, within the Oficina de Límites y Aguas Internacionales, are reports of other officers of the Mexican commission and the correspondence among García Conde, Salazar Ylarrequi, and the minister of foreign relations. This material addresses the problems of the commission, the condition of its instruments, and the daily progress of the survey. Also portrayed is the great care with which the Mexican government put together its commission. In addition there is in the ASRE a large file of papers under the title "Valle de la Mesilla" which contains correspondence concerning the Bartlett-García Conde line and the controversy it began.

Also in Mexico City are the files of the Archivo Histórico de la Defensa Nacional [AHDN], which shed much light on the careers of the military engineers who worked on the international survey. Unfortunately they contain little information regarding the survey itself, which is understandable since the Mexican commission worked under the aegis of the Secretaría de Relaciones Exteriores rather than that of the military. Similarly, research in the Archivo General de la Nación yielded little information regarding the international survey as the pertinent documents are housed in the ASRE.

An interesting view of the Lucas Alamán ministry formed under Santa Anna's last dictatorship and his handling of the boundary controversy is found in "Correspondencia con Embajadas y Legaciones," in the Archivo del Ministerio de Asuntos Exteriores, Madrid. Spain's observers in Mexico City were convinced that García Conde somehow had tricked Bartlett and that Santa Anna had no choice but to accept the Gadsden Treaty if he wanted to avoid war and remain in power. A portion, but by no means all, of this material can be found in duplicate in the ASRE in Mexico City.

The most important private manuscripts for the study of the survey are the William Hemsley Emory Papers at the Beinecke Library, Yale University. No one was more closely associated with the boundary on the United States side than Emory, whose influence was steady throughout the delineation of the line. This large collection also presents a good view of the Topographical Engineers and the role they played in drawing the new boundary. Of nearly equal importance are the Mexican Boundary Commission Papers of John Russell Bartlett at the John Carter Brown Library, Brown University. These contain the official dispatches from the Department of the Interior to Bartlett and a copy of the Official Journal of the Joint Commission until Bartlett's removal. There is also a large body of Bartlett's correspondence and his original journal from which he composed his *Personal Narrative*. Bartlett's image of his position as commissioner and his attitude toward the Topographical Engineers emerge clearly from this material. The Amiel Weeks Whipple Papers at the Oklahoma Historical Society, Oklahoma City, on the other hand, provide a different picture of Bartlett, as well as of Emory. This collection is comprised of Whipple's several journals kept while in the field and his correspondence with other officers of the Joint Commission. One could scarcely write the story of the Gila survey without them. Critical for an understanding of the endless quarrels of the Bartlett commission are the James Duncan Graham Papers at the Beinecke Library, Yale University. Graham's determination to scuttle the survey of the Bartlett-García Conde line is most interestingly revealed in his correspondence and memoranda.

An investigation of the Papers of Nicholas Trist, Library of Congress, Washington, is essential for an understanding of his role in negotiating the Treaty of Guadalupe Hidalgo. Trist's correspondence reveals his difficult decision to disobey his government and make a treaty when no one in Washington thought it possible. Of equal interest are the negotiations between Trist and the Mexican treaty commissioners as they worked their way toward a mutually acceptable international boundary. Complementary to the Trist Papers are the James Buchanan Papers at the Historical Society of Pennsylvania in Philadelphia. This is a large collection covering Buchanan's public career and is of particular interest in revealing what Buchanan desired in a treaty of peace with Mexico.

The Thomas Jefferson Rusk Papers at the Barker Texas History Center, University of Texas, demonstrate the keen desire of the South for a southern railroad to the Pacific. Rusk himself was untiring in this effort and was in close contact with Emory, Gray, and other members of the United States commission. A delightful perspective on the boundary survey is found in the George Clinton Gardner Papers at the De Golyer Library, Southern Methodist University. Gardner's unguarded letters to his family provide a not always flattering view of the senior members of the United States section, and most importantly explain the absence of Weller and Gray at the determination of the eastern end of the California line.

Of considerable value for unraveling the partisan politics that caused so much misery and delay within the United States commission are the Papers of Thomas Ewing at the Library of Congress, Washington, DC. Ewing emerges as determined to promote the cause of the Whig party at any cost and equally driven to undermine the Weller commission in California. Also of interest in attempting to understand the political partisanship that continually beset the commission are the John J. Crittenden Papers, the Thomas Corwin Papers, the William L. Marcy Papers, the John M. Clayton Papers, and the Martin Van Buren Papers, all in the Library of Congress. The Marcy Papers are of particular interest in approaching the question of the Gadsden Treaty. The William Bebb Papers, King Library, Miami University of Ohio, were also of some use for understanding the partisan politics of the era.

The Andrew Belcher Gray Papers in the Texas State Archives, Austin, unfortunately reveal little regarding his association with the survey, but do throw a bit of light on his earlier career. The Robert Blair Campbell Papers at the Barker Archives, University of Texas, are also of only minor value, but do touch on Emory's completion of the Río Grande survey while Campbell was commissioner. It is distressing that the William Carr Lane Papers in the Missouri Historical Society, St. Louis, offer so little to the story of the boundary survey. Aside from a few letters, he does not mention the survey or his striking pose at Doña Ana. While Lane wrote a cheerful journal of his travels in New Mexico as governor, the boundary controversy is entirely ignored. Also in the Missouri Historical Society are the Stephen Watts Kearny Papers that give a brief look at Emory during his war reconnaissance. The George Engelmann Papers at the Missouri Botanical Garden Library, St. Louis, naturally deal with Engelmann's oversight of the plant collecting associated with the survey, but also reveal a little of the character of the several members of the United States commission, and offer an interesting glimpse of the daily labors of the survey. The James Gadsden Papers were not consulted since they have been well researched in Paul Neff Garber's *The Gadsden Treaty*, and the actual negotiation of the treaty is easily found in the Despatches from United States Ministers to Mexico, Record Group 59, National Archives.

PUBLISHED PUBLIC DOCUMENTS

A large reservoir of material concerning the boundary survey can be found in the United States Government Serial Set. These House and Senate Executive Documents include reports from Bartlett, Gray, Graham, Emory, and other members of the United States commission. The reports contain much of the correspondence regarding the controversy over the southern boundary of New Mexico as well as the several disputes among the officers of the commission. The reports describe the work of the commission and contain maps of the various portions of the line. The most important of these documents is William Emory's *Report on the United States and Mexican Boundary Survey* ..., 34th Cong., 1st sess., 1857, S. Ex. Doc. 108 (Serial 832–34) consisting of three volumes in four parts. The first part is a narrative of the survey from the organization of the commission until the signing of the maps of the boundary in 1857, including a description of the country through which the line was drawn. It also contains pertinent correspondence of the United States section of the Joint Commission, but is flawed in that Emory seems loath to give much mention of the individual labors of other members of the survey team. The remainder of the report deals with the scientific efforts of the commission.

The *Report of the Secretary of the Interior* ..., 31st Cong., 1st sess., 1850, S. Ex. Doc. 34 (Serial 558) is in two parts and covers the survey of the California line. Gray's *Report of the Secretary of the Interior* ..., 33rd Cong., 2nd sess., 1855, S. Ex. Doc. 55 (Serial 752) is mainly a defense of his interpretation of the southern boundary of New Mexico. Graham's *Report of the Secretary of War* ..., 32nd Cong., 1st sess., 1852, S. Ex. Doc. 121 (Serial 627) fully supports Gray's line and attempts to discredit all of Bartlett's actions while commissioner. Bartlett's *Report of the Secretary of the Interior* ..., 32nd Cong., 2nd sess., 1853, S. Ex. Doc. 41 (Serial 665) is naturally a defense of the Bartlett-García Conde compromise line. For the sake of brevity the several other Senate Executive Documents will not be discussed here, but are found in the notes.

The *Congressional Globe* is of value for understanding the partisan politics that undermined the efforts of the commission and the debate on the southern boundary of New Mexico that Weller brought to the Senate floor. A few interesting letters from Bartlett are found in Lynda Lasswell Crist, ed., *The Papers of Jefferson Davis* (Baton Rouge: Louisiana State University Press, 1983). No one was more interested in a southern rail route than Davis.

The only published document directly concerning the survey on the part of Mexico is José Salazar Ylarregui's *Datos de los trabajos astronómicos y topográficos dispuestos en forma de diario* (México: Imp. de Juan R. Navarro, 1850) that unfortunately covers only the California line. It does provide an insight into the formation of the Mexican commission, its efforts in California and Salazar Ylarregui's view of the decisions of the Joint Commission. Of great importance for understanding the Mexican side of the negotiations leading to the new international boundary in the Treaty of Guadalupe Hidalgo is Antonio de la Peña y Reyes, ed., *Algunos documentos sobre el Tratado de Guadalupe y la situación de México durante la invasión americana*, No. 31 of *Archivo histórico diplomático mexicano* (México: Ed. Porrúa, 1971). This is composed of several government reports concerning the treaty, but of most value is the report of Couto, Cuevas, and Atristáin on their negotiations with Trist. The Comisión Internacional de Límites entre México y los Estados Unidos, *Memoria documentada del juicio de arbitraje del Chamizal* ...(3 vols.; México: Talleres de Artes Gráficas, Granja Experimental de Zoquipa, 1911), while dealing primarily with the later Chamizal dispute, contains a report by Agustín Díaz on his survey of a portion of the Río Grande that is not included in the Mexican Boundary Commission Papers in the Archivo de la Secretaría de Relaciones Exteriores. It also contains a brief report by Salazar Ylarregui on the survey of the Bartlett-García Conde line.

Of lesser value are Luis G. Cuevas, *Memoria del ministro de relaciones interiores y exteriores* ...(México: García Tores, 1849), Mariano Arista, *Memoria del secretario de estado y del despacho de guerra y marina* ...(México: García Tores, 1851), and Manuel Robles, *Memoria del secretario de estado y del despacho de guerra y marina* ...(México: García Tores, 1852) that provide a view of Mexico's political problems. A report by the Ministerio de Guerra y Marina, *Colonias militares. Proyecto para su establecimiento* ... (México: Imp. de I. Cumplido, 1848) contains a map of the military colonies along the Río Grande that proved useful in locating obscure points along the riverine boundary.

MEMOIRS AND CONTEMPORARY ACCOUNTS

The most valuable source in this genre is John Russell Bartlett's *Personal Narrative of Explorations and Incidents in Texas, New Mexico, California, Sonora, and Chihuahua, Connected with the United States and Mexican Boundary Commission, During the Years 1850, '51, '52, and '53* (New York: Appleton, 1854). Perhaps the most readable of all the travelogues dealing with the region, it is a detailed account of Bartlett's activities while commissioner and an apologia for his efforts. Of similar interest is Ross Calvin, ed., *Lieutenant Emory Reports: A Reprint of Lieutenant W. H. Emory's Notes of a Military Reconnoissance* (Albuquerque: University of New Mexico Press, 1951), which contains a biographical sketch of Emory, but does not include the scientific data of the original. These are available in Emory's *Notes of a Military Reconnoissance from Fort Leavenworth, in Missouri, to San Diego, in California, Including Part of the Arkansas, del Norte, and Gila Rivers*, 30th Cong., 1st sess., 1848, H. Ex. Doc. 41 (Serial 517). There is also Emory's *Notes on the Survey of the Boundary Line between Mexico and the United States* (Cincinnati: Morgan and Overend, 1851), a paper read before the American Association for the Advancement of Science, in which Emory reiterates his belief that surveying the line eastward from the mouth of the Gila would lose the rail route to the Pacific. A lively account that presents an interesting view of Bartlett's travels and difficulties with the Indians can be found in John C. Cremony, *Life Among the Apaches* (San Francisco: A. Roman, 1868). A fine complement to Whipple's journal covering his determination of the eastern end of the California line is William McPherson, ed., *From San Diego to the Colorado in 1849: The Journal and Maps of Cave J. Couts* (Los Angeles: Arthur M. Ellis, 1932). A brief biography of Andrew B. Gray can be found in L. R. Bailey, ed., *The Gray Report* (Los Angeles: Westernlore, 1963), a reprint of Gray's *Survey of a Southern Pacific R. R. on the 32nd Parallel ...* (Cincinnati: Wrightson, 1856). Of considerable utility for the end of the war and the beginning of negotiations leading to the treaty of peace is Winfield Scott, *Memoirs of Lieut.-General Scott, LL.D. Written by Himself* (New York: Sheldon & Co., 1864). Of lasting value and a delightful read is Josiah Gregg, *Commerce of the Prairies* (Norman: University of Oklahoma, 1954).

An invaluable source for revealing the character and personality of the men who played a role in Mexico's government and its boundary commission is Guillermo Prieto, *Memorias de mis tiempos* (México: Librería de la Vda. de C. Bouret, 1906). An excellent source for understanding Santa Anna's desire for an alliance with Spain is Buenaventura Vivó, *Memorias de Buenaventura Vivó, ministro de Méjico en España durante los años 1853, 1854 y 1855* (Madrid: Rivadeneyra, 1856). Important for an appreciation of the difficulties of the survey of the Big Bend area of the Río Grande is Emilio Langberg,

"Itinerario de la Espedición de San Carlos á Monclova el viejo hecha por el Coronel D. Emilio Langberg ...en el año de 1851," a manuscript in the Beinecke Library, Yale University. Pedro García Conde's *Ensayo estadístico sobre el Estado de Chihuahua* (Chihuahua: Imp. del Gobierno, a cargo de Cayetano Ramos, 1842) is of value in determining the resources of Chihuahua, but provides no scientific information of use to the study of the boundary survey. The three statistical surveys by José Agustín de Escudero, *Noticias estadísticas del estado de Chihuahua* (México: Juan Ojeda, 1834), *Noticias históricas y estadísticas de la antigua provincia del Nuevo-México* (México: Imp. de Laray, 1849), and *Noticias estadísticas de Sonora y Sinaloa ...* (México: Tip. de R. Rafael, 1849), while used by all those who argued over the Bartlett-García Conde line, are also of little real value.

BOOKS

The classic work on the Topographical Engineers is William H. Goetzmann, *Army Exploration in the American West 1803–1863* (New Haven: Yale University, 1959), in which Emory's war reconnaissance and the boundary survey are examined in detail. Lenard F. Brown's *Survey of the United States-Mexico Boundary 1849–1855* (Washington: National Park Service, 1969) inspired a close look at the actual work of the survey, but has a somewhat unusual organization. Odie B. Faulk, *Too Far North...Too Far South* (Los Angeles: Westernlore, 1967) is an attempt to cover the story of the survey, but contains a number of flaws. None of these authors seem to have had access to the Mexican Boundary Commission Papers in the Archivo de la Secretaría de Relaciones Exteriores. Manuel Orozco y Berra, *Apuntes para la historia de la geografía en México* (México: Imp. de Francisco Díaz de León, 1881) devotes one chapter to the survey, but did have access to the reports of the Mexican commission and interviewed several of its members. Robert V. Hine, *Bartlett's West: Drawing the Mexican Boundary* (New Haven: Yale University, 1968) is an excellent presentation of the skills of the draftsmen assigned to the commission, who produced some truly fine works. Ronnie C. Tyler's *The Big Bend: A History of the Last Texas Frontier* (Washington, DC: National Park Service, 1975) contains a fine treatment of the difficult survey of the Río Grande.

A very helpful work toward understanding the beginnings of the boundary controversy is Lawrence Martin's *Disturnell's Map* (Washington: G.P.O., 1937). Of considerable merit for an understanding of the cartographic results of the survey is Paula Rebert, *La Gran Línea: Mapping the United States-Mexico Boundary, 1849–1857* (Austin: University of Texas Press, 2001). Robert R. Russell, *Improvement of Communication with the Pacific Coast as an Issue in American Politics, 1783–1864* (Cedar Rapids: The Torch Press, 1948), remains an excellent study central to the question of the boundary survey.

David J. Weber, *The Mexican Frontier, 1821–1846: The American Southwest Under Mexico* (Albuquerque: University of New Mexico Press, 1982), explores the political situation in Mexico and that nation's difficulties with its northern frontier. Richard Bruce Winders, *Crisis in the Southwest: The United States, Mexico, and the Struggle over Texas* (Wilmington: Scholarly Resources, 2002), is valuable for an understanding of the political developments leading to the Mexican War. Of particular merit regarding the final stages of the war and the approach to the Treaty of Guadalupe Hidalgo is José María Roa Bárcena, *Recuerdos de la invasión norteamericana (1846–1848) por un joven de entonces* (México: Ed. Porrúa, 1947). Roa Bárcena had access to some materials that are no longer available. A companion volume is Ramón Alcaraz, et. al., *Apuntes para la historia de la guerra entre México y los Estados Unidos* (México: Tip. de Manuel Payno, 1848). Pertinent also for the end of the war and the negotiation of the treaty, and complementary to Roa Bárcena's work, is George Lockhart Rives, *The United States and Mexico, 1821–1848* (New York: Charles Scribner's Sons, 1913). On the war itself the classic work is Justin H. Smith, *The War with Mexico* (Gloucester, MA: Peter Smith, 1963).

Two excellent works that served as a foundation for this study are Norman A. Graebner, *Empire on the Pacific: A Study in American Continental Expansion* (New York: Ronald, 1955), and David M. Pletcher, *The Diplomacy of Annexation: Texas, Oregon, and the Mexican War* (Columbia: University of Missouri Press, 1973). Also of use in this regard is J. Fred Rippy, *The United States and Mexico* (New York: F. S. Crofts, 1931). A general work from the viewpoint of Mexico is Alberto María Carreño, *México y los Estados Unidos de América* (México: Imp. Victoria, 1922), which is based on Mexican archival material, but Carreño's footnotes do not effectively lead one to his sources. Of much greater value is the fine work of Luis G. Zorrilla, *Historia de las relaciones entre México y los Estados Unidos de América, 1800–1958* (México: Ed. Porrúa, 1965). Of lasting value for a general understanding from the Mexican perspective of the relations of the two nations is Josefina Zoraida Vázquez and Lorenzo Meyer, *The United States and Mexico* (Chicago: The University of Chicago Press, 1985). Equally useful is Angela Moyano Pahissa, *México y los Estados Unidos: Orígines de una relación, 1819–1861* (México: Secretaría de Educación Pública, 1985).

The best work on the many filibustering expeditions that bedeviled Mexico is Joseph A. Stout Jr., *Schemers & Dreamers: Filibustering in Mexico, 1848–1921* (Fort Worth: TCU Press, 2002). A well-researched work that deals with Mexico's political instability during the years of the boundary survey is Richard A. Johnson, *The Mexican Revolution of Ayutla, 1854–1855* (Rock Island: Augustana, 1939). Equally important is Francisco Bulnes, *Juárez y las revoluciones de Ayutla y de reforma* (México: Imp. de Murguia, 1905). Still of use is Paul Neff Garber, *The Gadsden Treaty* (Gloucester, MA: Peter Smith, 1959), but, employing no Mexican archival material, this work is somewhat one-sided.

A number of works are important in that they provide biographical information on members of the Joint Commission. Of these George W. Cullum's *Biographical Register of the Officers and Graduates of the United States Military Academy* (New York: J. F. Trow, 1850), and Alberto María Carreño's *Jefes del Ejército Mexicano en 1847* (México: Secretaría de Fomento, 1914), are useful for background on the military members of the commission. Francisco Sosa's *Biografías de mexicanos distinguidos* (México: Secretaría de Fomento, 1884) is also of considerable value. Two works by Francisco R. Almada, *Diccionario de historia, geografía y biografía chihuahuenses* (Chihuahua: Talleres Gráficos del Gobierno del Estado, 1927), and *Diccionario de historia, geografía y biografía sonorenses* (Chihuahua: Ruiz Sandoval, 1952), provided important biographical sketches of García Conde.

Juan López de Escalera, *Diccionario biográfico y de historia de México* (México: Editorial del Magisterio, 1964), was useful for background material on the lesser members of the Mexican commission. Of greater value in this regard was Santiago Ramírez, *Datos para la historia del Colegio de Minería recogidos y compilados bajo la forma de efemérides* (México: Imp. del Gobierno Federal, 1890), and Gabriel Cuevas, *El glorioso Colegio Militar Mexicano en un siglo (1824–1924)* (México: S. Turanzas del Valle, 1937). Information on the career of José Bernardo Couto is found in Ricardo Couto, *Homenaje a don José Bernardo Couto* (México: Ed. Porrúa, 1949), and in José Rojas Garcidueñas, *Don José Bernardo Couto, jurista, diplomático y escritor* (Xalapa: Universidad Veracruzana, 1964). The introduction to Luis G. Cuevas, *Porvenir de México: Introducción de Francisco Cuevas Cancino* (México: Ed. Jus, 1954), shed light on the life of Luis Gonzaga Cuevas. Of constant value for Mexican biography is the *Diccionario Porrúa de historia, biografía y geografía de México*. Tercera ed. (México: Ed. Porrúa, 1971).

ARTICLES

There are several articles that are of primary importance for understanding Nicholas Trist and his treaty. Louis Martin Sears, "Nicholas P. Trist: A Diplomat with Ideals," *Mississippi Valley Historical Review* XI (Jun., 1924), explains Trist's motives for proceeding to negotiate the Treaty of Guadalupe Hidalgo after his government had recalled him. Of equal utility is Norman A. Graebner, "Party Politics and the Trist Mission," *Journal of Southern History*, XIX (May, 1953), which explores the political atmosphere that led to Polk's appointment of Trist's secret mission to Mexico. A complementary article is

Robert A. Brent's "Reaction in the United States to Nicholas Trist's Mission to Mexico, 1847–48," *Revista de Historia de América*, XXXV-XXXVI (ene.-dic., 1953). Also of value is Jack Nortrup, "Nicholas Trist's Mission to Mexico: A Reinterpretation," *Southwestern Historical Quarterly*, LXXI (Jan., 1968). Eugene K. Chamberlin, "Nicholas Trist and Baja California," *Pacific Historical Review* XXXII (Feb., 1963), concludes that Trist was not responsible for his treaty's failure to obtain Baja California.

Regarding the boundary survey itself, the most complete view is found in William H. Goetzmann, "The United States-Mexican Boundary Survey, 1848–1853," *Southwestern Historical Quarterly*, LXII (Oct., 1958), although it does not cover the survey of the Gadsden line. Of long-standing merit is Lewis B. Lesley, "The International Survey from San Diego to the Gila River, 1849–1850," *California Historical Society Quarterly*, IX (Mar., 1930). Unfortunately none of these articles contains Mexican archival materials. The recent research of Harry P. Hewitt has remedied this, however. His "The Mexican Boundary Survey Team: Pedro García Conde in California," *Western Historical Quarterly*, XXI (May, 1990) fully demonstrates that the Mexican commission was every bit as active as that of the United States in the survey of the California line. Hewitt's "The Mexican Commission and Its Survey of the Rio Grande River Boundary, 1850–1854," *Southwestern Historical Quarterly*, XCIV (Apr., 1991), also based on the Mexican Boundary Commission Papers in the Archivo de la Secretaría de Relaciones Exteriores, ably shows the efforts of the Mexican section on that portion of the survey. Another informative article on the river survey is Ronnie C. Tyler, ed., "Exploring the Rio Grande: Lt. Duff C. Green's Report of 1852," *Arizona and the West*, X (Spring, 1968). Francis C. Kajencki, "Charles Radziminski and the United States-Mexican Boundary Survey," *New Mexico Historical Review*, LXIII (Jul., 1988), provides an interesting view of the Bartlett-Graham feud. The Mexican commissioner's role in the controversy over the southern boundary of New Mexico can be found in Joseph Richard Werne, "Pedro García Conde: el trazado de límites con Estados Unidos desde el punto de vista mexicana (1848–1853)," *Historia Mexicana*, XXXVI (jul.-sep., 1986). An excellent work for background information on the cartography of the area of the boundary survey is Carl I. Wheat, "Mapping the American West, 1540 to 1857," *Proceedings of the American Antiquarian Society*, LXIV (Apr., 1954).

Erwin H. Price, "The Election of 1848 in Ohio," *Ohio Archaeological and Historical Quarterly*, XXXVI (Apr., 1927), is most important for understanding the play of partisan politics on the United States commission. Of equal use is Edgar A. Holt, "Party Politics in Ohio 1848–1850," *Ohio Archaeological and Historical Quarterly*, XXXVIII (Apr., 1928). See also Joseph

Richard Werne, "Partisan Politics and the Mexican Boundary Survey, 1848–1853," *Southwestern Historical Quarterly*, XC (Apr., 1987).

There are a number of articles that deal with Mexico's political instability during the years of the international survey. Richard A. Johnson, "Santa Anna's Last Dictatorship, 1853–1855," *Southwestern Historical Quarterly*, XLI (Apr., 1938), illustrates the needs of the government that led to its acceptance of the Gadsden Treaty. Johnson's "Spanish-Mexican Diplomatic Relations, 1853–1855," *Hispanic American Historical Review*, XXI (Nov., 1941) reveals the dictator's failed diplomacy. Of a more general nature, but still quite useful is César Sepúlveda's "Historia y problemas de los límites de México," *Historia Mexicana*, VIII (jul.-sep., 1958). A number of articles by J. Fred Rippy provide an excellent background to the study of the Gadsden Treaty. Rippy's "A Ray of Light on the Gadsden Treaty," *Southwestern Historical Quarterly*, XXIV (Jan., 1921), and his "The Negotiation of the Gadsden Treaty," *Southwestern Historical Quarterly*, XXVII (Jul., 1923), are very useful for understanding the resolution of the boundary controversy. Rippy's "The Boundary of New Mexico and the Gadsden Treaty, "*Hispanic American Historical Review*, IV (Nov., 1921) is also an important work concerning the survey. The influence of armed incursions into Mexico upon that nation's relations with the United States is clearly demonstrated in Rippy's "Anglo-American Filibusters and the Gadsden Treaty," *Hispanic American Historical Review*, V (May, 1922). Finally, J. Fred Rippy's "The Indians of the Southwest in the Diplomacy of the United States and Mexico, 1848–1853," *Hispanic American Historical Review*, II (Aug., 1919) discusses the need of the United States to be released from its obligations to Mexico under Article XI of the Treaty of Guadalupe Hidalgo. Complementary to Rippy's work is P. M. Baldwin, "A Historical Note on the Boundaries of New Mexico," *New Mexico Historical Review*, V (Apr., 1930). On the Gadsden line itself see Joseph Richard Werne, "Major Emory and Captain Jiménez: Running the Gadsden Line," *Journal of the Southwest*, XXIX (Summer, 1987).

DISSERTATIONS

A few dissertations were consulted of which the most valuable was Norman A. Graebner, "The Treaty of Guadalupe Hidalgo: Its Background and Formation," (University of Chicago, 1949). Robert Arthur Brent, "Nicholas Philip Trist, Biography of a Disobedient Diplomat," (University of Virginia, 1950), was of equal utility. Alice Katherine Schuster, "Nicholas Philip Trist: Peace Mission to Mexico," (University of Pittsburgh, 1947), added to the material on Trist and his treaty. Paula Rebert, "Mapping the United States-Mexico Boundary, 1849–1857" (University of Wisconsin, 1994) is concerned primarily with the cartographic results of the survey. Of a different nature is

Paul Ingersoll Miller, "Thomas Ewing, Last of the Whigs," (The Ohio State University, 1933), which is of much value in understanding Ewing's position in the Whig party and his feud with Weller.

INDEX

north latitude, 58, 77; orders and plans for, 100, 113, 124–25, 146–47, 200; to presidio, 148; of Río Gila, confluence of Colorado and, 31; of Río Grande, 86, 114, 117–18; riverene, 78; of San Diego Bay, 28–29; suspension of, 127; travel: to Santa Cruz, 79; to Washington, 212; treaty, renegotiation of, 182–83

San Antonio road, 129–30

San Bernardino Springs, 198

Sánchez, Juan José, 178

San Diego: bay of, surveying, 28–29; boundary negotiation relating to, 6, 10–11

San Elceario, 60, 113, 117, 125

San Luis Springs, 198

San Miguel, 5, 11

Santa Anna, Antonio López de, 6, 163; boundary line, renegotiation of, 182; downfall of, 188; foreign policy of, 176–77, 188; García Conde, relationship with, 27; political instability of and lack of money, 181; return to power, 129, 175–77; Salazar Ylarregui, reinstatement of, 199; treaty, acceptance of amended, 186–88

Santa Cruz, 78–81, 198

Santa Rita, copper mines of, 166

Santa Rita del Cobre, 59, 69, 74, 76

Schaaf, Frederick, 96

Schott, Arthur: commission assignment, 143, 202; privations endured by, 208; surveying by, 145; data from, calculations for maps, 210

Scott, Winfield, 6

Seaton, Malcolm, 143

Senate Foreign Relations Committee, 142

Seward, William Henry, 136

Sierra del Tule, 209

slavery: issue in 1848 elections, 135–37; opponents of, 13–14

smallpox, 194

Smith, Edmund K., 194

Smith, Truman, 136

Smith, William Farrar, 61, 74–76

Socorro, 113, 125

Sonora Land and Mining Company, 227

Sonoran Desert (Sonora), 1–2, 10, 12, 187, 199

Sonoyta, 206, 208, 210

Southern Pacific Railroad, 227

Spain, political position regarding Mexico, 187–88; and Cuba, 177

Stephens, John Lloyd, 47

Strain, Isaac G., 49–51, 57

Stuart, Alexander: Emory, appointment of, 116; Graham and, 61–62, 72–73; dismissal of, 114–16; Gray, dismissal of, 104; McClellan, recall of, 51; surveying, involvement in: defense of 32° 22′ north latitude, 141, 170; delays, response to Mexico regarding, 84–86

Sumner, Edwin Vose, 163

survey, 97f, 121f, 168f–169f, 203f. See commission, Mexican; commission, United States'; Jiménez, Francisco; Joint United States and Mexican Boundary Commission; Michler, Nathaniel; surveyor, Mexican; surveyor, United States'; Whipple, Amiel Weeks

surveying equipment. See equipment, surveying

surveying party: assignments made, 143; hardships endured by, 119–22, 125–26, 143–45; lack of provisions, 98, 100–102, 118–19; travel and, 29, 94–96, 194, 200–202; immigrant interaction with, 30; survey work by, 202, 204; on California line, 30–31; field work completed, 211; on New Mexico border, division of labor, 59–60; on Río Gila, 101–2; suspension of, 62–63, 122, 206. See also commission, Mexican; commission, United States'; Joint United States and Mexican Boundary Commission

surveyor, Mexican. See Salazar Ylarregui, José

surveyor, United States'. See Emory, William Hemsley; Gray, Andrew Belcher

Talcott, Andrew, 69

Taylor, William A., 28

Taylor, Zachary, 13, 22, 137, 157

thirty-one degrees fifty-two minutes
(31° 52′) north latitude, 166; map
of, 168f–169f

thirty-one degrees forty-seven minutes
(31° 47′) north latitude, 195; map
of, 203f; survey of, completed, 197

thirty-one degrees twenty minutes (31°
20′) north latitude, 195; map of,
203f; north-south line to, survey initi-
ated, 197; survey of, completed, 199

thirty-second parallel: as boundary
line, 6, 10; as dividing line between
Californias, 5; railroad, potential
location along, 1

thirty-two degrees twenty-two minutes
(32° 22′) north latitude: as boundary
line: causing of jurisdictional dispute
of Mesilla Valley, 162; Gray, disputing validity of, 71–72; legitimacy of,
questioned per treaty, 140–42; of
New Mexico, 54–56; Stuart, support-
ing, 104; location of, determined, 58;
Graham, disputing, 61–62; map of,
168f–169f; western terminus of, 108

Thurber, George, 79, 104–5

Tillinghast, Otis H., 74

Tinajas Altas, 206, 210

Tinajas del Tule, 206, 210

Todos Santos, Bay of, 11

Topographical Engineers. See Corps of
Topographical Engineers

Tornel, José María, 176

transcontinental railroad. See railroad

treaty. See Gadsden Treaty; Treaty of
Guadalupe Hidalgo

Treaty, Gadsden. See Gadsden Treaty

Treaty of Guadalupe Hidalgo, xiii–xiv;
articles of: dispute over, 77; release
from XI of, 184–85; violation of XXI
of, 161; draft of, 11; interpretation
of, 182, 219–20; ratification of,
14–15; requirements of, 171; signed,
12; specifications of, 19

Trías, Ángel, 160f; background of,
161; defense of La Mesilla by, 163;
denial of annexation plot by, 178;

jurisdictional dispute over Mesilla
Valley, involvement in, 159–61

Trist, Nicholas P.: background of, 5;
commissioner appointment, 5; negotiations by, 5–9; quotation by, 1;
recall by Buchanan, 7–8; treaty:
interpretation of, by, 219–20; presentation to President by, 13–14; proposals and concessions, 10–12

Tucson, 80, 206

Turnbull, Charles, 194

United States: boundary commission
(See commission, United States');
boundary commissioner (See
Bartlett, John Russell; Campbell,
Robert Blair; Emory, William
Hemsley; Trist, Nicholas P.; Weller,
John B.); boundary line, renegotiation, 175, 184–85; economic growth
of, effect on Mexican migration, 228;
Mexico and: attempts to seize and/or
colonize northern, 227; effect on
international support for, 177–78;
position regarding jurisdiction of
Mesilla Valley, 162; trading partners
with, 229–30; military position of,
187; partisan politics in the: commissioner selection affected by,
33–34; effect of, on commission, xiii,
19, 23, 33, 129, 135–38, 222; support of survey, lack of, 19, 131, 224;
surveyor (See Emory, William
Hemsley; Gray, Andrew Belcher);
treaty: amendment and ratification,
185–86; ratification, 15

United States Army Corps of
Topographical Engineers. See Corps
of Topographical Engineers

United States Coast and Geodetic
Survey, 3, 143

Van Buren, Martin, 137

Vaudricourt, Augustus de: commission
assignment, 49; portrait of Bartlett,
46f; resignation of, 58; surveying by,
124

Villa del Altar, 202

Vivó, Buenaventura, 177–78, 187

von Hippel, Moritz: commission